D0152048

WITHDRAWN

REDWOOD

LIBRARY
NEWPORT
R.I.
Gift of
Robert Behra

A Woman to Deliver Her People

The Dan Danciger Publication Series

A Woman to Deliver Her People

JOANNA SOUTHCOTT AND ENGLISH MILLENARIANISM
IN AN ERA OF REVOLUTION

by James K. Hopkins

UNIVERSITY OF TEXAS PRESS, AUSTIN

Copyright © 1982 by the University of Texas Press
All rights reserved
Printed in the United States of America
First Edition, 1982

Requests for permission to reproduce material from this work
should be sent to Permissions, University of Texas Press,
Box 7819, Austin, Texas 78712

Library of Congress Cataloging in Publication Data
Hopkins, James K., 1941–
   A woman to deliver her people.
   (The Dan Danciger publication series)
   Bibliography: p.
   Includes index.
   1. Southcott, Joanna, 1750–1814. 2. Millennialism—
England—History—18th century. 3. Millennialism—
England—History—19th century. I. Title.
BF1815.S7H66   303.4'84   81-10462
ISBN 0-292-79017-1   AACR2

BF
1815
.S7
H66
1982

125215

NOV 0 2 2000

3

To Pat and Cathy

Contents

Acknowledgments

I have incurred many debts in the research and writing of this book. Standish Meacham of the University of Texas first encouraged my work on Joanna Southcott and her movement. He has maintained a lively interest in its progress over the years, for which I am very grateful. By precept and example, Stanford Lehmberg of the University of Minnesota provided a constant reminder of the highest standards of the academic profession. The Woodrow Wilson Foundation made possible a rewarding year at Cambridge University, where the late G. Kitson Clark shared with me a lifetime of reflection on early nineteenth-century England, as well as his deep compassion for and understanding of those, like Joanna Southcott, who have been unjustly relegated to the lunatic fringe of the past. Thomas Barnes of the University of California, Berkeley, made an early statement of belief in this study, for which I will always be indebted.

The librarians and staff of the Humanities Research Center at the University of Texas at Austin proved unfailingly helpful in assisting my research. June Moll and Sally Leach first guided me through the remarkable Joanna Southcott Collection. John Payne has maintained a warm interest in my work and kept me informed of new Southcottian acquisitions. I am also grateful to the librarians and staff of the Fondren and Bridwell libraries of Southern Methodist University and, in England, of the Bodleian Library, the British Library, the Cambridge University Library, the Gloucestershire Record Office, the Greater London Record Office, the Guildhall Library, the University of London Library, the Public Record Office, the John Rylands Library in Manchester, and the Worcestershire Record Office. I have been similarly well served by the reference and local history libraries in Ashton-Under-Lyne, Bradford, Exeter, Halifax, Huddersfield, Leeds, Manchester, Plymouth, Sheffield, and Stockport. I remember with particular pleasure my visits to Blockley, Gloucestershire, where Dr. and Mrs. A. W. Exell opened their home to me while I examined the Southcottian manuscripts in their care. I am grateful to the Sheffield City Librarian for allowing me to use material from the Wentworth Woodhouse Muniments (Fitz-william Papers).

I wish to thank my former colleagues in the London study center of Schiller College, Janie Ericsson and Mary Whitford, for their under-standing and encouragement. Without the hospitality of Miles and Anabel Donald and Rex and Zélide Cowan, several extended research visits to London would not have been possible. David Vincent made many evenings in Cambridge unforgettable with his enthusiasm for his important research in working-class autobiography. In the course of a visit to Exeter, E. W. Martin shared with me his knowledge of the pe-culiar and abiding intimacies of village life in Devon. Mrs. Richard Marker and Jim Edwards made my stay in Joanna's village, Gittisham, particularly stimulating. Charles Warnberg and Anne Fiedler read late drafts of the manuscript and left their own special imprint on this book.

I have been particularly fortunate in my colleagues in the Department of History at Southern Methodist University who have provided an at-mosphere both congenial and challenging in which to teach and write. Without the support of R. Hal Williams and David Weber, this book might well not exist and certainly not in its present form. A Council of the Humanities research grant from the university and a semester on leave helped bring my research to a conclusion.

Finally, I wish to thank Jane McKean Holahan, John Henson, and my parents for their many and varied contributions to the creation of this book. It is dedicated to my sister and daughter.

Introduction

This is a New thing Amongst mankind, for a woman to be the Greatest Prophet that ever came into the World, to bring man out of darkness, into My Marvellous light, and *make every Crooked path straight before You,* and bring every mountain to a plain, and *all dark Sayings shall* be *brought to light.*[1]

And what a proud, conceited fool must I be, to say of myself, I have more knowledge than the learned, and can tell them better than they know from my own wisdom. Shall I say I know it from philosophy, and do not understand one planet? Shall I say I know it from divinity, and never studied the Bible in my life, no further than I thought necessary for my own salvation? Shall I say I know it from other men's works, when I put no belief in any man's judgment but the Prophets and Apostles, and those who were inspired by the Lord? Shall I say I had the spirit of wisdom given me, when I never had any talents to boast of in my life, and was considered by all my worthy wise brothers and sisters the simplest of my father's house? And I always deemed myself the same; but the Lord hath chosen the weak foolish things of this world, to confound the great and mighty.[2]

A profound mood of expectation is an essential feature of the revolutionary mentality. The existing system of social, economic, and political relationships will be recast in the image and likeness of a vision sufficiently compelling to draw its adherents away from their daily routines into a life of hyperbole, one in which they and all their endeavors take on an outsized, heroic quality because of what it is they are to achieve. E. J. Hobsbawm has said that "utopianism is probably a necessary social device for generating the superhuman efforts without which no major revolution is achieved."[3] A twentieth-century poet and novelist, with some practical knowledge of revolution, agrees. "What moves me," Nikos Kazantzakis said of Russia, "is not the reality that they have achieved, but the reality which they long for, and do not know they cannot achieve. All human value rests in this chimera; for this intoxication, it is worthwhile to act and die."[4] In the waning decades of the eighteenth century, such a "social device," such a "chimera," was present in England, where a revolutionary situation did not exist, as well as in France, where one did. Though the circumstances of the English artisan and the French *sans culotte* were dramatically different, each in his distinctive way responded to a glittering vision of apocalyptic change.[5]

A follower of English prophet Richard Brothers wrote, "We live in a period distinguished by the most extraordinary events, one pregnant with the fate of Empires and Thrones—wonderful changes have already taken place, and still the portentous clouds thicken, and spread around the political horizon." The successful effort of the American colonies to throw off English domination had been a recent and stunning example. It was America which "first drew the sword in the cause of freedom." And its example did not go unnoticed. "The voice of Liberty was heard across the Atlantic, and the most astonishing revolution that history ever recorded soon followed." The pundits and politicians ascribed these singular events to various causes. "*One* may believe that in them he discovers the progress of reason—the *other* the prevalence of *French* atheism." Yet "others perhaps equally well informed, look to a higher origin, and beholding the hand of Providence—bid welcome to the accomplishment of ancient predictions, and revere the wonderful works of the GOD of heaven."[6]

The language and ideology of change have often been appropriated from the prophetic books of the Bible. The book of Revelation promises that Christ's Second Coming will somehow be combined with the appearance of a thousand years of felicity, the millennium. Form and content have sometimes been separated, as in the cases of Tom Paine and Robert Owen, both freethinkers, who rejected the Bible but incarnated its style and sense of irresistible optimism in their roles as secular prophets. The millennial tradition upon which they relied, and which Clarke Garrett and W. H. Oliver have so admirably described,[7] could precipitate social agitation, as it had most notably in England during the period of the Civil Wars, or confirm it in its course. Both effects were noticeable in the latter decades of the eighteenth century in English radicalism.

The English radical movement was shaped by a historically alienated element of society, for whom the past and its assumptions of an ordered, deferential society had little relevance. Dissenters were "remembered and condemned as sectaries and king killers."[8] In and yet not of eighteenth-century English society, they had the psychological leverage to reject all social categories and to provide an egalitarian vision of the future for early radical reform. Men like Richard Price and Joseph Priestley were the founders of "an indigenous and mature school of natural right politics, to which the French Revolution and its ideology came as a confirmation rather than an inspiration."[9] Although these were practical men, their imaginations could take flight when they contemplated the future. Priestley wrote in 1771, regardless of "the beginning of the world, the end will be glorious and paradisaical beyond what our imagination can now conceive." [10] "As I am a believer in Revelation," another said in a reply to Edmund Burke, "I, of course, live in the hope of better things; a millennium (not a fifth monarchy, Sir, of enthusiasts and fanatics), but a new heaven and a new earth in which dwelleth righteousness; or, to drop the eastern figure and use a more philosophic language, a state of equal liberty and equal justice for all men." [11]

With little reason to reverence the institutions of the past or present, Dissenters became increasingly visible as radical cadres in the late decades of the century. A contemporary observed, "Round the standard of 'Wilkes and Liberty' the nonconformists flocked in crowds. . . . A Dissenter and a Wilkite were synonymous terms." [12] As we know, John Wilkes was little more than a convenient and popular symbol, but he provided focus for the vague utopianism of many of his followers, a focus which sharpened with the onset of the American Revolution and attained perfect clarity during the first years of the French Revolution. The redoubtable Anna Barbaud observed in 1790: "It is to speculative people, fond of novel doctrines, and who by accustoming themselves to make the most fundamental truths the subject of discussion, have divested their minds of the reverence which is generally felt for opinions and practices long standing, that the world is ever to look for its improvement or reformation." [13] Isaac Kramnick argues that "millenial fervor" was fundamental to the radicalism of the dissenting tradition. "Their vision of a social order purged of barbaric and feudal iniquity [revived] among the dissenters the millenial dreams of their seventeenth century forebears." [14]

Tom Paine, who had grown up in the dissenting tradition, both stimulated and reflected this sense of dramatic, impending change. He wrote in *Common Sense*: "We have it in our power to begin the world over again. A situation, similar to the present, hath not happened since the days of Noah until now. The birthday of a new world is at hand." [15] Paine's rhetoric flashed like lightning against the backdrop of revealed religion, illuminating the American and French revolutions in an aspect familiar to every reader of the books of Daniel and Revelation. For free-thinkers like Paine and Thomas Holcroft, the dramatist, who shouted at William Godwin, "Hey for the New Jerusalem! The millennium! And peace and eternal beatitude be unto the soul of Thomas Paine," [16] such exclamations were intoxicating shibboleths, but for a large audience of Englishmen they had a literal significance.

William Blake wrote to his friend John Flaxman:

> . . . terrors appear'd in the Heavens above
> And in Hell beneath, & a mighty & awful change
>   threatened the Earth.
> The American War began. All its dark horrors
>   passed before my face
> Across the Atlantic to France. Then the French Revolution
>   commenc'd in thick clouds,
> And My Angels have told me that seeing such visions
>   I could not subsist on Earth.[17]

For Blake, Paine was possibly "an Inspired man"[18] but only to be expected at such a moment in time.

The American war and the events in France were so far outside the range of ordinary experience that intelligent men and women, confused and troubled, increasingly turned to the prophetic books of the Bible for solace and explanation. A dictionary of works on prophecy, published in 1835 and admittedly incomplete, has no fewer than 274 publications in England and Scotland between 1775 and 1815. In the period 1775–1789, there are 58 works mentioned, and from 1790 to 1804 the figure more than doubles, to 127.[19] And it is woefully incomplete. For example, none of Joanna Southcott's 65 publications are mentioned.

Observers on both sides of the Atlantic saw God's hand behind the great events taking place in America and Europe. A prominent colonial leader, Joseph Galloway, who had sought a rapprochement between the Colonies and Great Britain, wrote a commentary "upon such parts of the Revelation and other prophecies as immediately refer to the present times; in which the several allegorical types and expressions of those prophecies are translated into their literal meanings, and applied to their appropriate events." In the first pages of his work, Galloway explained, "I have been induced to search the *Scriptures alone,* for those prophetic marks which might possibly refer to the *present* critical and awful state of the world."[20] William Jones, "a friend to the plain old-fashioned doctrine of the Church of England" and a Fellow of the Royal Society, reflected on the "contagion" which had spread from the "discontented insurgents" of America to France. His work, published in 1790, was entitled *Popular Commotions Considered as Signs of the Approaching End of the World.*[21] Joseph Priestley, in his sermon *The Present State of Europe Compared with Ancient Prophecies,* said that if anything could be learned from the "language of prophecy" it was that "great calamities, such as the world has never yet experienced, will precede that happy state of things, in which 'the kingdoms of this world will become the kingdom of our Lord Jesus Christ.'" In his opinion, "the present disturbances in Europe are the beginning of those very calamitous times."[22]

Priestley, therefore, saw different forces at work across the Channel than did his fellow citizen of France and deputy to the Convention, the deist Tom Paine.[23] "Now, whatever we may think, as politicians," Priestley said, "I would, in this place, admonish you not to overlook the hand of God in the great scene that is now opening upon us. Nothing can ever come to pass without his appointment, or permission." The French Revolution, he believed, was the fulfillment of Revelation 11:13—"And the same hour was there a great earthquake, and the tenth part of the city fell, and in the earthquake were slain of men seven thousand: and the remnant were affrighted, and gave glory to the God of heaven." The earthquake symbolized a massive upset in the affairs of men, and France, the most powerful of the ten states on the Continent which had risen from the ruins of "the Papal dominions," the likeliest place for it to occur. Priestley's eye moved to Revelation 17:16 and found further confirmation of his views. The ten horns mentioned were the ten kings who had delivered "their power and strength unto the beast" (Revelation 17:13) and now "shall hate the whore, and shall make her desolate and naked, and shall eat her flesh, and burn her with fire." The "beast" and "whore" referred to the papacy whose shackles France was in the very act of casting off.[24]

It was the general understanding, based on Daniel and Revelation, that, amidst great upheaval, the Last Days would encompass the final overthrow of "Antichrist" or the "beast," the destruction of the Turkish Empire (the "King of the North" in Daniel 11), and the conversion of the Jews. Then would come the Second Advent. Opinion divided, however, on whether the latter would occur before or after the onset of the millennium. Premillennialists believed that Christ's Second Coming would inaugurate the thousand years while postmillennialists were equally certain that there would be "a spiritual millennium, consisting of the universal triumph of the gospel and the conversion of all nations in the thousand years *before* the coming of Christ."[25] After the millennium, Satan was to be released from his confinement and would set about "to deceive the nations." His lieutenants, Gog and Magog, would besiege the "camp of the saints" until finally they were destroyed by God. Then, John said, the devil will be "cast into the lake of fire and brimstone, where the beast and the false prophet *are*, and shall be tormented day and night for ever and ever" (Rev. 20:8, 10). The apostle described what awaited the faithful after the Judgment:

I John saw the holy city, new Jerusalem, coming down from God out of heaven, prepared as a bride adorned for her husband. And I heard a great voice out of heaven saying, Behold, the tabernacle of God *is* with men, and he will dwell with them, and they shall be his people, and God himself shall be with them, *and be* their God. And God shall wipe away all tears from their eyes; and there shall be no more death, neither sorrow, nor crying, neither shall there be any more pain: for the former things are passed away. And he that sat upon the throne said, Behold, I make all things new. And he said unto me, Write: for these words are true and faithful. (Rev. 21 : 1 – 5)

These reassuring words promising ultimate triumph were much needed by such men as Alexander Pirie, a liberal Scottish divine, who could gloomily observe that at "the end of this 18th century, the age of boasted light and improvement, a smoke from the bottomless pit has at once beclouded our sky—the spirits of devils have broke loose, and darkness has covered the earth and gross darkness the people." Yet, he added, "the Scriptures afford us strong consolation and good hope in the worst of times. Trusting in the Lord and keeping his way we need not fear, even now when the perilous times predicted are come." [26]

If the need for security and reassurance was great among these scholars and divines, who had an array of intellectual options before them, then how much greater must it have been in the shadowy world of the half-educated, for many of whom the Bible had long been the only accessible repository of knowledge. In 1540, at the command of Henry VIII, a copy of Coverdale's Great Bible had been placed in every church in the country. John Strype, one of the first biographers of Thomas Cranmer, who had written the preface to the second edition, described its effect:

It was wonderful to see with what joy this book of God was received, not only among the learned sort, and those that were noted for lovers of the reformation, but generally all England over, among all the vulgar and common people; . . . Everybody that could, bought the book, or busily read it, or got others to read it to them, if they could not themselves; and divers more elderly people learned to read on purpose. . . . When the king had allowed the Bible to be set forth to be read in all churches, immediately several poor men in the town of Chelmsford in Essex . . . bought the New Testament, and on Sundays sat reading it in the lower end of the Church: many would flock about it to hear their reading. [27]

Study of the Bible became the "national education," and the emphasis on individual interpretation meant that "each reader, even if a Churchman, became in some sort a Church to himself," [28] a development which was to prove most unhappy for Charles I and his party in the seventeenth century.

A hundred years later, many men and women of independent mind and intense but narrow perception still believed, as did Blake, that "every Natural Effect has a Spiritual Cause."[29] And they viewed the French Revolution as a natural catastrophe of incalculable magnitude—not unlike the way in which the previous generation had seen the Lisbon earthquake.[30] They had virtually no understanding or even awareness of the precipitating factors of the events in France. Such an appalling change could have but one explanation. It was brought about by God, and its portent could be found in the violent and grotesque imagery of the prophetic books of the Bible, particularly Daniel and Revelation.

Those who accepted the eschatological implications of contemporary events were subjected to an intense and relentless emotional pressure, which, when succumbed to, had the effect of sweeping away remaining barriers between the natural and supernatural worlds. Robert Southey described it as a time when "one madman printed his dreams, another his day-visions; one had seen an angel come out of the sun with a drawn sword in his hand, another has seen fiery dragons in the air, and hosts of angels in battle array."[31] Not since the Civil Wars had such a breach been made in the hard shell of everyday life. Blake felt himself "under the direction of Messengers from Heaven, Daily & Nightly." He understood, moreover, the trauma in the lives of those who resisted the forces at work upon them. "If we fear to do the dictates of our Angels, & tremble at the Tasks set before us; if we refuse to do Spiritual Acts. . . . Who can describe the dismal torments of such a state!" He himself had known this suffering and warned, "If you, who are organised by Divine Providence for Spiritual communion, Refuse, & bury your Talent in the Earth, . . . Sorrow & Desperation pursues you thro' life, & after death shame & confusion of face to eternity."[32] Blake's angels did not compel him to play a public role; those directing Joanna Southcott did.

Joanna was pursuing a career as a domestic servant and upholsteress in Exeter when in 1792, at the age of forty-two, she said that God had chosen her to announce the Second Coming. Her spiritual "communications" eventually filled sixty-five books and pamphlets, published from 1801 until her death in 1814, the year in which she announced that she was pregnant with a divinely conceived child who was to be called Shiloh. Joanna's following numbered in the tens of thousands, stretching from the West Country to the Midlands and the industrial cities of the north, with particular strength in London. Her appeal ranged widely. The Southcottians included country folk, like herself, whose needs were satisfied by a traditional piety, profoundly influenced by magic and superstition, in which biblical eschatology was a pervasively recognized and instinctively grasped key to an understanding of the true nature of events in America and France. Her support, however, came not only from the unsophisticated but also from those steeped in the rich and distinctive millennialist tradition in English thought reaching back to Joseph Mede, Thomas Brightman, and Isaac Newton in the seventeenth century and extending forward to her contemporaries Richard Hurd and Joseph Priestley. Educated followers, such as the Anglican clergymen, Thomas P. Foley, Thomas Webster, Stanhope Bruce, Samuel Eyre, and the learned Hoadley Ash, as well as Bermondsey paper manufacturer Elias Carpenter, famous engraver William Sharp, Colonel William Tooke Harwood, and Leeds merchant George Turner, became convinced of the legitimacy of Joanna's claims only after careful examination and investigation. Finally, her appeal also reflected new tensions developing in English society. Throughout England people were moving from the relative security of a rural economy to the new uncertainties of life in the capital and the manufacturing cities of the north, often in circumstances of unprecedented hardship. For many, the need for reassurance and the recovery of a sense of community was overwhelming. London, particularly, beckoned to the provinces and never had its appeal seemed so compelling as during the hard years of the wars with France. In 1800 its population reached 864,000 and by 1811 had climbed over a million.[33] Arthur Young wrote in 1771 of the new ease with which the transition from country to city was being made:

Young men and women in the country fix their eye on London as the last stage of their hope; they enter into service in the country for little else but to raise money enough to go to London, which was no such easy matter when a stage coach was four or five days creeping an hundred miles; and the fare and the expenses ran high. But now! a country fellow one hundred miles from London jumps on to a coachbox in the morning, and for eight or ten shillings gets to town by night, which makes a material difference; besides rendering the going up and down so easy that the numbers who have seen London are increased tenfold and of course ten times the boasts are sounded in the ears of country fools, to induce them to quit their healthy clean fields for a region of dirt, stink and noise. And the number of young women that fly thither is almost incredible.[34]

Joanna left Exeter for the metropolis in the late spring of 1801, joining the hegira of those in search of expanded opportunities. Unlike the prophetess, however, virtually all of those who traveled with her have vanished from our view.

Regardless of their background or learning, those who followed Joanna could agree on several propositions which would serve to sustain them on their journey—that in the Last Days they would be saved, that the earth would be transformed and made perfect, that salvation could occur at any moment, and that it would take place as a result of divine intervention. To apply several of Bryan Wilson's helpful categories, the Southcottian movement was, therefore, "revolutionist," if not revolutionary, in that its followers did not see a role for themselves as implementers of the new dispensation. There were significant "introversionist" aspects in the movement but, during her lifetime, Joanna's followers viewed themselves as members of a community which was separate from but still part of a sinful world, not one in withdrawal from it. Because of the preindustrial culture from which many of the believers came, not surprisingly, there was, additionally, a strong "thaumaturgical" element in their world view. For example, they gained reassurance and emotional release through dreams and visions and, in addition, were given (or, in some instances, purchased) a "seal," a folded sheet of paper bearing an inscription and Joanna's signature, which was interpreted by many to have magical properties, protecting the possessor against misfortune and, perhaps, guaranteeing long life and even immortality.[35]

However, contemporary observers dismissed Joanna simply as a fanatic, of interest, perhaps, as one of the more remarkable examples of what John Wesley had wrought upon the land. She served as a perfect foil for the malicious wit of Peter Pindar,[36] the genius of Gillray and Cruikshank, and the sardonic observations of Southey's Don Alvarez. By catching only Joanna's upturned face in their harsh glare, sketches of this kind left in darkness the multitudes of anonymous souls who gave her career its meaning. Observed from an unsympathetic point of view and deprived of context, Joanna inevitably withered into caricature. In 1820 a portrait of her appeared in R. S. Kirby's *Wonderful and Eccentric Museum; Or Magazine of Remarkable Characters, including All the Curiosities of Nature and Art, from the Remotest Period to the Present Time, Drawn from Every Authentic Source.* She found a place in *The Book of Wonderful Characters: Memoirs and Anecdotes of Remarkable and Eccentric Persons in All Ages and Countries,* in 1870, and five years later in John Timb's *English Eccentrics and Eccentricities.*

Recent scholarship has done something to correct this distortion. In 1956, G. R. Balleine provided the first extended treatment of Joanna and her movement. The usefulness of his book, however, is limited by its insular point of view and absence of notes.[37] Both E. P. Thompson, in his study of the English working class, and J. F. C. Harrison, in his work on the Owenites, suggested valuable new interpretations of the Southcottians.[38] It fell to Clarke Garrett to place the English millenarian tradition within a European context in his book *Respectable Folly.* Garrett summarized the state of scholarship on millenarianism over the previous twenty years and made important new contributions to our understanding of the careers of French prophetesses Suzanne Labrousse and

Catherine Theot and English prophet Richard Brothers. His eminently sensible and, often, wonderfully illuminating study offers a sound cautionary note. He reminds students of millenarianism that they travel across a riven landscape, mapped by scholars who have frequently applied a simplistic "socioeconomic" or "sociopsychological" explanation to a complex historical phenomenon. As a result, he says, those who have relied on such interpretations have, in significant measure, been led astray. He finds better balanced the work of scholars more sensitive to the multiplicity of factors and, particularly, the motive of genuine intellectual conviction which drove men and women in their pursuit of the millennium.

Garrett's book was followed by two others of genuine importance, W. H. Oliver's *Prophets and Millennialists* and, especially, J. F. C. Harrison's *The Second Coming*. Both works were stimulated by an earlier interest in Robert Owen and the millenarian culture of which he was a part. Like Garrett, Oliver is intent on rescuing the intellectual tradition of millenarianism from obscurity and misunderstanding. He argues that "in the later eighteenth and earlier nineteenth centuries the habit of looking at the world in a manner shaped by biblical prophecy was a normal and widespread activity."[39] While both Garrett and Oliver are rightly confident that they have made significant contributions to the history of ideas, Harrison is principally concerned with the popular manifestations of those ideas. His is a judicious and penetrating study in which he focuses not on the sophisticated advocates of millenarianism but rather on "the popular, largely self-educated, adventist millenarians." These were men and women whose antecedents can be found in the radical sects of the English Revolution rather than the divines of the seventeenth and eighteenth centuries. In his wide-ranging work, which includes sections on Richard Brothers, John Wroe, Zion Ward, Sir William Courteney, and the Mormons, as well as a lively supporting cast of minor characters, Harrison finds a sizable place for Joanna Southcott. His is the best treatment of the prophetess which has yet appeared. Drawing, in part, on my doctoral dissertation, "Joanna Southcott: A Study of Popular Religion and Radical Politics, 1789–1814," Professor Harrison offers a view of Joanna which is at once humane and generous and, moreover, illuminated by his appreciation of the many approaches which need be explored if she and her movement are to be fully understood. At the same time, Harrison concedes that his is but an "outline" of her career and that she "still awaits a modern published biography."[40]

Garrett, Oliver, and Harrison have convincingly demonstrated that millenarianism at both the educated and popular levels provided a recognized and widely accepted frame of reference for men and women at all levels of society on the Continent, in England, and in America. As a result, each is sceptical of the assumption that millenarian movements are composed of the poor and oppressed. From their vantage point, millenarian attitudes are seen as an acceptable intellectual option, having little, if any, correlation with the "chiliasm of despair." The real difficulty, as Garrett points out, is the lack of evidence which would allow the historian to come to convincing conclusions about the social composition of such movements. He writes, "The same sources that make possible remarkably full descriptions of the ideas of the millenarians and their responses to the events of the Revolution offer relatively few indications of the segments of society from which the millenarians drew their followers." Even casting Richard Brothers' appeal against the anguished years of 1794 and 1795, Garrett finds it impossible to determine "whether he attracted a significant proportion of attention among the English poor." As for Joanna Southcott, whose career "encompassed and transcended" Brothers' mission, Garrett suggests that here, too, the reductionists have been much too quick to suggest that her following came largely from the impoverished and psychologically vulnerable members of society.[41] With his emphasis on the "normalcy" of millenarian thinking, W. H. Oliver also warns against concluding that "prophetic and millennialist theorizing arose from tensions in the lives of individuals and in their society."[42] For his part, Harrison states flatly that none of the millenarian movements which he has studied, including that of Joanna Southcott, "had any substantial following among the very poor." In his view, "there is little to suggest that the disinherited and outcastes of society found solace or hope in millenarian belief."[43]

However, as Garrett, Oliver, and Harrison well understand, any historian working on millenarianism at this stage of inquiry must be tentative about many conclusions. What is necessary is further progress into a world which we are only beginning to understand, and a sense of humility is in the very grain of the undertaking. The burgeoning interest in the religious underworld of the eighteenth and nineteenth centuries only further points up how overlooked the subject has been. It is still true that "the history of popular and unorthodox religion in Great Britain—with the signal and often distracting exception of Methodism—has been grossly neglected."[44]

The purpose of this book is then, first, to build on the beginning that has been so successfully made by others. Second, it will attempt to place Joanna Southcott and her followers in a meaningful social and intellectual setting and, in so doing, to suggest the manner in which they came to reflect in a distinctive way the popular concerns of their generation. Particular attention will be paid to the millenarian influences on radical politics in the 1790s. By looking closely at the careers of William Tooke Harwood and William Sharp, I hope to demonstrate how the Southcottian movement came to serve as a mediating influence on the radical dreams of English men and women during the age of the French Revolution. Finally, and most importantly, it is hoped that this book will help restore to tens of thousands of ordinary souls a significant measure of the dignity and purpose that has long been denied them and is rightfully theirs.

A Woman to Deliver Her People

And, truly, what of good
ever have prophets brought to men?
Craft of many words,
　　only through
evil your message speaks.
　　Seers bring aye
terror, so to keep
　　men afraid.
—Aeschylus, Agamemnon

When hope goes, the joy of
living goes with it.
—Zola, Germinal

I

The Woman of Revelation

Having published to the world such wondrous prophecies, as many are at a loss to give credit to, and others judge it the disorder of a confused brain, I shall inform my readers, that my head was so disordered from my youth up, and so were the heads of my forefathers: Therefore, if the world judge, that a firm belief in the Lord, relying on all the truths of the Bible coming from men inspired by God, and the words left on record by our blessed Lord and Saviour, is madness to believe, I was born mad, and so was my mother before me.[1]

GITTISHAM

Joanna Southcott, the fourth daughter of William and Hannah Southcott, was born on April 25, 1750, at Tarford (or Taleford) in Devonshire, near Ottery St. Mary.[2] Not long after her birth, her family moved to Gittisham where Joanna spent her early life.[3]

Located some sixteen miles from Exeter, Gittisham is a small, picturesque village of great charm, in many ways unchanged since the eighteenth century. Richard Polwhele described it in 1797 in his history of Devonshire: "Its situation is healthy. The soil is strong and good, with clay on a gravelly bottom. A pleasant rivulet, that rises from various springs on the adjacent hills, . . . runs by Combehouse, and thence to Gittesham town." He was impressed by both the village and its inhabitants. It "is delightfully situated, and esteemed the cleanliest in the county. It is not large, but consists of many trim cottages: and the people are remarkably neat in their houses and in themselves. Nearly all the parish is divided into farms at rackrent, except a few remote tenements and some cottages and scattered fields at leafe."[4]

Combe, the manor house, stands out of sight of the cob-and-thatch houses of the village on the east side of the Otter Valley, just before the pastureland changes into forest. Even in 1797, Combe was considered to be "a very ancient building."[5] The house, in fact, dates from medieval times, having begun its existence as a thatched, wooden structure covered by ash wattles and cob. In the sixteenth century, the owner reconstructed it in stone. By the middle of the eighteenth century, when the Southcotts came to Gittisham, the house had attained its present, rather severe appearance with a stone-dressed, gabled central hall and adjoining wings. In addition, there were impressive stables south of the house which were to be torn down early in the nineteenth century.[6] Polwhele judged on his visit that "little art hath been employed in ornamenting this place: but few places are more capable of displaying to advantage the taste of the designer." He found the interior both attractive and functional. The surroundings proved equally congenial. "In its neighborhood are large commons, which afford delightful hunting, and abound with game, for that diversion."[7]

The parish church, "a neat structure," lies between the manor and the village. It houses the remains of two of the prominent families in the history of the community, the Beaumonts and the Putts.[8] On Sundays, Joanna and the Southcott family undoubtedly gathered with the rest of the inhabitants of the village to await the Putts, the "lords of the manor of Gittesham,"[9] with the men tugging their forelocks and the women curtsying to the squire and his family upon their arrival, as the villagers did until the early years of the twentieth century.[10] Perhaps the seating arrangement in the church was stratified by class as it was a few miles away in the Buckerell Church. A sketch from 1772 shows that at Buckerell the gentry and their servants were seated separately near the pulpit at the east end of the church, with the less important ranked behind them down the north and west aisles. The poor families were divided by sex. At the end of one aisle were "Vacant Seats for poor men" and at the other "Poor Women Seats." One of the best places was reserved for "Thomas Putt, Esqr.," who succeeded to Combe in 1757.[11]

When the Southcotts arrived in Gittisham, the squire of Combe was Reymundo Putt, a cousin of the second baronet, Thomas Putt, who had died without heir in 1721. Reymundo's son, Black Tom, renowned for his bad temper,[12] succeeded him. His domain included almost the whole parish and produced £1,700 a year. The family also owned other property in the county, as well as "several manors and estates" lying in Dorset, Somerset, and Cornwall.[13]

William Southcott, the father of Joanna, was one of the tenant farmers in this small, intimate world dominated by Squire Putt. A quick-tempered, vigorous man, William felt that he had fallen a long distance from his rightful place in the world. He told his children of an extraordinary sequence of misadventures which had blighted his prospects of a large inheritance from his grandfather. The story possessed all the elements of melodrama—an angry parting between William's father and grandfather, shipwreck, rescue, and a successful impersonation by another Southcott which deprived William's father of what should have been his. The unlucky man was finally drowned at sea. His wife promptly remarried, thereby losing the final claims upon her husband's inheritance. The too briefly grieving widow then allowed her new husband to dissipate the little that remained of her assets before her own premature death.[14]

If little else, each child of William Southcott was to inherit this sense of lost gentility, of having fallen beneath his or her proper station in life. Joanna wrote that when her father was the victim of some insult, an attorney, also named Southcott, "rose up and spoke very warmly, and said he would not see my father abused; for he was of as good a family as he, or either gentleman present; and was the first of the family that had ever known what it was to work." The lawyer said "the estate that belonged to my father had been in possession of the family for seven generations." He even offered to help William Southcott recover his property if he would go to London "and prove his grandfather's will." Joanna said he did not go because it "was in the time of war, when pressing was great both for landsmen and seamen, and my father was afraid he should be pressed, and therefore wished to defer it." Before the war's close, the attorney died and Joanna's father "gave up all thoughts of seeking after his estate, and thought his own hands should support him." Late in life William tormented himself with reflections on his lost inheritance. Without those thoughts, Joanna was to say, "He should be as other poor men were, nothing to reflect about; but now old age and poverty were come upon him, and he could not forget what he was entitled to."[15]

As a young man, there was little time for William Southcott to reflect idly on what might have been. Orphaned and friendless after his mother's death, he went as a servant to an uncle who taught him farming. At twenty-one he "took a farm."[16] An attractive young man, he relished the attention he received from the young girls in the neighborhood. Joanna said that he "married his first Wife out of pity, because he saw her upon a sick bed, and he was told she could not live without him." The first Mrs. Southcott did not have long to enjoy her inglorious conquest. As his wife lay dying, William Southcott's eye had already lighted on a successor whom he decided to court "as soon as decency would allow."[17] In the hard years to come, his second wife, Hannah, bore him six children and became the stabilizing influence in the family.

William Southcott's first farming venture began in a promising way but ended disastrously. By putting costly improvements into the land, he sometimes fell behind in his rent. A covetous neighbor offered to pay the rent in advance if Mr. Brooks, the owner of the farm, would devise some stratagem to dispossess the Southcotts. Brooks obliged with a plan. He stopped William Southcott on his way to Exeter market with his sheep and told him that although his rent was due he need not sell his flock unless it would bring a good price. Grateful for this concession, Southcott decided not to sell. Not long after his return from market, Brooks demanded the rent. Joanna's father was able to borrow the money but in anger decided to give up the farm "on the following Lady-day, and left all his labour for an enemy to reap the benefit of it." [18]

One of the factors which influenced Southcott in making his decision was the good reputation he enjoyed as a farmer. Joanna said proudly, "My father was allowed by every one to be as good a husbandman as ever ploughed an acre of ground." For this reason, other landlords had convinced him that they were eager to have him farm for them. When they made inquiries to Mr. Brooks, however, they were told that Joanna's father "was poor but honest," which convinced the neighboring magnates of the excellence of William Southcott's character but not of his capacity to put new improvements into their property. Finally, after Joanna's birth, Southcott "took a small farm at Gettisham, where the ground had been so impoverished for the want of dressing, that the first year they could not make the rent of the place." [19] Yet his local reputation remained excellent. According to Joanna, Squire Putt declared that "if there was an honest man in the parish it was my Father; and told my Father, when he was poorwarden and brought in his book of accounts at Easter, that he was peevishly honest, and therefore he must stand poor-warden another year." [20]

Misfortune did not bring out the best in William Southcott's character. He was susceptible to wild swings in mood which dominated the emotional atmosphere of his home. Hannah Southcott did her best to soften the effects of his erratic behavior. After one particularly unhappy episode, she counseled her family in words which revealed the tenuous basis of their security, "Children, why do you blame your Father? [I]f he is passionate he is compassionate, and he doth not do like many men, spend his time and his money in public houses, to bring you children to the parish." Indeed, there was much to be thankful for, she said. "He has been a hard-working, careful, industrious man, to keep you from the parish, that you might not suffer, as other poor apprentices do." [21]

Joanna's relationship with her father was particularly vexed. She remembered that he said of her, "My temper was such, and my care and industry so great, that no man but a devil could ever fall out with me." "Yet," she said, "he himself, when provoked to passions, without a cause, would fall out." Self-recrimination always followed. A servant remarked, "I never saw a man in such agonies in my life as he was, after he had done it." On one occasion, when Joanna had worked until midnight and her father had behaved badly, he insisted on waking her up to beg her forgiveness. She then sat for hours by his bedside, comforting him to sleep. On another occasion, he insisted that she run an errand at midnight to the pound house, a shed where apples were crushed for cider,[22] "more than two fields from the house we lived in." The moon was hidden behind clouds. When Joanna reached her destination, she mistook its outline for that of a man. Terrified, she heard some apples fall and believed "it was the spirit of the man that had been drowned in the well" nearby. Although Joanna managed to open the door of the pound house, she was nearly hysterical with fear. When she heard the sudden cry of owls and saw the moon unexpectedly shining against the door, she dropped her lantern, extinguishing it, and then, she said, "I . . . ran home as fast as I could run, without bolting the door, or locking the garden gate, but ran home through the lane, and thought I heard the footsteps of the spirit after me." When she arrived back at the farm, her father consolingly addressed her as "dear love." Joanna remembered, he "pitied my weakness, and did not blame me, but assured me I had seen no spirit, and it was nothing but the moon, that was hid in a cloud, that shined against the [door] jambs." But she deeply resented his benevolence. The onus, she felt, was on him for sending her out into the darkness where such terror was possible.[23]

One of Joanna's followers described how the relative circumstances of father and daughter had altered many years later, in 1797. William Southcott was "coming to Mr. Woolands' [the household of Joanna's employer] to have money of her, as he had no Employment. But as she had Given many pounds that Year before, and Knowing he would Keep on coming for money while he Knew she had Any; she asked Mrs. Wooland before him to lend her some money to give him. Mrs. Wooland gave meat to carry home, And gave him money; so that he said his Cup ran over. Joanna's Father was become a Child with Old Age And had lost all prudence in the Management of Money."[24] On the conscious level, Joanna remained throughout her life the dutiful, submissive daughter, keeping her father's house clean, which she particularly resented,[25] and supporting him. The pain inflicted on her in childhood, however, she could not forget. That other part of Joanna's personality, her "Spirit," prophesied the death of William Southcott. When he refused to cooperate by dying as predicted, the Devil admonished Joanna, "Thou Fool, it is an easy matter for thee to go in and choak thy Father, and then all thy Prophecies will appear true." The suggestion that she murder her father appalled Joanna, the devoted daughter. She thrust the terrible thought away and said, "My heart grew more in love for my

Father than ever. . . . so great was my love . . . that if he staid longer
from home then I expected I was miserable about him and went to seek
him (as I had determined in my heart to live and die with him)." [26] Indifferent to the terrible tensions at work within her, William Southcott
then complained that his daughter was too good to him. "Too much
oil," he said, "puts out the lamp." [27]

William and Hannah Southcott joined in encouraging the religious
development of their children. William Southcott insisted that they read
from the Bible each day and queried them frequently on the meaning of
individual passages. All except Joanna joined in answering his questions. "She felt, but could not describe: and all she appeared to know
was her own ignorance." Her usual recourse after one of these anxious
and humiliating sessions was to go to the fields or garden where she
wept in frustration at her inexplicable silence. [28] This verbal block, reinforced on a recurring basis, probably had its origins in Joanna's attitude
toward her father. It was sufficient to convince her siblings that she was
the least intelligent among them. [29]

Behind her wall of silence, the vulnerable young girl began to weave
the strands of an elaborate fantasy world which received unwitting support from the zeal of her mother, with whom Joanna could communicate, and the example of an aunt. "To all those who were in the habits
of friendship with my Mother," Joseph Southcott, Joanna's brother,
wrote, "it is well known, that she lived and died in the fear of God, with
the hope of a glorious resurrection through the merits of our Blessed
Savior." She was, her son said, "unwaried in her endeavours to inculcate
into the minds of her family, the principles of that Faith she herself embraced." [30] There is even some indication that Hannah Southcott herself
prophesied. [31] In any event, she firmly fixed in her daughter's mind an
abhorrence for sin. From an early age, Joanna said, "The fear of the
Lord was placed in me. . . . I not only feared sin, *but hate it*, and found
no pleasure in any thing but in the service of the Lord." [32] Hannah died
sometime before Joanna was twenty. [33] As she lay on her deathbed, she
told Joanna to commit herself to the ways of God. This was the turning
point in her daughter's life. Joanna recalled, "My Mother's Death sunk
deep into my heart. Since that, I may say I have been desirous to Live in
the Knowledge of the Lord but to my Shame I can reproach myself I
have forgot Him days without number and am an unworthy object of
His Loving Kindness." [34] Hannah Southcott's influence on her daughter
did not end with her death. According to Joanna, her mother communicated with her by three knocks on her bed at night approving her conduct, saying "something" about "Mr. Wesley and his preachers," and

answering Joanna's questions about "a future state," which, Hannah said, was all as described in Revelation.[35]

The one family figure who genuinely captured Joanna's imagination was her great-aunt Sarah. As a young girl, Sarah attracted many admirers with her beauty. She allowed herself only one love affair, however, and that an unhappy one. Her father broke off her engagement because he did not consider her suitor's prospects sufficiently promising. She turned to the consolations of religion, composing hymns and meditations which were later printed. But she "died of a broken heart . . . [when] she was about thirty; and the gentleman died about the same age." The book of meditations that Sarah had written survived the blighted romance. Hannah Southcott possessed a copy, and its contents made a lasting impression on Joanna. "Some of them," she said, "I learnt when a child, as I greatly delighted in them."[36] It is not difficult to see why a young girl, bullied into withdrawal from family life by her father, should have found comfort in these pious verses. Joanna said many years later that one of them, particularly, "seemed written upon my own heart."[37]

> Why should my passions mix with earth,
> And thus debase my heavenly birth?
> Why should I cleave to things below,
> And let my God and Saviour go?

By faith, Sarah found, man can reject the world and take his place among the saved, an aristocracy open to all believers.

> From earth's dull pleasures, and senseless mirth,
> Come thou my soul, in haste retire;
> Assume the grandeur of thy birth,
> And to thy nature heaven aspire.
> 'Tis heaven alone can make thee blest,
> Can every wish and want supply;
> My endless comforts ever blest
> Are all above the sky.

Joanna wrote that her aunt's meditations "have been a comfort and consolation to me, amidst the various troubles I have passed through, to bring my heart above this world."

The troubles began when she was fifteen or sixteen, "and began to be flattered by the world." Despite the good opinion of herself which resulted, she suffered constant frustration of her desires. "For everything I fixed my heart upon," Joanna said, "I was disappointed in, which made me turn all my thoughts, like my aunt Sarah," to religion. Her Spirit told her years later that, like her aunt, she had been fashioned in "a different way":

> I form'd thy heart to look to heaven above,
> In every sorrow thou hadst to pass through;
> I form'd thy heart, to bid the world adieu;
> I form'd thee like thy friend that's gone before,
> To be like Sarah thou hast mention'd here; [38]

Although there had been a charity school in Gittisham since early in the eighteenth century,[39] Joanna probably received little or no formal education. She herself said, "I am but a simple woman and was never brought to high learning."[40] She was not illiterate, as many believed,[41] though there had been little leisure or opportunity for self-improvement in her life. A critic supposed that she had devoted herself to the study of the Bible in her youth. "It is evident," he said, "that she received but a very illiberal education. Thus given up to the reading and study of the Scripture, she of course became very conversant with the Bible, and retained a great deal of it in her memory." Joanna admitted that she did not have a "learned education"[42] but denied that she diligently studied the Bible. "I was brought up to industry, from an early age," she said, "and had so much employment, that I had but little time for reading; neither did I give my mind to study the Scriptures."[43] To another who said, "You have got your Bible at your finger's end; you make the Bible your study," Joanna answered, "I have not studied the Bible these nine years." She remarked that the necessity of earning a living and the demands of her writing made such a task impossible.[44]

Even though Joanna could read, there is little evidence that books, other than the Bible and her aunt's hymns, exerted any significant influence on her development. She did say, "Many books of the works of men I have been ordered to read."[45] In fact, she read almost nothing. One of the few publications that Joanna actually admitted reading was Richard Knolles' *History of the Turks*, undoubtedly because of its eschatological implications. She attacked Paine's *Age of Reason*, although she denied having read anything else written by him.[46] When a follower sent her some of Brothers' prophecies, she returned them, saying, "I never read any books, at all; but write by the spirit as I am directed. I should not like to read any books to mix my senses with any works but those of the spirit by whom I write."[47] For information about the outside world, particularly news of catastrophe which helped confirm her conviction that the world had entered the Last Days, she relied on newspapers which probably, for the most part, were read to her.

Her handwriting was virtually illegible. Elias Carpenter, an early follower, who later separated from the Southcottians with much bitterness, said of Joanna, "The woman was as ignorant as can possibly be conceived; she could not write for any one to read; neither could she spell a word of two syllables, nor indeed many monosyllables." He said that, for example, she spelled the word because as "becos" and eyes as "i i."[48] Yet the spelling is regular and, according to Dr. R. E. A. Pool, seems "to reproduce, more or less phonetically, a West Country dialect." Dr. Pool found it possible to decipher Joanna's script, but it "had to be done by methods similar to the breaking of a simple cryptogram."[49] For this reason, Joanna had to teach several of her followers to read her script so that her writing could be transcribed for publication. This proved time-consuming and expensive. Later, she simply dictated to an amanuensis as she received her spiritual messages.

Despite the shortcomings in her education, and even her Spirit's judgment that her talents were "few,"[50] there is little question that Joanna possessed considerable ability. That she was to become the active center of a movement of tens of thousands of followers seems sufficient proof of this. One of her closest followers who was himself a Cambridge graduate and a fellow of Jesus College, the Reverend Thomas P. Foley, observed the prophetess on a daily basis over a period of years and found he had never met anyone with a "more sound Understanding than what she possesses."[51] On one occasion, Joanna's Spirit admitted that a measure of learning could be useful in helping her understand the time of tribulation which the country was entering. He exhorted Joanna to "call to thy remembrance the history of England, and what dreadful scenes of sorrow and misery, wars, and tumults one with the other, plague and pestilence, have been in the land, and what years of sorrow thou hast read of."[52] This suggests that she received at least the basic elements of an education.

The self-absorbed mood that runs throughout Joanna's writings encouraged candor about her own shortcomings. It seemed that the great liability of the Southcott family was pride, which had shattered its prosperity and unity and which Joanna believed she had inherited in abundance. She did everything she could to learn humility but without great success. "I never could conquer my own heart myself," she said, "for this war will ever continue, till we come out of ourselves, and come to the scripture rule, to cast away every weight." A second shortcoming was her obsession with clothes. Hannah Southcott criticized what her daughter wore but with little effect. "So deeply was my heart fixed upon the vanity of dress," Joanna recalled, "that I did not care how hard I worked, early and late, so long as I could earn money to get clothes to appear smart in." She said, "My father used warmly to reprove me, and say he was ashamed to see me, for a farmer's daughter to dress as I did." [53]

LOVERS

Joanna did not go unnoticed among the young men of the neighborhood. "When I was young in years," Joanna said, "I had many Lovers: but the first I indulged the company of was NOAH BISHOP, a farmer's son in Sidmouth." Her relationship with Noah established the pattern which her other romances followed. She was flattered by his attention; "I admired the nobleness of his spirit, and was convinced his passion was love, when he held me so strong by my hands, that . . . my hands and wrists [hurt] for many days." But she only succeeded in tormenting both herself and Noah with her mercurial shifts in mood. Working against her strong attraction for him were her own religious scruples. "All these ponderings in my heart drew my love almost to madness, that nothing but religion could keep me in my senses." When Noah retreated from her rebuffs, her ardor reasserted itself, "for I wished to awaken his passion to return again: for I had rather die with him than live without him." Made anxious by her indecisiveness, Joanna had gone to great lengths to meet Noah at the Sidmouth fair and revive their friendship. "But," she said, "for my life I could not; my hand and heart seemed as though they were bolted, and I desired my brother to go for the horse, and go home directly." [54] Afterward, Joanna recounted, "I went to service: and musing to myself repeatedly the hymns I have mentioned, and many others, I got the better of my foolish passion, though I could not blot his memory from my mind." [55]

Joanna was working for a Mr. Brown, a Honiton shopkeeper, when she met John Thomas, whom she thought "a man of fortune." She made it clear to him that her father, though a farmer, could give her nothing as a dowry. Thomas replied that this did not interest him. He was apprenticed to a serge maker and he told Joanna that his financial prospects were quite sufficient without contribution from her family. Thomas asked Joanna to marry him, offering to install her as a shopkeeper before his apprenticeship expired. With a young man's bravado, he attempted to impress Joanna with his affluence (as she remembered): "Money, my dear, I do not want; I have money enough for you and myself too: I have fifty pounds a year, which my uncle left me; I have money out at use, which my Father gave me, which I will call in, if you will be married, and place you in a shop before my time is out; for I had rather have you without a farthing, than any other woman with five hundred pounds." [56]

Hannah Southcott's death brought Thomas' hopes to an end. Joanna could think about nothing but spiritual matters. Relieved that she had an excuse to put John out of her mind, Joanna now believed herself liberated "from the burden of my doubts and fears." She decided to go "into the West Country." There she met another suitor, a Mr. Rigsby, who fell in love with her (Joanna said) at first glimpse in Black Torrington Church. Joanna refused his advances because he had an illegitimate child even though he possessed a "fortune" of sixty pounds a year. William Southcott, who did not know of Rigsby's philandering, raged at his daughter when he found out that she had rejected such a good catch. He asked Joanna how she could turn down "a handsome, genteel man" with such wealth. He then proceeded to give full range to his exasperation over Joanna's quixotic conduct, finally shouting at her: "I don't know what the devil thou dost like!" He believed that his daughter treated her suitors like chalk figures, erasing them when they no longer amused her. Joanna said that the husband she chose would have to be "of a more noble spirit than [Rigsby] was." William Southcott answered with acerb good sense that "he did not see any of these noble spirited men going." [57]

The final emotional attachment of her youth was to a handsome young man of good character named Peter West. As with Noah Bishop, she was alternately drawn and repelled by her feelings for him. And, as with Noah, she decided to break off the relationship: "I was thinking with myself, where is my foolish heart wandering? and was earnest in prayer that the Lord would not permit the love of the creature to draw my heart from my Creator, and that the Lord would not permit me to keep company with any man, that he had not ordained for my Husband." When she finally severed her relationship with Peter West, he disgustedly said, "These upright men get if you can; but I don't know where you will find them." Joanna reflected, "True I found his words; as true as he did mine; for upright men are very scarce." [58]

Joanna's inability to accept the mundane fate of a farmer's wife found further expression in the pleasure she took in the popular tales which circulated in the village. In addition to the entertainment provided, they often conveyed the follies of human relationships or pointed up a moral of general utility. Those that Joanna remembered in later life were the stories of amorous entanglements involving lovers from different levels of society. She had unusual interpretations of their characters and actions, which throw light on her psychological development. One of these was the famous story of Lord Burnet.

While Lord Burnet was out hunting, it went, his wife was caught in adultery with a page named Musgroves. A retainer hurried to inform his

master. The two lovers listened to a series of horn blasts announcing the
return of the outraged husband. Although Musgroves wanted to escape,
the noble lady dissuaded him. Upon his arrival, Lord Burnet threw open
the door of his chamber and found the adulterous pair still in bed. He
addressed Musgroves:

> Well, how dost thou like my bed, he cry'd?
> And how dost thou like my sheets?
> And how dost thou like my wedded lady,
> That lies in thy arms asleep?

The page's insouciant reply must have been very popular with the Gittisham villagers.

> O, well I like thy bed! he cri'd,
> And well I like thy sheets!
> But better I like thy wedded lady,
> That lieth in my arms asleep!

Lord Burnet then dispatched the lovers with his sword.

> So he kill'd the Lady and Musgrove—
> So merrily sings the bonny thrush,
> So sadly sings the Sparrow—
> So merrily sung Lord Burnet himself,
> For I shall be hang'd to-morrow.

Perhaps more disagreeable for Lord Burnet than contemplating his own
execution was the knowledge that he had promised the hand of his eldest daughter to the page who carried the ill tidings, if the appalling
disclosure proved true.[59]

Joanna believed the story to be an allegory. The wronged husband,
Lord Burnet, was, in fact, Christ; his deceitful wife represented the
Jews; the lusty Musgroves was Satan, and the page a symbol of the
faithful Christian. The edifying implications of the story were now
brought to light. The *arriviste* Jews had been both hypocritical and
faithless to their divine spouse and had received just retribution. Joanna's Spirit said:

> And so they [the Jews] all were wed to ME,
> That grandeur great I knew to be;
> That Lords and Ladies I'd make all,
> And so My Kingdom then should fall:
> But their adulterous hearts, I knew,
> That Love to ME they did not shew—

As she explained the symbolic role played by the adulterous wife, Joanna felt it necessary to make clear that the image could not possibly apply to her. "I knew I was innocent," she said, "for I have never suffered a man to come into my presence . . . ; neither would I suffer myself to look into the Street, fearing I should see a man." [60] She then offered further interpretation.

The first sound of the horn, alerting the lovers to the arrival of Lord Burnet, could only refer to the alarm that would awaken the nation at the Second Coming of Christ. The subsequent blast must be that of "the Horn of Redemption," heralding the promise made to man that "satan must, with his followers, now fall together." Satan, "the guilty lying wretch," responsible for the alienation of the Jews' devotion, was to be dealt with by an angry God as Lord Burnet had dealt with his wife and Musgroves. Even the murderer's execution and Christ's crucifixion could be successfully superimposed. "Lord Burnet's death is past already, in our SAVIOUR's being Crucified upon the Cross, after HE had cut off all the Brides [the Jews], that defiled His Bed, and defiled His Honor, by following after other Lovers, that were defiled by the arts of the devil." [61]

In a second story, a knight learned from the stars that his bride would be "an infant born of mean parents." Over the years, he attempted to have his future spouse put to death because "he could not bear to think that child should be the partner of his soul to complete his happiness." The reluctant bridegroom, however, grew contrite at his own perfidious conduct. Finally, not only did he pronounce himself reconciled to his humbly born bride but also, because he now realized that the match was ordained by God, "he married her, with raptures of joy and love." The Spirit provided the following monologue for the repentant hero:

> Pardon, said he in agony,
>   For wonders I behold!!!
> Millions of charms in thee must be,
>   My fluttering heart grows cold;
> When I look back upon the stroke,
>   How oft I've seek'd to slay
> The beauty bright before my sight,
>   That doth in wonders lay:
> Wonders at first to me did burst
>   When I the star beheld,
> That such an infant then was born
>   For me to cloath with gold.
> No beauty then to me was seen

> To see a helpless child,
> Born of such parents that were mean,
>   A Knight's heart to beguile;
> Ladies of fame I thought to claim,
>   In title great with me;
> Therefore the heavens I judg'd unkind,
>   To shew such destiny
> As did appear to me then clear,
>   To let myself down low;
> But by the wonders that are here,
>   No Knight so high can go.[62]

A third tale, "The Parable of the Hermit," presented another romantic triangle. Belinda loved Osmyn, "an officer in the Navy," who went off to sea. Orlando, the jealous rival, enlisted the aid of a hermit to steal a ring which Belinda promised Osmyn she would keep. The hermit, however, turned out to be Osmyn in disguise who managed to foil Orlando's machinations. "So will Satan be caught," Joanna said, "in the very trap he hath laid for others by the Goodness and Power of our blessed Lord."[63]

The sexual element in each of these stories both fascinated and repulsed Joanna, especially the sensational aspects of the tale of Lord Burnet. She confessed later that though compelled to publish the tale it had been very upsetting for her. She defended her action on the grounds that there were many examples of illicit love in the Bible.[64] Lord Burnet, his lady, and Musgroves the page shared with David and Bathsheba, for example, the same moral frailties. Inspiring lessons could be drawn from the former as well as the latter. These stories, and Joanna's relationship with her various suitors, reveal a fundamental tension in her personality between delight in a sexual situation in the abstract and horror of it in concrete, personal terms. In two of the three parables, the sexual relationship is between partners of vastly dissimilar social backgrounds. In her fantasy life, Joanna pictured herself as the beautiful young girl of humble circumstances who some day would be chosen by a "high-born" lover.

But, the high-born lover she sought did not exist. Joanna retreated from the decisive moment in each of her relationships, with all its sexual implications, into an interior world where the object of her desires had come to assume an ideal form. No mortal could have approximated this ideal and certainly not a young farmer or apprentice serge maker.

This interior image was the creation of her own peculiar psychological needs. Through her mother's influence, Joanna had developed a literal horror of sin. Sin was a category of opprobrium which became increasingly inclusive as she grew older. Yet, from the beginning it must have included any physical manifestations of sex, helping to explain her erratic behavior with Noah Bishop and the other young men attracted to her and to whom she was attracted. By repressing her natural impulses, she applied increasing pressure to the fantasy world which she had been elaborating since childhood.

THE SPIRIT

There was nothing unusual about Joanna's decision to enter domestic service. The primary motives of those who did so were security and the wish to rise socially and economically.[65] This was a course often followed by unmarried daughters of small farmers. An observer writing in 1766 bemoaned the fact that this principal source of recruitment seemed to be drying up:

Small farmers were the people that used to stock the country with the best of servants: these were the nurseries for breeding up industrious and virtuous young men and women; whereas the generality of servants now-a-days, are such as have had but little opportunity of learning how to do business so as to be fit to make good servants; . . . ; whilst those who rent small farms have generally wherewithal to give their children learning sufficient to qualify them to read virtuous books, and to know how to behave in a proper and decent manner. Besides, the girls have opportunities of learning at home how to brew, bake, cook, knit, sow, and get up linnen, &c., whereas poor people's children have not such advantages.[66]

There is no evidence in her writings of what duties Joanna performed as a servant. One source states that she labored "for many years" as a cook for a family in Exeter.[67] Through her employment in the households of several upholsterers, she became sufficiently proficient to consider setting up her own business. But in 1792, as she was entering the often emotionally difficult years of middle age, events from the outside world finally penetrated her fantasies. "One night I dreamt I saw men in the air, who pitched with their horses upon the earth," Joanna said. "The horses fought furious, and the men fought furious, and so frightened me that I awoke, and thought the French would land."[68] She began hearing "Voices" and having visions,[69] signifying that her fantasy life had finally attained an autonomous existence of its own.

It may be well to point out now that there is nothing inherently pathological about this so-called splitting of consciousness. The great mystics have enriched the literature of human experience with records of a similar kind of dialogue between themselves and God.[70] Blake, of course, serves as an excellent contemporary example. His friend, the artist Samuel Palmer, found him "of all men whom I ever knew, the most practically sane, steady, frugal and industrious."[71] Likewise, those who came in contact with Joanna, including Blake's friend William Sharp, found her normality one of the most compelling proofs for the authenticity of her claims.

Joanna's Spirit recalled to her the circumstances in which she first became aware that God had chosen her as the intermediary through which He would make His will known to the world:

Remember [the Spirit said] in what powerful manner thou wast visited by day and by night in 1792. And how the whole Bible broke in upon thee, as though Angels that were ministering Spirits were Sounding in thy Ears, that the End of all things was at hand. Reflect on the feelings of thy own heart, how hateful every appearance of Evil was in thy sight, and how thou sat drowned in tears, only to hear Innocent Songs, because they were not to My Honour and Glory. Remember how every oath went to thy heart. And in Church how thou was affected with the prayers and preaching, thy heart was then filled with the love of God, and an hatred to every Appearance of Evil. This was thy heart when the Sun of Righteousness first Arose on thee with power. All thou had'st felt before appeared but the break of day to the rising Sun, that then arose in thy heart with power.[72]

Joanna was at last able to live out her fantasy. She, the village maid, had finally been noticed by a high-born suitor, and an intensely jealous one at that.

> All to refuse, no man thou'lt chuse,
>   I know, to wed, but ME;
> So I'll appear thy husband here,
>   That every soul shall see.[73]
>
> . . . .
>
> As Lords have Stooped so low to wed
> I'll Stoop to Wed with thee.[74]

The Spirit called Noah Bishop "my rival foe."

> A Noah here, I'll now appear,
> And thy First Love now see:
> Because my [i.e., Joanna's] heart he did ensnare,
> And gain'd the love of thee.
> But it was I, that dwelt on high,
> Then kept thee from that man:
> For in the end, 'twas my intend,
> I, in that name should stand . . .[75]

In his love for Joanna, the Spirit had eliminated her suitors, as David, in his love for Bathsheba, had caused Uriah's death. "I slew the Man by love, by drawing her heart after ME. . . . This have I done with all her lovers, till I taught her heart to love ME, and ME only." The Spirit told Joanna, "What was of earth was earthly and sinful; but what is from the Spirit is spotless and innocent without sin unto salvation."[76] Joanna's interior ideal had thus fused with the image of a divine lover. The experience was accompanied by an intense emotional gratification. She described the range of her reactions during a visitation by the Spirit:

All of a sudden the Spirit entered in me with such power and fury, that my senses seemed lost; I felt as though I had power to shake the house down, and yet I felt as though I could walk in air, at the time the Spirit remained in me; but did not remember many words I said, as they were delivered with such fury that took my senses; but as soon as the Spirit had left me, I grew weak as before.[77]

She was to be the Bride of Christ when He returned to earth. A lambent eroticism flickered through her dreams:

At last she fell asleep with the strong breathings that were over her head which is impossible for her to describe, and which took her senses quite away—and whether awake or asleep she does not know; but she remembers that she was quite awake when she felt the hand of the LORD upon her; but in that heavenly and beautiful manner, that she felt joy unspeakable and full of glory. She felt herself laying as it were in heaven, in the hands of the LORD, and was afraid to move, fearing she should remove his heavenly hand, which she felt as perfect as ever woman felt the hand of her husband.[78]

Joanna described the charms of the "most beautiful and heavenly figure" that shared her bed:

He arose, and turned himself backward towards the feet of the bed, and his head almost reached the tester of the bed, but his face was towards me, which appeared with beauty and majesty, but pale as death. His hair was a flaxen color, all in disorder around his face. His face was covered with strong perspiration. . . . His locks were wet like the dew of the night, as though they had been taken out of a river. The collar of his shirt appeared unbuttoned, and the skin of his bosom appeared white as the driven snow.[79]

Minor infidelities sometimes occurred. Once Joanna exchanged kisses with a "Good looking" angel.[80] On another occasion, "I dreamt I was in bed, and thought some one lay close to me, and put their arm round me." "I thought," she said, "I would turn in my bed and see if anyone was by me. As I turned a good looking youth sprang off from the bed."[81]

From her childhood, Joanna's fantasies had encroached more and more on her apprehension of reality. Her awkward relationship with her father, the encouragement given her daydreams by her mother, and the example of her aunt have been described. Important, too, was the vague sense of lost gentility, of having fallen from a higher station in life, yet another unhappy legacy of William Southcott, which quite possibly made her more than usually sensitive to the misery and inequity of her situation. Her Spirit told her, "But let men discern the Sorrows of thy Life and then they will See what was thy Pondering thought in thy Early Age and where thou Looked to for Comfort when Disappointed in the world." [82]

At last, however, she had found that comfort which she desired. There was no longer the gnawing tension between her own psychological and sexual needs and their fulfillment. A perfect consummation was effected within her new role. She discovered herself to be the woman mentioned in the twelfth chapter of Revelation,[83] "a woman clothed with the sun, and the moon under her feet, and upon her head a crown of twelve stars: and she being with child cried, travailing in birth, and pained to be delivered." Having *become* the woman, Joanna also *became* lover and prospective mother, both of which she had been denied in reality.

POPULAR CULTURE

Joanna's confusion of her identity with that of a biblical figure, the Woman of Revelation, was a reflection not only of her own neurotic sensibilities but also of the disturbed international scene, which encouraged her belief that the world had entered the Last Days and that all the extraordinary characters of the prophetic books must soon be making their appearance. In a sense, however, the new career upon which Joanna was preparing to embark was only an exaggeration of a traditional role which the popular culture of Devonshire had long recognized and sustained. Joanna's local prestige was based upon her generally acknowledged success as a prophetess. "There was scarce any thing happened to the nation, or to particular families, or individuals, with whom she was acquainted," one of her employers said, "that she . . . did not inform me would happen before it did." [84] Joanna's accuracy in predicting the quality of the harvest, the life expectation of local notables, and the progress of the war with France had excited the admiration and the support of her neighbors but hardly their complete surprise. There had always been certain members of the community proficient at predicting future events, either by their mastery of arcane knowledge, such as astrologers or fortune tellers, or by supernatural inspiration, such as witches or wise women. In addition, dreams and visions were generally recognized as the medium through which intimations about the future were made known. Joanna's career, therefore, must be seen not only within the perspective of her own unusual psychological development in an age of social upheaval but also within that of the popular culture in which it had its roots.

The popular culture of Devonshire was an intriguing syncretism, combining both pagan and Christian traditions. The peasantry believed that cases of individual misfortune or communal catastrophe frequently had supernatural causes. They were intent on ordering their relationship with the spirit world so as to forestall or minimize the effects of such visitations. The ritual of Christianity intertwined comfortably with that of paganism to assist them in their purpose.

On occasion, the pagan tradition stood clearly revealed. Mrs. Anna Bray, a long-time resident of Devon and an acute, if somewhat condescending social observer, saw reapers at the end of harvest chanting incantations around one of their number, a "priest," who held an offering to the spirit of the harvest in his uplifted arms. On a clear day, she said, the liturgical celebrations of various groups of workers, conducted on hilltops, could be heard across the countryside. At other times, bizarre hybrids between paganism and Christianity resulted. To cure illness, for example, charms and herbs were prescribed by an old woman, "the charmer." If the difficulty was an "effusion of blood," the "charmer" would recite:

> Jesus was born in Bethlehem,
> Baptized in river Jordan, when
> The water was wild in the wood,
> The person was just and good,
> God spoke, and the water stood
> And so shall now thy blood—
> In the name of the Father, Son, [and Holy Ghost.]

The following was prescribed for a burn:

> Three angels came from the north, east, and west,
> One brought fire, another brought ice,
> And the third brought the Holy Ghost,
> So out fire and in frost.
> In the name, [of the Father, Son, and Holy Ghost.]

Sufferers from the "fits" asked for the church keys so that at midnight they could crawl under the communion table three times as a remedy for their illness. Those with a toothache sought relief by biting a tooth from a skull in the churchyard and carrying it with them throughout the year.[85] Amulets, usually worn around the neck, were particularly prized for both people and animals. In Devon a string of parchment with some suitable inscription, such as "This is a sign against evil demons" or "This sign is against witchcraft, putrid infection, and sudden death," found wide acceptance.[86]

One of the most prominent features in Joanna's immediate neighborhood was the well-known Rolling Stone, "a pagan sacred stone," which provides another fascinating example of the confluence of traditions. The stone is almost six feet long and a little over five feet wide, weighing about a ton, and lying at Putt's Corner on Gittisham Hill. Its origins are as obscure and tantalizing as those of similar stones at Avebury and Stonehenge. During Joanna's lifetime, it probably stood erect, a signal to travelers on the main roads from Honiton to Sidmouth and from Ottery St. Mary to Lyme Regis. To local people, however, the Rolling Stone had another and more awful significance. They believed that at midnight when the moon was full the stone rolled down to the River Sid, where the waters washed away blood stains remaining from human sacrifices. At the same time that this occurred, however, "an armed statue" in the church at Ottery St. Mary, where Joanna was baptized, would slip from its pedestal and patrol the aisles, suggesting that the church was not without its own defense against the old pagan rites.[87]

If the people of Devonshire accepted the ubiquitous presence of spirits in their world, dreams were respected as the medium through which they communicated to humans. Even someone as skeptical of superstition and as critical of the unorthodox as Mrs. Bray agreed that "there are spirits who walk the air as we do the earth; there are intelligences every where about us that, as winged messengers of God, perform His will, and yet we neither see nor understand them." She said: "All things are instruments of his Providence; and it is not our place to say which he may choose, or which he may reject, to fulfill his own unerring purposes. The dead may appear as they have appeared on earth; and who shall say it cannot be so? How many strong and right impulses sway the mind of him who seeks God, who knocks and it *is* opened to him; that prove themselves, in their results, to be no other than the secret counsels of His will for His servant's good!"[88] It is not surprising, therefore, that Joanna believed that "the Lord spake by dreams and visions of the night, and that the angels of the Lord are ministering spirits, to administer to the heirs of salvation." She described an incident "which [she said] convinced me the Lord was round our beds, and in our paths, the same now as he was in ages past, to day, yesterday, and for ever the same." The incident concerned an uncle, on the eve of a voyage, who told his father that he had a premonition of death. Upon completion of the outward leg of his journey, he wrote to his mother telling her that he intended to leave his ship and take another sailing for London. He received a letter from her in which she said that she had been told in a dream of his death. To ease her mind, he reconsidered his plans and stayed on the original ship. The captain, however, deviated from his course in order to win a race with another vessel into port, causing his ship to be dashed to destruction on rocks.[89]

The death of this "remarkably religious young man" and the manner in which it had been foreseen had a strong impact on Joanna. Because of "this singular instance, with many others, I never looked on no other than a sure sign the Lord was with us as in ages past." Another uncle neglected to visit a sick friend, a Mr. Dagworthy, who shared his interest in religious matters. "Their conversation was of things divine, and their observations and reflections on the wondrous works of Providence were deep, and deep were their writings." Unknown to Joanna's uncle, Dagworthy unexpectedly died. When he went to inquire after his friend's health, he "met his corpse at the door." According to Joanna: "This sudden shock so took my uncle's heart, that whether it was the death of Mr. Dagworthy, or the reflection of his own mind and heart because he had not gone and seen him sooner, remained unknown to all his friends, but the shock went deep, and a melancholy preyed on his spirits." He suddenly disappeared one morning, causing much consternation in the family. But his mother interpreted one of her dreams to mean that he had gone to sea and would return safely, which he did.[90]

Joanna heard of other dreams which confirmed her belief that those who ignored nocturnal warnings did so at their own peril. A servant girl working for Joanna's grandmother dreamed "that in Caddy-fields, between Ortrey [Ottery] and Fairmile, she was walking, and . . . met a Cat, sitting upon a gate, which scratched her upon the right breast till she bled to death." The girl was found later raped and murdered "at the very same place she dreamt the Cat met her." Another servant girl dreamed that she was stung to death by a serpent while walking on Sidbury Hill. Joanna's grandmother was concerned because of the fate of her previous servant and instructed someone to accompany her. The girl, however, refused to acknowledge that there was any reason for alarm. Of course, "she was found murdered at the very spot that she dreamt the Serpent met her; and was judged like the former, to be ravished first and murdered after." Joanna reconstructed a piece of advice her grandmother had given a skeptical maid, Molly Gardiner, on the subject of dreams:

Dreams are not always fables, Moll,
Though, some wonders they do tell—
For 'tis in dreams the Lord doth warn
A way that men do not discern.[91]

With these experiences weighing heavily upon her, Joanna not surprisingly said, "I was informed I should be shewed in dreams how the
things upon the Nation should come on."[92]

WITCHCRAFT

Undoubtedly the most vivid of all the fabulous creatures that stalked
the popular imagination was the witch. And perhaps nowhere in England was belief in this figure more firmly entrenched than in Devonshire. White witches used their powers for good, black witches for ill,
and there were even gray witches who had "the double power of either
overlooking or releasing."[93] Their medium of travel remained the conventional one, for witches. In a dream, one of Joanna's friends saw "a
woman in the Air that they said was a Witch and She Landed and came
into her Father's house and had a chain of Gold round her neck, which
no man Knew its worth."[94] Terrifying dreams could fade imperceptibly
into reality, recasting harmless neighbors or itinerants into striking new
figures of horror. A century before, in 1682, three women, Temperance
Lloyd, Mary Trembles, and Susanna Edwards, were executed for witchcraft in Exeter, followed two years later by Alicia Molland's trial and
death. These were perhaps the last such executions in England.[95] After
1736, when the witchcraft act of 1604 was repealed, legal machinery no
longer existed to convict a member of the community on the charge of
witchcraft. The repeal did little to alter the view that certain instances of
misfortune were caused by witches, a characteristic of English witchcraft beliefs which distinguished them from those on the Continent,
where witches were usually tried for heresy (i.e., devil worship).[96] A
study of witchcraft in Essex notes that "seventy percent of all accusations related to the death or illness of human beings, and most of the
others to injuries to animals."[97]

The pattern seems to have been that a poorer member of the community, almost always a woman, imposed a claim on another, for alms or
food, for example, which she had every expectation of being granted.
When refused, she might utter some obscure malediction at her un-
charitable neighbor, usually the head of the house. The neighbor, guilt-
ridden because of his action, would in time sustain an unexpected misfortune, an illness or death in his family or perhaps some affliction to

his animals, causing him to remember his altercation and to bring a charge of witchcraft against the person to whom he had been ungenerous, thus at the same time discharging his own guilt and finding a remedy for his suffering. Because the critical aspect in the relationship between the accuser and the accused was their personal enmity toward each other, larger catastrophes affecting a whole community, such as illness or famine, were almost never blamed on a witch but rather ascribed to God. There could be an exception, however. Under certain circumstances, as Joanna was to know, a community or neighborhood might come to feel that one individual stood in a malevolent relationship to it.[98]

In Devonshire, the popular belief in witchcraft was unusually deep-rooted and long-lived. Roger North, who attended the trial in Exeter in 1682, wrote: "The women were very old, decrepit, and impotent, and were brought to the assizes with as much noise and fury of the rabble against them as could be shewed on any occasion. The stories of their acts were in everyone's mouth, and they were not content to belie them in the country, but even in the city where they were to be tried miracles were fathered upon them, as that the judges' coach was fixed upon the castle bridge and the like. All which the country believed, and accordingly persecuted the wretched old creatures." "A less zeal in a city or kingdom," North said, "hath been the overture of defection and revolution, and if these women had been acquitted, it was thought that the country people would have committed some disorder."[99]

A century and a half later, Mrs. Bray said that "even in these days with the peasantry of Devon, witchcraft is still believed to be practised in the county, and that extraordinary circumstances or sufferings are brought about by the active agency and co-operation of the devil." "Indeed," she wrote, "our superstitions here are so numerous, and so rooted amongst the poor and the lower classes, that. . . .Witchcraft is still devoutly believed in by most of the peasantry of Devon." She was convinced that Joseph Glanville, the author of *Philosophical Considerations Touching Witches and Witchcraft* (1666), had gathered much of his material from the same locale in Devon which she was finding so fruitful.[100] It was Glanville who said, "Those that dare not bluntly say, There is No GOD, content themselves . . . to deny that there are Spirits and Witches."[101]

A story current in the neighborhood and which Mrs. Bray felt could have been taken from Glanville's work concerned "an old witch" who could transform herself into a hare. When she was in need of money, she sent her grandson to a huntsman who gave him sixpence for information about such game. Time after time, the huntsman and his pack of hounds would pursue the hare, but always fruitlessly. Finally, he suspected the deception and consulted the justice and a clergyman. Together, they were able to end the witch's game by confronting her just as she had changed back into human form. Although she was given an opportunity to repent, she later bewitched a young woman, "making her spit pins," and was burned at the stake.[102]

In another instance, a guide told Mrs. Bray that he had been bewitched by "an illminded old woman" for seventeen weeks. During this time, he never slept or felt sleepy, never ate, with the exception of one or two biscuits, and every night, beginning at midnight, he was tormented until six o'clock in the morning by the sensation of pins pricking him. Mrs. Bray also found that the "lower classes" believed the famous hero Sir Francis Drake to have been a wizard. According to them, he conjured up fire ships from small blocks of wood which he had thrown into the sea and with these defeated the Armada.[103]

Joanna shared the popular belief in witchcraft and confirmed its practice in Devonshire and other parts of the West Country. "Concerning Witchcraft," she said, "I am truly convinced it is practised by evil and wicked people, who are in a league with the devil, and without that no witchcraft can be wrought. But I know, that in Devonshire, witchcraft in an uncommon manner, was done." A family named Richard appealed to her for help to combat the stratagems of a local witch. There was evidence "that plainly proved it was witchcraft that was practised on both the stock and family; so that they were daily losing their cattle in a way that nothing but witchcraft could have accomplished. This continued some years before my visitation, and continued after Mr. Richard's being a believer desired me to inquire, if it were the will of the Lord to give me an Answer—if they could do anything to prevent these evil powers." Joanna consulted her Spirit. "I was answered, they should write on parchment, 'Holiness to the Lord,' and put it [around the head] inside the horses' bridles and the halters." Mr. Richard complied with her directive "and they lost no more cattle." "Afterwards," Joanna said, Mrs. Richard "was greatly afflicted with a pain in her head, and she wore the parchment with the words 'Holiness to the Lord,' round her head, under her cap. And she told Mrs. Taylor and myself, the pain had ceased since that time—and they had lost no more stock, though they had had the trial many years."[104] That these beleaguered souls approached Joanna for assistance indicates her acceptance as a wise woman or "charmer" in the neighborhood.

News came to Joanna one day of a coven of witches active in the Bristol area. "A woman from Bristol was here lately, and told us of a most wonderful witchcraft that was practised near them, which was done by twenty different people, who were formed together; and they had the Methodists to pray for those who were afflicted by these witchcrafts; but I do not find they received any benefit from them." [105] However, Joanna refused to attribute every unusual misfortune to witchcraft simply because its cause was difficult or impossible to determine. In this, she undoubtedly was exercising much greater discrimination than many of her neighbors. Continuing her description of the Bristol witches, she said:

I am giving you this information that I have heard of witchcraft, but I do not know from your account, that this is the case with Mr. and Mrs. ———, as there are many disorders which baffle the skill of medical men; and discern from the newspapers how 500 men in the army of Great Britain died in one month; on which it was remarked, that there must be some extraordinary disorders to cause such mortality. In Essex there has been a disorder, which carried people off in a very short time. If they survived the third day they got well, but very few who were attacked lived so long. The doctors could not find out the disorder; so we cannot say the disorder came from witchcraft, though the doctors may not know how to treat the disease. [106]

If some saw Joanna as a wise woman who could protect individual members of the community from witchcraft, others were convinced that she herself was a witch. Joanna believed that it was God who inspired her predictions of bad harvests. Her enemies, however, heard her prophecies as maledictions and saw her not as the handmaiden of the Lord but as a witch moved by a malign influence to act against the welfare of the neighborhood. Their accusations of witchcraft grew out of the adversary relationship which developed between Joanna and certain elements of the community, particularly the clergy, who refused to give her claims a sympathetic hearing. [107]

The bad harvests of 1799 and 1800, Joanna believed, were appropriate retribution on those who failed to take her prophecies seriously. In 1799, Joanna said, "The first week we had fine weather, and every appearance of a good harvest," which caused the local clergy to offer up thanksgivings. Then she was told by the Spirit, "The harvest would be like my father's blossom, that appeared beautiful in May, but the blight came and destroyed great part of it; and so would the floods come upon the harvest." The following Tuesday the rains came "and it is known to the public at large how it continued: prayers were publicly put up in Exeter, by all classes of people, that the Lord would stop the rain." Instead, "as men had refused to hear the words of the Lord, so he would refuse to hear their prayers." [108]

When she was told the following year that her letters to various Exeter clergymen had gone unread and that the chancellor of the diocese had burned the one which he had received, she was moved to prophesy that the harvest of 1800 "should be burnt up." At first, "they began to cry out, it was a good harvest, and dropped the price of corn a week before harvest, and said it was the finest harvest that ever was known." The opinion was that "wheat would be for six shillings a bushel, and barley for three." "Many," Joanna said, "began to curse me; and said, where were the prophecies now? I had prophesied of a bad harvest, but there never was a better; and I ought to be burnt." She could be sure of only one thing. If it was a good harvest, her inspiration could not be from God, "as he had so strongly affirmed the heat of his anger should hurt the harvest, as the Chancellor's anger burnt my letter." The boasting of the farmers was soon quieted. "Before one month was past in the harvest, the farmers began to change their words, and some said they had not two pecks an acre; and there was not corn enough in the land to last till Lady Day." The hardship was to become so widespread that the poor rioted in Exeter and throughout the county. "The spring following," Joanna said, "the turmoil rose all through Devonshire."[109] As a result of her successes, Joanna achieved a reputation of such magnitude that farmers based all their plans on her prophecies.[110]

At about this time, Joanna added even more to her local prestige by accurately predicting the death of Bishop Buller, who had become bishop of Exeter in December 1792.[111] Buller, too, had received a letter from Joanna and had ignored it. Some time before, he had had an interesting encounter with her father which had created a family sensation and which may have led Joanna to believe the bishop would courteously hear her claims, thereby making her even more resentful when he did not. William Southcott had arrived unexpectedly one day at Heavitree, a few miles outside Exeter, where his daughter was working. Joanna remembered that he

surprized us by saying he came in the Bishop's Carriage, at which we all laughed. He said, if he did not come in it, he rode behind it, which was true; for the Bishop had been out an airing, and his carriage overtook my father, when he ordered his coachman to stop, as he saw my father going towards Exeter, and enquired how far he was going: he said, to Heavy-tree, to Mr. Wooland's, to see his daughter; that he came from Getsham. The Bishop then ordered his servant to alight from his horse, and assist my father to get up behind his carriage. My father then enquired of the servant, who the gentleman was, that he might know how to return him thanks when he alighted. The servant answered, it was the Bishop of Exeter. My father said, he was glad he asked; or else he should have thanked his Honor, instead of his Lordship.

Joanna's employer, Mr. Wooland, told her father that "the servant only mocked him." It seemed improbable to him that the bishop would have "condescended, in that manner, to have stopped his coach to take up a poor man," although Buller "bore a most noble character." An inquiry, however, verified that it had indeed been the bishop.[112]

Joanna's prophecies were a form of execration of the "unbelieving world" which had rejected her. That "world" responded characteristically, smearing her with the charge of witchcraft. Joanna remembered that, when she prophesied the bad harvest of 1800, "I was . . . cursed by buyer and seller; both farmers and tradesmen boasted of the plenty, and called me fool and old witch, said that I deserved to be hanged for telling them they would be disappointed."[113] When her prophecies were fulfilled, however, attitudes changed. She received a gift of poultry from a Devon farmer, Mr. Cole, "who was Joanna's great opposer, and said she ought to be hanged, when she was in Devon; but now all the family are come in strong believers; *as the harvest in Devon has awakened many*."[114] There were always those who grudgingly recognized the truth of her prophecies but, Joanna said, "only *abuse me* at the same time and *call me an Old Witch*, in foretelling what will take place."[115] The reason that more of the "middling" victims of the bad harvest did not continue to denounce Joanna lay in the sheer enormity of the threat which she posed. The fulfillment of her prophecies meant that her claims must be regarded with solicitude if further disaster was to be averted.

Even so, her feelings of being unwanted, unappreciated, and unfairly deprived of authentic status in the community could never really be assuaged. She wrote in 1804 of "all the sorrow and sufferings . . . and the persecutions [she had] met with from an ungrateful[,] illnatured[,] and sinful world" from 1792 onward, feeling compelled to add, "I have often thought no woman living never went through so much unjust cruelty and ill treatment as I have."[116] A state of absolute polarity between Joanna and her opponents had thus emerged, well illustrated by some observations in the Exeter newspaper: "Her predictions were loud and frequent—full of comfort and happiness to her own subjects—dreadful denunciations of woe to the rebellious creatures that did not acknowledge her sovereignty, and trust to her prescience."[117]

ASTROLOGY

In her struggle for a distinct identity, Joanna had to compete with another who, with witches and wise women, had a firmly established place in the fabric of community life—the astrologer. Astrology did not lose its prestige as a scientific discipline until the middle of the seventeenth century, when the two bases upon which it rested, the immutability of the heavens and the disjunction of terrestrial and celestial bodies, were seriously disturbed. In discrediting the Ptolemaic conception of the universe, Copernicus, Galileo, and Newton dealt astrology a heavy blow. Since astrology is the study of the influence of the heavenly bodies on human affairs, once the discovery was made that the heavens were infinitely more varied than previously imagined, the task of calculating that influence no longer seemed as possible. Of greater impact, however, was the attack on the traditional distinction between the perfection of the heavens and the imperfection of the earth. When it was established that celestial bodies were subject to change, that comets, the immemorial symbols of impending disaster, were not unique phenomena but liable to discernible natural laws and that the earth was composed of the same materials as any other planet, it could no longer be seriously maintained that the heavens exercised *any* influence on the earth by virtue of a hierarchical superiority.[118]

If by the end of the seventeenth century astrology had lost its credibility with the educated, it still possessed considerable vitality among the people. The method by which the principles of astrology were spread on the popular level was the almanac. In the seventeenth century perhaps more than two thousand different almanacs were published, each selling on the average for twopence. The numbers of almanacs produced in the ten-year period following November 1663 approached three to four million. For the modest sum expended, the buyer received a record of astronomical events, a calendar, and an astrological forecast of the major occurrences in the new year. Also given was advice on which days were best "for bloodletting, purging and bathing; and [the almanac] showed right and wrong times for engaging in most kinds of agricultural operation, planting, sowing, mowing or gelding animals." In addition, by the beginning of the seventeenth century, interest in astrology was also reinforced by "a large, though indeterminate, number of low-level consultants scattered through the country, claiming to operate by astrological methods, and substantially patronized by a popular and unsophisticated clientele." As might be expected, "many of these were indistinguishable from the village wizards."[119]

Astrology tenaciously maintained its prestige on the popular level into the next century, although erosion had begun to set in. An argument used by Joanna's followers to support her claims was that the cover of the 1750 edition of Moore's Almanac depicted angels rejoicing, presumably at her birth.[120] But one of Joanna's followers asked her opinion about astrology. She answered, "Your ideas of astrology are like mine. I think it wrong: and in this, we ought to search the Scriptures for our guide,—not to seek after star-gazers, or astrologers." She cautioned a Mr. Wadman, who had been seduced by its claims, by citing examples from scripture which showed that men of good will relied on God for knowledge about the future and not on human calculation:

If Mr. Wadman has formerly studied the Planets, I think he ought to give it up. It is what I would not do for the world. Not that I think Mr. W. would do it, if he thought it was wrong. But, as I have no answer given me from the Lord, respecting it, I can only give you my opinion upon it. We know, in Daniel, it was not the wise men, as astrologers from any science of the planets, could tell the king his dream, or the interpretation thereof. But it was revealed to Daniel by the Lord. And in like manner to Abraham, concerning Sodom and Gomorrah; and concerning his having a son, it was by a revelation of the Lord. And the Angels being sent to him, that these things were made known to him. I do not find in the Scriptures that any of the prophets foretold any events by study, because it is said,—"the word of the Lord came to them:" and when Hezekiah was in danger of Sennacherib's army, he did not go to astrology to seek after the planets, to know what would be the events; but he went to the prophet Daniel, and the word of the Lord came to him from the prophet.

Joanna found in the Bible that "those who trusted in the Lord, sought the word of the Lord from the prophets. But when Saul rejected the word of the Lord, he went to the Witch of Endor; and those who did not rely upon the Lord, chose astrology to be led by." There was the case of a young minister who had

heard that his nativity had been cast at his birth, and that he was born under the influence of an evil Planet, wherein Satan would have power to tempt him to hang himself on such a day, and such an hour. Hearing this, he gave himself up to prayer, relying upon the Lord that he would keep him from falling into those dangers.

When the day was come, Satan's temptations were strong upon him, to hang himself; but he resisted, by trusting in the Lord. When inward temptations would not do, Satan appeared visibly to him,—and contended with him; and he contended with the devil till the hour was past; and then Satan and his temptation left him.

His friends hearing him disputing with someone in his room, whom they thought was a man with him, enquired who it was? He then related the whole, and said, evil planets had a power over those who did not rely upon the Lord; for his support and protection would counteract all their power. He said his temptations had been very great; and had he not trusted in the Lord, he should have hung himself; but now the time of his temptations were over, and he was happy to be freed from his power.[121]

Clearly, then, Joanna did subscribe to the belief that "evil planets had a power over those who did not rely upon the Lord." She believed, for example, that Satan lived in the moon. "There is a world in the moon," she said, "and in that world Satan dwells."[122]

The prophetess shared, too, the belief that comets were the harbingers of great events. The comet was a "sign." Even "mockers," Joanna felt, must realize "that the stars in the firmament that are placed as lights for man are now wearing out." Although vaguely aware that the appearance of a comet was no longer the unique event it had once seemed, she was certain that the comet of 1811 was the herald of the coming cataclysm. "For though men have given it a name that they say hath often appeared," her Spirit said, "I now tell thee it is a sign of much greater events than hath ever yet taken place." All would be blessed who saw "the unusual light" and inquired "into the meaning of this appearance." Religious men, her Spirit counseled, had the duty to ask "whether the sign was come to warn of severe events as a scourge to mankind, or whether the sign was of blessings to show mankind that I should change the scenes of sorrow and bring a glorious harvest to man." "For I now tell thee," he said, "this light which appears to thee like light from a fire issuing forward with a . . . flame, as if the substance of a fire was behind. . . . is the light appearing to show mankind the signs in the heavens in this day of their visitation." [123]

Joanna, therefore, accepted, at least partially, the claims of astrology; but she realized that humans could not be free and at the same time have their futures ordained for them by the stars. To be truly free meant that one had to be truly Christian, relying on trust in the Lord to circumvent the influence of the evil planets. Those without faith would be subject to all that had been ordained for them. Even a believer might have a difficult time. For this reason she presented the story of the minister as a warning to others who might be similarly tempted to taste the fruit of this dangerous knowledge. "What power of evil would he have destroyed," the Spirit asked, "or what power would he have conquered if he had gone on relying upon the planets, to shew him more and more what was decreed against him?" He would only "have given room for Satan's working the stronger to have told him these evils were decreed against him, and he must submit." [124]

But perhaps Joanna's most deep-seated objection to astrology lay in the challenge that it offered to her own prestige. "If a man can foretell future things by the stars," wondered William Bridge in the seventeenth century, "then what need of prophecy?" [125] This was the question which concerned Joanna, too. One of her secretaries caught her in a melancholy mood made worse "from our telling things of gipsies and people's telling of fortunes, which had been true." She said, "This worked a jealousy in Joanna's heart." The Spirit managed to reassure her, pointing out that any inspiration of the gypsies came from Satan. [126] And this was an inspiration perilous to pursue. One of Joanna's followers who himself prophesied learned from his Spirit, "I see the evil, how it worketh to draw the hearts of my labourers from me; but trust not to *astrologers* or *familiar spirits*; they are at work for hell, to deceive man." [127]

"COMMUNICATIONS" FROM THE SPIRIT

Joanna Southcott emerges from a preindustrial culture in which supernatural experiences were tightly woven into the warp of life. The compendium of such experiences was, of course, the Bible, which, in addition to reinforcing popular beliefs about such figures as witches, also offered in the prophetic books a number of alternative roles to that of the village wise woman or charmer. Certain pious women found these roles irresistibly attractive when the abnormal character of the times made it seem imperative that they be filled. A contemporary of Joanna in the West Country became known as the Cornish Trumpeter because she believed herself one of the seven trumpeters promised in the book of Revelation to announce the Second Coming.[128] Joanna, like her other contemporaries—Luckie Buchan, the leader of a small millennial sect in Scotland; Mother Ann Lee of the Shakers; and, in America, Jemima Wilkinson, "the Publick Universal Friend"—declared that she was the Woman of Revelation.[129] To justify her pretensions, Joanna asserted that the whole course of her life had anticipated this great moment. "So singular have my life been in this world, and so many remarkable things have happened in it, that it was nineteen years ago I was ordered to write my life, for it should go in print, and thousands should be convinced by it." [130]

Joanna would undoubtedly have remained a regional celebrity, as did the Cornish Trumpeter, with only a small devoted coterie of believers if she had not taken her savings and a selection from her writing to a printer in Exeter. In 1801 she published her first pamphlet, *The Strange Effects of Faith*.[131] Her writings consisted largely of "communications." These were messages with which the Spirit bombarded her ceaselessly—bolstering her new self-awareness, transmitting information about future events, annotating daily occurrences. Everything which was happening and which had happened to her had become invested with significance, and everything found its way onto paper. The results were at first circulated among selected confidants and later spilled into sixty-five books and pamphlets over a period of thirteen years, in all, some 4,500 printed pages. Much more remained in manuscript.

A fascinating aspect of this unlikely literary endeavor is that Joanna disclaimed any responsibility for it. To her, as to Suzanne Labrousse, the French prophetess, it was simply inadmissible that anyone with her humble attainments could be the author of the writings. Both her followers and critics agreed. The malicious asserted that one of her better-educated supporters performed the herculean labors of authorship. Joanna retorted that it was the work of her Spirit. The writings, she said, could not possibly be of her own invention. According to her, there was "no knowledge of myself to know, nor power to fulfill." She exclaimed, "I could as well have made the world, and formed the whole creation, as I could invent such writings of myself," continuing, "for I am not so wise as the world has made me." Not only was she not the author of the writings, but they also could not have been "the invention of any created human being." She made her case with force and impressive sincerity: "Without the Spirit I am nothing, without the Spirit I know nothing, and without the Spirit I can do nothing; so whether you judge the spirit good or bad, to that Spirit you must allude the whole; for I am a living witness against every man that says my writings are of my own invention, and I publicly affirm that such a man believes a lie, and the truth is not in him, who believes my writings are from myself." [132]

Joanna disclaimed any understanding of the communications she was given by the Spirit. At first, she took them down in her own hand. Later, as mentioned, because of the illegibility of her writing, she dictated to a secretary. On occasion, the flow of words broke off in midsentence. [133] Usually, however, the long, rambling, obscure communications poured forth uninterruptedly, most often in verse, amazing Joanna as much as her hearers by the quantity and the velocity with which they were delivered. A question of general concern was the matter of style. Could the Spirit of God really be speaking to mankind in verse and prose full of misspellings and grammatical mistakes (a question also asked of Suzanne Labrousse and Richard Brothers)? The printer even charged Joanna for such corrections on her first publication, announcing the fact on the title page. Joanna answered that God had adjusted His manner of communication to His instrument. [134] This was not to say that Joanna's vanity could not be stung by criticism, such as the sneer that hers "was Doggrel verse [mean, worthless]." She found the result unsatisfactory, however, when she tried to write "in the highest Language that I could think of." What God wanted was simplicity and innocence of expression, not "Eloquence full of offense." [135] In an original sense, Joanna was a popular writer, speaking in an idiom immediately comprehensible to those whose reading experience was circumscribed by Bunyan and the Bible and whose education had been as informal as her own. She said in 1801:

Simple as these books appeareth to some readers, they are too high for any man to climb to, and too deep for any one to fathom. Could ye behold the mysteries of them, ye would see they wanted neither eloquent language, brightness of speech, nor noble stile to set them forth, but depth of wisdom to understand them; and were they put into eloquent language, deeply spoken, and wisely placed, as though they came from men of learning, they would baffle all your belief, and men would judge it a cunning devised fable from some wise inspired penman.

But now to convince ye it is from the simple, and that the Lord hath dealt simply; yet, however simple this may appear, it is too strong for all your senses; ye could no more look into these three volumes of books, and see them clear, and keep your senses, than ye could stedfastly behold the burning sun, and not hurt your eyes; for the one is as much too strong for your senses, as the other is for your eyesight.[136]

The source of Joanna's literary impulse lay deep within her subconscious. Undoubtedly stirred by the achievement of her much admired Aunt Sarah, Joanna had ambitions which she refused to acknowledge to herself or others. Satan, in one of his several, protracted encounters with Joanna, offered her what presumably was the irresistible enticement, to make her "the first writer in the world" if she would support him in his warfare with God.[137] Her own creative experience—for that, of course, was what it was—bore a marked similarity to that of Blake. Blake told Crabb Robinson, the diarist, "I write when commanded by the spirits and the moment I have written I see the words fly abt the room in all directions. It is then published & the Spirits can read." Blake informed his patron, Thomas Butts, that he wrote "from immediate Dictation, twelve or sometimes twenty or thirty lines at a time, without Premeditation & even against my Will; the Time it has taken in writing was thus render'd Non Existent, & an immense Poem Exists which seems to be the Labour of a long Life, all produc'd without Labour or Study."[138] Like the poet, Joanna at times submitted only grudgingly to the pressure of her inspiration. On one early summer morning in 1803, the prophetess found herself behind in her daily tasks but sat down to transcribe a communication. "I obeyed with reluctance and wished to continue My work." Then, she said, "When I was writing my mind ran so much on my work that I grew restless and uneasy." Finally, "I . . . began to grow jealous of the Spirit though the [communication] was most beautiful."[139]

Now that automatic handwriting has been reduced to a parlor game, and we can read the accounts of contemporary literary figures who testify that their latest work of fiction came unordered from the subconscious,[140] the phenomenon which so affected the prophetess has lost much of its novelty. But for Joanna, Blake, and those who knew them, the experience was awesomely unique and remained central to their claims to have a special relationship with the world of spirits.

Despite periodic doubts, Joanna's certainty that she had been chosen by God for a great work remained unshakable. But it did not obviate the very human need for understanding and encouragement. For this, she turned to those who she believed would be most responsive, the Methodist community in Exeter.

II

The Reaction of the Churches

HUGH SAUNDERSON

Joanna Southcott has frequently been seen as a perverse manifestation of the Wesleyan movement. Richard Polwhele, an Anglican clergyman, even called the Southcottians a "Sect of Methodism."[1] Another clergyman accused Joanna of being sponsored in her literary activities by "a parcel of Methodist Parsons, [who] composed . . . them to impose on the Church Ministers, and teach them how to preach the Gospel."[2] However, the most influential source of the frequent misunderstanding about Joanna's relationship to Methodism was Robert Southey's essay "Account of Joanna Southcott," in which he described her as being "zealously attached" to Methodism.[3] E. P. Thompson accepts Southey's identification of Joanna with the Methodist movement in his discussion of the implications of her cult.[4] Similarly, Frederick Artz writes of Joanna as "the Methodist prophetess."[5]

At first, Joanna had high hopes that the Methodists would quickly rally to her side. "Had I been left to draw my own judgment, I should have thought the Methodists would have been *the first* that would have come in, because they pretend to preach of the visitation of the Lord." She discovered subsequently, however, that "they did not believe what they preached."[6] In her view, the wedge between words and belief was inserted when Methodism became successful and respectable. In the beginning, the Methodists had experienced nothing but "Scorn and Contempt and Persecution from the World." They were humble, as befitted a people chosen by God to do His work. But since becoming "Successful, Praised and applauded," and "being Judged Popular in the World [as well as] being Caresed by many of the Great," they were "filled . . . with pride and vain Glory."[7] For this reason, Joanna believed they were unresponsive to her. She said, "There is not a people in the world who hath caused me so much sorrow of heart as the methodists."[8] In July 1802, she wrote, "Do they not say they bless God for the manifestation of his Spirit and pretend to a Knowledge of God, but when the Knowledge of my Spirit comes with power they are as far from any Knowledge as the blind man is of colours."[9]

Joanna particularly abhorred George Whitefield's disciples, the Calvinistic Methodists, for their doctrine of an elect. One of her confidants spoke pointedly on the subject. The belief in an elect, he declared, "totally destroys all charity in the human heart, both to God and man." He found that "in their Public Worship they praise their Maker for electing them, and them only, to eternal life and happiness, and are quite insensible and indifferent to the fate of souls, whose numbers may be compared to the sands on the sea shore, thus brought into being by a decree of their Creator for no other purpose but to suffer eternal Torments." [10] Calvinism, Joanna remarked, condemned many to serve as soldiers in Satan's army. How could God so punish men for offenses they were in effect ordained to commit? [11] Joanna's adviser was chagrined that "the preachers of this horrid doctrine, some of whom have got themselves into the Church, are called popular preachers." He testified to their ubiquity: "Many have spread themselves into every part of the kingdom; they are to be found in every city and country village, whilst the Clergy of the Established Church are quite regardless of their flock, and suffer them to be carried away by these wolves in sheep's clothing." He was incensed by the passiveness of the clergy in the face of such a threat to the church, "as it is by neglect of duty in the Church Clergy, that these people have encreased and spread themselves every where." [12]

Three experiences influenced Joanna's ultimate estrangement from the Methodists: first, a disillusioning encounter with a Methodist preacher, the Reverend Hugh Saunderson; second, her rejection by the Exeter Methodist community; and, third, the apparent duplicity of a Calvinistic Methodist lay preacher, the Reverend Henry Tanner, to whom she had gone for advice.

Joanna's earliest contact with "Mr. Wesley's preachers" was sometime in 1782 or shortly afterward when she became involved with one of the more controversial and enigmatic figures in eighteenth-century Methodism, the Reverend Hugh Saunderson. Saunderson dealt the struggling Methodist community a heavy blow when he settled in Exeter after breaking with Wesley. Here, he "pitched his standard and declared open war" [13] against his former patron. The debate which has swirled around his career can now, perhaps, be settled with the help of Joanna's testimony. [14] She served as a witness of his conduct while he lodged in an Exeter household in which she worked as a servant. The preacher's scandalous behavior during the time that Joanna knew him was almost certainly a factor in her own final parting from the Methodist movement. Moreover, Saunderson's career demonstrates what unscrupulous use could be made of the superstitious fears which lay behind many popular conversions to Methodism.

For several years, Saunderson was one of Wesley's most valued if not always trusted lieutenants. Wesley regarded him particularly highly for his great effectiveness as a preacher. In 1773 the aged evangelist wrote to a follower in Ireland where Saunderson was preaching, "If you love me, hear Mr. Saunderson preach." He counseled Hannah Ball in Bristol later the same year: "I hope you will be able to speak to Mr. Saunderson [who was an assistant on the Oxford Circuit] without the least reserve. He has tasted of the pure love of God, and should be encouraged to hold it fast." The following year Wesley defended Saunderson from an attack made by Joseph Benson. "You fell upon Hugh Saunderson without rhyme or reason for contriving to supplant you at Edinburgh; whereas his staying there was not his choice but his cross." He reminded Benson: "Your congregations in Edinburgh are large: Hugh Saunderson's are larger still. Your preaching, and perhaps mine, has stirred up a sleepy people: his preaching has stirred them up still more. Our conversation has often quickened them: his has quickened them much more. 'But why does God work more by him that has far less sense than we?' To stain the pride of our wisdom. And hence not 'five or six girls' but 'the generality of the congregation' prefer his preaching to either yours or mine. They feel therein more of the power of God, though it has less of the wisdom of man." Wesley concluded his remarks, "Now, I see more than any single preacher can see, which of the preachers do most good, who have most fruit; and according to this, I form my estimate of them." In the fall of 1775, he wrote to his brother Charles: "When I was in Bristol, I ordered that Hugh Saunderson should preach on Thursday night. None but you should take his place. . . . Some much like, others much dislike, H. Saunderson; but his audience generally is not small."[15]

Wesley appeared resolute in his refusal to listen to the stories which pursued Saunderson. However, a follower who conceded that the preacher was "athirst for sanctification" told Saunderson bluntly: "Your youth, your natural propensity to gaiety and sprightliness, your unmarried state, and the pride of your own heart, will insensibly incline you to little fopperies in gesture and dress and little niceties about yourself; which will hurt your own soul, lessen your usefulness and make you ridiculous to others, if not guarded against." Wesley said benignly, "If you can guard Brother Saunderson against pride and the applause of well-meaning people, he will be a happy man and an useful labourer."[16]

But Wesley may not have been completely blind. Luke Tyerman, the biographer of Whitefield and Wesley, claims that Wesley addressed a letter of April 24, 1769, to Saunderson while the preacher resided in Ireland.[17] In it, Wesley asks that his correspondent "on this and every other occasion avoid all familiarity with women. This is a deadly poison both to them and you. You cannot be too wary in this respect; therefore begin from this hour." [18]

In 1773, Wesley and Saunderson traveled together on a proselytizing mission in Ireland. Saunderson's journal provides interesting detail about their progress through a largely hostile population. He wrote on May 3, 1773: "I came to Cork; Mr. Wesley gave the sacrament. . . . We lay that night at Charleville. In the morning set out for Limerick. Breakfasted with Mr. Coots, a gentleman worth £3,000 per year. Poor things! they were so fatigued with dancing last night that they could hardly be up at seven o'clock. This is not the way to Mount Zion. Yet they are a very agreeable family. The gentleman seems to have some desires for heaven." [19] When the two men reached Galway, Wesley preached "to a large congregation" which behaved, with one exception, decorously. Saunderson recorded, "At the last hymn one of Satan's children came with a great roar, as if he had just come from hell; but a gentleman laid hold of him and showed him the near way to the door." On May 19, 1773, they reached Sligo. Wesley said, "In the evening I preached in the market-house to such a congregation as has not been seen here for many years. Surely God is giving yet another call to the poor, stupid sinners of Sligo." Saunderson added, "Mr. Wesley left me in Sligo to preach in the evening, as the people desired it." Several times, circumstances compelled him to replace Wesley in the pulpit. On May 25, he wrote, "I was forced to preach in Mr. Wesley's place, as he had to go to another place." The next morning, he continued, "I preached again, and then set out to meet Mr. Wesley. He was not come at the hour appointed, so I sung and prayed to about 1,500 persons, and was just going to give out the text when he came." Saunderson described their last days together in Ireland:

Friday, July 2, was set apart for fasting and prayer. Mr. Wesley desired me to preach at five, which I did. We had a watch-night. It was a time of power. Sunday, July 4—At the sacrament I found it good to be there. At four I preached to a large congregation. . . . At five-thirty Mr. Wesley preached to a solemn congregation, and afterwards had a lovefeast. Monday, July 5—Ten at night we sailed from Dublin on board the *Free Mason*, Captain Shaw, and on Tuesday at five in the afternoon we cast anchor seven miles from Liverpool. Mr. Wesley and I made . . . our way on foot, and so got to town about eight; we were a little fatigued, but soon forgot it all. On Wednesday the 7th Mr. Wesley preached, and on Thursday he set out and left me here to preach for some days.

Saunderson's travels took him afterward to Chester, Manchester, Ashbourne, and Leicester. [20]

In June 1774, Wesley traveled to Edinburgh where Saunderson was preaching with great popular success. While walking to his lodgings, Wesley was served with a warrant for his arrest. The warrant accused Wesley of attempting to flee the city with Saunderson. A former member of the Methodist society in Edinburgh, George Sutherland, had charged "that Hugh Saunderson, one of John Wesley's preachers, had taken from his wife one hundred pounds in money and upwards of thirty pounds in goods, and had, besides that, terrified her into madness; so that, through the want of her help and the loss of business, he was damaged five hundred pounds." Because Sutherland feared that the two men "were preparing to fly the country . . . he desired his warrant to search for, seize, and incarcerate them in the Tolbooth till they should find security for their appearance." Wesley, quite literally, believed that the sheriff must have been under a malign influence in order to serve such a warrant. The matter was decided in favor of the defendants, however, and Sutherland was fined a thousand pounds.[21]

After this unsavory episode, Saunderson did not remain long in Wesley's good graces. Against instruction, he left his post at Bristol. Wesley wrote to Mary Bosanquet in May 1775, "Probably you know whether Mr. Saunderson is at Knaresborough. If he is, pray take up a cross for me. Write to him in my name, and tell him I desire him without delay or excuse to return to Bristol; otherwise he will disoblige me for ever." Two months later, he told Mary Lewis that Saunderson would not be reappointed to Bristol for a second year as would his colleague, John Murlin. "Two preachers never stay two years together in one place, unless one of them be a supernumerary. But I doubt his [Saunderson's] late behavior is another objection; for I am afraid the observations you make concerning it are but too well grounded."[22] In 1777, Wesley expelled Saunderson from the society. The preacher then went to Edinburgh where he managed to recapture his following. Wesley was in the Scottish city in May 1780 and recorded in his journal, "The rain hindered me from preaching at noon upon the Castle Hill. In the evening the house was well filled, and I was enabled to speak strong words. But I am not a preacher for the people of Edinburgh. Hugh Saunderson and Michael Fenwick are more to their taste."[23]

Two years later, in August 1782, Wesley arrived in Exeter on one of his tours. He observed sadly that "here poor Hugh Saunderson has pitched his standard and declared open war. Part of the society have joined him; the rest go on their way quietly to make their calling and election sure."[24]

At the time of Wesley's visit, Saunderson may have been living in the household of a Mr. Wills where Joanna worked as a servant. That Wills could be persuaded to accept a Methodist preacher as a lodger under any circumstances was a result of a bargain he had struck with Joanna. Still attractive in her early thirties, Joanna had been the object of several unwelcome advances made by Wills, who had been driven to thoughts of dalliance by the infidelities of his wife. He told Joanna, however, that his love for her was a "religious love." Joanna responded characteristically: "No tongue can paint the horror I felt, to hear of love from a married man."[25] Her Spirit was more understanding of Wills' motives: "At first he had no evil design, when he told thee thy religion made him respect thee; and I well knew it was thy religion, and the beauty he saw in thy mind, which made him love and esteem thee, having a wife so great an adultress, roving after every man, and seeing in thee so different a mind, drew his heart with cords of love."[26] Unappeased, Joanna threatened to leave. Wills prevented her by a kind of spiritual blackmail. "He threw himself into a violent passion, and said if I would stay he never would mention his love more; but if I went, never a methodist should come into his house again; but if I would stay he would maintain the preachers, that he knew I had a great regard for, as I thought them religious men."[27]

Joanna agreed to remain and Wills kept his promise, with disastrous consequences. He "took a methodist parson [Saunderson] into his house," Joanna said, "who declared himself a lover to the wife in my presence, and despised her husband, and wanted to set all the children against him." Saunderson's conduct left Joanna troubled and uncertain as to what course of action she should take. "I thought to get the man out of the house privately, by Mr. Wesley's preachers." But she was told "that Saunders[on] was turned out of their meetings."[28] Joanna faced an impasse. She could think of no tactful way to inform Wills of Saunderson's misconduct with his wife nor could she bring outside pressure on the preacher to leave. Apparently unsuspecting, Wills even maintained his guest "in a most extravagant manner." Joanna decided to confront the preacher directly. Saunderson pretended to think it was Joanna whom he was being accused of seducing. "He called the Three-one God to swear to those lies in one, which was that he had never touched me or kissed me in his life."[29] The only recourse that seemed open to her was to inform Wills by letter of the irregularity in his household. This, she hoped, would persuade him to evict Saunderson. But the maneuver backfired. Wills leapt to his wife's defense, calling her "a virtuous prudent woman." He said Joanna was "a wicked woman" because of her accusations of wrongdoing between his wife and Saunderson. Wills' face-saving duplicity could have astonished only Joanna. She sniffed, "I thought so ungrateful a man could not exist." But he then carried his revenge too far. Wills, Joanna said, "haunted me to the places where I went, to get me out of service." [30]

She had left Wills and gone to work for a minister named Marshall who dismissed her when Wills came to him with fabrications about her character and behavior.[31] So difficult did Wills make things for her that Joanna said, "I was obliged to go to law with him." She sued her former employer for defamation of character. Wills brought forward witnesses to support his slanderous accusations at a trial held in the guildhall. She was able to discredit their testimony by insisting that they were outsiders and arguing that Wills should produce members of his family to substantiate his allegations. "Mr. Wills would not purjure those in his own house, but he cared not how many he perjured out of his house." She asked that Wills' son testify, and "if he swore as these have, I will give up my cause." The son refused to defend his father, however, and Joanna won her case.[32]

Hugh Saunderson had in the meanwhile made serious inroads in the Methodist community in Exeter. Playing dexterously on the popular fears and superstitions of the people, he presented himself as a miracle worker with the power of life and death over both followers and adversaries. He encouraged just the sort of emotional hysteria which the sober, fastidious Wesley sought to avoid. Joanna attended Saunderson's class meetings and was at once attracted and repulsed by his pretensions: "He used to terrify all the people when he was in prayer; and was often telling what wondrous miracles he had wrought by prayer; and that he had, at a meeting, made the whole society lie stiff upon the floor, till he had got the evil spirits out of them; and I remember myself, once at a class meeting, a religious, good man shrieked out in such a manner as though he had sent an evil spirit into him; but I cannot say he ever had any power over me: only I used to think the room was full of spirits, when he was in prayer." Joanna's fellow servants in the Wills' household stood in terror of the renegade. They heard of a man from Plymouth who "had reproved Saunderson's conduct" and shortly thereafter died. Saunderson said that, in order to accomplish his critic's demise, he "had fasted and prayed three days and three nights, that the Lord would take vengeance on that man, and send him to eternity." This was not the only extraordinary incident attributed to him. Joanna declared, "Were I to go through all Saunderson's wonders and miracles that he told of, and all the wretched deeds that he did, I might fill many sheets of paper." [33]

Joanna accepted the fact that Saunderson performed "miracles." What she could not understand was how God could use an evil instrument to work such wonders. Her Spirit told her to open the Bible at random. It fell open at Revelation and she quickly saw that Saunderson was "the false prophet" who "worked miracles" until he and the Beast "were cast alive into a lake of fire burning with brimstone." Joanna now understood that Saunderson's supernatural acts were "wrought by devils." When she confronted him, he challenged her interpretation, telling Joanna he was inspired by God, "who gave him power to destroy all his enemies!!" Joanna recalled that he "said there never was a man so highly favoured of God as he was: and he would not thank God to make him any thing, if he would not make him greater than any man upon earth, and give him power above all men." She warned that if it was the devil and not God inspiring him "his end would be fatal in hell." Saunderson replied sardonically, "Yes, I will take care to get a good warm corner there." Shocked at his careless blasphemy, Joanna said she "never could bear him afterwards." [34]

Joanna rested content in the knowledge that Saunderson had not been chosen by God as His prophet. As for retribution for his conduct, she said simply that God was the judge, and her Spirit intoned, "the Great Assize for all draws near." [35] Saunderson's reign in Exeter was to come to an inglorious close. Joanna reported in May 1801, by way of an epitaph on their relationship, that "Saunderson[,] an abominable wicked preacher in the Methodist line who was some time at Exeter. . . . was driven with disgrace and infamy from Exeter, and is now a vagabond abroad if he is living." [36]

JOANNA SOUTHCOTT AND THE EXETER METHODISTS

Joanna had seen a faction of the Exeter Methodists embrace a man whom she considered the "false prophet," warned against in the book of Revelation. She must have presumed later, when she announced her own divine mission, that she would, at the very least, receive a hearing from her fellows in the Methodist society. In this expectation she was to be sorely disappointed.

At the guildhall trial, Mr. Wills' attorney called Joanna an "enthusiast," [37] a word with great emotive connotation, alluding as it did to the extravagant (and seditious) religiosity of the middle decades of the seventeenth century as well as to such contemporary manifestations as Methodism. Edmund Gibson, bishop of Lincoln, offered a useful definition of enthusiasm. Enthusiasm, he said, is "a strong persuasion on the mind of persons that they are guided in an extraordinary manner by immediate impressions and impulses of the Spirit of God." [38] For the enthusiast, like Joanna, the Bible was the record of the exemplary Christian experience, of a time when a perfect communion existed between people and the spirit of God. That this intimacy had been lost was the fault of the people and not God. Only the Methodists, it seemed to Joanna, had returned to the form and substance of apostolic Christianity. George Lavington, bishop of Exeter from 1747 to 1762 and a famous opponent of Methodism, complained of the Methodist assertion that "the Lord was in all their doings." He said: "Whatever errand they go about, though often not of the greatest significancy, it is still the LORD's DOING. Whether they are at home or Abroad, in good or evil plight, whether it rains or clears up, whether they escape a shower or are wetted by it, it is all owing to some divine direction, and made to answer some great purpose." [39]

The focus of the Methodist experience was the weekly class meeting, a gathering of five to twelve men and women (often segregated by sex) under the tutelage of a class leader. The latter's responsibility was "to advise, reprove, comfort or exhort, as occasion may require." [40] James Lackington, the famous London bookseller, described a typical class meeting in his autobiography. Early in his life, Lackington had been a devout Methodist. Later, he repudiated the movement but then suffered a change of heart and retired to Devon, where he supported several Methodist chapels. According to his account, the meeting began with a hymn. Afterward, the members knelt down and the class leader offered an extemporaneous prayer. Then the leader made a self-criticism of his behavior during the previous week. Having finished, "He enquired of all present, one after another, how they found the state of their souls." As one might expect, the moral climate was varied. "Some he found were full of faith and *assurance*, others had dreadful doubts and fears; some had horrid temptations." Most often, the members dwelled at excessive length on their shortcomings, "declaring that they were the most vile abandoned wretches on this side [of] hell, that they wondered why the earth did not open and swallow them up alive." The leader would then give a few words of encouragement or criticism to each of his spiritual charges. The meeting concluded with more prayers and singing. [41]

The Methodist class meetings were thus characterized by a highly charged emotional atmosphere in which members were applauded for the candor of their disclosures and supported in their moral infirmities by the fellowship of the group. Certainly, in this kind of environment, Joanna must have felt, she would receive a sympathetic hearing. She began going to Methodist services but also remained scrupulous in her attendance at the Established Church. She said: "I attended constantly my church, forenoons and afternoons, and received the Sacrament. At the same time I also attended Mr. Westley's preachers at eight o'clock in the mornings and at six in the evenings; these hours not interfering with the service of the established church; but did not then join their society, though I was much invited to do so."[42] Her brother, Joseph, was alarmed at the turn she had taken. He said, "I . . . thought my Sister so far possessed of methodism, from her very strong propensities for reading and perusing the Bible, that I was afraid her intellects might be hurt."[43]

The Methodist society which Joanna finally joined had been established in Exeter at an early date. In November 1739, John and Charles Wesley had traveled to Tiverton in Devon to console the widow of their recently deceased brother, Samuel, who had been headmaster at Blundell's School. While in Tiverton, John Wesley received an invitation to preach in Exeter from a friend of Samuel. He delivered a sermon on Sunday morning at St. Mary Arches. His topic was "the Kingdom of God is not meat and drink; but righteousness, and peace, and joy in the Holy Ghost." The rector would not let him preach in the afternoon, however. "Not," he told Wesley, "that you preach any false doctrine. I allow all that you have said is true. And it is the doctrine of the Church of England. But it is not guarded; it is dangerous. It may lead people into enthusiasm or despair." Charles Wesley said he preached in 1743 "to about a thousand sinners, mostly gentlemen and ladies, with some clergy," in what was believed to be the first open-air sermon given in Exeter since the Middle Ages. Whitefield may have had a third of the city as his audience the same year.[44]

This auspicious beginning received a serious setback from the great anti-Methodist riots in Exeter in 1745. A contemporary pamphlet asserted that two hundred men and women were "put in peril of their lives, some so beaten and bruised that they begged to be killed outright." The normally cynical *Morning Post* described in the issue of May 16, 1745, what took place:

In Exeter the Methodists had a meeting house behind the Guildhall, and on May 6th the mob gathered at the door, and pelted those who entered with potatoes, mud and dung. On coming out, the congregation were all beaten, without exception. Many were trampled under foot, many fled without their hats and wigs, and some without coats or with half of them torn to tatters. Some of the women were lamed, and others stripped naked and rolled most indecently in the kennel [gutter], their faces being besmeared with lampblack, flour, and dirt. This disgraceful mob consisted of some thousands of cowardly blackguards, and the disturbance was continued till midnight.[45]

The society in Exeter struggled on with a handful of members until late in the century. In 1776, Wesley wrote to a new preacher, "I am glad to hear that you are ordered to Exeter: there seems to be a particular providence in this. We have a small Society there, which is but lately formed, and stands in need of every help." Two years later he said to the same correspondent, "I am glad to hear that the work of God begins to prosper even in poor Exeter."[46] The Methodists obtained a permanent meeting place, Musgrave's Alley Chapel, in 1778 or 1779, which they were to use for thirty-four years. Wesley wrote a note encouraging his Exeter following on their initiative: "It seems to me that this is a very providential thing, and that you did well not to let the opportunity slip. There is no doubt but our brethern at the Conference will readily consent to your asking the assistance of your neighbours for your preaching house, and the time appears to be now approaching when poor Exeter will lift up its head."[47]

By 1782, when the Reverend Hugh Saunderson caused the society to divide, the Methodists still numbered only 30 to 35 members.[48] Wesley's final despairing note came on his last visit to the city on August 31, 1789:

We set out at three in a lovely morning, and reached Exeter between twelve and one. Here the scene was much changed: many of the people were scattered, and the rest faint and dead enough. The preaching house was swiftly running to ruin, the rain running through the room into it amain, and five or six tenants living in the house were noisy enough, having none to control them. We called earnestly upon God to arise and maintain his own cause. He did so in the evening congregation (which was much larger than usual), while I strongly enforced the parable of the sower; and the dread of God seemed to rest on the whole congregation.[49]

In 1798 the membership had climbed to 70 and by 1815 reached 291.[50] But Exeter and Devon were never to be strongholds of Methodism.

The date that Joanna formally joined the Exeter Methodists is somewhat unclear. She became a member at Christmas of either 1791 or 1792. In a pamphlet published in 1802, she herself said, "At Christmas, 1792, by divine command, I was ordered to join the society, for ends I should know hereafter, for something should happen in the class meeting, which would be the means of convincing the people [of her claims]."[51] And there was good reason to be optimistic. Joanna's class leader was John Eastlake, whom the historian of the Exeter Methodists remembered "as the 'father of the Society,' a man of saintly character and manners, and a pattern of meek and simple goodness."[52]

The Spirit instructed Joanna to tell her fellow class members of her experiences. This caused the troubled woman great apprehension. "No one spoke of past experience in a class meeting; how should I go to act different from others?" Her Spirit answered abruptly, "If thou art afraid to speak of the goodness of God, I will take it from thee. For now thou art comforted, strengthen thy brethren." Unfortunately for Joanna, her "brethren" were not edified by the revelations she had to make, particularly in view of the awkward way she disclosed them. "I thought they might judge me simple, and I was much confused whilst I was speaking," Joanna admitted. Greatly depressed by the results of her initiative, the following day she prayed earnestly for enlightenment. "I was answered the people at the meeting were malicious against me; hearing me speak so much of the goodness of God, they had been in prayer that the Lord would take it from me." Joanna became disconcerted at this intelligence. "[I] said to myself, *it cannot be*; they are too religious men, and Mr. E[astlake], I know to be too good a man." It was not Eastlake, however, but "the rest." For their sake, Eastlake "wished me out of the society, fearing I should hurt the people." The Spirit told Joanna that the class leader had not informed her personally "because he was afraid to offend thee." This was too much for Joanna. She broke down sobbing and determined to abandon her enterprise. "But the more I thought to give it up, the more the Bible broke in upon me, and seemed as though I had ministers preaching in my ears." Her emotional turmoil lasted for the remainder of the week. Finally,

I was powerfully told that I should go to the class meeting, and tell the people what had happened unto me; and what was also in their hearts and thoughts concerning me. This I trembled to do, but being threatened that the Lord would withdraw his spirit from me, if I did not do as I was commanded. This made me go with trembling steps, and when I came I thought many times I should have fainted at the meeting, as the class leader began with these words—let us come to the purpose of things that are present, and say no more of the things which are past.—This took all fortitude from me and I thought of leaving the meeting, as I grew faint, but was answered I should not—and then the Lord restored my courage, and I told them I thought it was the powers of darkness that had given me such an account of them, that such things as before-mentioned were in their hearts and minds concerning me to set me against them. But finding the class leader was silent, and the men looking one upon another with confusion in their countenances; I began to grow jealous, and thought to myself what can all this mean? I was answered by the spirit I should leave the meeting *for good.*

Eastlake tried to persuade Joanna to rejoin the society. The Spirit agreed and told her "to go and reprove them." She was in agony at the reception she knew would greet her. The thought of it "chilled my heart and soul within me; well knowing if they had been offended with my speaking of the goodness of God to me, they would be much more offended if I went to reprove them." Before she returned to the class meeting, however, the Spirit informed her that he was only testing her submissiveness, as he had that of Abraham in telling him to kill his son Isaac: "I only did it to try thy obedience; and as far as thou hadst it in thy heart to obey, so far will I reward thee. For now will I swear unto thee as I did unto Abraham, that I will make with thee an everlasting covenant, and I will save thee with an everlasting salvation. Thou shalt prophecy in my name, and I will bear thee witness." [53]

HENRY TANNER

After the distressing rebuff she received from Eastlake and his class, Joanna went for advice to the Reverend Henry Tanner, a Calvinistic Methodist lay preacher who combined zealous participation in church affairs with full-time employment in an Exeter mill. Tanner is one of the few members of Joanna's circle in Exeter about whom we know very much. After his death in 1805 at the age of eighty-seven, a diary, some letters, and a fragment of an autobiography were found among his personal papers. They were published together as a book in the hope that proceeds from the sales would add substantively to the support of his widow and daughter, who were left indigent at his death. The autobiography makes compelling reading because of the very ordinariness of the life which stands revealed. Undistinguished by either outstanding personal gifts or good fortune, Tanner often found himself in severe economic straits. Poor and devout, he differed little from thousands of others of his generation who remain anonymous.

By his own account, Tanner was a wastrel as a young man. The turning point in his life occurred when he heard George Whitefield preach in Plymouth. Whitefield was conducting a service in an open field. His voice carried to Tanner and several of his fellow workmen in a nearby shipyard. They thought the preacher mad and decided to go over and bully him. The men were running toward the sound of Whitefield's voice when they suddenly saw him, arms outstretched, exhorting sinners to follow Christ. Tanner stopped abruptly, profoundly moved at what he saw and heard. "Every sentence in Mr. Whitefield's sermon was delivered in such a divine, pathetic, and energetic strain, as cut me to the heart." At the close of work the next day, Tanner threw down his tools and hurried to hear Whitefield speak again. He got as near to him as possible, this time in order to protect the preacher from malcontents. Again he was deeply stirred. "I thought I beheld heaven in his very looks. My heart was melted at once." The Calvinist preached on those who crucified Christ. He said to the crowd, "I suppose that you are reflecting in your minds on the cruelty of those inhuman butchers, who embrued their hands in innocent blood." Then, suddenly, he turned and

stared directly at Tanner, crying out, "Sinner! thou art the man that crucified the Son of God." Tanner never forgot his reaction. "I knew not
whether to stand or fall. My sins seemed all to stare me in my face. I was
at once convicted. My heart bursting, mine eyes gushing forth floods
of tears. I dreaded the . . . wrath of God, and expected that it would
instantly fall upon me." Then Whitefield stretched out his hands and
invited sinners to repent. "Come to Jesus," he said. "Come just as you
are. Come thou Jerusalem sinner. Jesus bids me call, and invite thee to
come. He saith himself, all that do come, he will in no wise cast out." At
this point the great preacher's voice must have begun to quicken. "Here
is grace to pardon you; a fountain to cleanse you: a righteousness to
cloath you; a full, finished, complete salvation for you in his blood.
Come, sinner; come, come, come, my master bids you come. Now is the
accepted time; now is the day of salvation. Hark! how he calls you."
Tanner answered the call. "I at once thought that, like Israel at the Red
Sea, being delivered from spiritual Egypt, and mine enemies, like the
Egyptians, floating as dead carcases before me, I had nothing to do
more but to walk towards heaven in a continued sunshine." [54]

Sustained by the immutable egoism of the saved, Tanner came to accept the disappointments of his life as divine visitations meant to test his
faith rather than any indication of personal shortcomings. His first wife
became an alcoholic after his conversion and sold most of their belong-
ings in order to support her addiction. But he learned from prayer that
"*these light afflictions are but for a moment, which work out for his
people a far more exceeding and eternal weight of glory*." With his
clothes and furniture gone, his child uncared for, even forced to rent a
furnished room "and . . . that I could not easily obtain; for few cared to
have a drunken woman near them," Tanner's equanimity remained in-
tact. "I have often thought how wonderful the goodness of God in these
dreadful afflictions, for I can truly say my soul thrived under all." He
entreated his wife to join him in prayer. He "found her not only totally
averse; but she threatened to cleave me down the head with the hatchet,
if I attempted to pray in her presence." Her behavior finally became so
disreputable that no one would rent lodgings to them. He was forced to
convert a lumber room, without heat and swarming with rats, into a
dwelling place, using old sails for beds. It was tolerable because Christ
had lived in even more humble surroundings. When anger at his wife for
bringing them to such a state threatened to overcome him, it subsided
because "the great consideration which constantly wrought upon my
mind, was the distinguishing grace of God, which made all the difference between my conduct and that of my poor wife." He was among
the chosen; she was not. Some time later, the magistrate considered her

public behavior so disgraceful that he ordered her confined in the work-house. "I ruminated on the situation of my poor wife," Tanner said, "in whom I saw the emblem of a sinner, dragged away from the obstinate commission of sin, to an eternal prison, from whence there is no redemption." He exclaimed, "Oh! Lord! how gracious wert thou to my soul, in those seasons. Thy presence softened all. 'Sweet pleasure, mingled with the pain.' I found I could do all things, and bear all things, while my Lord was with me."[55]

Tanner's wife ran away to Ireland with a marine, leaving him alone with four children, but was drowned in passage. He managed to conceal his delight only from himself. Unlike other men, he said, he felt no joy in being delivered from such a burden, only sorrow, not personal grief but rather regret which all Christians should feel over a soul that has been lost. He elaborated on this theme in what can only be described as loving detail:

But is it not enough, to make the very blood chill, and every face gather paleness to behold an immortal soul, hurried into eternity, in the full career of sin, and passing through the watery grave, to an abyss of everlasting woe? Fancy, you see the once stupid soul now thoroughly awakened to the horrors of eternity; under a load of irremissible sins, and transgressions; with no jovial, no drunken companions, to bear out in laughter, the misery; but fiends, and damned spirits, insulting over, and to aggravate the torment, the dreadful recollection of having long despised Jesus, and his sweet gospel of mercy.

Tanner speculated on the distress which his wife must have felt at "my long abused kindness, my earnest pressing exhortations, and tears, and entreaties."[56]

While Tanner may have rid himself of a number of debilitating habits by his conversion, he seems to have become a thoroughly disagreeable human being in the process. As men and women surrendered their anti-social or self-destructive tendencies under the terrifying pressure of a conversion experience, many gave up something infinitely precious, the richness of their individuality, and became, in their "new birth," unfeeling and self-righteous, seeing themselves and others as stereotypes of good and evil rather than as distinct human beings.

In Tanner's case, nothing connected with his life seems to have retained any freshness or originality. Even the lovely Devon landscape had no other purpose than to teach a moral lesson. He wrote of a journey he made from Plymouth to Exeter: "The unevenness of the road, the hills, the vales, and miry ground over which I had to pass in my journey, presented me with an epitome of the Christian's experience in his journey through life. The mountains and hills of care and difficulty with which I have to contend in my passage to glory, can only be surmounted by un-limited confidence in my All-sufficient Saviour, and by having the ever-lasting arms of omnipotence underneath me." Tanner said on another journey, "I wanted to spiritualize every object mine eyes beheld." Noth-ing was to be admired for its own merits. The beauties encountered were only "trifles . . . the little gewgaws of time and sense, [which] often detain the traveller, and attract the carnal mind, please the curious ear, and entertain the lustful eye." The effect of such distractions could be disastrous. "So that the looking one way and travelling another, I have often stept into pits of water and mire, (the Christian understands the allegory,) and have fallen into the dirt, and stained my garment, which made me ashamed to meet any person." As he approached the town of Ashburton, endangered by heavy rains and a slippery road, his thoughts turned to the journey's end: "What storms of temptation and showers of persecution, mountains of difficulties and valleys of distress, am I called to encounter in this world, because I do not belong to it! But all these things only excite me more diligently to run the race that is set before me, and create in me a greater longing to be at home in the sweet enjoyment of my Lord." [57]

Although he complains of physical ailments constantly in his diary, Tanner's constitution was remarkably durable. In 1775, when he was fifty-nine, he rose each morning, prayed for two hours, and then worked long hours at a mill in Exeter, frequently traveling to Topsham to preach in the evenings. An entry in his diary for January 5, 1775, describes a typical day:

Rose at four, because of going to work at six. O how wonderfully had my dear Lord refreshed my weak and frail body in a few hours sleep; and even in sleep, dreamed I was doing my dear Lord's work. God is faithful to his word and promise, "Strength shall be equal to the day;" and Oh! how could I do less than spend my hours in prayer and praises! Lord, increase my faith! At day-dawn went to work, and a very hard day's work was before me: my lawful business employed my head and hands very severely till half-past five; but, glory be to God, my heart was kept great part of the day in ejaculatory prayer. Came home and changed clothes, and, though very weary, set out for Topsham; and at seven preached from Luke, viii.20 and following verses. I had soon forgot my toil and pain, and my good God gave me great enlargement of soul, &c. [58]

Tanner's oratorical gifts were probably somewhat above the ordinary. One "very crowded congregation" was "struck with awe-some trem-bling" at his performance in the pulpit. On another occasion, "My dear Lord gave me great freedom and power, and the children of God re-joiced." But there were times, too, when he "lacked power" or was "almost shut up." He began preaching in Plymouth and continued after he settled in Exeter, where he found much new wickedness to combat. To make his self-appointed task more difficult, he found himself hated by "all sorts of men in this Sodom." But much more troubling to Tanner than the personal malice he encountered was the rich profusion of heresies in Exeter. He inveighed against Arians, Arminians, Socinians, Antinomians, and Papists, all of whom had to be stamped out "in this wicked city." For all his efforts, he received little material compensation. Tanner wrote to a friend in May 1789:

I preached eighteen years, and did not receive eighteenpence; but laboured hard with head, heart, and hands, . . . to the support of my family and the necessity of the church, because they were poor. Since that, one year, with great difficulty, they raised for me twelve pounds six shillings, (and one year only:) then it was reduced to four pounds ten shillings; until last year, 1788, when two or three members who are in better circumstances in life were added to the church: these raised, and caused to be raised, twenty-two pounds ten shillings and sixpence, with what they got from country friends, &c. But this year it will be some pounds deficient, because some payers are gone from Exeter; and half of this goes for house-rent, rates, and taxes; and my manual labour, as to worldly things, is quite done, being in the seventy-second year of my age, and my body very infirm.[59]

Upon his arrival in Exeter from Plymouth, Tanner found "a little despised society" of Methodists.[60] In 1772 he built the Tabernacle, a meeting place for the Calvinistic Methodists in the city.[61] Twenty-one years later, sometime in 1793, Joanna approached this pious, limited man in hopes of a sympathetic hearing. Two accounts of what transpired between them emerged, one from Joanna and the other from Tanner's daughter, who gave her version after her father's death to Joanna's opponent, a Reverend Mr. Smith, author of *The Lying Prophetess Detected*. The statement which Miss Tanner presented to Smith read as follows:

Joanna Southcott had been a member, before she turned prophetess, of the church, under the charge of that herald of truth and good soldier of Jesus Christ, the Rev. Mr. Tanner, of Exeter: after being an absentee for sometime from the tabernacle, she waited on the venerable minister, and informed him of the spirit of prophecy, that was given her, which she had committed to writing, and sealed up with seven seals, and left at a place, which she named, and the Spirit had directed her to bring it to Mr. Tanner. After hearing what she had to say, Mr. Tanner answered—"Joanna, you are a deluded woman; I will not receive the papers;" and endeavoured to convince her, that her revelations and inspirations were unscriptural. At this answer, she was much irritated, and discovered herself as a deranged person; saying, she was the woman spoken of in the Revelation, &c. &c. Mr. Tanner thought it prudent to say but little; her looks and manner evidently proved she could not bear it.[62]

Joanna denounced this version of their encounter. "There is no truth in the whole of this assertion, only of my going to Mr. Tanner." She said, "I have living witnesses to prove the truth of what I assert." Joanna then offered her account:

In 1793, I was ordered to go to Mr. Tanner, and tell him of the visitation I had in 1792, of what the Lord would do upon the earth; and I told him that Mr. Wesley's people had said that my visitation was from the devil. Mr. Tanner immediately answered me, "Then they were all unconverted people[." H]e believed my visitation to be from the Lord; and what I told him was hastening on, he said he believed it was; for he himself had had many warnings, that awful things were coming on: but he said, he could not say his warnings were so clear to him to shew how the Lord would go on from nation to nation; or whereto these things would end was not so clearly made known to him as it was to me, from what I told him of my visitation. He asked me to bring him the writings of my visitation the year before; but I told him that I could not; as they were left at Plymtree, sealed up, and were not to be opened as yet. I never carried Mr. Tanner any writings; neither did I ever ask him to receive any; nor did I tell him how many seals were upon them; . . . I did not tell Mr. Tanner that I was the woman spoken of in the Revelation; for at that time the Scriptures were not explained to me. I only told him of my visitation, to warn us of what was coming upon the earth, which he affirmed he believed was from the Lord; and the assertions they have brought forward are entirely false. Mr. Tanner asked for my writings, which I refused, being ordered not to have them opened at that time. They say that Mr. Tanner thought it prudent to say but little to me; and that I was much irritated. This is false; for I was as much at my ease with Mr. Tanner, as ever I was in conversation with anyone; we entered into deep conversation of what happened to me at the end of the American War. I told him of the scriptures I opened to then, which were the xxviii and the xxx chapters of Isaiah, and the xxx of Jeremiah, and many other scriptures that I told him of. He said that all these things alluded to the present time, and what he believed was hastening on; he asked me to call upon him again, and he should be glad to see me at any time. Mrs. Tanner was part of the time in the room with us; and she joined with her husband in all he said; but as to Miss Tanner, I know nothing about her, as I do not remember ever seeing her in my life, to know her.[63]

Of the two versions, Joanna's is probably the accurate one. No one was more conscious than she of the importance of her credibility. The reason that the prophetess moved frequently from household to household in Exeter and its neighborhood was to increase the number who could attest to her veracity and good character. In December 1804, a "trial" was held in Bermondsey at Joanna's insistence in order to establish beyond doubt her reputation for truthfulness. A number of witnesses from Exeter attended, corroborating Joanna's account of her life in the city.[64] It was because of her sensitivity concerning her reputation that she was so quick to take up cudgels with anyone, like Smith, who accused her of falsifying some aspect of her career. If she was ever caught in a lie, Joanna knew, all her claims would be open to question.

Joanna, therefore, would undoubtedly have produced the "living witnesses" to substantiate her account if it had seemed necessary. On the other hand, she was probably not telling the whole truth about her feelings toward Tanner. At some later point, after their first encounter, their relationship must have deteriorated dramatically, perhaps because Joanna refused to leave the Established Church and submit herself to his spiritual ministrations. This is the most probable cause of her rejection of the Calvinistic position. Joanna could never rise above a personal grievance. She excoriated both kinds of Methodism, Wesley's Arminianism as well as Whitefield's Calvinism, the first because of her rejection by Eastlake's class and the second, probably, because of some antipathy developing out of her relationship with Tanner, Exeter's leading advocate of the Calvinistic persuasion. As for Tanner, it is easy to imagine how the preacher's attitude toward Joanna could have completely altered if (for whatever reason) he became convinced that she was not one of the elect. His developing hostility toward Joanna might, in turn, have distorted his daughter's recollection of their early relationship.

Joanna herself realized how involved her personal feelings were in her estrangement from the Methodists. She said, "I was deeply wounded with the conduct of the Methodists, who said that my writings were not from the Lord." Joanna wanted to be generous and forgiving toward them but found it impossible. "I wished to forgive all injuries; but said, to my shame, I could not forget them, . . . I wished them [the Methodists] to be buried in oblivion, never to be remembered any more." The Spirit told her to describe her feelings in verse.

> But, Oh, the follies of my heart!
>   Why do these thoughts arise?
> And every injury done to me
>   Lie spread before my eyes;
> All past offences now appear
>   As strong within my view
> As though they were this moment done,
>   And old things now were new.[65]

Joanna's alliance with the Methodist movement was, finally, only a much regretted dalliance. "As high as the Heavens are from the Earth, so high are my Writings from the thoughts, knowledge, and under-standings of the Methodists." [66] She said, "My religion is that of the es-tablished Church of England." [67] Her avowed purpose was to bring all back to the "standard of the Church." [68]

CONSEQUENCES

The mutual hostility between Joanna and the Methodists had important consequences. Because they appealed to much the same audience, it became difficult, if not impossible, for a man or woman to worship both as a Southcottian and as a Methodist. When Joanna traveled to Stockton-on-Tees in 1803, a division occurred in the Methodist society there "as well as at other Places." She said, "Those that believe in my writings, and of the near approach of Christ's Kingdom gave up their Chapel to me and it was thronged with many hundreds if not a thou-sand." [69] Specific cases arose in which believers were either expelled from Methodist societies or forced to surrender their allegiance to Jo-anna in order to remain. She received word that a prominent supporter, Thomas Senior, had been "turned out of the Society of the Methodists for believing in Joanna's mission." [70] In May 1797, there was an instance in which the Methodists managed successfully to discredit the proph-etess in the eyes of one of their number. "The Methodists [she was in-formed] had persuaded Mr. Manley out of every belief, and told him of many false reports, that I had prophesied falsely. This provoked me to anger against their religion, finding they were full of lies." [71]

Her abrasive encounters with Methodist preachers helped to widen the gap between her following and the society. She was "provoked by the Methodist Preachers at Stockton who Said all I had told them was false. . . . [while] others Said my Prophecies were from the Devil." [72] A Calvinistic Methodist impugned her motives, as well as all those "who have constantly read the books as they were published, from the begin-ning of the year 1801, to this day." According to this logic, a supporter said, if she were guilty of duplicity, then "all and every one [of her read-ers], whether hundred or thousands, must be implicated in the deceit." Indignantly he said of such narrow critics, "These are the men that call themselves the Elect, and claim the heavens as their own!" [73] In 1804, she wrote in a pamphlet, *A Warning to the World*, that a "methodist preacher" had charged that her writings were from the devil, conceding only that she had accurately predicted the war against France; "not one thing else" would come true, he claimed. As a result, Joanna's hold on her self-confidence became tenuous until she accurately prophesied that a dying relative would survive even though "given over by the apothecary." She believed this to be a sign that she could disdain such "opposition." "This wondrous work of the LORD strengthened my faith against every opposition of man, as I was well convinced none but a God could have set such signs before me."[74] Joanna underlined her attitude toward her onetime mentors by telling of a dream of rotten cucumbers which, the Spirit explained, referred to "the Methodist preachers, who went to set forth their rotten wisdom, their rotten understanding."[75]

Finally, the Spirit compared the Methodists to the Jews, who in the beginning had possessed the truth but had wandered into alien ways:

> And Westley's calling was from me
> But in his calling few abide
> And like the Jews, as first Is said
> They said that they were Abraham's seed
> But in his faith did ne'er abide
> Save but a few that turned to me
> And as the Methodists, now be
> There are a few of Westley's faith
> Before the Gospel as it saith
> That I in Spirit work in man
> And so they are guided by his plan
> But for the others they do lie
> Just like the Jews when they did cry
> That they were all of Abraham's Seed.[76]

Joanna expressed no surprise at the animus of the Methodists against her. In 1796 and 1797, she said, she had been "foretold of the unbelief of the Methodists in general." She could not help but wonder, nevertheless, "how it is possible that men called Christians can see the judgments that have been already in our land, and see the distressed situation our country is now in, with the sword hanging over our heads," without realizing the implications. "This appears marvellous in my eyes; yet it verifies and fulfils my prophecies."[77]

CHURCH AND CLERGY

If the Methodists were not to cooperate in the accomplishment of Joanna's mission, then whom had God chosen for this task? "The clergy of the Church of England," the prophetess said, were to bring in "the good fruit . . . and from them the good fruit would spring." "Back to the Church," Joanna declared, "all must come."[78] By this exhortation, she meant that all sects were to seek in her the avenue of reconciliation to the Church of England.

Thomas Macaulay once wrote that if Joanna had been a Catholic living in Italy she would have founded "an order of barefooted Carmel-
ites."[79] Unfortunately for Joanna, her allegiance was to Canterbury
rather than Rome and the Church of England proved unaccommodat-
ing toward her and her following. The prophetess struggled against its
obduracy throughout her career. The clergy of the Established Church,
Joanna believed, had a great role to play in the accomplishment of her
mission. Alone, she could not awaken the nation from its slumber. Only
they could confirm and amplify the importance of her message: "But as
the Lord hath appointed Ministers as shepherds to their flocks, so all
who read this book, if they cannot understand it, ought in duty to appeal to their Ministers; for they have as much right to demand their
judgment, as the Ministers have to demand their money for preaching."[80]

Joanna made innumerable overtures to the hierarchy and clergy in
hopes that a hearing for her experiences and claims would be forthcoming. In the beginning of her first pamphlet the prophetess even said that
"if any twelve Ministers, who are worthy and good men, will prove
these writings come from the Devil and his foreknowledge of things;
and explain clearly to me those mysteries of the Bible that I shall pro-
pose to them; I will refrain from further printing: But if they cannot, I
shall go on, till I have made public all the mysteries of the Bible—the
times which are to come—and what shall happen till Christ's Kingdom
be established."[81] At first, she had asked members of the clergy in Exeter to examine her writings. Then, at the "trial" staged in 1804 to evalu-
ate the authenticity of her claims, "the bishops and clergy were invited,
by private letters and in the public Newspapers, to come forward and
judge for themselves." She suggested that, if the bishops could not come,
they produce twenty-four clergymen "from different dioceses" who
would be joined by a similar number of her choosing, and upon their
decision she would rest her case.[82]

The reaction to her appeals was sufficiently hostile to alienate Joanna
from the clergy, if not from the church: "The letters were returned by
the ministers with such infamous and blasphemous language, as though
the devil had either guided their hands or hearts. For such letters, from
men that were worthy the name of men, I should think could never be
penned; for many of the expressions are so low, illiterate, and indecent,
that it appears to me what we call in Devonshire Billingsgate Language."[83] A Reverend Mr. Draper claimed that he spoke for "the *sentiments of the clergy* at large" in saying that Joanna's writings were blasphemous. The only biblical figure in the Bible which she resembled, he
declared, was Jezebel.[84] Those replies which she received at the beginning of her London "trial" shared the same "general tendency" of

"mockery" and "condemnation of prophecy." Several of the clergymen's letters "were of that indecent description, that delicacy prevents their being at all brought forward to public notice." So vile were they, that it was felt the Society for the Suppression of Vice should expose "some of these clergy to public disgrace and shame."[85]

The ministers invited to come forward in Exeter had "all refused." Her "fair and generous offer" to the hierarchy in London that they appoint twenty-four ministers to sit in judgment of her was treated in a similarly cavalier fashion.[86] The sacrament was denied to Joanna's followers.[87] One minister offered perhaps the unkindest cut of all when he returned Joanna's "last Book" with caustic observations on her rhymes. "War and years are also Rhyme for appears. Oh fie! fie! what a poor, barren Language, must this make THE ENGLISH APPEAR!"[88]

Of twenty thousand clergymen in England, a follower said, in the beginning only three professed to believe in Joanna's mission.[89] One who chose not to be included was the Reverend Joseph Pomeroy, vicar of St. Kews, Bodmin, Cornwall. Joanna believed that Pomeroy had given her conspicuous encouragement in Exeter until the appearance of her first pamphlet in 1801, which provoked such ridicule from his fellow parsons that he ignominiously withdrew his support from her. She and her followers haunted him for the remainder of her life in the hopes that he would admit his error and reassume his role as her adviser and even, perhaps, become her consort. In this, however, they were to be disappointed.

Joanna's followers were under no illusions as to why she was spurned by the clergy "both in and out of the establishment." Many of them, they knew, could offer no objection to the prophetess' arguments but only to her. "An untutored female to be the conveyancer of divine truths, was repugnant to worldly wisdom, repugnant to learned pride." But Elias Carpenter recalled that Christ had associated with "contemptible persons." Perhaps the clergy, he said, did not consider such men as the apostles—"men of low character, no learning, of the meanest occupations, destitute of every thing that gives estimation in life, publicans and sinners"—worthy of their time and consideration. "Could it be possible," he asked, "for any well-educated body of people to receive truths from the leader [either Christ or Joanna] of such a disgusting rabble." The clergy's answer seemed to be, "Certainly not!"[90]

The refusal of the clergy to cooperate with Joanna was a serious setback, not only for her personally but also, she was certain, for the nation at large. The prophetess believed that the bad harvests, the dismal progress of the war with France, all the catastrophes befalling England were visitations from God, sent in punishment for the clergy's disbelief in her mission. England was being betrayed by its priests who told the people their prayers were well received when, in fact, they were not. In doing this, clergymen were mistakenly seen "as earthly gods." [91] Joanna wrote to Pomeroy in 1804, telling him that in three years God would bring "a total famine" on England "if you and the clergy go on, as they are going on." [92] The consequences for Pomeroy and his colleagues would be grim indeed unless they accepted her claims and informed the people. "If I am mocked by the shepherds," the Spirit said, "their end shall be fatal; if they refuse to warn their sheep, and they perish in their sins, their blood will I require of the shepherds' hands. But if the shepherds give the warning, and the people refuse to take it, then the shepherds shall save their souls alive, and every man's sin shall be upon his own head." [93]

As it grew increasingly clear that she was to receive no significant support from this source, the rhetoric of her anticlericalism became more and more strident. She said: "If I were in Turkey I should find more humanity amongst the priests there than I have found in England. In the first place I intreated them, as though my soul and body depended upon their advice to know from what Spirit my writings came; yet they refused to give it; or even to hear me." [94] The clergy, however, were indifferent, interested in neither the glory of God nor the good of mankind. They "only Preach for *Hire* and *Reward*." [95] In a pamphlet published in 1804 she forcefully reasserted that the shepherds were apathetic and full of avarice. If they dismissed Joanna's claims, they cared not whether "tens of thousands" were led astray by her writings, or, if they conceded them, they refused to bring any enlightenment to the "tens of millions" who had never heard of the prophetess. "It is all one to the bishops and clergy, while they are fed as fat horses at the full; and while they can have the fleece they care not what becomes of the sheep." "This," the prophetess said, "is Joanna Southcott's opinion of the clergy; and by experience can prove it true." [96]

Her outrage expanded even more impressively when she compared the opulence and indigence of the hierarchy with the abysmal condition of the poor. She found the parable of the young man who refused to give up his riches and follow Christ particularly suited to illustrate her views on the bishops:

What honor can there be due to the bishop[s] from me, when I consider the thousands a year they are paid to be faithful Shepherds of the Lord, to take care of his Flock? And Christ died to set them an example, to follow his footsteps. Now if Christ so loved the world, as to die for man; and become poor, that we, through his poverty, might be made rich; ought not the bishops, that are made rich by the Gospel, to take care of Christ's flock that is committed to their care? Now I ask the Bishop, who came to Christ that he refused to hear, or whom he sent empty away?[97]

The attitude of the clergy toward the poor was of critical importance. The clergy "are part of the government of England, and ought to stand between the king and his people."[98] But necessities which would have sustained the poor were devoured by "the Priests, and their wifes."[99] Most criminal of all, however, was the clergy's refusal to even acknowledge the deprivations which the poor were suffering. If they did, Joanna said, then they would have to recognize that God had sent His judgments on a sinful nation. But the clergy persisted in claiming that no unusual hardship existed. The Spirit sarcastically asked that these deluded men prove their assertion

by bringing peace and plenty into their land, and feed the bowels of the starving poor; or my charges will come heavy against them; and my judgments must be great in the land, if they starve the poor in the midst of plenty: then now that plenty I charge them to shew, and let the prices be like the former years; or let them know the curse pronounced against them, for oppression to the poor. So if they affirm their words to be true, that there is a plenty in your land, they must allow my judgments just to bring a curse upon the land: and they are pulling my judgments down. So if they bring charges against my work, and deny my judgments, I shall bring my charges against their cruelty: and let them know, he that sheweth no mercy shall find judgment without mercy.[100]

Joanna could not understand how men could be so blind. But the clergy were not the only ones to blame. She wrote to a Mr. Warren on October 22, 1807: "I am astonished to hear the ignorance there is in mankind when they see the heavy affliction that our nation is now under, and our commerce and trading so much stopped that thousands are complaining, in different parts of the kingdom they are almost starving for want of labour, and yet they are inquiring where are the judgments."[101]

Finally, one of Joanna's followers suggested how alien the idea of "hired Teachers" was to the ideal of early Christianity, which the Southcottians sought to practice: "In the original Apostolic Assemblies All met together and prophesied, One by One, that All might learn and be comforted; but are not hired Teachers contrary to that Spirit, which ought not to be quenched, and which Ecclesiastics, coming forth in the power of human Learning, too frequently do, and make the Church worldly?"[102] In an early pamphlet, *The Answer of the Lord to the Powers of Darkness*, the Spirit said, "*It is no Love to Me that man aspireth to be a bishop[,] a chancellor, an archdeacon, or a shepherd of the flock, it is their love to themselves, for they all preach for hire.*"[103]

Joanna's purpose was to vivify the institutional church rather than to sap its strength further. Like Wesley, she had no intention of founding a competing sect. As in Wesley's case, however, the momentum of a separate movement became irresistible because the human need was so vast and unsatisfied. When the Church of England proved largely unsympathetic to Joanna, as it had to Methodism, the Southcottians founded their own chapels. Yet always, Joanna insisted, she knew herself to be a good and devoted daughter of the church. And it was for the church that she hoped to recover the poor and all those whose spiritual, emotional, and intellectual needs had been so resoundingly neglected. However, in order to understand the nature of her success, it is necessary to look carefully at the pressures on the society from which she and her followers in Exeter, and throughout the country, came.

III

Exeter and Elsewhere: The Background

[I] dreamed I was on a high mountain, and saw the sky as bright as noon day sun, and two men come out of the clouds, with long robes of purple and scarlet, with crowns of gold on their heads and swords in their hands, standing in the sky. Two men came out with heavy horses, and spoke to those that stood on the clouds, and soon after rode away, like lightning in the air. Soon after, I saw the men on horseback coming out of the clouds, as fast as they could, till the whole skies was covered with men in armour and spears glittering in the air. I thought, I looked down, and saw the world in confusion, men in armour riding fast. This dream alarmed me; and I was meditating with what divine majesty and splendor our dear Redeemer was coming into the world. Once he came meek and lowly, persecuted by men; but now he will come, as a prince and a king, conquering and to conquer.[1]

THE FARM LABORER

Millennial movements embody the aspirations of the poor—men and women defeated by the world in which they live. For such people, the measure of their despair is that the promise of Christ's imminent coming offers their only hope of deliverance from suffering. Calculating the numbers who flocked to prophets in England during the period of the French Revolution and Napoleonic Wars is, in part, an exercise in the arithmetic of human misery.

Joanna Southcott wrote to a friend on July 19, 1803, describing the reception she had received on a recent visit to Exeter:

The number of Enquirers and Believers were daily and Hourly visiting me that I had scarce time many days to eat my meat. Some came nineteen miles to see me, others Thirty miles and all expressed the greatest satisfaction from every thing they had seen and heard. . . . Many Learned men and well conversant with the Scriptures in Devenshire affirmed that no one who Knew the Bible and believed it and weighed it with my Writings and seeing the truth of Both together could not Doubt its being from the Lord as the words of the Prophet Joel.[2]

But the poor were especially prominent among those Joanna saw. "It is affecting to see how the Poor are Praying and Desirous for Christ's Kingdom and wishing for the time" of His coming.[3] The transformation of these distressed men and women into Southcottians was an experience forged out of despair. High prices, unemployment, and a series of bad harvests combined to create widespread and unprecedented suffering in Exeter and the countryside, especially after the beginning of the French wars in 1792.

Catastrophe of some kind is a usual prologue to millennial movements. Norman Cohn, in his study of revolutionary millennial movements in the Middle Ages, found that "again and again . . . a particular outbreak . . . took place against a background of disaster."[4] Vittorio Lanternari observes, "Everywhere, in primitive as in highly developed societies, the messianic movement emerges from a crisis, to offer spiritual redemption."[5] The illiterate and semi-educated frequently become the rank and file of such movements because they are the ones on whom the wars, earthquakes, famines, plagues—whatever the particular calamity—fall the hardest and who are least able to understand them. The difficulty which these men and women have in rationalizing their suffering renders them peculiarly vulnerable to the appeals of millennial prophets, themselves subject to the same stresses as their followers, who assure them of the redemptive character of their tribulations and the prospect of an early and dramatic release.

As a domestic servant and the daughter of a tenant farmer, Joanna stood near the bottom of the social scale described by agriculturist Charles Vancouver during his tour of Devon in 1807. Echoing the admiration of an earlier visitor for the county's inhabitants, Vancouver reported to the Board of Agriculture: "There is an openness of heart and mildness of character in the inhabitants of Devonshire, which probably is not to be excelled in any part of England. A general urbanity of manners, and desire to please and meet the wishes of the stranger, prevail among all classes of the community, from the peer to the peasant; even in those who compose the lower order of society, and among whom we are to find both male and female servants."[6]

The peer and the peasant stood at opposite ends of a society which had five distinct levels. The first was the gentry, "all Nobleman, Knights, and Esquires." The second consisted of the merchants, most of whom lived in Exeter or principal towns of the county and were engaged in the clothing trade, the increasingly fragile support of Devonshire's economic life. The third class, the yeomanry, consisted of farmers and freeholders. A farmer could be either a leaseholder for a term, which meant he had purchased tenure of his land for a long but fixed period of time, often ninety-nine years, or a rackrenter, such as Joanna's father, which meant that he was unable to afford the purchase of a leasehold and therefore paid rent on his land for periods of seven, fourteen, or twenty-one years, although longer or shorter terms could also be arranged. By contrast, a freeholder held his land without any fixed tenure and, in fact, could be a leaseholder who possessed lifetime tenure of his land. The fourth class was composed of artificers and mechanics. Their skills were found in the clothing industry as well as in building trades where they might be employed as slaters (those who covered houses with slates from the quarries indigenous to the region), masons, or thatchers.[7]

The day laborers were "the last and lowest Class of the Inhabitants." In the 1770s, William Chapple, a Devon agriculturist, judged their condition to have greatly deteriorated within his own lifetime: "Now the high Price of Provisions in Proportion to their Wages, and the Duties charg'd on Soap, Candles, Salt, and other Necessaries of Life, will permit them to keep but few *Holidays*; unless compell'd thereto by the want of Employment, and to turn them into *fasting* Days by their want of Bread." He saw a great difference "even within the last 30 or 40 Years":

Most of those Country Villages, wherein Chearfulness and a kind of rustic Gaiety, might be observ'd among the poor Labourers within our Remembrance, have at present a very different Appearance, and exhibit all the Marks of Poverty and Distress: Instead of that Sprightliness and Alacrity with which they heretofore perform'd their daily Task, and earn'd a competent Supply of homely Food for themselves and Families, we now perceive a kind of heavy Gloom on every Face; and instead of having now-and-then (as they formerly had) in a Summer Evening, before Harvest-time came on, an Hour's Recreation after finishing the Work of the Day,—they must now endeavour to supply, if possible, the Deficiency of their scanty Wages (being scarce sufficient to purchase two-thirds of the Provisions it would have bought 25 Years since), by assisting their craving Families in some Employment at home, or otherwise send them supperless to Bed.[8]

The fundamental cause of the day-laborer's plight, according to Chapple, was the shift from small farming units to larger ones. He admitted that there were compelling economic reasons to support such a change. A small farm required proportionally more workers than a large one. The landlord made little, if anything, on the cottage rents, which usually were just enough to pay the repairs and window tax. Turning acreage over to grazing was more profitable than cultivating it. Chapple agreed, therefore, that large farms had "their peculiar Advantages both to the Proprietor and the Publick." He argued, however, "that the Strength and Riches of every Country, depend on the Number of the labouring Part of its Inha[b]itants;—that Persons employ'd in Agriculture or Manufactures, must have Bread to eat, as well as Houses to dwell in;—and that for the Sake of a little present Gain by enlarging their Farms, they are famishing their Poor, discouraging Marriage, diminishing the Number of Labourers, Manufacturers and Artificers, and depopulating and impoverishing their Country." This injured the community and "must ultimately tend to the Loss and Disadvantage of themselves and their Posterity." He believed that the farm laborers had actually been better off as villeins, "for tho' they, and all they had, were the Property, and at the Command of their Lords, they had Liberty to till their little Allotments of Ground, and perhaps seldom wanted that Bread to which their Obedience and Servility intitled them."⁹

Charles Vancouver found in his survey thirty-five years later that the outdoor laborer was paid "7s. per week winter and summer, and from a quarter to three pints of drink daily." At harvest and hay-time the wages were not increased, "although the additional exertions at those seasons are amply compensated by board, and very extraordinary drinks and sittings over ale and cider." The laborer could also buy bread-corn, wheat, and barley at reduced prices. In addition, he and his family were often given land by the farmer to plant potatoes, which enabled them to keep a pig. On smaller farms, the laborer had to be satisfied with 3s. 6d. per week and his maintenance. There were some, although not around Exeter, who only worked for one day during the harvest, receiving board and drink and the promise that they would be invited the following Christmas to the farmer's house for the harvest party, which lasted for two or three days. Vancouver acknowledged that "the price of labour has certainly not kept pace with the depreciation in the value of money within the last 20 years," but he believed that the opportunity to buy provisions under the market price, housing, and ground for potatoes combined to offset the decrease in buying power.¹⁰

That Chapple rather than Vancouver was correct in his assessment of the farm laborer's condition was demonstrated by the sharp rise in poor rates in every part of Devon in the second half of the eighteenth century. Sir Frederick Eden found compelling evidence in 1795 of the distress experienced by the farm laborer in the parish of Clyst St. George. Every man in the parish was an agricultural laborer. The average wage was a shilling a day and cider. In addition, the men received meat during the corn harvest. But it was all pitifully inadequate. He wrote in *The State of the Poor* (1797):

No labourer can at present maintain himself, wife, and children on his earnings. All have relief from the parish in money, or corn at a reduced price. Before the war wheaten bread and cheese, and about twice a week meat, were their usual food; now barley bread and no meat. They have of late made great use of potatoes. An industrious healthy man can earn 8s. a week by piece work on an average throughout the year. Labourers' children are often bound out as apprentices at 8 years of age to the farmers. Prior to the present scarcity a laborer, if his wife was healthy, could maintain two young children on his 6s. a week and liquor without any parochial relief. A very few years ago laborers thought themselves disgraced by receiving aid from the parish, but this sense of shame is now totally extinguished.[11]

In those parishes which were not exclusively agricultural, wives of farm laborers supplemented the family income by spinning wool. Their daily earnings were 6d. to 7d. a day, or £9 2s. 6d. annually, a figure which represented half of their husbands' annual wages. This was often all that kept the family from the workhouse. With the failure of the serge industry during the Napoleonic Wars, this source of income was removed and the laborers and their families had to live solely on their agricultural earnings. The successive number of bad harvests was the final blow for many families.[12]

THE WEAVERS

The gradual decline in the condition of the farm laborer in the second half of the eighteenth century was matched by that of the weaver and other dependents of the serge industry whose economic fortunes were tied to those of the city of Exeter.

At the end of the seventeenth century, Exeter had been the leading city of southwest England and one of the three most populous, affluent, and active cities in the provinces. Only Bristol and Norwich were larger and wealthier, and only the ports of Bristol and Hull were busier. Exeter's principal markets were Holland, Flanders, and Germany. The city's reach extended as far as Norway and Newfoundland and the Canary Islands. By the close of the eighteenth century, however, the city was reduced to the status of a market town and its trade restricted to the surrounding countryside. The rise and fall of Exeter's fortunes closely corresponded with the fluctuations of the serge industry with which its economy was almost completely identified.[13]

Perhaps with some exaggeration, a contemporary said that in 1700 four out of five people in Exeter were employed in the serge industry. Serge was particularly valued in the international marketplace because it was an intermediate fabric, lighter and cheaper than broadcloth but more long wearing than the lighter Norwich stuffs. The wool was imported by sea from Sussex, Kent, and Spain, as well as from the neighboring countryside, and spun into yarn under the supervision of master weavers or by master spinners. Their efforts were supplemented by the "multitude of independent spinners in the small farms round about, bringing their surplus yarn to market each week." Once the serge was fabricated it was sold in the Serge Market or to individual merchants who then had it finished and dyed before exporting. By the middle of the eighteenth century, although the industry's decline was well advanced, the city had established a monopoly of the kingdom's serge export.[14]

As the woolen industry grew, it created a chasm between the lower and middle classes. W. G. Hoskins has written, "Unlike the thrusting men of Lancashire and Yorkshire, who believed all things possible and saw outstanding achievement all around them for their emulation, the inhabitants of Exeter accepted their station in life without question." The reason lay in the fact that the laboring population of the city had at an early date become economic dependents of the merchant class. By the eighteenth century the distance between master and man had become psychologically unbridgeable. As far back as 1330, the arable land of Devonshire was almost entirely enclosed. According to Professor Hoskins, "this had probably resulted in the appearance, by the middle of the sixteenth century, of a considerable class of landless households who drifted into towns like Exeter and Tiverton to provide a body of cheap labour dependent entirely on a wage for their subsistence." Balanced as these men and women were on the knife edge of catastrophe, they eventually lost possession of the looms and spindles which alone gave them a measure of independence from the merchants who provided them with their raw materials.[15]

The merchant capitalist who exploited these circumstances first made his appearance in the middle years of the sixteenth century, to import wool when local supplies were no longer adequate. At the same time, Devonshire became an attractive place to invest when a new and profitable kind of fabric was developed requiring the long wools used in southwest England. Since the skill involved was not great but the raw materials were expensive, the industry was soon dominated by entrepreneurs living in Exeter and Tiverton. The result was "a concentration of control in the hands of a comparatively few men, instead of a system of small independent craftsmen such as persisted, for example, in the West Riding of Yorkshire." By 1700 the merchants had formed an almost hereditary class which was literally impenetrable. Hoskins has said, "There were no Peter Blundells [a seventeenth-century success] in eighteenth century Exeter to rise from carrier's boy to first merchant in the town."[16]

After 1713, in the face of a challenge to the domestic market by Yorkshire and the foreign market by Norwich, the serge industry of Exeter went into a state of decline. Norwich, particularly, demonstrated its competitive mettle by producing a cheaper and more attractive fabric and aggressively merchandising it in the continental market where Exeter had for so long reigned unchallenged.[17] From the middle of the eighteenth century, however, there was a period of renewal which lasted until the American war, and the outbreak of the French Revolutionary wars in 1793 finally shattered the Exeter industry beyond recovery.

Although, when disaster struck, a large number of the unemployed were at first absorbed into shopkeeping and personal service trades, the consequences for the city of the debility and destruction of the serge industry were inexorable and at best could only be delayed. In order to keep Exeter serge competitive in a diminishing world market, the wages of the weavers were progressively lowered from almost nine shillings a week in 1750 to eight in 1787 and seven in 1791. In 1766 the harvest failed and a serious food riot occurred. From that year prices rose, unemployment increased, and a chronic sense of uncertainty replaced the relative security of the first half of the century. Between the years 1762–1765 and 1790–1793, the price of bread rose 30 percent, meat 60 percent, butter 50 percent, cheese 34 percent, milk 43 percent, coal (approximately) 11 percent, and pease 57 percent. In general, the cost of food, which was three-quarters of the budget of most families, rose 40–50 percent over these thirty years while wages remained roughly the same. This meant that many of those employed in the serge industry experienced a drop of real income of approximately 50 percent. For others it was about 30 percent.[18]

All this was only a prelude to the suffering of the war years, 1793–1814, when twenty of twenty-two harvests failed.[19] In 1796 there were mob riots over the high cost of food. A contemporary, Alexander Jenkins, described the circumstances in which "the common people" felt it necessary to resort to civil insurrection:

The price of Provisions, especially Wheat, advancing greatly, creating much murmuring, and dissatisfaction among the common people, who judging the evil to have arisen from nefarious practices of the opulent Millers (whom they suspected of engrossing great quantities of grain) collected in a mob, and proceeded to *Belle Marsh-Mills*, near *Chudleigh*, which they partly demolished, plundered what grain they could find, and furiously insulted, and ill treated the proprietor, *Mr. Balle*. For this offence, one *Mr. Campion*, a blacksmith, of *Drewsteignton*, was apprehended as a ringleader, committed to gaol, and on trial, being convicted, was sentenced to be executed near the spot where the crime was committed.[20]

In order to intimidate the condemned man's supporters and sympathizers, the Light Dragoons, two troops of volunteer cavalry, two companies of volunteer soldiers, "and several others of the neighbouring Volunteers" accompanied him to his execution. This formidable retinue was still not considered sufficient to prevent a rescue attempt. Therefore, the authorities instructed a battalion of militia with two pieces of artillery to appear.[21] Although there was no disturbance at the execution, the military continued as the effective government of the city for a number of years.[22]

The plight of the people continued to worsen. Joanna remembered the effects of the disastrous harvest of 1800, the year in which she prepared her first pamphlet for publication: "As soon as the harvest was over in 1800, the poor began to complain what martyrs they had been, and sold all they could part with to go through the dearth of 1799; but now they said there was another year come, in which they should be starved to death; and many, I was told, dropped down dead in the streets for want."[23] Joanna wrote to a clergyman in March 1800 "that it was universally observed in Devonshire, that a guinea would go farther in Housekeeping in 1799 than one guinea and half would in 1800." She said that "all vegetables were treble the price of the year before, butter double, and cheese and animal food in proportion."[24] Jenkins agreed that "every necessary article of life advanced to such an enormous price, that the resemblance nearly appeared of an actual famine!"[25] Hoskins argues, "1800 was the critical year"; in addition to the terrible inflation, "trade was at its worst; large numbers of the population were without any visible means of subsistence."[26]

With the continued upward surge of the cost of wheat, barley, meat, and potatoes, further disturbances seemed inevitable. The price increases, Jenkins said, "occasioned great murmurings, and clamours, especially among the middling, and lower classes of society, who had hitherto borne their sufferings with an unexampled patience. They loudly exclaimed, without exaggeration, on the distresses of themselves and families, and flocked to the markets in such numbers, that the Mayor . . . was obliged to order out the constables to protect the country people, as the populace, driven almost to despair, crouded on them." To embitter the situation further, Jenkins noted that, on July 28, a fire destroyed thirteen houses, "inhabited chiefly by *poor Weavers*." Thereby, "a number of poor families were reduced to great distress."[27]

The final result was that the poor, "no longer able to provide proper sustenance for their families," acted by marching into the countryside to confront "the principal Landholders and Farmers" with the demand that they sign an agreement authorizing the sale of their wheat and other necessities at reduced cost. Jenkins felt that they had a good deal of justification. In his opinion, "many cruel, avaricious persons" by "their hoarding and monopolizing" had at least in part induced the high cost of necessities in Exeter.[28] Joanna must have sympathized with the popular response for she too felt that the farmers were hoarding grain in order to get a higher market price. She wrote, "A great clamour was raised against the Farmers, who were charged with exercising the fatal power of raising the prices until nearly FAMINE fell on all the poor, as many died for want!" "It is a question that is yet to be answered," she said, "how a small selfish body of men could resist the powerful government of Britain, and compel [by their hoarding] the rulers of the Land to send Millions of Gold to purchase Grain [from abroad]." Assured of her answer, she asked, "Can any Man say that Misery like this ever fell on this Land for one hundred years past: the Quartern Loaf to be above Two Shillings!"[29]

The city authorities had to exert themselves to the utmost to bring the situation back under control. "Most of the householders in the city were sworn as additional constables, and the mob being prevented from holding any more meetings, by the vigilance of the Mayor, quietness in some degree, was restored." Private subscriptions and government subsidies were combined to purchase fish, wheat, and rice from abroad so that they could be sold at nominal price to the hungry. In addition, a cheaper kind of bread was sold in the parish churches. By these steps, the authorities hoped that violence could be averted.[30]

At almost this moment, in January 1801, Joanna published her first book, *The Strange Effects of Faith*, in Exeter. This was a compilation of communications and prophecies dating from 1792 which she asserted were divinely inspired. With her announcement that the Second Coming was at hand, the Exeter poor could see the dreadful tribulations they were undergoing in a new light. Their hardships were not to be resolved by their own action, which, in any case, had become almost impossible because of the energy of the military and municipal authorities. In this and later pamphlets, Joanna stressed the inevitability of human suffering. The "high prices and great dearth" in the land were divine judgments on a sinful world. Those who disagreed, "the unbelievers," were deliberately attempting to discredit her prophecies in order to obscure the fact that deliverance was at hand for the believers. Of her adversaries, she said: "It appeareth to me as though the unbelievers are studying how they can harden men's hearts in sin, telling them there are no judgments, while we are surrounded by judgments; telling them there is no sorrow, while our land is surrounded with sorrows: and should I speak the language of my own heart, I should say these men are as full of lies and aggravation as the devil, to say the harvest is good, when the corn is risen here more than double the price it was last year." [31]

Recruits to Joanna's cult in Devonshire, therefore, sprang from circumstances of insecurity, economic deprivation, and social immobility. The effective response of the authorities to the civil disturbances made it clear that even by collective action the poor could not significantly improve their situation. It was possible, however, to transcend if not to change the world in which they lived. Vanquished in their competition for the goods of the world, the poor, as Southcottians, were able to alter the context of their unequal struggle and find victory at last over "unbelievers" and "the World" in spiritual terms, thus redeeming the long agony which their lives had become; for only believers would reign with Christ at His coming.

One can detect a note of surprised triumph as the West Country Southcottians surveyed the new dispositions and confirmed that they were on the high ground. "So great is the faith of many in Devonshire," Joanna said, "that they rather rejoiced then grieved at the ridicule of unbelievers." [32] Colonies of Southcottians grew up in Crewkerne, Dowlish, Tiverton, Crediton, Ashburton, Totnes, Brixham, and Plymouth, as well as in Exeter. [33]

It was Exeter, however, with which Joanna personally identified. She remembered that afterward, in the course of a month-long visit, "there was more then 100 Signed their names whilst I was in Exeter and I sealed more then 400." [34] When compared with the city's population of something over 16,000, it appears that approximately one in thirty formally acknowledged his or her millennial beliefs in the space of a single month. Adjustments must be made, however, for those in the number who came from the countryside surrounding the city. Still, this is a startling figure.

In 1813, Joanna wrote a letter to one of her former employers in Exeter in which she described how she had been liberated from poverty through her trust in the promises of God. In doing so, she caught the desperate hope of those for whom life in the real world had become impossible: "What various Scenes and changes of Life have my Strange Effects of faith brought me to. [Y]ou Know the manner of my Situation in Exeter was mean and Low, that I worked early and Late to Support myself and to go on with my Writings that I often experienced Hunger and Want but I was answered in 1801 that was the Last year I Should ever Know what Poverty was and I bless the Lord from my inmost Soul from what I have experienced of the truth of the words, for the Lord has blessed me in my basket and in my store." [35]

OUTSIDE DEVONSHIRE

In December 1801, seven men with whom Joanna had been corresponding traveled to Exeter to interview her. One, Peter Morrison, was from Liverpool. A second, John Wilson, came from Kentish Town, a London suburb. The remaining five included three Church of England clergymen, the Reverend Thomas P. Foley, member of an established Worcestershire family and rector of Old Swinford, near Stourbridge; the Reverend Thomas Webster, lecturer at two London churches; and the Reverend Stanhope Bruce, vicar of Inglesham, Gloucestershire. Finally, there were George Turner, a Leeds merchant who himself was a prophet and visionary, and William Sharp, perhaps the most outstanding engraver of the age and at one time a prominent radical figure in London.[36]

Satisfied with the results of their inquiry, Joanna's visitors urged her to leave Exeter and come to London. She agreed, arriving in the capital on May 20, 1802.[37] Once in London, Joanna had a base from which she could address a national rather than a regional audience. Her publications continued to spill from the press. Aided greatly by several of Joanna's proselytizing trips, the Southcottian movement spread from the West Country and London into the fertile soil of the Midlands and the north.

There, as in Exeter, profound economic hardship was to be an endemic feature of Southcottian recruitment. Unlike Exeter, however, London and the growing manufacturing cities harbored populations in transition from the relative security of a rural economy to new uncertainties of life, presenting special and remorseless pressures which made the human need for connection, reassurance, and explanation for suffering that much more urgent. For example, a student of Leeds Southcottianism believes that Joanna's success can only be understood against the background "of the first chaotic decades of headlong urbanization and industrialisation."[38] Whether the believers lived in the north or south, whether they were victims of economic hardship or social dislocation, or both, their world was one overwhelmed by catastrophe. In a broadsheet distributed in Yorkshire, George Turner reminded his readers that in 1801, the year he traveled from Leeds to Exeter to interview Joanna, "all must acknowledge it was in a time of great distress, scarcity and war, calamities which the nation then laboured under; so much so, that the cry was throughout the nation for bread and peace."[39]

If bread was in short supply, so was peace. The Treaty of Amiens in 1802 resolved little, and on May 17, 1803, Great Britain declared war against France. By the winter of the following year, French troops had been strung out along the coast from Ostend to Boulogne, and Napoleon was laying plans for an invasion of the country. In the summer of 1804, a force of 100,000 men had been assembled at Boulogne accompanied by hundreds of barges designed to carry them across the channel. With the emperor's great "Army of England" preparing to descend on the island, something like hysteria seized large sections of the population, suggesting another factor behind Joanna's astonishing recruiting success in the early years of the movement: fear of a French invasion.

To many, there seemed little question that the French would land. Only when and where were undetermined as well as the outcome of what would undoubtedly be the mightiest and bloodiest struggle the English people had ever faced. On January 12, 1804, Joanna learned that the French had been seen off the coast and were expected to land each day.[40] A month later she discovered that George Turner's son-in-law had sent news from Nottingham that the French were in Scotland.[41] For his part, Turner felt certain that he knew where the first blows would fall. He wrote to Henry Addington, the prime minister, that "Portsmouth, Chatham, and London will be the three places of attack from Buonaparte."[42] Regardless of place or time, the consequences would prove horrifying, and London would suffer the most. The Spirit told Joanna, "Nine parts of the Inhabitants of London will perish; as the streets will be filled with dead Bodies, French as well as English."[43]

Nothing in the way of defense or retaliation could be accomplished, however, until the government understood that Napoleon and his forces were only mercenaries in the employ of the nation's real adversary, Satan. The English were "relying on their Fleets and Armies" when they should be "trusting in the God of their Salvation."[44] Men unaided by divine guidance could never hope to repel the attacks of Satan's legions. Yet they refused to see the truth. A Southcottian preacher warned that the Volunteers, an untrained force especially recruited in 1803 to protect the country from invasion, would not be capable of withstanding a French onslaught. He then had the unhappy experience of seeing his meeting dissolve into "a general scene of tumult" as a result of his remarks.[45] Yet there was reason to be optimistic if the true nature of the danger came to be understood, and appropriate measures were taken. The Volunteers needed to be divided into "two Companies," those who possessed a "seal," a sign of Southcottian belief, and those who did not. "When it appears that the French are too strong, and Likely to overcome the [unsealed] Soldiers," then the believers would be thrown into the breech, and "they shall gain the Victory."[46] But it would be "more by Faith than the Sword" that success would be achieved.[47]

When the final struggle did come, those who owned one of Joanna's "seals" would be spared. Her Spirit intoned, "If I permit them to land in the City of London, I shall fill the places With the dead bodies *of the Enemy, and of those that are Enemies to me, and my Coming.*" The enemy, then, consisted not only of the French but also of "those who are Enemies to thy Prophecies." The unbelievers would perish "till the Cities be full of the Bodies of the dead."[48] No room existed for compromise. Those who were not with the prophetess were against her, and prospects looked distinctly gloomy for the latter. Unbelievers in Leeds, Sheffield, Birmingham, Manchester, indeed all the "cities" whose population rejected Joanna's message, would, she seemed to be saying, be stacked like cordwood in the streets as in London. Moreover, Joanna's followers alone would be warned of the time of the French descent and, as a result, be able to make preparations. She wrote to William Sharp that he should warn only the believers that the time was drawing close, "and . . . you must settle all your affairs in London, as fast as you can, that you may be able to leave it at a Week's Warning."[49] When it was thought the French were in Scotland, even then her Spirit said the believers were not to worry "for as distant as Scotland is from London, so distant they will hear their Dangers before they come upon them—and then they may flee for safety, 'to the Town or Country,' where I shall order thee to go."[50]

GROWTH AND GEOGRAPHICAL AND SOCIAL DISTRIBUTION

As one would imagine, the numbers of believers did not grow at a uniform rate. When Joanna first burst upon the scene in 1801, she was able to take maximum advantage of the unusual hardship which prevailed in Exeter and various parts of the country, and, later, she offered dramatic reassurance to those who lived in daily anxiety of a French invasion. There were other, individual reasons that might compel one to become a Southcottian, which will be explored later, but the interplay of Joanna's claims with these phenomena was fundamental to the movement's spectacular growth in the first months and years of its existence as her following climbed from a handful of supporters to thousands. The prophetess wrote to Mrs. Taylor on January 2, 1804, "I have an opportunity of sending you a few lines but not time to send you a long letter as I have been every day for this week past . . . signing and sealing, upwards of two thousand in a few days." She said that another three hundred had entered their names on an assistant's list "so you may Judge how my time is employ'd and my Friends for me," adding that she and others were working furiously to make the large numbers of "seals" required.[51] But, with the invasion scare past, much of the urgency of Joanna's appeal evaporated.

After her break with Elias Carpenter in 1805, Joanna instituted a second sealing (and, later, a third) which was intended as something of a loyalty test to her leadership.[52] Those who had already been "sealed" were asked, but not required, to sign their names a second time on the lists of believers. The results, however, were disappointing. "Few" signed a second time and "few" new recruits emerged.[53] On September 11, 1808, Joanna reported the disappointing developments to a friend. The second sealing had attracted only 1,298 new recruits and those who signed the lists again numbered only 4,673, making a total of 5,971. "From this small number returned," she wrote, "we may see what a falling away there has been among the sealed, when we consider that 14,000 were sealed before."[54] The movement labored forward, apparently little affected by the years of scarcity in 1810–1813, with Joanna writing "a short account of the Friends" on July 22, 1812:

You enquire how the work is going on amongst the Friends. I am happy to inform you that a Spirit of enquiry seem to be rose at most places around the Friends in Yorkshire. Our Leeds' Friends give an account of an increase to the Church, and that the Friends appear very lively in their faith at Halifax, Stockport, & round them, at Doncaster, Thorne, and the villages round, in Somersetshire, Ilminster, and about two Miles from thence. Friend Baker holds a meeting which is well attended from all the villages round[;] at Plymouth Dock there is a little circle & more joining them; our meeting in London is pretty well attended[,] some coming in every month tho' considering such a body of People the number is but few, but still they increase. Another little Church have been within a few months at Deptford about six miles from London which is well attended.[55]

It was not until the last year of Joanna's life that the movement regained and, indeed, surpassed the extraordinary recruitment of the first years. In the incandescent months of 1814 Joanna could jubilantly report to George Turner that "the Chapels are crowded." On April 10 of that year, she said, communion had been given to "between six hundred and seven hundred" in one of her London meeting places.[56]

Lists of believers survive which, though incomplete, offer a remarkable tool with which to analyze the geographical and social distribution of the Southcottian movement.[57] The importance of the lists was the highest. "By the lists," Joanna said, "I shall know who are the true believers and who are not."[58] After obvious duplications have been removed, the names of 7,249 men and women living in 140 towns and villages across England appear on the lists. Another 10 believers lived outside the country: 8 in Ireland, 1 in Belgium, and 1 in Swedish Pomerania. Of the total, 2,676 (37 percent) were men, and 4,539 (63 percent) women. The Southcottian strongholds were in Devon (849, 12 percent), Somerset (719, 10 percent), London (2,083, 29 percent), Lancashire (583, 8 percent), and Yorkshire (1,755, 24 percent). Its antipodes were Alnwick in the north and Plymouth in the southwest, with a widespread following in Somerset and incidental though significant support in Kent in the south and appreciable strength in the Midlands, most importantly in Mansfield, Newark, and Nottingham in Nottinghamshire, Chesterfield in Derbyshire, and Leicester. Wales and Scotland were entirely untouched; East Anglia almost so. The largest individual followings were at Sheffield in Yorkshire (350), Dowlish (374), and Crewkerne (265) in Somerset, Gravesend in Kent (211), and Ashton-Under-Lyne in Lancashire (200).[59]

Contemporary trade directories can be of assistance in discovering the occupations of a small number of the movement. Trade directories consisted of the names, occupations, and sometimes, as in the case of London, the addresses of local tradesmen. In the London lists of believers, the addresses as well as the names of some 1,300 Southcottians appear. Only 8 of them can be definitely placed in *Holden's Triennial Directory, 1809–1811*. One is a baker, a second is a dealer in natural and artificial curiosities, a third is a wife of a pewterer, a fourth is a cheesemonger, a fifth is a tailor, a sixth is a hat manufacturer, a seventh is a watchmaker, and an eighth is a brushmaker and turner. Several others may not have completely vanished. Of these, one was perhaps an attorney, another a watchmaker, a third a flax and hemp dresser. But the remaining hundreds of believers either had addresses which were different from those they submitted to the sect, or they were not in London at the time the directory was compiled, or they were working, if indeed they were employed, at tasks presumably inferior to those of their fellow Southcottians listed in the directory.

It is possible, however, to locate 1,127 of the believers in the London metropolitan area with a degree of confidence and to make some speculation about the nature of their employment. Thirty-two percent lived on the South Bank, in Southwark (17 percent), Lambeth (9 percent), and Bermondsey (6 percent). Second only to Southwark, Westminster housed the largest numbers of believers (13 percent). Significant representation can also be found in the City (9 percent), Holborn (8 percent), Stepney (6 percent), Finsbury (5 percent), and Walworth (4 percent).[60]

North of the river, a Southcottian might be found working as a small shopkeeper in the City or Westminster or perhaps as a weaver in Spitalsfields in the east. The South Bank, according to George Rudé, had be-

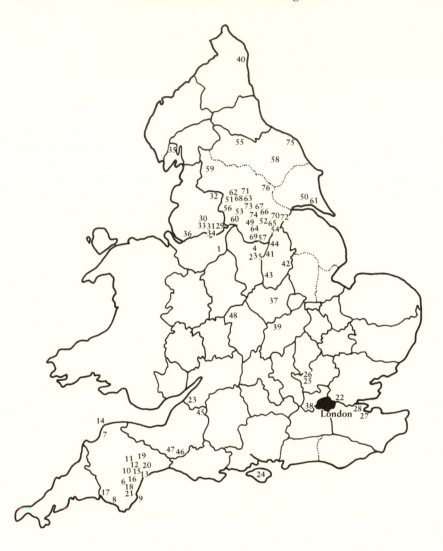

Geographical Distribution of the Southcottian Movement: Towns with
a population of five or more believers have been located with the aid of
the *Atlas of Britain and Northern Ireland* (Oxford, 1963) and other
references. Names are listed as they appear on the Southcottian scrolls
and lists.

London	(2,083)

Cheshire
1. Macclesfield (35)

Derbyshire
2. Ashover (11)
3. Blackwell (15)
4. Chesterfield (71)
5. Pinxton (8)

Devon
6. Ashburton (50)
7. Barnstaple (17)
8. Bigbury (90)
9. Brixham (100)
10. Christow (6)
11. Crediton (33)
12. Exeter (145)
13. Exmouth (21)
14. Ilfracombe (20)
15. Kenn (27)
16. Newton Abbot (11)
17. Plymouth (169)
18. Staverton (12)
19. Tiverton (62)
20. Topsham (10)
21. Totnes (57)

Essex
22. Rainham (5)

Gloucestershire
23. Bristol (67)

Hampshire
24. Isle of Wight (5)

Hertfordshire
25. Gaddesden (23)
26. Little Gaddesden (16)

Kent
27. Chatham (27)
28. Gravesend (211)

Lancashire
29. Ashton-Under-
Lyne (200)
30. Bury (42)
31. Clayton (33)
32. Coln (36)
33. Manchester (43)
34. Stockport (121)
35. Sunny Bank (9)
36. Warrington (87)

Leicestershire
37. Leicester (44)

Middlesex
38. Teddington (125)

Northamptonshire
39. Welford (14)

Northumberland
40. Alnwick (20)

Nottinghamshire
41. Mansfield (84)
42. Newark (81)
43. Nottingham (56)
44. Worksop (14)

Somerset
45. Bath (75)
46. Crewkerne (265)
47. Dowlish (374)

Warwickshire
48. Birmingham (8)

Yorkshire
49. Barnsley (58)
50. Beverley (5)
51. Bradford (125)
52. Brodsworth (39)
53. Cowms (52)
54. Doncaster (54)
55. Gilling (5)
56. Halifax (6)
57. Hatfield Woodhouse (56)
58. Helmsley (13)
59. Horton (78)
60. Huddersfield (107)
61. Hull (26)
62. Idle
& Idle Thorpe (63)
63. Leeds (186)
64. Little Houghton (16)
65. Marr (20)
66. Pontefract (62)
67. Potovens (76)
68. Pudsey (39)
69. Sheffield (350)
70. Stainforth (33)
71. Stockton (25)
72. Thorne (120)
73. Thornhill Lees (56)
74. Wakefield (21)
75. Whitby (31)
76. York (27)

come "a refuse dump for some of the dirtier trades that had been kept out of the City."[61] There, Southcottians could well have been located in the timberyards of Lambeth, among the soapmakers and petty tradesmen in Southwark, and the tanneries of Bermondsey. Perhaps some fished the Thames or, if attracted to a life with wider horizons and possessed of greater daring, they turned to the sea. Swan Lofgren gave his address as "mariner" while Stephen Dalby and Robert Whithead came to Joanna from a ship called the *Bromsberg* (or *Bransberg*). There is other evidence that a number of soldiers possessed seals, but only one is identified in the London lists—Frank Kent who lived in the Royal Military Asylum in Chelsea. One other follower (besides Swan Lofgren), Henry Ewington, was singled out by occupation, apparently because of its prestige. He is identified as a "Teacher of Arithmetic from Bath." Female believers in the metropolis might have worked with their husbands, pursued some independent activity, worked for wages, or found employment as domestic servants in the fashionable squares of the West End, as did, undoubtedly, Ann Earl, who gave an address off Grosvenor Square; Mary Ward and Ann Folkard, who lived near Hanover Square; and Sarah Smith, who resided a few blocks away on Prince's Street, Cavendish Square.

The overwhelming number of London believers were humble souls, many living in impoverished circumstances. In the first years of the nineteenth century, the poorest sections of the city could be readily identified by the evidence of typhus. According to the *Report on Contagious Fever in London* of 1818, these areas were "Shadwell, White-chapel, Bethnal Green . . . Shoreditch, St. Luke's, about Old Street and Golden Lane and Cow Cross and Saffron Hill. Near Smithfield and also St. Giles, the neighborhood of Clare Market and Drury Lane and the parish of St. Clements and also very much in . . . St. George's, Southwark, Kent Street and the Borough."[62] Southcottians lived in all these places. However, there is only one example of a believer who had unmistakably fallen from the ranks of the industrious poor. Benjamin Benson gave his address as St. Clement Dane's workhouse. A second believer, Elizabeth Hodder, said she lived at 16 Workhouse Lane, Deptford.

One of the most active colonies of Southcottians was on Gibralter Row, St. George's, Southwark. The street connected Prospect Place and Pleasant Place and was only a few minutes away from Joanna's chapel on Duke Street and Elias Carpenter's "House of God" near the Elephant and Castle. As one looks at the names of those who lived on the street, and the dates when they became believers, it is impossible not to feel, at last, an instinctive and overwhelming sense of intimacy with the world of Joanna's followers. The usual categories of "the poor," "the miserable," "the lower orders," "the 'other' London," at best masks of our own ignorance, seem peculiarly crude when applied to the vitality, the "life" of a London street during these years. It is easy to hear passionate discussion raging within individual houses and throughout the neighborhood, to see Joanna's books being read and exchanged, to sympathize with those who quickly succumbed to the prophetess' appeal, and to wonder about those who held out for days or weeks or years. It is as close as we are ever likely to get to the community life of ordinary believers.

In the spring of 1809, Zecharia and Letitia Lowick at No. 42 Gibralter Row were the first on the street to become convinced of Joanna's claims. At the beginning of April the following year, Sarah Shrimpton at No. 13 accepted a seal. All was quiet until February 3, 1811 when James Lowick of No. 42 joined. Two years later Ann Callingham of the same address followed. In the summer of 1813, Edward Dixon of No. 12 became a member. On Easter Sunday, April 10, 1814, at the height of Joanna's recruiting success, 301 believers received their seals. Among them were Nanny and William Allford, Thomas Henry, and Jane Slight, all of No. 2. John Lowick of No. 42 joined his family as a believer on the same day. Another new recruit on this exceptional occasion was Martha Froom(e) who lived a block away on Pitt Street. With her decision, she joined a family member, Mary Ann, who had accepted her seal the previous February and lived on the same street.

It cannot definitely be established in the cities outside London whether names which appear both in the local trade directories and on the lists of believers are the same.[63] Neither the names of provincial believers nor in many cases the names of those in the trade directories have addresses. Nevertheless, the Sheffield directory for 1817 has the names of thirty-four men and two women which were the same as those of Sheffield believers. Most were artisans, men engaged in such trades as penknife cutter, file manufacturer, razor manufacturer, and sickle maker. There were, however, several grocers, a butcher, and a shoemaker. In the Leeds directory of 1817, there are the names of twenty men—none, any, or all of whom may have been Southcottians. These include three dressers, two butchers, two merchants, a milk dealer, a druggist, a flax spinner, a wheelwright, and a shear maker. The Bristol directory for 1813 has the names of eight men and three women which were listed among the Bristol believers. The three women were, respectively, a grocer, a milliner and dressmaker, and a basket maker. In Bath there was a fisherman and a teacher of arithmetic; in Bradford, a grocer and a hatter; in Exeter, an attorney; in Manchester, a shoemaker and an earthenware dealer; in Nottingham, one who may have been a blacking maker or a musician and music seller.

Sometimes refugees from the upper reaches of the economic and social strata did make their way into Joanna's world. The prophetess wrote in 1802 that there were "many genteel people" coming daily to make inquiries in Exeter about her cause.[64] The Reverend Thomas P. Foley claimed in 1808 that the Bristol believers had managed to capture a family with an income "near £9000 a year."[65] Joanna possessed similar good news for Foley two years later when she informed him that a "Man of Property" had joined the movement.[66] At her second "trial" on January 12, 1803, there were eleven judges, of whom only one, William Sharp, the engraver, was listed as "esquire," although the names included George Turner, a merchant, Elias Carpenter, the owner of a paper mill, and William Roundell Wetherell, a surgeon. Among the twelve members of the "jury" was William Layton Winter, described as a "gentleman." Also in attendance were the three Church of England clergymen, Bruce, Webster, and Foley.[67] Sufficient representation from the professions, the clergy, business, and the gentry existed to enable the *Edinburgh Review* to assert that "it is by no means true, as sometimes represented, that the sect has been confined to the lowest and most ignorant persons."[68] One of Joanna's most active opponents admitted that she had in her following "men of parts and great abilities."[69] *Chambers Encyclopedia* echoed this view years later. In the 1867 edition, it reported that among the thousands who joined Joanna's cause "were men of good education and respectable position in society."[70] Nevertheless, the conversion of someone well-to-do remained sufficiently exceptional to be worthy of comment.

Falling beneath these comparative few was the vast bulk of the movement. At lower levels were the small farmers, married women without employment, the self-employed, soldiers and sailors, and all those working for wages. Typical of them was a Leeds printer, Samuel Jowett, who had been a prominent figure in the movement during Joanna's lifetime and more than a half century after her death described himself as "a poor old man," telling a correspondent, "Should you write me again, please omit the Esq. you have attached to my name. I have not any right to it, . . ."[71] Yet further down were those who left no trace even in the literature of the movement but were merely summarized by Joanna as well as her social superiors as "the poor." Elizabeth Foley, the clergyman's wife, wrote on October 13, 1803, from Worcestershire, "Not one of the *Rich* has come in here during Mrs. Southcott's Stay to Sign for Christ's Kingdom to be Establish'd, and for Satan's to be destroyed." This only confirmed the gospel admonition, she said, that it was easier for a camel to pass through the eye of a needle than a rich man to enter the Kingdom of Heaven.[72] Her husband records in his journal incidents when he gave away Joanna's books "to a poor person" and "to a poor woman."[73] Some years after Joanna's death, a Yorkshire follower who had been a class leader with the Methodists before his conversion was eagerly presented to a group of believers and given a leadership role because, his sponsor said, "We were a poor illiterate set."[74] On May 19, 1829, the Reverend Thomas P. Foley wrote to a Manchester acquaintance that "almost in every part of the Kingdom, where there are any Believers in our Heavenly and Glorious Cause, . . . many of them are exceeding Poor, and are Suffering greatly." "In every place," he said, "we are called upon, most strongly, to help them as far as we can, according to our circumstances." However, he lamented, "It is impossible for a few Individuals to do much Especially if they have Large famileys of their own."[75]

Although it is simplistic to assume that the poor were inevitably the rank and file of millenarian movements during this period, it is equally perilous to deny them a place in its membership. The assertion that "there is little to suggest that the disinherited and outcastes of society found solace or hope in millenarian belief" and that the Southcottians and other contemporary millenarian groups did not have "any substantial following among the very poor"[76] goes too far in its effort to redress the balance. The circumstances of the beginning of Joanna's public career in Exeter in 1801, as well as other evidence, lead to the conclusion that some and probably many Southcottians were chiliasts, drawn to the movement because it offered an escape from suffering.

The size of the Southcottian movement is impossible to determine with any real exactitude, but again there are clues which we can follow. The more than seven thousand names on the lists of the believers were probably but not necessarily "sealed," the "sealed" representing the core of Joanna's following.[77] This figure is about one-third of the total number "sealed" by February 1815. According to Southcottian records, the increments proceeded in the following manner. In 1803 there were only 58; in January 1804, 8,134; in 1808, 14,105; and in 1815, 20,505.[78] Some, however, were "sealed" twice, as previously indicated, thus (apparently) causing the figures to be inflated.[79] This by no means represents the total number of adherents to the Southcottian cause. The "sealing" was stopped at various times at the command of the Spirit. The names of many believers never found their way onto the lists. For example, only 8 Birmingham Southcottians appear on the surviving lists, but in a letter to a Birmingham newspaper in 1814, a clergyman wrote that the local society had more than 500 believers and was growing rapidly.[80] The London *Encyclopedia* made the remarkable claim that Joanna's following in London and its environs alone was 100,000.[81] Another neutral source declared that, in all, the Southcottians numbered 50,000.[82] Joanna's adversaries estimated her support in lower figures but still larger than the 20,000 "sealed." In January 1805, one of them wrote to the *Evangelical Magazine* that the Southcottians had 20,000–30,000 followers.[83] Lewis Mayer, a notorious opponent of the prophetess, said in 1806 that he had been informed there were more than 11,000 believers in the metropolis,[84] although the names of only 2,000 Londoners appear on the surviving lists. In 1814, Elias Carpenter, once a close supporter of the prophetess but grown bitter after being expelled from the movement, claimed that the Southcottian membership had reached 40,000.[85] There is no indication of what evidence, if any, these various estimates are based upon. Undeniably, however, the movement gave the impression of having great strength. That this impression had even more substance than suggested by the just quoted figures comes from two further pieces of evidence. At the bottom of a Southcottian broadside dated February 22, 1838, is the stunning inscription: "Where this prayer lies for SIGNING, already signed OVER Four Hundred and Fifty Thousand!!!"[86] This undoubtedly referred to one of the scrolls, perhaps a complete collection of them, which believers, even if they never received a seal, signed for Satan's overthrow. The existence of the scroll or scrolls is independently verified by a later writer who visited a household of London Southcottians and saw a "parchment document," which, he was told, possessed "over four hundred and fifty thousand signatures."[87] Needless to say, even the suggestion of a following of this magnitude throws the question of the importance of the Southcottian movement into an extraordinary new light.

These figures of tens of thousands, perhaps hundreds of thousands, of followers are in no way surprising when the size of the audience Joanna reached with her publications is considered. Both individual editions and additional printings of her works were apparently published in a thousand copies each.[88] Surviving issues of her sixty-five publications in the University of Texas Southcott Collection reveal that one, *Sound an Alarm in My Holy Mountain*, went through nine editions, seven others went through four editions, two through three editions, and eight through two editions. Forty-eight other pamphlets stopped with one edition.[89] Also, the first edition of her publication *A Word to the Wise* went through a second printing, as well as a second and third edition. Together, these total 108,000 copies published from 1801 to 1816. And this must be considered a conservative figure. Other editions may have been issued which have not survived, as well as additional printings of individual editions. Since many of Joanna's followers were "poor," copies of her works were undoubtedly passed from hand to hand, considerably increasing the circulation. In this regard, a bookseller noted, "so greedily were the writings . . . sought after by the poorer classes that almost all the copies were worn out at the time by continual thumbing and reading."[90] The prices ranged from fourpence for a twenty-two–page pamphlet to three shillings for a hundred-page pamphlet. Most cost one to two shillings.

These figures, remarkable though they are, do not stand comparison with the sales of Tom Paine's *Rights of Man*, which, in its various editions, sold 200,000 copies within the year following its publication, or with the Cheap Repository Tracts, which sold 300,000 copies in the first six weeks they became available. On the other hand, Burke's *Reflections on the Revolution in France* at three shillings a copy sold a comparatively modest 30,000 copies in the first two years after publication.[91] The most important conclusion to be drawn from these publication figures and estimates of the size of her following is that the Southcottians were not a coterie of cranks and eccentrics subsisting on the margins of society but a people reflecting in a distinctive way the popular concerns of their generation.

A SENSE OF COMMUNITY

The much larger proportion of women over men in the Southcottian movement, 63 percent to 37 percent, is partly explained by the fact that women are usually more numerous than men in any religious movement, regardless of its character.[92] But several other factors should be considered. First, there is the obvious feminist appeal of the sect. God had selected a woman, not a man, through which to reveal Himself. One of Joanna's critics complained that when the Spirit said, "I am in the woman's form," it means "Christ has changed his sex, and is made a woman."[93] Joanna herself recognized that an unusual number of women were flocking to her cause. She found it difficult to explain because "the Lord never promised any wondrous working to convince the unbelief of women."[94] But what Joanna offered was the emancipation of women from the burden of the Fall, of Eve's role in tempting Adam to sin. As the woman "*at first plucked the fruit, and brought the knowledge of the evil fruit; so at last she must bring the knowledge of the good fruit.*"[95] In her, women found a deliverer from the inferior status bequeathed to them by the Christian tradition. Her Spirit saw her career as another in the series of "great Victories gain'd by Women."[96]

Second, women were perhaps more vulnerable to the psychological toll of the new industrialism and often were exposed to it in numbers disproportionate to those of men, particularly in the cotton mills where their nimble fingers, smaller bodies, and malleable dispositions made them more suitable than men for the tedious work. For example, in 1816, of 10,000 employed by forty-one Scottish mills, 3,146 were men and 6,854 were women. The remaining 4,581 were male and female children under eighteen. Similarly, the labor force of forty-eight Manchester mills revealed a distribution of two-to-one, women over men.[97]

Third, it is likely that Joanna recruited a significant following from the huge domestic servant population in England. In addition to the natural affinity which existed between Joanna and female domestic servants, such women were perhaps more acutely aware of repressive class distinctions because of the nature of their work and were, therefore, more eager to have these distinctions erased. Bryan Wilson has advanced this argument in his study of the Christadelphians, another adventist sect. In an analysis of their membership records for 1883 – 1884, he found that "the largest single classification was that of domestic servant."[98] Adding some support to this speculation about the Southcottians is the apparently high percentage of single women (and men) in the sect. Only 2,305 (32 percent) of the believers are readily identifiable as members of family units. This leaves 68 percent who may have had no immediate family attachments or were the only members of their families to join the movement—1,764 (66 percent) of the men and 3,146 (69 percent) of the women.[99] If, as seems quite possible, many of these women were single and they had to earn a living, their options were severely limited. Laurence Sterne underlined this when he advised his unmarried sister to either learn dressmaking to support herself or find a place as a servant with the nobility.[100] For those of the laboring classes who were without husbands, the factories also offered an alternative.

Regardless of the route taken, into dressmaking, domestic service, the factories, or a genteel spinsterhood, such women were unusually exposed and defenseless to the terror of their world, a terror which might well be assuaged as Joanna's had been. The example of Joanna's single life was seen as exemplary by so many female believers that a man traveled from London to Leeds to ask her if she forbade marriage. Although she hotly denied the suggestion, she admitted that, for female believers, her "seal" could bear the connotation of a marriage ring. A divine spouse might easily *guarantee* the protection which married women rightly expected but were disappointed in receiving from their earthly husbands. The Spirit said, "As a husband is empowered to avenge an insult offered to his Wife by the union of the hand in Marriage, so am I empowered as a Husband to avenge the injuries offered to those that give their hands to ME." [101] George Turner said in 1819 there were no fewer than 1,556 women waiting "to *be married to the Lord*." [102]

The local leadership of the movement came from these humble men and women who flocked to the chapel or the meeting room, in London, Leeds, Manchester, Birmingham, Exeter, and the scores of other towns and villages. With few exceptions, it did not include the clergy of the Church of England or the Dissenting sects. [103] "We are plain men," they said, "aspiring to no other pretensions than a zeal for honesty and truth." Therefore, "we have done nothing artfully, nor deceitfully; neither will we consent thereto, nor conceal it where we find it done. This cause, in which we are engaged, we consider as a cause of honour; and in it we know of neither fraud nor collusion. The object of our pursuit is truth; and the truth we are determined to stand by; and to expose whoever makes lies his refuge. We contend for the honour of Joanna, and of ourselves; . . . we contend for justice and for truth; we contend for the glory of God, and for the good of mankind." [104] They and their fellows represented a cross section of the denominations. Of "the different sects," the Spirit said, "there is not found believers enough in Any one to Join together in My work." [105]

Although the government kept the Southcottians under its scrutiny, the movement was largely ignored by the church and the educated classes, taking root in the emotional and intellectual needs of the "lower orders." The rewards for believers were considerable. They experienced a delicious sense of being different, of counting for something distinctive and important in a world which too often had debased the dignity of themselves and their labor. They were able to reconstruct the old patterns of community, broken by the harsh judgments of the city or the marketplace, as they assembled at this last redoubt. Joanna urged her followers on in their withdrawal, counseling them not to marry [106] or even socialize with unbelievers. She asked, "Could an unbeliever enjoy the company of believers,—or believers enjoy the company of unbelievers?" [107] Carpenter, like Robert Owen an owner rather than a worker, also like Owen could better articulate the sense of community which these maimed men and women sought and found: "The frequenters of playhouses and cardtables, &c. may sneer at us, and pity our mopish amusements; but, I am persuaded, that not one amongst their merry tribe was ever so thoroughly happy as we were: others, may brand it as superstition and enthusiasm; if they please, it may remain so in their estimation. Through the grace of God, we found what we sought, *happiness*; and that out of which, I trust, we shall not be easily reasoned by the one, or laughed by the other." [108]

IV

Old Wine in New Bottles

THOMAS P. FOLEY

The congeries of believers throughout the country were unified only by their belief in Joanna. The Southcottians left no equivalent of the careful organizational structure of the Methodists which enabled them to flourish after Wesley's departure from the scene.[1] One of Joanna's followers stressed the importance of her role. Looking sadly at the disarray of the movement after her death, he said, "No one has had authority to give any directions for the guidance of her followers—all have been left to follow their own views and opinions."[2]

Standing at the center of the movement, Joanna was compelled to advise and exhort an enormous following, a task seemingly far beyond the capacities of the woman who stumbled so pathetically in dealing with her Methodist class in Exeter. But now that she could look out at the spreading sea of upturned faces, she felt unsuspected new sources of strength emerging within herself. As the prophetess prepared to address a meeting in London, she reflected on the changes in her audience and within herself: "I felt myself deeply affected, as the beginning of my Visitation came Strongly to my mind, and when I began, all my Religious acquaintence were against me. [B]ut now to see so large a multitude gathered together as Believers with me, Affected me greatly, and it came strong to my remembrance on a Sudden . . . the Grain of Mustard Seed that was the least of all seeds before it came to a large Tree for the Birds to lodge in the branches thereof."[3]

In the "multitude" attracted to Joanna were three dissimilar figures, the Reverend Thomas P. Foley, Jane Townley, and her servant, Ann Underwood, whose ardent support helped soften the trials of leadership and who provided both an emotional and administrative context which made it possible for the prophetess to deal effectively with her vast new responsibilities.

Foley's conversion to Joanna's cause stirred critics to a rich and volatile mixture of rage, indignation, ridicule, and simple disbelief. That a man of such eminent respectability could be so ensnared was both terrifying and absurd, particularly in view of the fact that Foley came from a wealthy and influential Worcestershire family which sent its sons into Parliament, the army, business, and the clergy. The clergyman acknowledged that he was one "who had been accustom'd to move in higher Circles of life."[4] He attended Cambridge where his good looks, and private income, coupled with "gay and dissipated" habits enabled him to cut a vivid figure, one enhanced in the memory of an acquaintance by his wearing of a scarlet coat, considered the height of fashion in London but much frowned upon by college authorities. He subsequently took his M.A. in 1782, became a fellow of Jesus College, and obtained a college living at an early date. Later he accepted the offer of a more valuable living at Old Swinford from his family.[5] There, with a wife and growing family, he attempted to moderate his self-indulgent ways although his account books reveal that he borrowed money from the Reverend Stanhope Bruce and John Wilson and on one occasion even "borrow'd from Joanna Two Guineas towards Housekeepg."[6] Certainly he continued to delight in the social pleasures of his class, sometimes distressing his parishioners at Old Swinford when he appeared at funerals with a surplice thrown over his hunting clothes.[7]

Because of his flamboyant personal style and his family connections, he became a highly visible figure whose opinion mattered in the county. Possessing "a character for liberality," he managed to shock Joseph Priestley when he wrote to the reformer of his "satisfaction" at the abuses which had been heaped upon him in nearby Birmingham.[8] Priestley had stirred local opinion by his religious views, his membership in the Birmingham Lunar Society, and his active role in the reform movement. For three days in July 1791 the Birmingham mob turned on Dissenters and their property, destroying, among other things, Priestley's books, manuscripts, and his laboratory.

Already a believer in the prophet Richard Brothers, Foley first heard of Joanna in the early spring of 1801. There were "some extraordinary accounts of her . . . in circulation" which made him eagerly place orders with his bookseller for her publications. He received the first three parts of *Strange Effects of Faith* in June and read them with great care, comparing each with appropriate parts of scripture. "I found them so consistent therewith, and so agreeable to *common sense*; at the same time opening to my view a new scene that I was wonderfully struck with them. In my opinion, there is a *greater Body* of Spiritual Light given to the World in these Writings than was ever given since the Bible was completed." He began corresponding with Joanna, and at Christmas, as previously mentioned, went to Exeter with two other Anglican clergymen—Thomas Webster, then of St. George's, the Borough, London, and Stanhope Bruce, of Inglesham, Gloucestershire—as well as William Sharp and John Wilson to interview her and to "see whether Joanna Southcott was an Impostor or not." George Turner from Leeds and Peter Morrison of Liverpool joined them. Despite the Exeter bishop's opinion that the prophetess was mad, Foley and his friends became convinced that Joanna "was truly *pious, honest* and industrious" as well as of sound mind. They witnessed her dictating her communications from her Spirit and found "ample proof" that her prophecies on Napoleon, the harvests, "and many other events equally extraordinary" had come true. The seven men remained in Exeter a week and then returned to London with her writings. Foley and the others who lived outside the city went back to their homes.[9] On April 3, 1802, he wrote to William Phillips that he had "circulated as far as I possibly could *my full and decided belief in Joanna Southcott & Richard Brothers.*"[10]

On May 22, the clergyman was back in London at Joanna's command, although seemingly in need of further proof of the authenticity of her claims. Despite his protestations to the contrary, Foley could not have been completely convinced by his visit to Exeter, for he told a decidedly different story of his conversion to his friend William Mathew, senior fellow and bursar of Jesus College. While in London, Foley wrote, he dined with a party of friends who brought up the topic of Joanna. They agreed she was an impostor and decided to carry out a thoroughly sophomoric prank. The next morning, pretending to be believers in need of counsel, Foley and his companions called on Joanna who, nevertheless, quickly saw through their charade. She then stunned the group by observing that one of their number from the previous evening's revels was missing. She proceeded to inform them that their friend became ill after he returned home from their party, and that he would soon be dead. Foley wrote to Mathew, "I confess that her words had made a deep impression, and I hastened to the house of my friend." He found him critically ill, and several days later Joanna's prophecy was fulfilled. "After his funeral," Foley said, "I again sought an interview with Joanna Southcott, and professed myself a convert."[11] Thus was to begin an association which lasted until Joanna's death in 1814.

In order to better understand why Foley may have been unusually susceptible to Joanna's arguments, it is not unreasonable to suppose that underneath the surface of this gentle, devout, and relentlessly convivial man burned a keen sense of grievance at the disadvantages facing a younger son of a famous family. His alliance with Joanna could well offer a host of new prospects, both for personal advancement and for a sense of importance in an age which seemed intent on relegating him to the role of bystander and which, at the same time, offered his relatives in politics and the military such fabulously heightened possibilities. If he would suggest nothing consciously to support this speculation, his dreams, which he candidly recalled, offer some telling evidence in its behalf. In one, the clergyman remembered, I "flew upon the most Grand & Magnificent church I ever beheld, and I thought it far Exceeded all I ever saw or Read of in Splendor & Glory." [12] Such a splendid establishment, with a suitable ecclesiastical retinue, would unquestionably mean a glittering appointment in the coming Kingdom of God, one to which a prominent believer such as Foley might legitimately aspire. Foley's dreams became more filled with incident, and violence, when he contemplated the threat that Napoleon, the Beast of Revelation, offered to the faithful. Casting himself in a heroic role, one that could well have been usurped in reality by his brother, a colonel in the army,[13] Foley dreamed that, after a battle between the English and French, he and others had taken Napoleon into custody. The emperor provoked his captors by throwing missiles at them, and Foley responded with equal aggressiveness. "I seized a short Bludgeon that lay by me & I kept my eye steadily fixed on Buonaparte's Eye, and never quitted it an instant & this prevented the mischief he intended me—I . . . then secured his Arms & called to my companions to come and kill him; or else, he would kill us." [14] On another night, he dreamed he was playing a game with Napoleon "Life for Life." Whoever was victorious could have the other executed. "Happily," he reported, "I came off Victorious, and great shouts were given by the Spectators." [15]

But the fulfillment of these dreams depended, in part, on his success in convincing the nation's leaders of the wisdom of his beliefs. On February 26, 1802, two months after his visit to Exeter, Foley fell asleep and saw himself "in a large Room with many of the First People in this Kingdom" along with "several of the Members of the late Administration," including Pitt and Dundas. He spoke to them about Joanna and Richard Brothers but with mixed results.[16] A less equivocal response awaited from the eminent in his own family. His uncle, Lord Foley, in time disinherited him, and another relative, a member of Parliament with whom he had enjoyed a close relationship over the years, judged him mad for his beliefs.[17]

Although Foley and his wife, Elizabeth, lived with and kept house for Joanna in London during the winter and spring of 1803 and stayed with her in Leeds for seven weeks in the summer and fall,[18] over the years Foley spent most of his time at his home in Old Swinford. There he battled with his curate who led a parish movement to have him suspended because of his allegiance to Joanna, finally gaining the upper hand only after a successful interview with his bishop,[19] and tried, with intermittent success, to stir local interest in the prophetess.

It was to be Foley's cross that his recruiting efforts in his own parish stood in sharp and unhappy contrast with the movement's growth elsewhere, particularly in Yorkshire. But then, conditions were vastly different in the tightly knit, socially reassuring world of rural society and the desperately alienating existence of a bustling industrial city and its satellites. To an inhabitant of Old Swinford, a world transformed might have much less appeal than to a citizen of Leeds. Foley lamented to Mrs. Taylor on October 31, 1803, that Joanna's "reception at Leeds" proved "very different from what it was here. At this place they were almost *all mockers* & full of lies—and in Yorkshire there are crowds of Believers." [20] Five weeks later his wife, Elizabeth, confirmed that in Leeds "Believers . . . encrease in multitudes daily." [21] But progress continued to remain sluggish in Old Swinford. A little over a year later Foley wrote, "Indeed all is perfectly tranquil here at present—very few Enquirers concerning Joanna or her writings—and scarcely a Book sold." [22] A year afterward, he repeated the old refrain once again, writing that the cause "is spreading rapidly in Yorkshire, and many are added to the Sealed Number—Here I am truly sorry to say but few come to solicit seals." [23] But the gloom could lift. In the summer of 1805, Foley reported that on successive Sundays he had "considerably more than 100" believers to preach to and there were meetings three times a week at Stourbridge and Upper Swinford.[24] The original pattern always reasserted itself, however. In a letter to Peter Morrison in August of the following year, he commented, "I have the happiness to inform you that the Glorious Cause is spreading in Ireland—in & around Bristol—and also in Gloucestershire where many Quakers have joined us with Zeal & Enthusiasm." Yet, "in this part of the World we make but little Progress," although "now & then I have a few who come to sign their Names & Request Seals." [25]

Two other episodes, the first rather comic, managed to upset the gentle rhythms of Foley's country life. He made a twenty-guinea wager with a local magistrate, Major Pidcock, that after Louis XVI's death, France would never again have a monarch. Napoleon's coronation in December 1804 convinced Pidcock that he had won the wager. Foley disagreed: "I am as fully confident that I have *not lost* my wager, as you can possibly be that you have *won* it." Joanna came to his assistance, supplying the argument that, if Napoleon was now king, why couldn't the French emigrés who seemed to throng the streets of London go home to France to reclaim their property. Unconvinced, the major challenged Foley to a duel, which the clergyman wisely declined, but their rancorous disagreement went on for months.[26] Second, Foley received a disturbing letter from E. J. Field on April 14, 1808, outlining the serious financial difficulties into which their friend and fellow believer John Wilson had fallen. Wilson did not want Joanna or Sharp to know of his desperation and, through Field, begged Foley's advice. Field said, "It is absolutely needfull for him to be in some place of refuge till the Storm is blown over." He asked Foley if he could provide an "asylum" for Wilson from his creditors and business partners who "took a most unfair & villinanous advantage of him." Foley replied that it was "a dagger to my heart" to hear that Field did not want to inform Joanna of the situation, and asked how can he "forget all the dangers & difficulties which he has so often escaped from by the goodness of the Lord thro' His chosen Servant Joanna." All this was a ploy, he wrote, on the part of Satan "to divide us." Foley's parting advice was that Wilson must go to Joanna and tell her the whole story.[27]

From his conversion until Joanna's death, Foley's support remained unflagging. He preached and wrote effectively for the cause, sustained a valued correspondence with Joanna and other important figures throughout the years, and, when called upon, enthusiastically administered the sacraments.

JANE TOWNLEY, ANN UNDERWOOD, AND RICHARD LAW

During the first two years after leaving Exeter, Joanna led a vagabond existence, staying at the homes of several prominent supporters both in London and outside, traveling in the Midlands and Yorkshire, spending seven months in Leeds and a number of weeks in Bristol, as well as making a trip back to Exeter for a month-long visit.[28] In the spring of 1804 she met two women, Jane Townley and her servant, Ann Underwood, who brought her travels to an end.

Miss Townley was a woman of independent fortune who had suffered from fragile health until six years before when she came under the care of a physician who put her on the path to recovery. During her illness she was sustained by the conviction that she would live to see Christ's return to earth. She first heard of Joanna in May 1803 and read her books, which confirmed her in her beliefs. A year later she wrote to her friend the Bishop of London, "When I heard of Joanna Southcott's prophecies, last May, I thought it my duty to Read them, and Judge for myself, whether they Corresponded with the Scriptures." She became "fully convinced that her Communications could only come from a

God."[29] Having discovered that the prophetess planned to return to London, Miss Townley invited her to stay at her house at Weston Place and subsequently, along with her maid, Ann Underwood, accompanied Joanna to Gloucestershire and Bristol. The three came to recognize the advantages of a shared living arrangement. Afterward, they established themselves at Blockley in the Cotswolds at a place called Rock Cottage, remaining there until 1813.[30]

Joanna was now free from financial worries and, as importantly, had acquired two sympathetic and adoring companions who assumed the extraordinary secretarial demands of a movement of thousands of followers.[31] The two women responded, sometimes independently but for the most part at Joanna's direction, to endless inquiries from believers and nonbelievers. Counseling, exhorting, admonishing, and persuading, the letters poured out, usually in Ann Underwood's hand and with Joanna's signature appended at the end. On occasion, Miss Townley might attempt to clarify some misunderstanding that Joanna had unwittingly encouraged,[32] but neither she nor Ann Underwood ever saw themselves as anything but faithful and privileged acolytes.

Dealing with correspondence, as important and onerous a task as it was, paled in comparison with an even more important charge. According to Miss Townley, from the first days of 1792, Joanna had herself transcribed the communications from her Spirit "free from erazures and alterations." Even so, her writing proved "illegible to every one besides herself." After June 17, 1804, she began dictating to Townley and Underwood.[33] The dual responsibilities of transcribing correspondence as well as the communications proved staggering. Within five days Miss Townley wrote to Joanna's Exeter friend and former employer, Mrs. Taylor, "I find the task [too] hard for me."[34] Nevertheless, the women persevered, sometimes being helped by other believers. The task eased somewhat by January 1806 when Underwood finally learned to read Joanna's writing "with perfect facility." Yet, Miss Townley said, "She is the only person capable of so doing."[35]

Ann Underwood remains an insubstantial figure. She was industrious and loyal, a widow with children, whose self-effacement remained so complete that only once did she inspire comment, and then merely a gentle reproof that she became "nervous" under pressure.[36] Yet, as Joanna's principal secretary, Ann was one of the best known figures in the movement. The beauty of her handwriting was instantly recognized in "many thousands of homes throughout the country."[37] Only rarely, however, did she express her own views. An isolated example exists in a letter to Joshua Lowe, a Birmingham believer. Lowe wrote to her of his sister's "melancholy state of mind," to which Ann replied sympathetically that mental instability was on the increase, indeed had reached alarming proportions among religious men and women. From the symptoms indicated in the letter, Ann agreed that Lowe's sister "is under mental derangement but derangement appears in various forms[.] Therefore her being able to converse is no proof of her sanity[.] That all derangement proceeds from the working of evil spirits is my Idea. Some may have a short Frenzy produced by fever in the Brain and recover from it[.] But where the people gradually sink into Lowness of·Spirits and then endeavour to make away with themselves, appear to me to be from the evil power and therefore in these cases confinement or continual watching is necessary." Insanity, she added, was not confined to a particular religious group. "We have heard of persons of every denomination of every sect and party of religion that have suffered from this dreadful calamity and have put an end to their existance." "Therefore," she said, "it is nothing more than the common lot of all men that some have fell under the fatal malady."[38] For a Christian, this was a remarkably tolerant and enlightened view of a suicide.

Although little more is known about Jane Townley than her servant, she comes briefly to life because of a series of oddly compelling love letters written to her by Richard Law, a flaxdresser who joined the movement in its first years. The illumination he gives to Miss Townley, and himself, possesses a feverish, often bizarre quality; but, alone in the Southcottian correspondence, his letters abandon the usual devout and high-minded commonplaces and speak in a passionate, angry, unmistakably individual voice. The surviving letters, all from Law, begin in 1816 after a thirteen-year break in their relationship, and in the throes of bitterness and disillusion that swept many of the believers after Joanna's death. They combine a flesh-crawling mendicancy with both a continuing hope that she will accept his love and a keening sadness for all the years lost to them.

On May 10, 1816, Law wrote to her from Doncaster, "You have drove me mad[;] you have made me run distracted, and you have bewitched me out of my wits, as all my letters to you will most clearly testify." "Nevertheless," he said, "I may be fully restored again if you will consent to a reconciliation." Her refusal to comply drove him to write again, "Inexorable Jane, what if Heaven should be barred to you as you have barred yourself from me," and then he proceeded to chide her on her nunlike habits. "Come, come don't puff yourself up about your virginity." Such "foolish celibacy" only meant that "many a brave and proper man goes Wifeless and Childless to the Grave." It is she who is his "rightfull partner," and there is still time for her to realize it and for the two of them to find happiness together.[39]

Further provoked by her unyielding attitude, he then blamed his an-
guish on Joanna and, it seems, the difference in their classes. "For
though the Witch is dead," he wrote on June 23, 1816, "her spells yet
continue, and are set with the most infernal art." He said, "You were
easily caught by the fascinating delusion, because you was unskilled in
the way of Religion." A year and a half later he charged that Joanna had
once told her not to write to him, implying that it had not served the
prophetess' purpose for her irreplaceable benefactor and aide to marry
Law. As her stony silence continued, he compared the poor, those like
himself who had known and knew bitter poverty, with the rich, Jane
Townley's class, much to the latter's disadvantage. He wrote to her:

How vain and contemptible does this world appear to me, especially that part
of it called the Wealthy[;] how greedy they are of what they call riches, yet lofty
withal and expect all the Poor to worship them[;] but why should we worship a
person or be afraid to speak Truth to a Person because he may have gold[.] A
sincere man will not fear gold nor worship gold, he will fear God and worship
Him only. I would not wantonly affront a rich Person but I should esteem my
Poor friend before him. The poor are far more benevolent than the rich. They
frequently lend their all and give there all, but if a rich man possesses thousands, meets his friend and spiritual acquaintance in distress, he will rather
mock his misery than [relieve] his wants. Perhaps he may tender him a small
silver mite which the humility of the poor Friend [forces] him to accept while his
blood runs cold within him at the solemn mockery of his Poverty.[40]

Even though Law could say, "In Christ I am everything and possess
all Things," he concluded by asking Jane Townley for thirty pounds.
Five days later he wrote to Ann Underwood, whom he hoped would be
"a Friend at Court," and told her of just how desperate things were.
Effusions of love for her mistress evaporated in face of the sufferings he
felt necessary to describe. "I have often been in dreadfull want, and in
extream need[.] Often hunger [has] driven me from London." "When
provision was at the dearest," he said, "I have been obliged to languish
on three shillings per week without a single friendly invitation. I have
often walked London streets seeking employment till for want of food, I
have been ready to fall down on the pavement, and I have gone home
trembling with a palpitation of heart." In desperation he had fled the
city for the country but found conditions little improved. Indeed, there
was little to choose between the two. "The last time I came through
London two years since, I lost 3 pounds in seeking employment, and
was obliged to leave it near the depth of winter, with scarce enough in
my Pocket for 3 days Journies." At the same time, "the country every
[where] was in a very shocking state. I wander'd 8 weeks in the shortest
days thro' dark Tempests and most awfull roads . . . subsisting on tur-

nips[,] bread[,] and a little milk[,] reserving my money to pay for a
night's lodging." The next day he wrote to Jane Townley, "God is no
respecter of Persons[;] the Poor and the Rich are both a like to Him."
Unhappily for Law, Jane Townley was not equally blind to class distinctions or at least not in his case. He continued to importune her for
money and probably fell victim to a last, extravagant religious fantasy
in which he became "a Bishop and Priest of Salem."[41] What emerges
clearly is that, like a member of a religious order, Jane Townley obe-
diently served her superior and found her emotional needs gratified by
love of God, not man, however affected she may have once been by
Law's ardent attentions.

LEADERSHIP

Although uneducated, Joanna possessed unusual reserves of energy and
a fund of common sense acquired over a lifetime of capable performance of her duties as a servant. These attributes, combined with her
new sense of self-confidence, the prestige afforded by her claims, re-
sourcefulness and patience in the face of opposition, and not incon-
siderable skills as a speaker and propagandist, provided the leadership
qualities required by the movement.

Upon her arrival in London, in 1802, Joanna plunged into a mael-
strom of activity. Writing back to her friend Mrs. Taylor, in Devonshire,
she said, "Ever since I came to London I have been constantly employ'd
in writing either to put in print, or for private Instructions to my
Friends; or else I have had opposers to Contend with . . . to support the
Cause of Truth."[42] On a typical occasion Foley asked the prophetess if
she had any enclosures for a letter he was posting but found her "so
loaded & overwhelmed with business that she begged me to finish it—
and that she would write soon to her dear friends herself."[43] She invited
leading believers to London in January 1803 and December 1804 for
her second and third "trials" (the first having been in Exeter at Christmas 1801), to which the clergy were invited and which were meant to
establish the authenticity of her claims beyond doubt.

At first, Joanna naively believed that all who accepted her claims
would coexist harmoniously. Thus, when local disagreements broke
out, she was not prepared to deal with them effectively. A companion
said, "Joanna was deeply affected to hear the discord amongst the Believers, and in fact almost Stumbled that such Strife and contention
Should be amongst them, and that they were not all united together in
Christian Love and unity one with the other."[44] Evidence that Joanna
could learn to deal sensibly with such difficult situations comes from a

letter she wrote on October 25, 1805, to William Tozer, the preacher in her London chapel on Duke Street. Tozer and the London Southcottians needed guidance after the bitter secession of Elias Carpenter, a Bermondsey paper manufacturer. In order to prevent unauthorized worshippers and curiosity seekers from attending the service, Joanna suggested that the believers be admitted only if they possessed tickets, a procedure she remembered from her association with the Methodists. She wrote:

If you take my advice, and the sealed people who wish to attend you join you in it, I think it will prevent great confusion amongst the people if they all took their seats, and every one had a ticket for their seats, then the people who may come out of curiosity, or to make any disturbance, will be prevented from filling the place with disorderly people, as they cannot go into any place of worship to take away the seats from those who have taken them. This keeps all churches and places of worship in order, and by this conduct, I think you will all agree with me, it will prevent a riotous people from assembling to interrupt those who wish to meet seriously together, and assemble themselves together to hear and judge for themselves, the Scripture pointed out for the coming of the Lord, and the truth of the prophecies made known and explained with the Scriptures of truth.[45]

Joanna long held out hopes that the Established Church could be persuaded to embrace her following. In order to gain recognition, she continuously circularized bishops and clergy but was almost always completely ignored. Finally bowing to the inevitable, she sanctioned independent worship among her believers. In a letter written on December 2, 1811, she warned about the legal pitfalls of this course:

I have heard of late that many have been *fined for Speaking or Preaching Without being Licensed*. I must lay the cause before you. If there is anyone amongst the Believers that would like to take it upon himself to be *Licensed as a Preacher* he must be Licensed as a Protestant Dissenter, and the place where he Speak[s] must be Licensed also. And then it is a place of worship but if there is no one Licensed as a Preacher I do not see any occasion to License the room for so small a number as attend at present and if you meet together to read the writings and compare them with the Scriptures and neither use Prayer or Hymns they cannot hurt you for that. [B]ut using Prayer or Hymns makes it a Place of Worship for which if you have not a License they can fine you.[46]

Joanna's correspondents were not all concerned with organizational problems or dissension among themselves. Frequently, they consulted the prophetess about practical matters, revealing their confidence in the soundness of her judgment. Mrs. Taylor solicited Joanna's help over a legal dispute between her husband and a man named Mills who claimed he was overcharged for upholstering materials he had bought from the Taylors. Joanna summarized the situation as she understood it, approving of Mr. Taylor's offer to apply to another upholsterer for arbitration and reassuring her friends that she found Mills' behavior reprehensible. If the law upheld him, she said, "then every Man that wish[es] to cheat a Tradesman out of his Money may make a pretence he hath bought his goods too dear." She reminded the Taylors that Mills had known the price of the goods beforehand and only after receiving them did he accuse Taylor of being overcharged. If the law upheld him, then "all Business must be at an end."[47] In any event, Joanna did not have strong confidence in the courts. She once advised Foley to stay away from the law over another financial matter, warning that hundreds of pounds are gone "when once you get into their Claws. I myself have seen so much of it, that I am frightened at the Idea of it."[48]

One of the most painful hurdles that Joanna had to clear was her fear of public speaking. From early childhood, she had great difficulty in expressing herself before others. But with growing confidence, she was now able to perform this function effectively. At a gathering with her London believers, she at first felt unable "to know how to Speak to the People at all . . . yet I felt a feeling in my heart that I could by no means refrain from Speaking." Once she began, she was able to proceed with passionate intensity: "I exhorted the People to be like the Wise Virgins, waiting to enter in with the Bridegroom and . . . as man Clamoured for the blood of our Saviour so must we now join hand and heart to Clamour for Satan's destruction by our Petitions to the Lord to do it for us. . . . I exhorted them to be in Love and unity with each other and the Strong to bear the infirmities of the weak and not let little things Kindle Strife amongst them to give Satan advantage over them." Finally, "I exhorted them all to be Steadfast in their faith. Hoping if they Lived till the Coming of the Lord that they would be waiting like the Wise Virgins to enter in with the Bridegroom . . . but if they Died before the time I hoped they would come with the Lord in Glory." At her brother's funeral, Jane Townley said that Joanna gave "a very clear and beautiful Exhortation, to be Ready and Watch for the time when they might be taken like her Brother." Miss Townley was impressed and deeply moved by the prophetess' remarks. "She spoke very clear and distinct. [T]here was not a dry eye in the room after She had entreated the Lord would Bless and Keep them all stedfast in faith."[49] On another occasion, Foley recorded in his diary that Joanna spoke to a group of believers "in a most forcible and animated speech."[50]

Sometimes, however, problems exceeded Joanna's capacity. Even with her immense local influence, she found the dissensions which erupted among the Exeter Southcottians intractable. On December 6, 1806, Joanna wrote to G. Woolcott in Exeter, approving of the meetings of the believers which were taking place. "For as knife sharpens knife, so does a man his friend; and by these meetings in different places many have been strengthened and established. Therefore as you have began, I wish you to continue." But the prophetess did not grant a request to set up a chapel. "As to establishing a place of worship with any alterations to the Prayers of the Church, it is not approved of by God or man." Anyway, she said, there was always the difficulty of finding a suitable minister. "Ye know in Exeter how deeply a man's character would be scrutinized, who began to be a preacher to the people." In order to face the mockery which would greet his efforts, he would have to "be endowed with every Christian patience and fortitude." Joanna had a particular objection to the nominee suggested, Mr. Portbury. "I am sorry to say . . . though he appears zealous in the cause, yet the rashness of his passions is such, as I fear would do more hurt than good to be at the head of a people." Therefore, "I do not think establishing a church for the present in such a place as Exeter, would be of any kind of good. And yet, by your meeting together, you may, in time, get an united Church to join together." [51]

The situation continued to simmer, however. In 1809, Jane Townley wrote that "the contention there is at Exeter amongst the Believers is quite dreadful and the Lord alone can make peace amongst them." Exacerbating the situation was the fact that Portbury had gained the support of the Taylors, who had once employed Joanna and subsequently become converts to her cause. This development greatly distressed Miss Townley. "The Taylors were partial to him as he has a very cleaver head and thought us too much prejudiced against him but I fear to their [un]easiness they will find they had better have Kept him at a distance for if he has not every thing his own way, his violence and insolence is great." Despite the attempts made by Joanna and her lieutenant to mollify the squabbling factions in Exeter, and elsewhere, there was frequently little to show for it. "We do all we can to Keep peace by Bearing and forbearing, and Softening on all sides, but the Lord alone can make Harmony amongst them." [52]

When dissensions at Exeter and elsewhere became too disquieting, Joanna could always look to Leeds as a model of the kind of Christian fellowship she hoped would prevail throughout her movement. She wrote to a supporter, "I wish I could make you all be united together in Love as they are at Leeds[;] I never hear of no discord from them, . . . and they have Thousands to attend them in many places and yet they are united together in Brotherly Love." She said, "I shall be happy when I hear it so at every place but as it is not, we must bear with patience what we cannot mend and bear Infirmities one of another," adding, "I wish you to avoid discord as much as possible." [53]

Joanna believed that she was the chosen instrument of God. As such, she defended the correctness of her views not on the basis of her own acuity but because of the infallibility of the Spirit who guided her. This belief gave the prophetess an invincible certitude, enabling her to behave quite ruthlessly to those who differed with her. After she read a communication on the nature of the Fall to a gathering in Leeds, in which she placed the heaviest blame on Satan, a man stood up and disagreed with her, asserting that the responsibility for the Fall lay with Adam and Eve. Several of Joanna's supporters remonstrated with him, stressing the exclusive culpability of the devil. Joanna, too, attempted to dissuade him from his opposition. When he refused to accede to her authority, she said, "I then told him to quit the room, as he was a *friend to the Devil*; as I had invited my friends there to take my leave of them, and would not be interrupted by his contention; as I had proposed to spend the day with my friends only; for many had come from a great distance to see me." The stubborn soul refused to leave as the prophetess had ordered. Then, one of her followers suggested that "every man that is against him, let him hold up his hand." Joanna triumphantly reported, "Immediately every man in the room held up his hand, to shew they were all against him; and he was immediately put out of the room, as an enemy to the human race, and a friend to the Devil." [54] The overwhelming show of support may have been influenced by the fate of two men who had set out for Leeds to contend with the prophetess. "A sudden stoke of death" felled them both. The Spirit claimed that "my angels" had served a "death warrant" on the two would-be adversaries because of their "insolence." [55] Stories such as these must certainly have helped render Joanna's authority unassailable in many quarters.

Other indications existed of the ascendancy she attained over her followers. Jane Townley, the prophetess' closest associate, declared after her death, "I obeyed her in all things; as any one must have obeyed the Duke of Wellington, who was an officer in his army; without taking in question the duty assigned to him. Thus, as no responsibility rested upon me, I had only to obey the commands given through her during her lifetime." [56] The Reverend Thomas P. Foley wrote to defecting Southcottian Elias Carpenter that he relied on the prophetess "for directions how to act, as I shall not take any step of my own in this momentous cause without consulting her; having found now for near four years past every Direction given to me by the Spirit thro' her to be most accurately True & correct." The clergyman's happiness would continue as long as he was "*faithful & obedient*." [57] Joanna convinced her principal Leeds supporter, George Turner, that he was led by an evil spirit and that he should respond only to the dictates of *her* Spirit. Joanna's Spirit put the issue succinctly. Both she and her followers would escape Satan's wiles *"if thou followest my directions, and they follow the directions given to thee."* [58]

The best evidence of Joanna's autocratic control, however, came over the matter of Peter Morrison. Morrison was a cotton printer from Liverpool who had been one of the original seven to visit Joanna in Exeter. After becoming convinced of her claims, he returned home as an active proselytizer for the cause in Liverpool and the surrounding areas. At first her hopes for him were high,[59] but his conduct grew "disgraceful"[60] and he came to take an increasingly independent line, daring even to enlighten his hearers with his own prophecies. Joanna grew furious. Calling herself "mortified and grieved" over his prophesying, she wrote to him, "I cannot stand joined with any that will not follow the directions that are given to Me[;] I have nothing to do with those that go on by a Spirit of their own, in opposition to the directions given to Me." She added, "I have been often ordered to reprove the violence of your temper, the wrongness of your judgment and the harshness of your Words." If he persisted in his deviation, she said, "then no longer say you are joined with Me."[61]

Morrison's conduct improved and Joanna came to the realization that he had "friends" as well as "foes" but, she said, "I am always carefull who I listen to."[62] Nevertheless, charges of misconduct and "erroneous judgment"[63] continued to flow in. She attempted to be fair, still hoping he would mend his ways. "It would give me great pleasure if you could clear yourself of the whole, for I can assure you, it give[s] me pain to be under the necessity of reproving you so often." If "innocent," she said, "I give you an opportunity of clearing yourself" by going to the places from which the complaints originated and persuading critics that he had reformed or that the allegations were false.[64] At the end, she felt it necessary to forbid him to preach.[65] Morrison was not the only Southcottian preacher to feel Joanna's lash,[66] but, with the exception of Elias Carpenter, he proved the most troublesome.

Finally, the absolute authority of the prophetess was confirmed by an oath "required of Joanna Southcott and her friends," in which her Spirit asked, "Wilt thou swear by Him that liveth—thou wilt obey, in all things, my strict Commands to thee—and it is not all the Powers of Earth and Hell, shall make thee turn to the right or the left,—but my Command, the living Lord of Heaven and Earth thou wilt obey?" Because the Spirit made his will known through Joanna, the oath amounted to an act of fealty to the prophetess.[67]

The most striking example of Joanna's effectiveness as a proselytizer was the success of her visit to Yorkshire in the fall and winter of 1803. Upon her arrival, the prophetess stayed in the country about eight miles from Leeds. She "was visited from morning until evening by large companies of the Surrounding Inhabitants, and Several Gentlemen and Ladies." On Sunday a "Country Lady" asked Joanna to call at her house. There she talked freely with "two Ladies and two Gentlemen, one of them a minister of the Church of England." She was then asked if she would address the large number who had gathered to hear her in the kitchen. "Before the servants could finish their dinners," Joanna told Carpenter, "the large Kitchine was thronged with some hundreds." In order to be heard, Joanna climbed up on a table "and tole them the truth of my Prophecies from 1792 to this day, and explained many of the Scriptures." She began "going through the Visions" when the clergyman informed her "there were some thousands out of doors." The huge crowd pleaded with Joanna to address them in the courtyard of the house. She agreed, walking outside and standing on the steps, so that they could see and hear her. The gravity of her listeners greatly impressed Joanna. After tea, she visited another house where she again found a "large company." The following day she traveled five miles "to a Mr. Dixon's where [she said] I met a large Company, the most Serious I have ever seen." The day afterward she had an interview with a Church of England clergyman who rode three miles through a heavy rain to talk with her. Joanna found that "he was truly convinced the Calling was of God as all my Writings were like the ways and wisdom of the Lord." She went from Leeds to Stockton in Cheshire where the response continued to be overwhelming. Joanna informed Carpenter, "It is fruitless to tell you the thousands that has flocked to hear me." [68] At Halifax in Yorkshire, she spoke to a "multitude" estimated variously at fifteen thousand, nine thousand, or six thousand people. Joanna thought the last figure the most realistic. [69]

THE SEALS

The *Leeds Mercury* grudgingly noted Joanna's presence in the locality. "In announcing the arrival of distinguished personages, we have to mention, that JOHANNA SOUTHCOTE, the celebrated *Prophetess of Exeter*, has, in pursuance of her mission, arrived in Leeds." The newspaper said wonderingly: "It is not more strange than true, that Johanna's disciples are numerous both in Leeds and many other parts of the Kingdom, and all of them as [sincerely] believe in the marvellous prophecies of this *Lady of Exeter* as ever did good Catholic in the miracles wrought at the shrine of the Lady of Loretta." According to the newspaper, "The object of her visit is to distribute CELESTIAL SEALS to the faithful; and as these seals, like the Agis of Minerva, will protect the possessor from all danger even at the cannon's mouth, we recommend the Volunteers to lay in a stock preparatory to the arrival of Bonaparte and his sharp-shooters." The *Mercury* offered the information that the seals "may be had without money and without price, and only one thing is wanting to give them full efficacy, namely Faith!!"[70]

The "seal" was indeed the shibboleth of the Southcottian movement. A slip of paper with the believer's name at the top and Joanna's signature at the bottom, it contained the following inscription:

The
Sealed of the Lord, the Elect Precious
Man's Redemption to Inherit the
Tree of Life
To be made Heirs of God, & Joint Heirs
With
Jesus Christ[71]

The paper was then folded over and closed with a seal which Joanna had once found while sweeping out a house in Exeter. The letters I C were incised upon it,[72] causing the prophetess to believe that they signified the words *Jesus Christ*. Joanna justified the "sealing" from a passage in Revelation which reads, "Hurt not the earth, neither the sea, nor the trees, till we have sealed the servants of God." Eventually the sealed, Joanna believed, would reach the number of 144,000.[73]

The "seal," the folded, sealed paper, was endowed with extraordinary properties. The believers who possessed them were protected from the workings of Satan, which meant, in effect, from all the real and imagined terrors which beset them. One who signed himself "A BELIEVER" wrote in the *Leeds Mercury* that "the Sealing is the Way the Lord has appointed for his obedient Servants to escape this hellish Fury, and Judgments which will cause Desolation on the Earth."[74] The expression "seal of safety" recurs again and again in Joanna's writings. At a time of profound emotional disorientation, the seal held out the promise of personal security, even, perhaps, personal immortality. The *Leeds Mercury* said that devout possessors of the seals "will in the opinion of the Prophetess live at least a thousand years!"[75] In a letter dated May 2, 1805, Joanna confessed herself "astonished" at the falsehood that "the sealed shall 'live for ever and never see death.'"[76] That this belief gained widespread circulation is attested by the reaction to the murder of a Mr. Joachim, one of the sealed, in London. "The Believers are much

hurt to hear, as they thought the Seals were a Safety from All Dangers."
Joanna felt called upon to admonish her following: "And now let this be
a *Caution to all Believers, not to run theirselves into Dangers* but let
them remember how oft I have warned them, to avoid Dangers every
way. But if they Simply Suppose the Seals were made as a wall about
them that no Dangers could come near them, then my warning and
Caution would be in vain, but let them all discern from this how Dangers are laying in wait for the *Just* and the *unjust*, for *Believers* and
unbelievers." [77]

If the seal was not powerful enough to protect believers from a random misadventure, it would, according to Joanna, offer other protection. She said that in the event Napoleon invaded England only the
sealed could be confident of survival.[78] Joanna's reassurance on this
point came in 1804, a timely moment, with Napoleon's great army
poised at Boulogne, seemingly ready to descend upon England. Many of
the believers ordered that, if they died before Christ's return to earth,
their seals were to be buried with them so that their souls would go
directly to heaven.[79] There were also reassuring reports of believers'
being saved from the misadventures of foreign battle or shipwreck by
possession of a seal.[80]

Excitement to obtain the seals became intense. In 1803, the "sealed"
numbered only 58. A year later, the names of 8,144 recipients had been
recorded "besides those who are blotted out—and some Lists are not
yet gathered in."[81] E. P. Thompson has compared the "market in seals
. . . to the late medieval market in relics of the Cross."[82]

Many believed that Joanna herself was trafficking in the seals.[83] Robert Currier from Salisbury sent to the prophetess' agent asking for a
"half a Hundred of your seals" and the "price."[84] The smell of scandal
made its way into every recess of society. It was particularly appreciated
by the sensitive nostrils of Lord Byron, who wrote John Murray, "I
should like to buy one of her seals: if salvation can be had at half-a-
guinea a head, the landlord of the Crown and Anchor should be ashamed
of himself for charging double for tickets to a mere terrestrial banquet."[85] The prophetess found these charges deeply troubling. Joanna
dreamed that she was approached by a woman who made the shrewd
observation, "I see yours is a money business, and I will give you half a
guinea." In her dream, the prophetess hotly denied that the seals were
for sale and told the woman that she despised her money.[86] George
Turner verified that the seals were given away and not sold. He said, "I
affirm and declare to all the world, that the Seals are a free gift, without
money and without price." Moreover, "no one is authorized to seal by
the command of the Lord, or to use that seal . . . but by the hand of

Joanna Southcott." [87] Foley denied that he had ever sold any seals and took out an advertisement on May 5, 1809, in the *Worcester Herald* defending the prophetess from such accusations. [88] Another follower declared in 1842 that "not a single farthing" was "ever charged for one." [89]

The truth was that, although neither Joanna nor her close advisers countenanced the selling of the seals, the relatively limited supply and the enormous demand led to frequent sales. A correspondent who called himself, ungrammatically, "AMICUS RELIGIO," wrote in the *Leeds Mercury*: "That money has been given for these *passports to Heaven* I do positively assert, but that they are publicly or openly sold, I am not prepared to affirm." [90] In a letter to the *Sunday Monitor*, a London paper, a correspondent stated unequivocally "that the sale of the seals was public and notorious" and "that *many* of the *present* followers of Mrs. S. were purchasers." [91]

Joanna was herself acquainted with an instance in which one of her lieutenants, a Mr. Middelton, was accused of selling a seal to a man and his sister-in-law. If true, she cried anathema on both seller and the two buyers, writing: "If Mr. Middelton received any money for his trouble for filling up the Seals and delivering them, then he is entirely cut off from having anything to do in the work for the future, because he sinned knowingly—that no money at all should be taken for the Seals, and those who would not willingly take the trouble to do it freely, are not to deliver them at all." As for the buyers: "If the man gave any money for his Seal, and that of his sister, they would be of no use to them, but a curse instead of a blessing, if he does not now deliver up both his Seal and his sister's, for each of which he says he paid Mr. Middelton a sixpence. . . . for no Seal that was ever purchased with money must be kept." [92] Perhaps the most convincing defense of her rectitude was Foley's suggestion, which she agreed to, that, if any of the thousands of sealed paid money for their seals, they should make their cases known publicly. [93]

Joanna admitted that at first she had not discriminated among those to whom she gave the seals. Until 1803, "believers, unbelievers, and children" were allowed to have them. [94] Afterward, however, she introduced a system of screening. Those who desired seals were examined on their knowledge of her publications. One of Joanna's followers wrote to her, asking if a substitute could examine initiates in his place. She replied, "As to the Sealing, if you can Trust your Friend, that he Will Examine them Whether they are believers from reading my Books . . . , he may take their names . . . during your absence to be put upon your list when you return." [95] In 1804, the Spirit warned: "Let no man sign his name, till he hath read this Book [*Sound an Alarm in My Holy*

Mountain] and judged for himself. Then, they, who are clearly *convinced* the Calling is of GOD, and they are desirous for MY Kingdom to come, and MY Will to be done on Earth, as it is in Heaven . . . ; let their names be entered, and Seals be given them."[96] Not only must the book be read, it had to be owned. "If they had [the book] and parted with it, still that would not do." She conceded that a married couple need possess only one copy, "but if there are twenty in one family, and they all want seals, they must each produce their book, or buy one at the time; and the Lord has again strictly commanded they must keep the book by them, and this order must on no account be departed from."[97] Therefore, after 1803, the thousands who signified their intention to join the Southcottian movement by accepting the seals did not do so lightly. All had to give convincing proof of their familiarity with Joanna's writings and of their belief in the Second Advent. In 1810 a believer said that no one was allowed to sign his name to the lists unless he possessed a copy of another of Joanna's pamphlets, *A Caution and Instruction to the Sealed*, published three years before.[98]

The question of the sealing of children was raised and, under the new formulation, Joanna recommended equally careful scrutiny of them. In response to an enquirer, she wrote, "As to the little girl; you must be the best judge of her understanding." The real issue was whether a child, regardless of age, could fully understand the significance of receiving a seal. "There is more in some children at Eleven, than in Others fourteen or fifteen, it does not always go by the age," she said. If a young believer could "have sense enough to know what she believes from the Instruction of her parents, & what she have read, I do by no means wish to keep her back; But let her have a seal."[99]

ORGANIZATION

In part because of the very logic of Joanna's appeal, which based itself on the imminence of Christ's Second Coming, and partly because it was not her intention to found a separate sect, the organization of the Southcottian movement never attained genuine maturity. To the outsider, however, that which existed seemed worthy of no little apprehension. One observer wrote in an open letter to the Archbishop of Canterbury, "The system of imposture was *regularly organized* [emphasis added], men of a similar character with the *priests of Jeroboam* were appointed to promulgate the sacred character which this woman had impiously assumed."[100] Southcottian chapels sprang up in every county in the country, and Joanna involved herself in virtually all the details of their management.[101] There are no indications that Joanna actually appointed preachers but ample evidence, as the cases of Peter Morrison and Portbury suggest, that when informed of their shortcomings she was quick to reprove them, to intercede, if necessary, when factions nominated a particularly unsuitable candidate and to encourage those who performed well.

Although Joanna remained desperately eager to bring clergy from the Church of England into the movement, the few who joined were ill-suited to appeal successfully to the typical Southcottian. The differences in social class between the two and the inhibiting influence of Anglican liturgy and ritual, if strictly observed, could prove all but insurmountable barriers. Joanna wrote to Foley complaining about his brother clergyman, the Reverend Samuel Eyre, who although "a very worthy[,] good man" was having difficulties in dealing successfully with the Bristol believers. As "a Church Minister," she told Foley, "he is under so many restrictions that the people are not satisfied [because] he can only read the works to them." "Many of them," according to her, "have been in the Methodist [connection], and they wish a meeting to be established where Prayer and Singing can be used, and an exhortation from the [Southcottian] works and the Scriptures in the form of a Sermon, as is used in other meetings." If this were done "in a public manner," then "many would join the cause."[102] Much more successful were three Yorkshire preachers, all former Methodists, who better understood the personal and religious needs of the believers. One, Thomas Senior, had been a class leader in Leeds, and he "has often thousands to hear him." A second, Samuel Hirst, attracted similar throngs to his meetings. But the prophetess reserved her highest praise for a Mr. Slake who, she said, was "the finest preacher I ever heard."[103] Even so, Joanna never found an advocate from any quarter as stirring as a Whitefield or a Wesley to promote her cause.

It appears that the Southcottian preachers were assigned districts,[104] after the Methodist example, and were expected to remain there as long as Joanna felt it necessary.[105] The three Church of England divines, Foley, Webster, and Bruce, however, did not labor under any such strictures. Because Joanna saw baptism as a necessary prerequisite for recruitment and would only endorse the form used by the Church of England, the three clergymen "went up and down the country" baptizing "crowds."[106]

Despite her efforts to bring both church and chapel to the "standard of truth," the obdurate refusal of either to respond to her appeal meant an inevitable hemorrhage of followers to separate meeting places where Joanna's message could be properly appreciated and absorbed. The meeting place might be either an independent chapel, often a rented room, or the home of a believer. In the summer of 1805 her Spirit told the prophetess that believers could not receive the sacrament in any of the Anglican churches in London but only at Carpenter's chapel, which was called the House of God. The explanation was that, "if men deny the fulfillment of my Gospel, they cannot administer the sacrament aright." The Spirit said that Elias Carpenter "is the only one in [London] who is gone out in my name to give the sacrament expecting my coming again." [107] By administering the sacrament herself, as she had begun to do,[108] and authorizing lay preachers, such as Carpenter, to do the same, she continued increasing the distance between her movement and the Established Church. This meant, inevitably, not only the establishment of separate places of worship but also a distinctive ritual and liturgy, of which the following examples provide evidence.

Joanna attended a ceremony at one of her London chapels on September 2, 1808, at which candidates were interviewed and given their seals. She walked to the chapel in inclement weather with John Wilson, who "told . . . of the Victory gained over the French in Portugal by General Wellesley." Joanna said, "the Guns were fired and we saw the flags on the Ships in the River in token of the Victory." They reached their destination and found a service in progress. Afterward, the unbelievers were asked to leave. Joanna's visit had not been expected, and she was pleased that "though the Storms of rain was very great, . . . the meeting was full and most of the Friends that I knew were present." There were seventy-four believers to receive their seals. "Some that had not Signed were examined at the Altar." Joanna said: "After the examination was over and they had answered to the Questions put to them by Mr. Tozer, the Seals were closed. [A]nd after the Bread and Wine had been distributed, Mr. Tozer called the names of the People to whom the Seals belonged which were handed by the Friends to their respective owners." [109]

A service of the believers is described in more detail in a pamphlet published in 1803. In this, as in everything, Joanna attempted to be scrupulously orthodox. She prayed constantly that her activities might be free "from all false doctrine, heresy, and schism." [110] A friend even invited the Society for the Suppression of Vice to search Joanna's writings for "false doctrine." [111] The service included a ritual with "wine and cakes." The wine was poured into a cup. Joanna drank first and then the clergymen present passed the cup around, first to the women because Christ was coming "to redeem the Fall of women" and then to the men in the order of their standing in the society. After drinking, each believer repeated:

May I drink deep into the Spirit of Christ;
And may his Blood cleanse me from all sin!

Although not considered a sacrament, the drinking of the wine conferred "a double portion" of the Spirit on the communicant. After all had drunk, the cup was returned and Joanna said, "As we all have drank in one cup, may we drink into one faith, and may that faith be in Christ!" Following this, the prophetess delivered a homily to the believers on her experiences. The "ceremony" concluded when Joanna gave cakes to the women "which they broke among one another in token of love and friendship." Next they were given to the men. "All was a scene of joy and mirth, in the midst of which Joanna took a final leave of her friends and retired." [112] Not included in this account is the singing of hymns which became a popular feature of Southcottian services. The hymns were composed from Joanna's writings and became so popular that in 1814 a large collection entered its fourth edition. [113]

Unquestionably, one of the most spectacular Southcottian meetings took place in London on January 12, 1804. Under the supervision of Elias Carpenter, followers with artisan skills converted an enormous loft so that it would hold "upwards of 1000 people." They made an altar at one end of the vast room by taking a large table, covering it with a white cloth, and putting three silver candlesticks on either end. Standing in rows between the candlesticks were decanters filled with wine, along with bowls and plates. A large silver urn flanked by two silver cups completed the setting. A follower recorded that all in all "it had a Beautifull and Solemn appearance." Carpenter and his friends then created a particularly stunning effect by placing lamps and candles on the timbers running across the loft. [114]

More remarkable than the meeting place, however, was the character of the assemblage. Joanna's bookseller, E. J. Field, wrote that "such an astonishing Body of people met togather on such a Solemn Purpose has been Seldom seen in any Nation." He was probably right. There were Italian, Swiss, French, and English followers as well as a group of German members of the Moravian Brotherhood. Some were communicants of the Church of England, others Roman Catholics, Dissenters, or followers of Wesley or Whitefield. A single Quaker came and, even, "one American Indian." Field found himself overcome when copies of hymns were passed around and this extraordinary congregation began to sing. "My Soul was so filled with Heavenly Joy at the Sight, to see so many *Sects* of people of *Different Nations*—all Getting Rid (as it were) of their Old Religious predjudices, and all apparantly uniting in one Common Bond of Love and Friendship." He said, "It Really made such a

Deep Impression on me and Many others, that when we would have Sung, the Tears of our Love and Grattitude Choak'd our utterance, to see so many Men of Different Persuasions united, that Really we felt ourselvs unworthy to behold such a Sight." [115]

This was the first "uplifting of the Hands" service which came to be a regular feature of Southcottian worship, held each year on January twelfth at six o'clock in the evening. Those who gathered in the huge loft on the inaugural occasion were all sealed and had come "to petition with uplifted hands for Christ's Kingdom to come and Satan's power to be cut off." The hour-and-a-half meeting consisted of one of Joanna's invocations, the Lord's Prayer, and the reading, in this case by Elias Carpenter, of the second and third chapters of Ezekiel, as well as a selection from Joanna's work *Sound an Alarm* and additional prayers and hymns. The communion service took place at seven o'clock. For it, a German believer made a thousand loaves of bread "of the Finest Hertfordshire Flour he could purchase." Only two baskets remained afterward, suggesting that the room may well have held as many believers as intended by Carpenter and his assistants. Close to half-past seven, the ceremony came to its climax when the hundreds of believers stood and said slowly three times, with hands raised at each repetition:

> The—will—of—the—Lord—be—done
> Come—Lord—Jesus—O—come—quickly

Altogether, it must have been a vastly impressive occasion. [116]

Even though there were other examples of attendance as large as at the London meeting, for the most part a typical gathering probably numbered under a hundred souls. A higher figure proved worthy of comment. The Reverend Thomas P. Foley wrote to a friend on January 22, 1810, "My Thursday Meetings are well attended having near a 100 most evenings." [117] Believers read from selections of scripture which were meant to support their views, [118] sang hymns, adapted parts of the Church liturgy to their own needs, [119] and frequently participated in some form of a communion service the first Sunday of every month. The forms of communion varied because of the different religious backgrounds of the believers. What was important was that there be "all one design and end." Because of this, Joanna's Spirit gave her no instructions "to reprove the Dissenters" for their ritual "as the Lord looks more to the heart than the forms." [120] She said, "If the friends are dissenters[,] I must leave them to administer it in their own form and if there are different sects meet together[,] I wish them to be united in one heart and mind in what form they wish to Receive it." Nevertheless, the form which she most preferred was that of the Church of England. She wrote to a friend that "the only Instructions" she ever received concerning the Sacrament were that the Prayer of Absolution not be read. Otherwise, she said, the Anglican service might be followed for the understandable if rather lame reason, "I always was accustomed to the Church." She realized that this might pose difficulties "if none of the People belonged to the Church." Nevertheless, even if they were "at a loss," she said, "in that manner I was ordered to proceed, for I can see no words to be more proper in Delivering the Bread than what is spoken in the Church service." Later in the same letter she moved back to a more ecumenical position by stating that, "if others are of a Different mind" and find that "other words may be more suitable," then she would not object.[121]

Joanna did not wish the believers to cultivate idiosyncrasy in dress or social habits. Either would set them apart from other Christians and make them especially susceptible to ridicule. The prophetess forbade the public wearing of any kind of distinctive clothing or distinguishing mark.[122] At the same time, she was quick to encourage "respectable" dress. When her Exeter friends, the Taylors, were coming to London for her second "trial," she wrote to them, "I must beg to remind you & Mr. Taylor to bring *your Gloves* with You." In the same letter the prophetess related that she had ordered all the women attending to attire themselves in especially made white cambric muslin dresses "in token of their Innocence that was betrayed."[123] As for deportment, she saw no harm in the faithful enjoying normal social pastimes, including card playing, but, she said, "I do not recommend the believers proposing it themselves," and warned, "there is a danger of drawing the mind and heart after these amusements, which may steal on imperceptibly more and more till they become dangerous."[124]

Just as there was little significant alteration in liturgy, Joanna offered virtually no doctrinal innovation. Her role, as that of the Roman pope, was to teach from and interpret the received word and to serve as the voice by which God continued to reveal His will to the faithful.

On November 16, 1802, Joanna defended herself to the Reverend Mr. Bull of Saffron Walden by saying, "I have not added to the Scriptures nor taken from them but explained their meaning."[125] Her theology was, for the most part, an unexceptional restatement of usual millenarian beliefs. It was made interesting neither by intimations of heresy nor—with the single exception of the importance claimed for an unlettered woman and, by extension, her sex in the working out of God's will on heaven and earth—by even significant deviation.[126] Whether Church of England or Dissenter, believers could confidently repeat the Southcottian creed: "We believe there will be a New Heaven, as declared by the Spirit, and a New Earth, wherein dwelleth Righteousness. We believe that Man will be created anew in Hart and Life. We believe there is a Time to come for the Millenial World, a Rest for the People of GOD; that he will destroy the Works of the Devil, and send his Holy Spirit up—on the Sons of Men." [127]

The "great article of faith" of the Southcottians was "that the Kingdom of Christ is just at hand, and that Johanna is to be the great instrument of introducing it." [128] A twentieth-century follower claimed a role of wider significance for the prophetess when she said, "the central feature of her mission" was "the great part to be played by woman in subduing the forces of evil and hastening by spiritual election the coming of the Kingdom of Christ in this world." [129] A third source puts the matter more succinctly by calling her a "thorough feminist." [130] Nevertheless, Joanna was not the formulator of a new theological dispensation. Her followers, however, did subscribe to a certain body of belief which, though obvious in its appeal to women, was not intended to have feminist overtones. Rather, it offered a distinctive application of scripture to contemporary events so that the believers of both sexes might find edification and, finally, their salvation.

The key to the Southcottian canon lay in the third chapter of Genesis where God tells the serpent, "I will put enmity between thee and the woman, and between thy seed and her seed. It shall bruise thy head, and thou shalt bruise his head." The "woman" chosen to fulfill this promise, or the "second Eve" as Christ was the "second Adam," was, the prophetess claimed, the "woman" mentioned in the fourteenth chapter of Revelation. Cast in this role by God, Joanna became the instrument chosen to make known the coming of His Kingdom, which would appear at the end of Satan's six-thousand-year reign on earth, the "shadow" of the six days it had taken God to create the world. The succeeding thousand years of God's rule would then culminate in the Day of Judgment, at which time those being judged would bring forward two testimonies, the first concerning the evil suffered by mankind under Satan's reign and the second, by contrast, demonstrating the benevolence of God's millennial rule. This "evidence" would prove conclusively that Satan "was the root of evil upon earth." With the verdict rendered, those who had fallen under Satan's influence would at last permit the scales to drop from their eyes, repent, and revolt against their evil monarch. In His infinite mercy, Christ would extend His forgiveness even to these erring souls, and ultimately they too might join the saints, those who had never surrendered to Satan's wiles. [131]

The woman's "seed" consisted of Joanna's followers, who alone recognized the true character of events and joined with her in praying for

Satan's downfall (thus bruising his "head") and the establishment of the Kingdom of God. In return for their fidelity, each received the seal which would provide protection against evil. Finally, Christ's coming would be marked by judgments which were necessary to convince the nations of the world of the folly of their allegiance to Satan, and to hasten their repentance. God's selection of Joanna to redeem the failure of the original Eve proved, however, that England would be "the happy nation . . . first redeemed." [132]

If anything could be said to distinguish Southcottian beliefs, it was their "mild universalism." [133] Joanna was as much a democrat in her view of who was eligible for salvation as Tom Paine was in his opinion of who should have the franchise. Nor did being saved depend on adherence to her movement. At a meeting at Tozer's London chapel on September 2, 1808, she said, "There were Thousands in this [world] now of good people that might die, and never hear of the Visitation to me, and yet they would go to Glory." [134] Nothing enraged her more than the belief in a spiritual aristocracy. As a result, throughout her career, she waged relentless combat against the elitist doctrines of the Calvinists.

THE WORD MADE FLESH

Joanna's message reached its audience in a variety of ways. Her publications were either sold or given away in the many thousands. In 1803 and 1804 she traveled extensively in the West and North, visiting Bristol, Exeter, Stockport, Leeds, and other communities in the surrounding areas. It was said that "people would walk scores of miles to obtain a sight of the 'woman clothed in the sun,' or to borrow one of her books." [135] Her preachers, of course, were active in her behalf, converting new members to the cause and sustaining recruits in their faith in meeting places and Southcottian chapels across the country. In addition, the believers might distribute broadsides in huge numbers to highlight a particularly important section of a new publication, to respond to a critic's barb, or to simply bring news of some event or development in the movement to the largest possible numbers.

E. J. Field wrote to Mrs. Taylor on March 10, 1803, of what seems to have been a typical distribution effort. According to him, Peter Morrison had been given seven thousand handbills to circulate in London, and a few in Exeter and Leeds; Elias Carpenter received two thousand to spread around "his Populous Neighbourhood"; William Layton Winter, a "gentleman," had one thousand which he gave to his groom to circulate "in various parts." Others were delivered "on Horseback to every Gentleman's House Round his part." Winter also hired a man to go to Brixton in Surrey and Ilford in Essex "to Leave a Bill at every house upon the Road." Field reported with pleasure that Richard Law and a friend were responsible for printing and distributing two thousand and "have been very Industrious & active in Dispersing them in various parts." Another believer, Thomas Stephens, went to the bank, the Royal Exchange, Whitechapel, and other places in London, giving out some five hundred. Sharp hired a man to distribute a thousand through Hampstead and Highgate. A clergyman gave out five hundred, as did a publican. And so it went.[136]

Occasionally other opportunities, somewhat more unusual, could present themselves. If a coachman, for example, became a believer, it is easy to imagine the opportunities he might have to promote Joanna's interests. Writing to Charles Taylor in Exeter about a pending visit to his home in Old Swinford, Foley gave the times of the coaches from Birmingham and suggested that Taylor make contact with "Belles the Coachman [who] is a Sealed Brother & a firm Believer in dear Joanna's Divine mission & Inspired works."[137] On the route from Gittisham to Exeter, Joanna befriended a guard on a mail coach who "became a firm believer in me, and offered every assistance to support my writings."[138] There was a third occasion in which Joanna was taken home "by a Coachman that was a true believer and had a longing desire to drive Me."[139]

If Edmund Baker's following at Teddington in Middlesex can be taken as an indication, most believers placed heavy reliance on Joanna's publications for their instruction. Baker's congregation was typical in its size, numbering 125 members. It was somewhat unusual in that there was a higher percentage of both male believers and family units than prevailed in the movement as a whole. Of the 123 believers who can be identified, 69 were women (56 percent) and 54 were men (44 percent). Only 44—25 women (20 percent) and 19 men (15 percent)—appear without "family" affiliation on Baker's list of followers. Of particular interest is that Baker's records reveal which of Joanna's works individual members possessed, from her first publication in 1801 until the appearance of her fifty-fourth work, *The Controversy of the Spirit with the Worldly Wise*, in 1811. Eight of the thirty-five "families" possessed copies of fifty or more of Joanna's publications. Three had between thirty and thirty-nine of her canon, six between twenty and twenty-nine, six between ten and nineteen, and twelve had fewer than ten. Only two couples did not possess any of the prophetess' works. Of the "single" followers, four men and one of the women had a complete run of the publications. Most of the women possessed only two to five of her works. Three women did not own any of the publications while only one man did not. In all, Baker's flock had in its possession 1,460 copies of Joanna's works, an average of 12 for each member.[140]

Despite her enemies' repeated assertions to the contrary,[141] Joanna realized few monetary rewards from the movement she had created. Her early publications were financed from her own small savings and donations from believers. Sometimes loans were necessary.[142] After April 1804, when she began living with Jane Townley and Ann Underwood, Miss Townley provided the principal support for Joanna. However, the prophetess received an annuity of 250 pounds from another believer toward the end of her life, giving her a significant degree of independence from her patroness if she had desired it. Her relative lack of affluence is suggested by the provisions of her will, in which she left a life income of 10 pounds a year to a sister and her brother, and 10 pound grants to a sister-in-law and a niece (with another 15 pounds when she became twenty-one). These coupled with "tokens of love" to old friends did not amount "to more than a thousand pounds." The remainder of her estate was to go to Townley and Underwood. In a later codicil she explained that she and her two friends had "a joint interest" in the published books "and all debts and credits appertaining thereto."[143]

The proceeds from the sale of her books were for the most part consumed by continuing publication expenses.[144] She was willing to sell her books through the post but generally relied on a network of vendors who purchased the publications from her and then resold them, realizing a profit on the individual transactions.[145] For example, on one publication, the vendors paid Joanna 1s. 9d. for each copy but then were permitted to resell them at 2s. 3d.[146] Not that there were large sums to be made. According to E. J. Field, one of her sellers went into the drapery business "for the present" because expenses had been great and the return on investment slow. In 1807, Field wrote to Peter Morrison, "I think it will be a long time before they are about to Print another Book. The printing of so many thousand has already cost them such a sum of Money, that few have a Conception [of]."[147] One who attempted to forego her commission was told by Joanna that she had already done enough for the cause and should not make further sacrifices. In the same letter, however, Joanna encouraged her to order fifty copies of her most recent book ("as it is not worth while to send a smaller parcel on account of the Carriage"), which she believed would sell briskly. "I think it is a Book that may be much sought after as it is greatly liked everywhere & it fills the believer's mouths with arguments to confound gainsayers."[148] Nor was the prophetess above a little bargaining in order to move her publications more rapidly. When she heard that her agent in Stourbridge had quit and subsequently warned the local people not to buy her works, Joanna wrote to Foley and promised that she would send more books to him if he could persuade the believers to subscribe for them. Then, she attempted to make her proposal more attractive by volunteering to pay the postage out of her profits. What she did not want was "to send them to lay dead when they will be wanted at other places." [149]

Foley's account book offers a prosaic but unique record of the financial side of the Southcottian movement. He distributed publications sent to him from London or Exeter to local vendors for resale; he sold and gave away certain titles himself; and he arranged for the printing of some of his own and Joanna's writings. Most of the financial transactions ranged from one to twenty pounds and only infrequently are more sizable sums of money mentioned. On July 1, 1803, the clergyman received two hundred books from Field, including fifty copies of *A Word in Season to a Sinking Kingdom*, for the sum of £8.14.7. The next day he notes that he distributed several of the publications in the neighborhood for resale. On October 28, he recorded that Mr. Child, Joanna's Stourbridge agent, owed Joanna £17.6 for publications he had received directly from her. Larger figures appear in his accounts from time to time. A year later Miss Townley sent Foley £150 for printing expenses in Stourbridge. On August 20, 1808, according to Foley's figures, he had in stock £792.15 worth of Joanna's books. [150]

Distribution and accounting problems took up significant amounts of Joanna's time. She wrote to one of her agents that "my Books have gone off very irregular" and added, "I shall be glad to know what there is left of every thousand in your hands that I may know how to reprint *the First again* or any of the thousands that may be nearly out." [151] Through apparent inefficiency her correspondent had lost track of the size of her stock. At least, Joanna could not believe that she "will designedly cheat me." [152] The prophetess then decided that her booksellers should report to her on a monthly basis. This seemed to work much more satisfactorily, as she informed one of them: "I am much obliged to you for sending me the statement of your account; I find . . . that yours is prefectly right, according to what we have down since we took the Books in our own hands." She severed connections with E. J. Field, who refused to agree to this system and then absconded with the assets he had in hand. [153]

This last development proved a sad conclusion to a once successful career. Field had been a staymaker whose financial complaints were sufficiently loud, and his services considered sufficiently valuable, that he, alone among the Southcottian booksellers, was put on a regular salary.

Joanna fixed it at a guinea and a half a week but she estimated that his annual income was more than 100 pounds a year.[154] Before his flight, the investment could seem worthwhile. The Reverend Thomas P. Foley had on one occasion been able to write that Field's time was "most delightfully employed in answering questions upon the Prophecies & Visions—and about ten days ago he had *one order* for *fifty whole sets* of Joanna's Divine Works."[155]

Thus, the foundations were established. Writing, advising, speaking, traveling, organizing were achievements of extraordinary dimension for a woman of Joanna's experience. The prophetess had managed to project the voice of her Spirit far outside her native Devonshire and, in so doing, to excite a response that was to profoundly affect large numbers of a generation of English men and women. If there was a voice of the inarticulate in the first years of the nineteenth century in England, it was Joanna's.

V

True Believers

THE SPIRIT OF PROPHECY

The earnest men and women who became Southcottians gave one or more of several reasons for their conversion. First, they found the experience described in Joanna's writings persuasive and, as a result, her claims credible. Second, they sought a new principle of religious authority, thereby recognizing the inherent contradiction of a number of Christian sects claiming to possess the truth. In Joanna, all denominations might find a new center. Third, many had had some sort of mystical experience which acquired legitimacy and significance only through their belief in Joanna. Finally, they desired the world they knew to be utterly transformed, a desire which found its strongest expression in the lives of the poor.

Joanna's audience was as stunned by the profusion and prolixity of her publications as she was herself. Once her credibility had been established, there seemed no other explanation than the one that she offered. God Himself was the author of her writings. Theodore Turpin, one of Joanna's most active lieutenants, preached at various Southcottian chapels from 1812 to 1814 and began one of his sermons: "My brethren, examine the writings of Joanna, and point out any one passage or page, which you blame, and if scripture proof cannot be found for the passage, then it is time enough to find fault; but if, on the other hand, those writings can be proved to be good by the scriptures, you must then be convinced, it is the Spirit of Jesus which visits this woman that is come to reveal the sayings in the scriptures."[1] Many were indeed convinced. A letter appeared in the *Sunday Monitor* in which a believer said that "I have repeatedly examined and compared the pages of Mrs. SOUTHCOTT's books with those of the Old and New Testament for more than *seven years*, and I most solemnly declare, as a man, as a member of the Church of England, as by law established; and as a believer in the revealed will of GOD, that both, *that is*, the Bible and Mrs. SOUTH-COTT's books are dictated, or directed by one and the same spirit."[2] The Spirit opened the eyes of a Mr. Nesbitt, who had been reading her books since March 1803: "Being in the habit of constant reading Mrs.

Southcott's publications, I can truly say, with David, they have made those that attentively pursue them wiser than their teachers, and have opened to us such a view of the Divine economy and wisdom in creation and preservation, as lifts the mind, as it were, out of itself, and expands it evidently on every side."[3] Daniel Roberts, a Quaker and coal-mine owner who traced his lineage back to William Tyndale, remembered that he became a believer upon reading Joanna's first book, *The Strange Effects of Faith*. "For my part," he declared, "I am astonished that every one who has access to her books, is not instantly convinced that they are written by inspiration."[4]

Another believer, W. B. Harrison, agreed with Roberts and expressed equal amazement that any reader could resist the truth of Joanna's experience and the resulting implications. "I hereby declare it to be my solemn conviction, that *not a single individual* in this christian land, has ever gone into an investigation of Joanna Southcott's character and writings, free from prejudice, and with a sincere desire to come to a knowledge of the truth, without being convinced that her calling was divine."[5] One of the convinced, describing himself as an "obscure individual," said that he found the "system" of the prophetess "grounded firmly upon the Scriptures, supported by new revelations," and that it "produced on all who rightly received it reformation of Morals and spirituality of Mind."[6] A Unitarian told Joanna that "after seeing thy books" he had burned his own and that he knew "how the Deists and Atheists have been convinced by thy writings."[7]

A believer who knew a good deal about the "Deists and Atheists" proved one of Joanna's more satisfying conquests because, she said, he "lives at a distance from me and I never saw him in my Life." In a letter to Mr. Taylor on August 29, 1805, she reconstructed the circumstances of the conversion in interesting detail. Her new follower, she was told, had come "very near the borders of Deism" as a result of reading the works of Voltaire, Bolingbroke, Hume, and similar authors. Moreover, he had frequented the company of "Sophists[,] Atheists[,] & Deists," which added more uncertainty to his outlook. Then he "accidently" read some of Joanna's works, compared them with the Old and New Testaments, and "was struck with wonder & amazement" at how Joanna's writings explained enigmatical passages in the Bible, becoming convinced that she was led by the same spirit which inspired the biblical prophets. His beliefs hardened when he learned of the accuracy of her prophecies of "the Fever in America[,] the Rebellion in Ireland[,] the Mutiny in the Fleet[,] the Harvests of 1799 & 1800[,] the conquest of Italy by the French[,] the Quarrels in Spain[,] Germany[,] & England[,] the states of Families & individuals & private conversation of different

People, [and] . . . various other matters that could be known only by the Lord." He asked, "Who could be the Author, but the Spirit of Prophecy which is the Spirit of Jesus Christ?" In his estimation, the only reason that the prophetess had not gained universal acceptance was because her mission "comes in so mean a garb." He said, "This affronts the Great[,] the High[,] & the Learned."[8]

The prophetess' books even reached across to Ireland, where they had some slight impact. On June 4, 1806, a Mr. Baylee in Limerick wrote to the Reverend Thomas P. Foley that his small circle believed Joanna's Spirit was from God: "They all agreed the Matter contained in these Books was the most Extraordinary they had ever heard and Brady declared before his Preacher that he thought Mrs. Southcott Should get every Encouragement and that if signing his name could be any use he would do it."[9]

Unlike the fellow traveler of the Deists, the Irish believers, and many others who were convinced of the truth of Joanna's claims by her writings alone, some felt compelled to seek out the prophetess before making up their minds. Elias Carpenter, one of the most important of the early followers, knew several of the men who first approached Joanna in Exeter "and highly esteemed them for the liberality of their minds, and universal benevolence of their dispositions," but he could not accept Joanna's pretensions until he had talked with her. Their meeting prepared him for the prophetess' writings, which he considered "sufficient to convince every candid and unprejudiced mind." According to Carpenter, "many pious people" had come to the conclusion that the end of the world was at hand and by esoteric calculations had predicted when it would occur. Their efforts "little interested" him "because they seem only the opinion of fellow-mortals, who appear not to have better grounds than others have for a contrary one." This was not the case with Joanna, an "untutored female." "She pretends to no knowledge, frequently declaring herself unable to explain what she writes: and, in fact, she often gives proof that she understands not its purport so well as those to whom it is read. Had it been otherwise, we should have had none of those strong evidences of the reality of the work. Her being unable to explain what she writes, and to write so as others can read, are two circumstances which afford me the highest satisfaction."[10]

To her critics, Joanna's writings were "rhapsodies of ignorance."[11] For her supporters, however, the prophetess' rough, ungrammatical style provided the most compelling possible setting for the absolute candor with which she wrote and the remarkable character of her experiences. Carpenter felt that Joanna's mode of expression was important because it so clearly revealed her limitations. With such manifest shortcomings he believed she could not possibly have the wit to be an impostor. Others considered her style significant because it circumscribed those elements of society with whom God was especially concerned, the poor and unlettered. Theodore Turpin compared the failure of the Jews to understand Christ, "who was born of a mean virgin and laid in a manger," with that of "the clergy and the great men" who refused to listen to Joanna.[12]

With an impressive lack of apology, Joanna expressed herself in the language spoken by most Englishmen. In so doing, she called forth readers who were attracted not only by what she said but also by the way in which she said it. Stimulated by her example, some of them were even prepared to speak out in their own voices to defend her claims. In a pamphlet entitled *A Vindication of Joanna Southcott's Writings*, John Crossley offered no excuses for his plain speech: "So far as I am informed I have wrote truth, and if my superiors will not take the pains to inform me better, I must remain as I am, and as to the style, it is adapted to the comprehension of multitudes, who, like myself, not only are unlearned, but must remain so."[13] A Manchester Southcottian declared himself outraged that proud and haughty men should disdain to notice the divine truths uttered by Joanna, simply because she was "a poor[,] illiterate woman." He felt it necessary to challenge her adversaries despite his own handicaps, which included the fact that he had a large family to support, had never written anything for the public before, and had known little formal schooling. "I have received no education but what I obtained at a common country school, in the Peak of Derbyshire." Nevertheless, he decided to refute the Reverend Thomas Stone, "a scholar of St. John's College, Cambridge," who denied that there could be latter-day prophets. "He possesses all the advantages of a good education, which I do not," the believer said, "and if a learned education will enable a person to attain a superior knowledge of Divine things, he ought to be able to put me into the shade." But, "I fear him not, as I feel I have truth and justice on my side." Being a working man with limited leisure time, he warned "that if this letter should fall into the hands of Mr. Stone," and the clergyman replied to it, "I shall not consider myself under any obligation to notice it by a further publication."[14]

Joanna's Spirit explained why the educated were so reluctant to be persuaded. He told her that "learning puffs up Men with Pride because the Love of preeminence above others is their Object more than Thier Love of Truth."[15] One of her most relentless enemies was, in a sense, right when he said that she "held in mental bonds an amazing proportion of the stupid part of the English nation."[16] So dominant became the association of humble men and women, such as John Crossley and the Manchester believer, with the Southcottian movement that it was charged in 1805 that "no men of Learning or piety" had become "converts."[17] But there was the occasional exception, proving that not all of Joanna's followers were as unsophisticated as her critics supposed.

The prophetess achieved one of her greatest triumphs with the conversion of the Reverend Hoadley Ash, doctor of divinity, a man both learned and pious and the son of a prebendary of Winchester. The dean and chapter of Winchester appointed Ash perpetual curate of Crewkerne and Misterton in 1775.[18] This part of Somerset, and particularly Crewkerne, Chard, Dowlish, and Ilminster, became a hotbed of Southcottian activity with a "cottage of worship" established in virtually every village in the locality.[19]

Ash's conversion was to result in bitter estrangement from his parishioners. A letter he wrote to Joanna on September 28, 1807, suggests, however, that there would be few immediate regrets. He had met the prophetess for the first time five days before, and the effect proved overwhelming. After he left Joanna, her communications "vibrated" upon his ears, and, he said, "A happier night I never enjoyed in this world—they have left a fragrance upon my mind, and the remembrance of them is sweet." In his letter, Ash described himself to her as "a new disciple of Christ, who has been educated only a month in your school" but one who had become "fully convinced" from what he had read of her writings "that the hand of God, the Divine Spirit, inspired every page of it." He read the two publications which were required for the sealed and "found that every step I took, the Word of God out of your mouth was a clear burning light unto my feet, and a glorious lamp unto my path." At last, he wrote, his search had ended. What learning had not revealed to him, an unlearned woman would. "For a space of more than thirty-seven years I have diligently searched the Scriptures in seven different languages, and have consulted all the commentators, with the hope of finding the truth." But the highroad of learning had not brought him to his destination. Another route became necessary. "I am more and more convinced that the learned, as they may fancy themselves, are grasping at shadows, the substance of which only appears in your Writings—*Prophetic* publications. In every page that I have opened, I clearly see the finger of God." He candidly addressed the question of why God had chosen to reveal Himself "through a weak, low, simple and illiterate woman." The answer lay in his recognition that the good news of Christ's first coming had been told "to a few simple shepherds." Was it not reasonable to suppose that the Saviour would similarly make known His Second Coming "to the meek and lowly in spirit" so "that the poor in understanding might have the Gospel preached unto them"?[20]

CERTAINTY IN AN UNCERTAIN WORLD

Men and women turned to Joanna in need of an infallible guide through the physical and spiritual dangers of the climactic age in the world's history. Confidence in the religious institutions of the kingdom, both the Church of England and the Dissenting sects, had seeped away in the face of the innumerable differences of opinion between and within the denominations. If, as many people believed, Christ was soon to return to earth in the circumstances described in the Bible, then it was inconceivable that God would not make His plans known through an unimpeachable authority. Thus the quarreling Christian churches could join ranks and prepare themselves and their followers for the moment of His coming. W. B. Harrison said, "We live in an age when the whole civilized world appears to be on the eve of some great and important change." According to him, "the members of the church of England think their doctrines right, the Wesleyan Methodists think the same, and so do the Calvinists, and many others." "As all these bodies of christians draw their doctrines and opinions from the written word of God," Harrison said, "there is no authority to which they can appeal to decide the correctness of their respective views and creeds." He asked, "What part then of the christian church can have supreme authority over the whole body, so as to direct and prepare them for the second coming of our Lord?" There had to be a herald like John the Baptist to announce Christ's Second Coming. "Without it there is no standard to which we can appeal, there is no one possessing general influence, there is no one to prepare us effectually for the great and important change."[21] Another follower, William Roundell Wetherell, declared that God had manifested Himself to a woman whose mission would be "to perform the grand Work of reconciling all differences in Religion, and bringing the whole World under one Faith; to clear up every Mystery, and make the Nations unite in Brotherly Love, bringing them together as One Fold under One Shepherd; then will every one know God, and be taught by his Spirit."[22] Harrison and Wetherell agreed that only Joanna could be the one chosen for this role of ending the internecine rivalry among the Christian sects. Elias Carpenter concurred with them: "I firmly believe that this persecuted system will be found ultimately to destroy all cavilling disputations of divided professors, blending them into one fold, under the one great Shepherd."[23]

A remarkable number of those seeking and discovering in the Southcottian movement a solution to the puzzle of competing religious claims were Methodists. A fascinating clue as to why this should be so comes in a letter written by the Reverend Thomas P. Foley. According to him, George Turner, one of the seven who had interviewed Joanna in Exeter in 1801 and a prominent Yorkshire merchant and brother of a former Leeds mayor,[24] had a dream which proved influential in preparing the conversion of Wesley's followers into Southcottians, as well as apparently serving as a catalyst for his own interest in Joanna. Turner dreamed that he was sitting down by the fire to read when the door opened, revealing the figure of the long-dead John Wesley. Wesley was dressed in a hat, a gray, curling wig which hung down to his shoulders, a black gown, and leather shoes and black stockings. His face and hands glowed with a "bright" light, and, according to the merchant, "he appeared . . . younger than when I last saw him before his Death." Wesley turned toward him, looked above his head, and then spoke: "Inform my Brethren that it is the Will of the Lord that they obey the Word of God which is made known. I am happy. Jesus is God. I know many of my Brethren will believe."[25]

Turner told two traveling Methodist preachers of his experience and they asked what "Word of God" had Wesley meant. The men claimed it must be the Bible, but Turner demurred and suggested the two pray for enlightenment. Just then, Joanna's first prophecies appeared, sending Turner on a journey that was to see him become the leading Yorkshire supporter of the Southcottian cause. As important as the dream was for him personally, it was of equal significance for many others. The account of his meeting with Wesley "was printed in hand bills at Liverpool & given away at the Meeting-house Doors, there & likewise dispersed through the Kingdom." It appeared to many that Wesley had anointed Joanna as his successor. Thus it seemed, Foley said, because "*many*" Methodists "have signed their names to the Lord's roll & have received seals, and are joined to our blessed & Glorious Cause"—their way to the "one fold" opened by Turner's dream.[26]

DREAMS AND VISIONS

Like Turner, many men and women were undergoing new and perplexing experiences. They had little idea of their origins or how to deal with them. In her first book, *The Strange Effects of Faith*, Joanna remembered the injunction "Quench not the Spirit; despise not prophecy; for the time is come, that your women shall prophesy, your young men shall dream dreams, your old men shall see visions; for the day of the Lord is at hand."[27] According to Elias Carpenter, "very many persons in the present day" were having such mystical encounters.[28] A number recognized their affinity with Joanna and beseeched her for advice and support.[29] Several had experiences as unusual as Joanna's own. In a pamphlet published in 1804, the prophetess said, "There are Four, who have written to me, that they are the CHRISTS."[30] The experience of most of those who approached her, however, was slightly less extraordinary. For example, James Copley, a weaver from near Bradford, finished his work late one night in December 1806 when he heard "the sound of bells, or voices speaking as bells sounding." At first he thought it was simply the noise of men working in the nearby furnaces, but he came to the door of his house and a voice called out: "Oh earth! Oh earth! Oh inhabitants of the earth!" If Copley's account was accurate, Joanna's Spirit said, then what he heard was "the lamentation of mine angels, who lament the fall of man, to see their blindness, their ignorance, and hardness of heart."[31]

An Exeter believer, "a young man of good character," wrote to Joanna of the similarity of their experiences. He too received communications from a mystical presence and was tormented by evil spirits. He told Joanna in his letter: "Sunday as I was washing myself in the dyehouse, I saw an appearance to me, a man came into the dye-house with a drawn sword in his hand. He said—'Now then, will you desist writing?' I said—'No,' and ran into the house." He returned to the dyehouse three hours later and the same figure threatened his life unless he promised never again to write down a communication. The young man attempted to hit him with a stick, but his adversary vanished. Joanna added: "In this manner the evil spirits appeared to him by night and by day with all manner of oaths and blasphemy appearing in various shapes, sometimes like men, sometimes like four-footed beasts, always threatening him if he did not desist from writing, and desiring him to do as they bid him, but he always answered, 'he would not.'" God permitted Satan to terrify the young man in such a variety of ways because only then would men begin to realize who was the cause of their earthly miseries.[32]

Joanna admitted that if she alone had been afflicted by such experiences she deserved to be condemned. "But," the Spirit reminded her, "now discern the hearts of others, and in different parts of the kingdom does Satan pursue various ways to show you all what is his working in man, and from whence persecution arises."[33] In a letter of October 1807, Joanna advised how to deal with such evil spirits: "You mention Mrs. Scanes being still tormented with evil spirits, but if she answers them, it should be in strong words from the Scriptures, to tell them what a wretched state they have brought themselves into, and to demand in the name of the Lord why they trouble her." Joanna observed that a difference always existed between a visitation by an evil spirit and one by a heavenly spirit. If the former, one had a distinctly disagreeable sensation, but if the latter, "There is a heavenly joy within, . . . which takes all fear and terror from us." According to Joanna, "This I always experienced—my fears to vanish and my comforts to increase when I am visited by the Lord or good spirits; but when the evil spirits came to assault me I always felt fear, terror, and dread, and though the devil may come as an angel of light, yet he brings a horror and fear with him." The prophetess gave further instructions for Mrs. Scanes and then reminded her correspondent, "But these things are common amongst believers and unbelievers. I never heard so many people who complained of these kind of visitations in all my life as I have heard of lately amongst all sorts of people." [34]

Yet another instance came to Joanna's attention, this one interesting because of the very practical benefits promised the believer and his future clients. A Mr. Torrens wrote to her, describing a dream he had of three sheep which provided him with an inexhaustible supply of meat. "I had a large case Knife in my hand and cut off about four pounds from the shoulder of one of them [they were hanging, heads off and disembowelled] which was immediately made whole again." A spirit informed him, "For what you have done, you and the Generations to the end of the world shall never want and ye shall have it in your power to reduce meat to a penny a pound and whatever you dispose of or sell Shall be replaced without any Human assistance." Joanna replied to him that the three sheep were "Moses, Job and the Son of God."

> But as the voice thou heard'st at first
> If you have faith now Keep it fast
> And in the end all meat you'll see
> Reduced as low as need to be
> And Peace and Plenty will abound. [35]

However, the most interesting and important of the visionaries who attached themselves to Joanna's following was Joseph Prescott. Prescott began having visions in 1793 when he was eight years old. The feature which distinguished him from others was that he possessed a modest artistic ability and painted in watercolors the images he saw. [36] In 1803 he came to the attention of Elias Carpenter, who took him from a workhouse and employed him in his paper mill.

The youth had excellent natural parts [Carpenter said], but wholly uncultivated; never having had any instruction, he could read but very imperfectly. I took him from Christ-Church workhouse. He, with five other lads, were daily employed at a glass manufactory altogether for 18s. per week. His growth having been greatly checked, I strove to improve it, by making him work in the garden, and other employment which had air and exercise; this, with good living, soon materially altered his appearance. His temper was good, his mind cheerful, but volatile and giddy to excess; yet, while with me, free from any known vice. He was very ingenious, apt to learn, and, having musical instruments about the house, from seeing others perform, he learned to finger them, and, by the same means, to play the flute. In fact, he was always in action. When I first took him he was about fourteen years old, but so small as by some supposed not to exceed ten years.[37]

The interest which Carpenter took in the welfare of a workhouse boy was not exceptional for him. Energetic and ambitious, having started out at fourteen in a merchant's countinghouse in Antigua, Carpenter had met with considerable success in life and felt an obligation to assist those less fortunate than himself. He spent two hours each evening teaching the basic skills of arithmetic, writing, and reading to his workers and their families, who numbered about fifty. He provided free "books, pens, slates, and all other requisites." These activities left him little time for rest, but, he said, "I had an ample reward in a well-regulated manufactory." The local parson constantly reminded the workers how well off they were "and actually preached a sermon on the manufactory once a week."[38]

Carpenter came to know some of Joanna's followers in London and on July 14, 1802, invited the prophetess and her friends to his house. He then felt "a command to descend from the tree of worldly pursuits, and advocate the cause of which she was an instrument." He believed Joanna "had teachings from the Lord, to instruct us how he will prepare the inhabitants of the earth for the latter day glory."[39] Carpenter regarded Joseph Prescott and another visionary, known as Jerusha, as his special finds and, thus, marks of divine approbation of his role in the Southcottian movement. He took Joseph into his house to live on February 28, 1803. Within four months, the boy had drawn a number of visions which, Carpenter believed, confirmed Joanna's mission. The most striking evidence came when Joseph reported that he saw a dove fly through a window, station itself before Joanna, and then disappear. He then heard a voice say, "That is the Spirit of God, which influences Joanna Southcott."[40]

A believer who called himself "Amraphel" wrote a pamphlet in which he reported that Joseph's "extraordinary productions of the pencil, and pen," confirmed Joanna's role in announcing the imminence of "a new order of things . . . , when Purity, Peace, and Felicity" will prevail.[41] In the summer of 1803, Joanna took Joseph's pictures with her on a trip to Exeter in order to display them for the edification of the people.[42] Her friends argued that this activity was taking up too much of her time. The Spirit countered their criticism, telling Joanna, "I ordered the visions to be drawn for thee, to be made public, and shewn to all who wished to see them."[43] In the end, they were placed around the walls of Carpenter's chapel, the House of God.[44]

Joanna first saw one of Joseph's watercolors on March 6, 1803, a week after he left the workhouse in Carpenter's charge. She said, "This youth is very happy in his present situation, as he has *now free liberty* given him to execute these heavenly visions."[45] According to Catherine Carpenter, they remained for "two, three, four, or more days, during which he is perfectly collected, and able to give a rational answer to any question asked."[46] Once Joseph had painted what he had seen, it was explained by Joanna's Spirit. Four of Joseph's visions, and the explanations of them, are particularly interesting.

On March 7, 1803, at "just about ten o'clock," Joseph's eyes were directed to a section of Carpenter's paper mill. Suddenly everything darkened. Before him appeared a view of the heavens. Dominating the scene was a horseman astride a gray horse, "exceeding in size all he had ever seen." The rider was "*the Lord*," dressed in extraordinary fashion. Around his shoulders rested "a large loose flowing robe of a red color: underneath which He had a close garment of bright purple, a broad sash over the right shoulder, and under the left arm, of the same color. Upon his head was a crown of twelve stars, and four arches with a star between each arch, and one on the top of each arch, and four stars in a cluster on the top of the ball: and in his right hand a *sword* large and broad, which he held perpendicularly: with the other hand he appeared to guide the horse." Surrounding the two figures was a nimbus of clouds, which enclosed "an immense number of angelic faces, of various sizes, at various distances, and apparently of different ages." Together they "shouted": "*Glory to thee, O Lord. Ride Forth, Mighty God, conquering and to conquer.*"[47]

Two weeks later Joseph turned toward the sound of a voice and saw another remarkable scene. A figure of Christ with arms outstretched, dressed in a heavily decorated gown, and with almost feminine features stood facing four young men. Each of the four had a highly individual appearance: one was a "black," another was "a dark person, like one of us, with whiskers," the third "a fair man," and the fourth "a copper colour." The first and fourth figures had trumpets; the second and third, a harp and a lyre. Beside each stood a flag, one of which was white "with a broad black's face on it," and another, standing by the bearded man, was, apparently, the American flag. It had "red and white stripes, with a square of blue in one corner, with thirteen stars brilliant, as if of diamonds." The third flag possessed a number of unusual configurations. It was white "with half moons, swords, stars, and snakes or serpents, all in variegated colours." The fourth possessed a similarity to the English flag. It was blue "with white and red stripes or crosses, somewhat like the English colours." To this representative group and to "millions of people . . . of the same kind as they were," who were also meant to be represented in the picture, Christ announced, "*I will be known in all hearts, throughout the whole world, from the emperor on the throne, to the meanest subject, on the earth.*"[48]

A third vision occurred close to eight o'clock on Friday, June 3, while Joseph was busy at the mill assisting workmen in preparing size for paper. He saw before him the Last Judgment. His watercolor of the scene teems with activity. In the background are a multitude of faces, many darkened. An unprepossessing figure in the upper middle portion of the canvas is God, and on His left and right are angels holding open a book. A larger figure, reclining and to the lower left of the deity, reads from a long, curling list. Beneath the huge cloud formation supporting the assemblage is what is meant to be "a very confused appearance of the earth." Numbers of people are seen rising from their graves. "Some in a kind of light mantle, were going toward a hill, which was light and shining" on the right side of the "Celestial Being" while others, seeming to be "bodies formed of clay," moved to the left side. "The place where they were assembled was dark and gloomy." Beside them flames are erupting. Close to the fire is a small dark figure, the devil, drawing aim with a bow and arrow on the white figure above him. Serrating the horizon are "a number of rough hills, with gloomy black clouds, from which issued flashes of lightening in different places," and in the middle of the canvas, standing on the edge of the cloud bank, are two figures, one dressed in silvery mail, holding a linked chain, to which is attached "a wretched being in human form, in appearance miserable, ragged, and dirty." This "infernal figure" apparently either has been or is about to be condemned to the endless torments of the flames below.[49]

Joseph's paintings, though important and fascinating, are largely devoid of artistic merit. An exception is a superbly drawn three-masted schooner, the *Faith*, which is anchored between a glowering, irregularly shaped mass, "The Rock of Ages," and a lightly tinted coastline, the Promised Land. An angel transports passengers from the rock to the ship. Above them are billowing dark clouds, broken by two white figures, one at the top of the picture and the other at the upper right. The first is an angel blowing a trumpet and the second a "Being like our Saviour, encircled by a splendid light."⁵⁰ The picture speaks eloquently of the spiritual migration which thousands of Southcottians were at that moment making.

Yet another visionary whom Carpenter supported was the poor soul known as Jerusha. "A humble, pious Christian," he was "a man of a timid nature, feeble in body, and equally so in mind; but the fear of God was uniformly before his eyes." In addition, he was "very poor." He and Carpenter met in September 1803, when Jerusha was sixty-three. The critical moment in Jerusha's life had come in November 1793, when he dreamed he was walking down a street, reflecting on the disorders which were taking place in France. Suddenly before him appeared twelve angels dressed in white. "He . . . thought himself involved in blood and slaughter, which so terrified him, that he fell down to pray." In the following eleven years, he continued to have disturbing dreams of a similar nature. "Sometimes he thought they concerned himself alone, that great evils would befal him here, and that his happiness hereafter was very doubtful; at other times, he feared evil was coming upon the nation, which, from his abhorrence to what had passed in a neighbouring one, was nearly as distressing to his feelings." Finally, he decided to attend a Southcottian meeting, although at first he had considered Joanna's writings and Joseph Prescott's paintings to be blasphemous. At the door to the Southcottian meeting place, he met "the very female he had seen in his dream, in November, 1793," and who had haunted his imagination since. The woman refused him admission, "the room being then filled with inquirers." He felt this was a judgment upon him for criticizing "the Cause of God." The old man contemplated suicide if he were turned away again. The next time, however, he was allowed in. While at the meeting, Jerusha professed his belief in the prophetess and received a seal. As had happened to Joanna, he began to communicate with a spirit who gave him the following message about the prophetess "as fast as I could write it":

> Come, see Joanna, see the saint arise!
> Burst earthly prison, soar above the skies,
> To that bright world where joys immortal grow,
> And life's unfathom'd pleasures ever flow;
> There, rob'd in white, she'll join the heav'nly train,
> The ransom'd throng for whom the lamb was slain:
> She'll share the glory of the sealed race,
> And bask, and triumph, in the God of Grace.⁵¹

Carpenter expressed the same amazement over Jerusha's sudden fluency as Joanna's friends had over hers: "Although there may be nothing in the style to attract the notice of such as pride themselves in their correct taste in composition, yet, to those who knew the man's simplicity, the whole was extraordinary; for, he was so deficient in learning, that he was unable to read a paragraph in the newspaper for others to understand him." Carpenter added, "I should be glad to put to the trial . . . the brightest in the united kingdoms; for I believe there exists not one who could give, off hand, as fast as a ready penman could possibly write, a number of lines on a subject, with which he was unacquainted." Carpenter felt that Jerusha's output could not be matched even if a month was given a competitor for each hour the old man spent in writing. "On any parts which were obscure, explanation was entreated, and generally immediately returned in thirty, fifty, or a hundred, lines in verse." [52]

Despite his qualifications, Jerusha did not present a threat to Joanna's preeminence in the movement. "Those who had closely investigated, considered there was nothing but what confirmed her mission." Jerusha, Carpenter believed, "was one among many who were spiritually visited, to testify the reality of the Lord's dealings with her." [53] Carpenter elaborated on this another time when he said that "very many persons in the present day" shared Joseph and Jerusha's visionary experiences. "To most or all of these persons," he said, "certain things of a private nature have been given, which, in a remarkable manner . . . have come true." [54]

Carpenter's break with the Southcottians came principally over Joseph Prescott, who began flattering his patron until Carpenter became restive under Joanna's absolute rule. He bitterly recalled, "In the year 1805, she had an unaccountable fit of being invested with some supreme authority; and directed certain proceedings against me for supposed acts of disobedience." A "grand jury" of twelve men assembled and received the charges "on the second floor of a Holborn lodging house." The jurors accused him of communicating with Satan through Joseph. According to Carpenter, "those that were of her party believed every thing through the youth was from an evil source." [55]

One of the principals in these developments was William Tozer, a crude, uneducated but powerful figure who had recently arrived in London from Devon and who played a particularly disruptive role by first backing Carpenter and then throwing his support to Joanna. Carpenter wrote that in the middle of the year Tozer

came from the country . . . to publicly tell the inhabitants of the metropolis, that nothing was to be received but through this woman, and that I was leading people by the devil; that, had he not come to town, all were going, headlong, to the infernal regions. The simple people were as alarmed, as though his satanic majesty had, personally, appeared; for he impiously said he was spiritually taught by God, whilst I dared make no pretensions, but to be an explainer of spiritual teaching. And, notwithstanding his illiterateness, his gross language, and repulsive manners, he prejudiced two-thirds of the people's minds against, what, if understood, they would have firmly held as the pearl of great price, and made a breach which has never yet been healed.

Carpenter, the aggrieved victim, felt he had sacrificed "my friends, property, prospects . . . apparently for nothing."[56] Although the Spirit said that "he hath many to Stand by him,"[57] by the middle of 1807 Carpenter's support had completely disappeared. Scarcely a week passed that his windows were not smashed by Joanna's followers, still irate over his apostasy. In 1814, he wrote: "Nine years have . . . passed without being wanted; for, wherever any knew me, even to the farthest part of Yorkshire, she has blackened me in the vilest and most infamous manner; and they who have heard and believed this envenomed slander have taken an equally active part in diffusing it to others, to display their fidelity."[58]

SWEDENBORG

At this point it may be well to point out that behind Joanna's hostility toward Joseph and other "false prophets" was her fear of a challenge to her position. The Spirit trumpeted, "So now awake, Oh Zion, put on thy beautiful garments, O Jerusalem, for now shall your light break forth as the morning, and I will make the light as clear as the noon day sun." Much was promised. "If ye obey the woman's voice as Jacob did, ye shall be prevailing Israels, for as princes ye shall have power with God, and shall have power over men." But there was a condition. No one must "turn back to any other prophet."[59] Joanna discovered that another besides Joseph Prescott was tempting the believers away, this time, a long-dead prophet, Emanuel Swedenborg, who, to some, offered a more persuasive ratification of the experiences being undergone by themselves and other distressed souls than did the prophetess.

Joanna was hostile to the influence of the Swedish philosopher Swedenborg as she had been to that of witches, astrologers, and gypsy fortune tellers in Devon. A Swedenborgian church, the Church of the New Jerusalem, was founded in London after Swedenborg's death in 1772. William Blake was one of eighty people to attend the first General Conference of the church in April 1789, and the Swedish mystic was to play an important role in the development of the poet's thought. Blake wrote:

O Swedenborg! strongest of men, the Samson shorn by the Churches,
Shewing the Transgressors in Hell, the proud Warriors in Heaven,
Heaven as a Punisher, & Hell as One Under Punishment.[60]

It is highly unlikely but not impossible that Joanna had heard of Swedenborg while she was still in Devonshire. As far as she was concerned,
however, he was only another false prophet sent by Satan to distract the
people from her. And like the others, he had to be refuted. She engaged
in correspondence with a disciple of Swedenborg, an establishment clergyman "who at times varied in his opinions about Joanna." He believed,
"according to the system of that author, that this world was to be re-
generated, without any particular character to come forth." But how
could Swedenborg's prophecies be taken seriously when he "wrote thirty
years before Joanna's Revelations were to be given"? And had not God
deliberately refrained from revealing the future until his visitation to
Joanna in order "to prevent the Powers of Darkness having any foreknowledge of the Divine Plan of Human Redemption, which in that
case, the arts of hell would endeavour to defeat"? Therefore, "it must
. . . be clear to the rational mind, that no spiritual writer could have any
knowledge of what was to take place at a future period, concerning this
event." Indeed, men should stop being "double minded," follow Joanna
alone, and abase themselves before God before it was too late.[61]

Joanna was not unsympathetic to the plight of those who had fallen
into Swedenborg's net: "I do not marvel at [them] being no judge of me
as long as they believe in Swedenborg; for, believe me, Sir, had I read his
writings some years back, and given the least credit to them, I should
have been like a ship overmasted, whose topsails are too heavy for the
bottom, and being in danger of overturning." She felt he "ought to be
read as you would read an Arabian Night's Entertainment." Joanna,
however, had nothing to offer in the way of analysis or criticism and it
seems highly unlikely that she ever actually read any of Swedenborg's
writings. "I have heard some of them read," was all that she would
say.[62]

The reason Joanna imagined she would have been "a ship overmasted" if she had come in contact with Swedenborg's work early in life
was deeply rooted in her own experience. She never doubted that the
Spirit who guided her actions and dictated her writings had its origin
outside herself. The tension lay in whether it was good or evil. Was she
being manipulated and deceived by the devil or was she faithfully carrying out God's will? Joanna was never entirely free from the torment resulting from this anxiety, and she took refuge in the belief that if all she
had said and done was inspired by Satan, her life was a blasphemy of

such magnitude that God could have no option but to strike her down. If she lived, it must be with God's approval. In addition, though Satan might have certain intimations of the future, only God could be certain as to what was to transpire. As she said, false prophets prophesy falsely. Thus, as long as her prophecies continued to be fulfilled, she could push her self-doubts to the side. Her emotional stability, however, depended on her conviction that there were only two spirits with which she had to contend. When Joanna told her sister Susannah Carter that her writings must be from the Lord if they were not from the devil, Susannah answered, "They might be from neither as there were many Spirits Invisible which we could not account for." Joanna became greatly agitated. "This threw my mind as one in a Fever. As Meat trieth the stomach so her words tried me. I begun to grow Jealous for myself and all the Prophets—thinking If there was such Knowledge and Wisdom in Spirits Invisible that were not of God. What rock had we to trust to?" The Spirit came to her rescue, saying he would rather have her die than draw back just because "thy Sister hath filled thy mind of some confusion of Spirits that are not from me nor from the Devil." [63]

Joanna thought she would have found this same "confusion of Spirits" if she had been a believer in Swedenborg.

My head would have been filled with so many different ideas of spirits, that I should not have known where to fix my anchor but in a steady faith in the Word of God, which made a steady balance in my heart. For had I not believed the Bible in its perfect truth, and relied on all the words and promises of God, I should have fainted many years ago; therefore I see the wisdom in the Spirit that directs me . . . to read no book but the Bible, for that teaches us there are but two masters. Our Saviour said we cannot serve them both. . . . So, if we draw near to God he will draw near to us, and if we resist the Devil he must fly from us. So, relying on the written Word of God, I found an anchor to fix my faith upon, being assured that by serving the one I must shun the other. But had I judged there were various kinds of spirits to draw our minds and drown our senses, there would be no room left for reason.

Swedenborg offered nothing but uncertainty to his followers. "Instead of the God of truth leading you into every truth, he says you are led you know not where. Instead of men and devils, saints and angels, this man tells you all were created men at first upon the earth." In addition, he stood accused of unorthodoxy. "Here the Bible is firmly denied and some new plan formed which no man can trust to." [64] There was a choice to be made by Swedenborg's followers between their heresiarch and the Bible. Those who gave up their faith in the scriptures were warned that they would be tossed and turned and "carried away by every kind of Doctrine," their security splintering "on the Strange inventions of mens' minds who vary from the Word of Truth." Such men will "put their own wisdom on what they see and hear, making the word of truth, which is the Bible of no effect." [65]

Joanna abhorred the very idea of heresy, as we have seen. She believed that her role was to give the many sects a rallying point from which they could return to the "standard of the church." During her reflections on Swedenborg, the Spirit noted her praying "to be kept free from all false doctrine, heresy, and schism, and all contempt of *My Words* and Commandments." [66] To Joanna, the world was a battleground between the forces of God and the forces of Satan. Neither her faith nor her state of mind would support any modification of this alignment. She believed that the map of the spiritual world drawn by Swedenborg was overly subtle and led him and his followers from orthodoxy into heresy. "Were I to believe Swedenborg's works," she said, "I should be of no religion at all." [67]

Nevertheless, Joanna freely conceded that her understanding of Swedenborg might be imperfect. "But how far my judgment of the book is right I know not." As always, the Spirit reassured her. "Right is thy judgment concerning Swedenborg," he said; "the writings which come from him are, as thou sayest, Satan coming as an angel of light, or as a cunning crafty invention of some new plan of salvation." [68] The Spirit admitted, however, that "some strange things were brought before his view," but he generally found Swedenborg's account of his mystical experiences unconvincing:

> But oh! the heavenly joys he does now shew;
> No likely pictures does he draw at all,
> Faint are his colours, and too faint for all,
> 'Tis like the daylight that's nearly gone,
> And so that daylight he has shewn to man

The reason for allowing Swedenborg his tantalizing but incomplete glimpses of the heavenly world was to show that, although humans can achieve much on their own initiative, the final heights are denied them without the assistance and favor of God.

> That I such wondrous writers do let go,
> That men their faith and wisdom might shew.
> But now their wisdom I'll pronounce it dead,
> If men can e'er believe a word he said
> Concerning the Heavenly Host above,
> When my disciples I did so dearly love,

And yet to them I never did reveal,
The heavenly mansions I did all conceal;
Then how should I reveal it to that man?
I ask. For me, what wonders has he done,
That he should come so favourite great of Heaven? [69]

POOR MEN DREAM

Joanna's final and most compelling appeal was her promise that the world which damaged and defeated so many would soon be swept away. "The purpose [of my prophecies]," she stated, "is to warn the whole World at large, that *the second coming of Christ is nigh at hand*." [70] It was this penultimate event for which the poor waited. When Christ came, they, the humble, would then be raised high and the rich brought low. The despair from which this hope derived is best illustrated by an epitaph on a tombstone which a believer copied down and put away in his notebook:

> This World's a City full of crooked Streets
> Death is the Market Place where each one meets
> If Life were only Merchandise to buy
> The Rich would Live, the poor alone would die. [71]

It was not Joanna's intention to set the rich and the poor against each other. She directed her message to both. Her Spirit said, "I made the rich, I made the poor / And both alike to ME." [72] Joanna believed that the two extremes of society, and indeed all intermediate levels, were linked together in their distress, equally intense but qualitatively different. The mental suffering of the affluent and learned joined them with the physical suffering of the poor and uneducated in one potential community of believers.

> The husbandman, discern his plan,
>   He labours to get bread;
> The wise and learned in your land
>   They labour, as I've said;
> The counsellor here let him appear
>   His trials to go through,
> He labours more than he can bear
>   Without some pain, I know;
> The clergy see, alike they be,
>   They labour all to gain
> The livings that are given they,

> And often feel much pain;
> Now to the king I next shall come,
> He labours just the same,
> And oft with pain, I will maintain,
> To guide and guard your land;
> In council here for to appear
> The parliament all see,
> How in their heads they labour here,
> For I do now tell thee,
> They labour more for earthly store,
> Or grandeur for to shine,
> Than the poor man that ploughs your land,
> I tell thee, in their minds.
> So all alike the path is strait,
> In sorrow men go on.[73]

Reflecting her strong ties to the paternalistic world of village society, Joanna's Spirit charged the rich anew with their responsibility to the poor:

> I've shewed my love to every man;
> The rich I bless'd with earthly store;
> If they act right I'll bless them more;
> If faithful stewards they will be,
> In order guard my family,
> And guide my substance with such care,
> That no complaining I may hear
> From those that I have plac'd below;
> A good account I bid them shew;
> For all the earth is surely mine,
> I've fixed the stewards in mankind.[74]

Joanna hoped that the rich would be the first to respond to her call, perhaps because she believed that she was now entitled to reclaim what she felt was her rightful place in their society. But disappointment waited.

> The way 'tis done, let all discern,
> The great invited first;
> But they refus'd, and then I chus'd
> The lower class to burst.[75]

A transformed world had no appeal for the rich, as it did for the poor.

Joanna discovered that many of the "stewards" were more concerned about their great titles and raising their "pride and Grandeur heigh"[76] than they were about their brothers and sisters, the poor. Although Joanna accepted the hierarchical nature of society, she believed in it only as long as every class fulfilled its functions. In Gittisham, Squire Putt's despotism was unquestioned because it was benevolent. In the world outside the village, she found that the rich refused to intervene and set right the inequities which beset the lower orders. Because they failed in their responsibilities to their charges, the rich were no longer worthy of their place in society. They too would know physical suffering and, quite literally, a fall from their lofty perches. "I will tell thee what I mean, by cutting off the under Branches: that is the lower class of people: as one branch groweth after another: just so are the stations of mankind: the under branches are cut off already by poverty and the sword; that is, the major part of them. Now, they are going farther—to the second and third Class of people by cutting [off] their substance, then where do vain men think to come down, when the tree is pruned through? What Branches will they stand on?"[77]

The Spirit told Joanna "with what contempt" those whose approval she courted "looked upon one that was so mean and low as they judged thee." And the great "judged the Lord another such as theirselves."[78] Neither the affluent nor the comfortable God they worshipped could be bothered with someone of Joanna's class. This rejection was sufficient for the prophetess to recognize her enduring constituency, the poor. "Know amongst the Believers," she said, "there are many Poor, that must be Sufferers from a long Continuance of Dearth of bread, which I Promised to Prevent if faith was found in man."[79] The Spirit reassured her on the subject of his own origins. "It was given to lower the pride of the great that I was born of poor parents, and laid in a manger to bring men to that humble mind; and, if they would be partakers with *Me* in my kingdom and reign with *Me*, they must become humble with *Me*."[80] The battlelines were thus drawn. The Spirit accused the rich, "Ye starve the poor and so they die."[81] But God promised that He had "chosen the weak foolish things of this world to confound the great and learned,"[82] reminding the rich that "my Gospel was brought in by poor men and fishermen, men unlearned in the world; and by such my Kingdom will be brought in: for now is coming the fulfillment of the whole; the meek shall be exalted; the proud shall be abased; and the meek shall inherit the earth."[83] Yet the poor were not to have special favors. If they, like the rich, mocked Joanna's warnings, then "let them not complain of suffering nor of famine."[84]

Joanna recognized the special difficulties which the church had in communicating with her natural audience. The Spirit said, "This folly I see in the church, teaching people fine speeches, and learning, that the poor do not understand."[85] She avoided its mistake by addressing the poor in a language which was comprehensible to them, thereby conveniently turning her own shortcomings in the eyes of the rich to advantage. But she realized the limited circulation that her publications must have among the poor because of their cost. An enemy who had purchased Joanna's *Second Book of Wonders* observed that "it is for such pernicious trash that the poor are tempted to expend that money which they want for the necessities of their families."[86]

Because of the expense of acquiring her numerous publications, Joanna issued a special pamphlet in 1803 which was intended to be a synopsis of her writings and was to be given away. On the first page, she said: "Now as my Prophecies are many and extend to large Volumes, that the Poor cannot buy them, if they should wish to know the meaning of them, I shall now explain them in a small compass for the sake of the poor, that no excuse may be found, that they could not afford to buy to judge for themselves. I now print this little Book *to give* the Poor, by the bounty of the Rich."[87] The topics which she raised were the imminence of the Second Coming, the place which she held in the biblical tradition of prophets, the cause-and-effect relationship between Satan and the misery of mortals, the history of her mystical experiences, and the promise which the millennium offered. Joanna concluded by naming herself one of the three most important women who had ever lived, the other two being Eve and the Virgin Mary. On September 4, 1803, Joanna wrote to the Reverend Stanhope Bruce that the book meant for the poor "will be a key to all my other books." She said, "As soon as the book is out, the Rev. Mr. Foley will send some to you, for your disposal, to give to whom you think proper, in your own parish, or the neighbouring parishes around; as I am ordered to have them spread as much as possible, that the coming of the Lord may be made known."[88]

Perhaps unconsciously, Joanna began to bolster her position as an advocate of the poor. She told of an incident in which she refused to visit some "great" relatives with whom she felt uncomfortable in favor of staying with the poor, who accepted and respected her.[89] But there was little need for Joanna to verify her right to speak of and for the poor. The prophetess' audiences recognized her as a fellow victim. When she lashed out at the rich for their self-indulgence, it was with a sense of outrage of all those like herself whose often precarious, always hard-earned livelihoods depended on their patronage. The best example appears in a pamphlet published in 1804. There Joanna attacked ladies of fashion, who ruin their fortunes in the works of the devil, by gambling at cards, operas, balls, assemblies, masquerades, and every catalogue of vice, that the devil can invent. These are very well to be supported, and every luxury and extravagance are very well to be upholded, till their shattered fortunes are gone; and the poor, honest, industrious tradesmen, are often ruined by their extravagancies; for they not only run through their own fortunes, but they *run through the fortunes of others*, and then think it very well to say *they are broke, therefore the people must forgive them*, and they remain as *gentlemen the same*, and with impudence and confidence demand it, because of their *Rank and Title*.[90]

Christians were aware from their Bibles that the poor would always be with them, but never in memory had they been so visible. All around her, Joanna saw the dreadful blight of poverty. "The Prospect on every side is gloomy for the unbelievers. Trade ruined. Scarce any employment for the Poor in the manufacturing Towns."[91] She wrote, "I hear the cries of the poor, complaining they are starving to death, for want of food. It is almost incredible to believe they can keep life in the manner they now live: every station of men are full of complaints, unless it be the rich and great."[92] The "dearth of provisions" and the wartime taxes were the nails being driven into the cross of their martyrdom. As in Exeter, high prices made a grim situation desperate. The highest that Joanna had ever known corn was 8 shillings a bushel. In 1800, it had risen to 25 shillings a bushel, a 300 percent increase. Similarly, meat which had been 2d. to 3d. a pound in 1792 had climbed to 8d. and 9d. a pound. Other items were "Double Beer," from 2½d. and 3d. to 6d. and 8d.; wine ⅙d. to 4d. and 6d. a bottle. "Everything else" advanced "in proportion." Taxes, too, were crushing. Those "upon Houses, Windows, and everything" had gone up "more than trebel." But, worst of all, "labour that was then plenty for the Poor have been taken from their hands."[93] The poor, Joanna said, were "born to be the negroes here."[94]

Occasionally, an outsider obtained a glimpse into this dark world of poverty and suffering. While out walking, William Frend happened by chance to hear the conversation of a group of poor women which both shocked and haunted him. A Dissenter and reformer, Frend was expelled from Cambridge for his writings. He had translated some books of the Old Testament for Joseph Priestley and was often to appear in William Godwin's circle, which included several Southcottians. In the course of his walk, Frend said he

joined company with two men of the village, who, being employed by the woolstaplers to let out spinning to the poor, had lately received orders to lower the value of labour. We were talking on this subject, when the exclamation of a groupe of poor women going to market, overhearing our conversation made an impression on my mind, which all the eloquence of the houses of lords and commons cannot efface. We are to be sconced three-pence in the shilling [they said], let others work for me, I'll not. We are to be sconced a fourth part of our labour. What is all this for? [Frend commented:] I did not dare to tell them what it was for, nor to add insult to misery. What is the beheading of a monarch to them? What is the navigation of the Scheldt to them? What is the freedom of a great nation [France] to them but reason for joy? Yet the debating only on these subjects has reached their cottages. They are already sconced threepence in the shilling. What must be their fate, when we suffer under the most odious scourge of the human race [war], and the accumulation of taxes takes away half of that daily bread, which is scarce sufficient at present for their support?

He then turned his ire on a willful, unfeeling government: "Oh! that I had the warning voice of an ancient prophet, that I might penetrate into the inmost recesses of palaces, and appall the haranguers of senates! I would use no other language than that of the poor market women. I would cry aloud in the ears of the first magistrate, we are sconced three-pence in the shilling, the fourth part of our labour, for what?" Thousands can resist this cry of desperation, the reformer ended, because "threepence in the shilling for spinning conveys no ideas to them. They know not what a cottage is[;] they know not how the poor live, how they make up their scanty meal." He implored "some one in our house of commons" to tell his colleagues "what the deduction of three-pence in the shilling occasions among the myriads of England."[95]

One of the "myriads of England," Thomas Taylor, a follower of Richard Brothers, spoke in a similarly anguished voice to those who had failed in their responsibilities to the poor: "It is your duty, who live in plenty, to seek out, enquire for, and relieve the poor and distressed. *But instead of this*, you will hardly acknowledge them as worthy of your notice, or composed of the same flesh and blood as yourselves. *Hence it is*, that the poor are oppressed, crying *daily* for food and raiment, have scarcely a hogstye to dwell in, and cannot with all their industry acquire the common necessaries of life." Taylor attacked the self-indulgence and immorality of the age, the exploitation of native peoples, the war, the merchants for their participation in the slave trade; but, he saved his greatest wrath for enclosing landlords: "You wealthy and opulent possessors of property, who dwell in the country, what right have you to lay house to house, field to field, and one village to another; taking away the commonright of the poor, in turning a beast out into the field, gathering wood, and not suffering them even to *glean* in your enclosures, without first taking your leave." His conception of "right" possessed a logic which had little in common with the value system of capitalism, and his anger grew ever more expansive:

What right have you to purchase so much land to lay out in parks and pleasure gardens, and thereby prevent the lands from being cultivated, the fruits of the earth being increased, and the labourer from having employment.

Why ought not the poor to have an opportunity to increase, as well as you in attempting to grasp at all the possessions, and govern all the people in your neighborhood?

What right have you to get a sanction from Government to enclose Common-fields, and take away the right of the poor in this manner; and oblige every inferior possessor of property, who is defenceless to comply with your terms.

[But a means of redress existed:] KNOW YOU, that the cries of the Widow, Fatherless Children, and the defenceless oppressed Poor, are come up into the ears of the Lord of *Hosts*. He is ready to undertake their cause: and if you repent not of your evil deeds, *He will consume you*, with the breath of his mouth.[96]

In an equally passionate but more homely vein, one of the most successful of Joanna's Yorkshire preachers, Thomas Senior, who spoke to "thousands" on the Southcottian circuit, recounted a dream which, again, reflected the bitterness and desire for revenge which could be felt so intensely by those at the bottom of society. Senior saw himself in a room where "the rich and great [were] feasting and Drinking." To his left "were a few Poor . . . sitting in trouble." He said, "The Rich looked upon them worse than if they had been dogs." Then, in his dream, Senior finally blurted out to them, "The scenes are going to be changed. The Haughty disdainful looks of the rich are going to be brought down. And the Poor is going to be Exalted." The preacher's words resulted in "the whole of the Rich" being "put in confusion."[97]

As did Frend, Taylor, and Senior, Joanna raged at the insensitivity of those with full stomachs and a livelihood to the plight of the poor. In a letter to a clergyman, she wrote: "If the Bad Harvests and the high price of provisions Starve the poor that they suffer Martyrdom for want, you have not felt it, and I will tell you why you have not felt it, by a Hardened unfeeling heart, that never thinks of your fellow Creatures, how they Live and what they must suffer to see the price of Corn so high and other things in proportion." The prophetess told the parson sitting securely behind his deanery window, "I will tell you I have seen their distresses. I have heard their complaining."[98]

Her confidant, Jane Townley, wrote to Mrs. Taylor in Exeter on September 4, 1804, of Joanna's anxiety. Despite news of a good crop, Miss Townley said, "Bread is dear, and the poor Man with his Family are suffering [so that] the rich may get large rents." She reported that Joanna, the farmer's daughter, had declared that "if corn is more than 5 shillings a bushell, the harvest must be very bad or the Farmers a den of thieves, to rob the poor from blessings the Lord hath sent." The cause of high prices, it seemed clear, was that the rich "are . . . eating up the Poor as they would eat up bread."[99]

However, not all of the poor were convinced of the sincerity of Joanna's identification with them and their plight. At least one embittered former Southcottian, Richard Law, considered her a simple opportunist. "But you being a Person of Property," he wrote to Jane Townley, "she coaxed you on to the end as she did . . . others possessing Property." He charged that "at first" she embraced "the usefull and upright poor" because "she was glad to profit by their labours." "As she grew stronger," Law said, "she would not suffer them to remain among the Prelates and Dignitaries of her new Church, but she pushed them out to put Gentlemen in their room." With much the same rancor of a disillusioned political supporter who had not gotten a promised appointment, Law accused the prophetess of being "the most ungrateful woman that ever was befriended by man." He said, "Many a rich present she got thro' the instrumentality of such men as myself, but she forgot us in her will nor even left us a single trinket to keep for her sake." In the same letter, Law declared that Joanna's destination would also be that of her affluent friends. He told Jane Townley, "Mother is gone to Hell, and . . . her gentlemen and ladies will soon follow her."[100] It must be remembered, however, that Law was writing after Joanna's death, that he believed the prophetess had prevented his marriage to Jane Townley, and that he was one of those who himself had been deprived of a leadership role in the movement.

Certainly, however, Law was correct in seeing that Joanna's fame and new prestige offered opportunities of mingling in a world which previously had existed only in her fantasies. An enemy composed a rhyme for her:

> What better, then, to prophecy, and tell
> Of things to come, of heav'n, of earth, and hell?
> What better can invention name on earth,
> To line my pockets with Peruvian worth?
> A few years back in humbler paths I walk'd,
> Bow'd to the rich! and with poor people talk'd.
> But, see the change false prophecies have wrought,
> How high in wond'rous works my name is brought.
> I now, forgetful of my wonted state,
> Talk with the rich—am courted by the great.

. . . .
Do not, good Master, frowning, thus complain,
From lisping childhood I thy slave have been;
Brought thousands to believe thee, rich and poor,
But spare me, and I'll bring some thousands more.[101]

Despite defections and denunciations, however, Joanna never forgot her principal constituency, those, like her, who wore the badge of suffering. She offered many of the poor what was indispensable for their emotional survival and was in tragically short supply in a country gripped by war and widespread social and economic dislocation—hope.

According to Joanna, both the believing and unbelieving poor were suffering the same deprivations. The difference lay in their attitude toward the hardships they experienced. For the unbelievers, life was a barely endurable agony, happily terminated by death. The believers, however, "have a different Prospect before them[.] Knowing though they have the Storms first to pass through yet they can *look forward to the glorious prize* in the *end*." [102] This was a world "where no Enemy can assault you and no Sorrows come near unto you." [103] Joanna told the callous parson that if the poor "were without Help and without Hope" she would prefer to die rather than witness their continued suffering. She harangued him for his skeptical attitude toward her mission which benefited no one. "Now as you cannot give them Help to deliver them from their burden you must be of a wretched make to wish to take the Hope from them that the Lord hath so mercifully condescended to give to His People that are now Longing for the Coming of their Lord." With hope, people could endure. "This is my Happiness," Joanna said, "and this is the Happiness of all true Believers." [104]

Unlike Richard Brothers, Joanna did not offer a detailed blueprint of the millennial kingdom. However, the Spirit told of the "golden days" the believers would see.[105] They were described in terms which could easily be understood within the life experience of Joanna's audience:

Then all your swords to ploughshares you may turn,
To plough with plenty your delightful land;
And all your spears for pruning hooks may be,
To prune with pleasure your delightful trees.
No thistles then shall hurt the reaper's hand;
But peace and plenty flow throughout your land.
No prickly thorns to hurt the binder's care;
For God will bind in bundle ev'ry tare;
And all the foxes he away will take,
That doth so spoil and hurt the tender grape.[106]

The Spirit said, "I will throw down and build up until every house is made pleasant for man. Gardens and vineyards shall join to their houses. I will throw down your towns and build them anew, with gardens and fruitful vines to every man's dwelling."[107] Joanna seemed to be making a specific appeal to the poor when she said that the wealthy unbelievers would be dispossessed upon Christ's return.[108]

The prophetess was well aware of the fine acquisitive instinct motivating many of her followers. Some impatient ones had joined because of "the Loaves and fishes" which they believed would be their "present reward." Others, somewhat less pragmatic, were content to work as "faithful Labourers in the Vineyard" until ultimately they too would receive their reward.[109] The Spirit admonished those in the first group who were too eager for material acquisitions. If this was their only desire, they would be destroyed.[110] But for those whose behavior was more circumspect, an abundance of good things, including personal riches, awaited in the New Jerusalem:

> Your houses I shall build anew,
> And palaces bring to your view;
> For golden mines I have in store,
> The foaming seas shall send on shore
> Millions of treasure hid therein,
> And mines of di'monds shall be seen,
> Of pearls, and ev'ry precious stone,
> I've mines conceal'd from men unknown,
> I've gold of ophir, that shall come
> To build Jerusalem up again.[111]

The believers would even "be fed with royal dainties."[112]

However, there was not to be an immediate expropriation of the rich as some believed. This became clear when the news reached the prophetess that the egregious Peter Morrison was telling his audiences in the north that "all the Property and Land belonging to the Rich would be taken away and given to the Sealed People." Once again, as so many times since the Christian message had made its way across Europe, the egalitarian vision rose up, glittering, irresistible, alive, as always possessed of the promise of touching and transforming the lives of the wretched of the earth. And it was a vision, this time, with some slight, evanescent reality. To her horror, Joanna learned that the "sealed people" working on the property of Sir Thomas White had been discharged "because they had been laying out who was to have this part of his Estate, and that part, as the Rich were to be taken out of the way." She angrily asserted that raising such expectations on the part of the believers was "dangerous" because it distracted their attention from the coming of Christ's kingdom "to a present reward of earthly greatness and Grandeur." It was the City of God that must first be sought by the believers "and then all other blessings will be added to them." Then, she made a shrewd hit. "If all happiness laid in earthly greatness and that be all [the believers] have in view, the Rich and Great possess this already." Since the rich had obviously not responded to Joanna's message, leaving their lives tragically incomplete, what good were possessions if they simply blinded their owners to the truth. Anyway, she asked her errant preacher, why should God condemn the rich "for enjoying the things that you are teaching the others to long for"? Spiritual and material well being were not incompatible in Joanna's eyes, far from it. But, as always, the spirit came before the flesh.[113]

For those in Joanna's following not numbered among the poor and who had much to lose if all was to be swept away at the Second Coming, Joanna offered perceptive advice. "No one," she observed, is "to think that trade and business will cease in our land after the deliverance comes of the clouds that now hang over us." She added, "All kinds of trade will go on the same." This was an important issue. When Richard Brothers announced that he would proceed to the Holy Land in order to build the New Jerusalem, the prophet exhorted his propertied followers to throw over their possessions and accompany him. According to Joanna, "Many people have been ruined thereby." In the vision of the new world which Joanna held up, private property, at least that of the believers, was to be protected. One had to be astute in planning, however. The prophetess told a follower that God "never directs any man's property what he shall do. In these things we are left to judge for ourselves, and you must be the best judge whether you can sell the estate to an advantage to do you good; but as you ask my advice, I shall tell you what I should do myself, unless I was distressed, and obliged to sell my estate[:] I must say I should not sell it if it was land, for, come what will, that will stand; but if it be in houses, or the greater value of it be in a house, I should sell it as soon as I could get its worth."[114] Daniel Roberts, the wealthy Quaker, appealed directly to Joanna for advice on his particular circumstances. The Spirit reassured him that, unless the destruction was general, "He hath nothing to fear of losing his mines." As to the loss of family and friends, he would receive spiritual rewards which would "repay that loss."[115]

As the Southcottians gathered together in London, the growing manufacuring cities of the Midlands and the north, and the small towns and villages of the West Country, they raised their voices to sing of that which transfixed their aspirations and dreams, the coming of a new world:

> CHRIST'S SECOND COMING is at hand,
>   In MIGHT and POW'R 'twill be;
> For CHRIST will *Renovate* the land,
>   And set the captive free.
>
> Then wars on earth shall be no more,
>   All tears HE'LL wipe away:
> The *Lame*, the *Blind*, *Infirm*, and *Poor*,
>   Will bless that happy day.
>
> For *Paradise* will be restor'd,
>   And earth resemble heav'n';
> JEHOVAH . . . will be ador'd,
>   And satan hence be driv'n.
>
> Oh read your BIBLES, there you'll see
>   The day is near at hand,
> For GOD hath fix'd the firm decree,
>   He will REDEEM the land.[116]

Yet the crucial question remained. How was the transfer of power to take place? How was the old world to be destroyed and the new world, for which thousands yearned, to be raised in its stead? Joanna's Spirit had urged her, "Tell the Weak to be Strong in the Lord, and in the power of His might."[117] But must believers deal directly with the forces of evil which had infiltrated all earthly institutions by taking to the streets and attempting to pull down the government, as the Fifth Monarchy men had done in the seventeenth century? Or were they simply to wait patiently for Christ or one of His emissaries to deliver them from injustice and suffering, thus posing no active threat to society? In the late years of the eighteenth century, both these active and passive strands were woven through the careers of William Sharp and William Tooke Harwood, two leading members of the Society for Constitutional Information, one of the most prominent radical societies in London. Both Sharp and Harwood were to become Southcottians. An understanding of the milieu from which they emerge and the sometimes intricate course of their careers will help us to see another and most critical aspect of the psychology of those whose journey to the New Jerusalem was endangered by the enchantments of politicians, such as Tom Paine, and a prophet, Richard Brothers.

VI

The Politics of the Millennium

As the world has seen an age of Reason and an age of Infidelity, so also shall the world see an age of Prophecy.[1]

INFIDELS AND MILLENARIANS

On March 9, 1801, the Duke of Portland wrote to Earl Fitzwilliam, the lord lieutenant of Yorkshire, that he had received a disturbing letter from Bradford. The duke's Yorkshire correspondent warned of the appearance of a religious sect in the neighborhood "which is likely to become mischievous to H. M.'s Government." He said, "These People are yet not numerous, but they increase daily," and concluded by telling Portland that "their principal tenet is that Christ has commenc'd his second Kingdom, & that all submission to civil government is at an end."[2]

Nine days later a meeting of magistrates was held in Leeds to look into "a variety of reports" suggesting "that an Insurrection was in contemplation among the lower orders of the people."[3] Behind these stories, as E. P. Thompson has found, lay a network of illegal trade union activity and probably some sort of Jacobin conspiracy associated with the tragic figure of Colonel Despard, who was to be executed for his part in a military conspiracy.[4] Certainly the magistrates concluded that there was substance to the reports. Apparent evidence existed of meetings being held and oaths taken for purposes which could only be described as "extremely dangerous." A decision was made to ask for military aid and, particularly, a contingent of cavalry.[5] The next day Fitzwilliam received a second letter from Bradford which sought to clarify the original report. It seemed that the "Sect of Fanatics" were followers of prophet Richard Brothers, whose cause had been taken up by George Turner, the prominent Leeds merchant who, the source said, "appears to have been the first Encourager of the Doctrines of Mr. Brothers & his Followers in this County." The "principal leader" was a weaver named Zaccheus Robinson. For a number of years, he said, Robinson had been a significant figure among the local Methodists but was converted to the "New Jerusalemites" by Turner. The members of Brothers' sect met in private houses and read prophecies and parts of the Bible which supported their views. Fitzwilliam's informant offered the consoling information that, "as to their setting themselves against all human Laws & Ordinances, nothing of that sort has yet appear'd publicly amongst them, whatever they may do in private." Less encouraging, however, was the very real possibility "that there is a Communication kept up amongst these societies throughout the Kingdom."[6]

It may or may not have been that the radicals exciting the fears of the Leeds magistrates and the enthusiasts supporting Brothers had some connection. If confusion had arisen between them, however, it would have been highly understandable, given the mutable character of popular politics in the last decade of the century.

It has been recently argued that the "ideology of the reformers of the 1790s . . . was purely political and materialistic," resulting in a "separation of the political and religious enthusiasms of the day." Unlike their predecessors in the previous century, "the reformers had in fact moved beyond religion."[7] On the contrary, however, the radical culture of the age was still strongly nourished by men whose perspective on political change was shaped by religion. This chapter will attempt to demonstrate why the reform societies made such a powerful appeal to millenarians and, second, why disciples of John Horne Tooke and Tom Paine could then shift their allegiance to Richard Brothers and Joanna Southcott without contradicting the logic of their beliefs.

In the early fall of 1790, the Society for Constitutional Information (S.C.I.), the oldest and most influential of the reform societies, had become demoralized and impotent. The unlikely rescuer was Edmund Burke, whose *Reflections on the Revolution in France* restored the necessary ballast of controversy to the radical societies and, of absolutely crucial importance, elicited Tom Paine's *The Rights of Man*, which became the Bible of the reform movement. Paine's book sparked back to life the S.C.I., of which he had been an honorary member since December 17, 1787. He even attempted to give the S.C.I. one thousand pounds of his royalties. So germane was his book to the revival of the society that in 1794 the Secret Committee of the House of Commons judged that "the period from which it appears . . . material to trace in this view the proceedings of the Society for Constitutional Information, is that of the publication of the pamphlet so well known under the title of 'Rights of Man,' by Thomas Paine." The society happily identified itself with Paine and his work, voting him thanks "for his most masterly book" which lay bare the "Sophistries of hireling Scribblers." Older, conservative members fell away and were replaced by men of more radical sentiments. In the first half of 1792, the S.C.I. stood preeminent among the reform societies and served as tutor to the newly founded London Corresponding Society (L.C.S.), which, unlike the S.C.I., was genuinely democratic in its composition, and the popular societies in Sheffield, Norwich, Manchester, and elsewhere in the country.[8]

Paine's work, so important in revitalizing the floundering reform movement and so fundamental in the making of working-class consciousness, had a significance which it is difficult to exaggerate. For this reason, when Paine articulated his unorthodox, but hardly unusual, religious views in *The Age of Reason*, his prestige as a reformer ensured that deism and radical politics would become enduring bedfellows. P. A. Brown notes that "Paine's deism . . . was accepted by many as part of a democrat's faith."[9] The language in which infidels couched their aspirations, however, remained that of Bunyan and the Bible. Of "the early radical consciousness," Edward Royle has said, "ideas which might today be expressed purely in economic terms were then often given a religious and sectarian form, and the ultra-radical leaders were notoriously 'infidel' or 'atheistic' in their opinions." Paine bore the principal responsibility for this development. "Radicalism in religion and politics was forged into a single infidel tradition, and the apostle of this tradition in England, France and America was Thomas Paine."[10]

In an important respect, however, Paine's impact, because of its very magnitude, has obscured the variety of motivations which inspired men to commit themselves to radical politics in the 1790s. There were those prominently engaged in radical activities who were susceptible to Paine's influence at certain points and deeply antagonistic at others. Because their beliefs were soon to lose relevance, they have often been ignored or little understood. These were men who not only talked the language of religion but also still believed it. Two of the more prominent, William Sharp and William Tooke Harwood, are of particular interest because they became leading figures in the Southcottian movement and were among the prophetess' closest advisers. Both Sharp, perhaps the most famous and talented engraver of his day,[11] and Harwood, in 1794 a captain of dragoons and an intimate friend of William Godwin and John Horne Tooke, were leading members of the Society for Constitutional Information. Harwood had been a member since May 28, 1791.[12] At a meeting almost a year later, on March 23, 1792, Harwood was in the chair when John Horne Tooke nominated Sharp for membership in the society. The motion was seconded by William Bonney.[13] Within two and a half years, both Horne Tooke and Bonney stood accused of high treason for their radical activities and Sharp had been taken into custody for "treasonable practices."[14]

The utopian strain in radicalism, whether infidel, which traced its antecedents to the necessitarian doctrines of the French *philosophes*, or Christian, which took its inspiration from the prophetic books of the Bible, owed much to the French Revolution. Royle writes of the infidel debt, "It was the French Revolution which set English freethought alight."[15] But others, like Harwood and Sharp, felt themselves confirmed in their religious attitudes by the events in France and strenuously sought to counter the infidel influence in radical politics. The Reverend Joseph Lomas Towers, a millenarian, wrote, "Of those, in whose bosoms joy beats the highest, on account of the great and glorious events which produced the French revolution, a large part, we know in point of fact, were persons attached to religion and zealous for its interests."[16] He acknowledged, moreover, that he undertook his work, *Illustrations of Prophecy*, because reflection on miracles and prophecy, the two pillars on which Christian belief rested, seemed "peculiarly called for at a period, when the disciples of infidelity are so active and so successful in the gaining of proselytes."[17] The important role that millenarians played in the radical societies of the 1790s, their uneasy coexistence with the infidels, and the ultimate falling out between the two factions are important themes in the shaping of the English radical tradition, and, for the purposes of this study, indispensable for an understanding of those among them who ultimately found their way into the Southcottian movement.

ILLUSTRATIONS OF PROPHECY

The Reverend Joseph Lomas Towers' remarkable and virtually forgotten work, *Illustrations of Prophecy*, offers a compelling insight into the minds of those who for religious reasons traveled from passive acceptance of the immutability of injustice and corruption to an active role in bringing about change through reform activity. Beyond any number of other works on prophecy pouring from the presses, his is particularly worthy of interest because he was the son of the "militantly reformist"[18] Reverend Dr. Joseph Towers who was an active member of the Society for Constitutional Information and a leading Dissenting preacher in London. While the coadjutor of Richard Price at Newington Green, Dr. Towers became one of those who published a reply to Burke.[19] It had been Price's sermon which provided the occasion for Burke's *Reflections on the Revolution in France*. Price, like Priestley, is an excellent example of the Dissenting minister who saw more behind the reform movement than the labor and aspirations of men. He had prophesied that "it may not perhaps be too extravagant to imagine that . . . the progress of improvement will not cease till it has excluded from the earth, not only VICE and WAR, but even DEATH itself, and restored the PARADISAICAL state, which according to the MOSAIC history, preceded our present state." He placed himself squarely in the millenarian camp in his address at the Old Jewry which took place on April 25, 1787. He could see the "Millennium hastening": "We see the clouds scattering. The shades of night are departing. The day dawns; and the Sun of righteousness will soon rise with the healing in his wings." [20]

Dr. Towers' son published *Illustrations of Prophecy* anonymously in 1796, although he had probably written it two years earlier. On the title page he promised to elucidate "many predictions, which occur in Isaiah, Daniel, the Writings of the Evangelists, and the Book of Revelation; And which are thought to foretell, among other Great Events, The Revolution in France, The Overthrow of the Papal Power, and of Ecclesiastical Tyranny, the Downfal[l] of Civil Despotism, And the subsequent Melioration of the State of the World." Pitt's government quickly suppressed the two-volume work because it "was judged inimical to the existing order of things." [21]

That *Illustrations of Prophecy* could have caused the government a measure of genuine concern deserves comment. Revolutionary activity had found its inspiration in the prophetic books of the Bible before in English history. Towers did not temporize, affirming "that the prophetical books of Daniel and of John are in a considerable degree of a political and revolutionary nature." [22] Who could be certain that contemporary counterparts of Venner and his Fifth Monarchy Men, springing from the popular societies or some other cell of disaffection and stirred by publications such as Towers', might not pose a threat to public order? The solicitor general raised this hoary but still frightening specter at Thomas Hardy's trial. "The idea," he said, "that by the establishment of the Rights of Man, universal peace would be established throughout the world," is "an enthusiasm dangerous in the highest degree." It was "as dangerous to government as any that ever existed," he said,

as dangerous as the enthusiasm of the millenarians, or Fifth Monarchy-men, who in the last century occasioned some disturbance, not very violent, indeed, in this country, under an impression upon their minds that Christ was to come to establish his own government upon earth, and that there was to be universal peace and good-will among men; what they called the kingdom of the saints. Under that impression they made an insurrection in the reign of Charles the second, which was suppressed after the death of a few people. There had been an insurrection of the same nature under the government of Cromwell, which also was soon suppressed; but the persons concerned in these transactions, to the very last persisted in their enthusiasm, and some of those executed in the reign of Charles 2nd, protested in their last moments, that if they had been deceived, they had been deceived by heaven. When the minds of men are capable of being worked up to such blasphemous expressions, it is not possible to say to what length they may not go. Their sincerely entertaining such ideas, does not at all lessen the danger of them; does not at all lessen the necessity for the government of the country to take the means of repressing them, and punishing the delinquents in the severest manner. If men should take it into their heads that the community of goods is part of the christian religion, and should upon that ground take the goods of their neighbours, they must be punished as robbers, because it is impossible to preserve the peace of society by any other means.[23]

A member of the London Corresponding Society gave evidence which encouraged the fear that there was a link between religious and radical enthusiasm. He said, "There are certain religious societies in the kingdom, almost in every town, whose sentiments lead them strictly to republicanism." They were "numerous" in Leeds, Birmingham, Liverpool, Bristol, Manchester, Derbyshire, Hull, and "particularly" in London. In fact, "the society in London are just now beginning to organize themselves agreeable to the principles of France." He was even able to supply the information that they met on Mondays and Thursdays.[24]

This testimony was given further credibility by W. H. Reid, who provided significant detail about the relationship between the infidels and millenarians in the London Corresponding Society. Reid asserted that the L.C.S. had been converted to infidelity by Tom Paine's *The Age of Reason*, which became known as "the *New Holy Bible*" of the society. "A *Deist* and a good *Democrat*," he said, "seemed to have been universally compounded." According to Reid, infidels in the L.C.S. found fertile recruiting among religious enthusiasts who saw the French Revolution as the fulfillment of scriptural prophecy. Especially around Spitalfields, he found that "the French system of politics insensibly attached itself to the auxiliary ideas of prophecies." And, congratulating the government on its handling of Richard Brothers, Reid said: "Prophecies, relative to the destruction of almost every kingdom and empire in the world, teemed from the British press, some of them in weekly numbers, till government, perfectly aware of the tendency of these inflammatory means, prudently transferred the prince of prophets [Richard Brothers] to a madhouse."[25]

WILLIAM TOOKE HARWOOD

The careers of William Tooke Harwood and William Sharp provide evidence of the manner in which millenarian beliefs and radical political activity could dynamically interact with each other in the 1790s. Towers stated unequivocally in his work that during the Last Days Christians could not remain supine in the face of an anti-Christian government, if they valued their souls. He accused Pitt's government of using Robert Fleming's commentary on prophecy, *Apocalyptical Key. An Extraordinary Discourse on the Rise and Fall of the Papacy; or the Pouring Out of the Vials*, first appearing in 1701 and then reprinted in 1793,[26] to justify its otherwise indefensible conduct toward France. But, worst of all, the "friends of freedom" had allowed it to happen. Towers compared this apathy with that of the "placemen and pensioners and expectants" who were working energetically to undermine "the liberties of my country."[27] Clearly, Christians who understood the underlying significance of events would have to involve themselves in the struggle against corruption and tyranny in the government, and an obvious place to do so was within the reform societies.

Harwood had joined the Society for Constitutional Information a year before Sharp, and both had been nominated to membership by John Horne Tooke, who linked the tradition of "Wilkes and Liberty" with the radicalism of the 1790s. A man whose career abounded in contradictions—a clergyman without a vocation, a radical who ridiculed Tom Paine and allowed himself to be returned from the rotten borough of Old Sarum, a philologist convicted for libel, a lawyer by inclination and ability but refused admission to the bar—Horne Tooke was above all a brilliant conversationalist whose Sunday dinners at Wimbledon attracted some of the most interesting men and women of the age. William Hazlitt said, "His intellect was like a bow of polished steel, from which he shot sharp-pointed poisoned arrows at his friends in private, at his enemies in public." At Wimbledon, "he sat like a king at his own table, and gave law to his guests—and to the world!"[28]

Harwood was introduced to this extraordinary, if ultimately superficial man by his uncle, William Tooke of Purley, a rich, retired, politically sensitive business man whose last name John Horne adopted in 1782 in anticipation of becoming his heir. As a young man, William Tooke had resolved that upon making fifty thousand pounds he would turn his back on commerce, a resolution he kept. Tooke followed the usual pattern of moving to the country to enjoy the fortune he had made. He purchased the estate of Purley, near Croydon, to which John Horne Tooke frequently repaired for the pleasure of riding on the Downs in the morning and playing cards in the evening, and which he immortalized in the title of his best known work, *The Diversions of Purley*. Although William Tooke supported radical causes with his time as well as his money—he backed the fortunes of Wilkes until his break with Horne Tooke and was treasurer of the Bill of Rights Society—he did not allow scruple to interfere with a profitable financial venture. When he and an associate invested money in a West Indian plantation, they had to endure Horne Tooke's gasp of outrage over the fact "that two such great sticklers for liberty, should buy and sell their fellow creatures!" [29]

The older man valued Horne Tooke's personal advice, agreed with his political views, and basked in the reflected glow of his brilliance. As time passed, however, he grew more and more uneasy under his protégé's careless familiarity, which probably had its origins in Horne Tooke's desire to show his independence from a man whom all the world knew had given him such great expectations. Their relationship deteriorated to the point that in 1788 William Tooke threatened to leave his fortune to his nephew William Tooke Harwood. This was the first time that Horne Tooke had heard of Harwood and he immediately insisted that the young man be produced and the matter settled. An amicable arrangement resulted whereby it was agreed that Harwood and Horne Tooke would be made joint heirs in the estate. [30]

William Tooke Harwood was from Norwich, as was William Godwin. Like Sheffield, Norwich enjoyed great prestige in the radical movement because of the early and lasting commitment of its reform societies. Harwood knew many of those active in the Norwich circle but, undoubtedly because of his unusual relationship with Horne Tooke, entered the reform movement in London and never became a member of a Norwich society. [31] Harwood and Horne Tooke became intimate friends. At Horne Tooke's trial, Harwood said that he was in the habit of visiting him "frequently, from day to day." [32] Two others who often dined at Horne Tooke's table and with whom Harwood was on close personal terms were William Godwin and Thomas Holcroft. In 1796, Harwood married Thomas Holcroft's eldest daughter, Ann. [33]

It seems at least arguable that Holcroft and Godwin reinforced or perhaps even inspired Harwood's millenarian beliefs, although both were avowed atheists. First of all, the two men themselves enjoyed a virtually symbiotic relationship. Holcroft met Godwin sometime around 1787 [34] and remained his closest friend for almost twenty years. [35] They had a profound influence on each other. A biographer of Godwin has said their relationship "quickened Holcroft's nascent republicanism and intensified Godwin's religious scepticism." [36] Godwin, the former Sandemanian minister, himself wrote, "In my thirty-first year I became acquainted with Mr. Thomas Holcroft, and it was probably in consequence of our mutual conversations that I became two years after an unbeliever, and in my thirty-sixth year an atheist." Their rapport matured to the point that Godwin said, ". . . the principles afterwards developed in my Political Justice . . . were the almost constant topic of conversation between Holcroft and myself." [37] Second, in *Political Justice*, the testament of the middle-class reform societies, Godwin (and Holcroft) asserted that, once the truth was made known and communicated, men would have it in their power to bring about a new world. Truth, if only it was listened to, would reveal the idiocy of kings and priests being exalted over their equals. Indeed, everything that stood between humans and the prospect of their perfection was susceptible to its inexorable erosion. Leslie Stephen once wrote, "Godwin believes as firmly as any early Christian in the speedy revelation of a new Jerusalem, four-square and perfect in its plan." [38]

No English radical was more committed to this utopian vision than Holcroft. He exclaimed to Godwin after helping *The Rights of Man* through the press, "Hey for the New Jerusalem! The millennium! And peace and eternal beatitude be unto the soul of Thomas Paine." [39] Hazlitt said that Holcroft "was among the foremost and most ardent of those who indulged their imaginations in contemplating such an Utopian or ideal state of society." He described the world that lay within his friend's dreams: "He believed that wars, bloodshed, and national animosities, would cease; that peace and goodwill would reign among men; . . . every man would be a brother . . . that laws and punishments would cease with the cause that produces them, the commission of crime . . . all would cheerfully labour for the good of all." In Holcroft's utopia, "the labour . . . requisite to produce the necessaries of life, would be equally divided among the members of such a community, and the remainder of their time would be spent in the pursuit of science, in the cultivation of the noblest arts, and in the most refined social and intellectual enjoyments." Hazlitt hit a good deal closer to the truth than he realized when in concluding his comments on the dramatist's "wild and visionary" schemes he said that Holcroft should be no more persecuted for his fantasies than someone who had "written a treatise on the Millennium." [40]

In this compelling vision of an earthly millennium, we find a conjunction between the aspirations of the infidel (or, more accurately, the atheist) and the millenarian, between Godwin and Holcroft, on the one hand, and Harwood and Sharp, on the other. This is more than coincidental. There is evidence of a number of personal encounters during these years among the four men which suggests, perhaps, an acknowledged sympathy of purpose. Harwood and Sharp (and, of course, Holcroft) appear frequently in Godwin's diary, beginning in the fall of

1792—Sharp possibly fifty-nine times and Harwood, either he or his wife individually or the two of them together, no fewer than eighty-seven times.[41]

Several entries offer intriguing evidence linking infidels and millenarians together in radicalism. On May 14, 1791, Godwin went to dinner at the home of Brand Hollis, another of the fourteen original members of the Society for Constitutional Information, and wrote afterward: "Scott a believer in spiritual intercourses lends Paine £40, to aid the publication of his pamphlet." This *may* have been John Scott, a lawyer, who was a member of the S.C.I. Possibly, this is the Scott, also a lawyer, who later became a leading Southcottian. The following year, on December 23, 1792, ten months after Sharp became a member of the S.C.I., Godwin noted, "Dine at H. Tooke's, with Sharpe engraver, & Jardine, talk of ideas & revolutions." Two years later on March 13, 1794, he and his dinner companions joined in "talk of politics & religion." Until 1799, it must be assumed that the "Towers" who appears in his diary is usually Dr. Towers, but after the reformer's death that year, the "Towers" mentioned could either be the Reverend Joseph Lomas Towers or a "Capt. Towers." If it is the Reverend Towers, then we have a link between the authors of *Illustrations of Prophecy* and the *Principles of Political Justice*.

Godwin had a strong belief in the futility of political associations but Sharp, Holcroft, and Harwood made common cause in the Society for Constitutional Information. The crown brought forth the minutes of fifty-nine meetings of the S.C.I. as evidence in the state trials of Thomas Hardy and John Horne Tooke in 1794. They reveal that Harwood, although at the time commanding a troop in the ninth regiment of dragoons, attended twenty-three of the meetings. Sharp can positively be identified at twenty-two; a high degree of probability exists that he is frequently the "Mr. Sharp[e]" present on twenty-two other occasions. The attendance sometimes dropped as low as five or six at the meetings, but the average was about ten. The regular presence of at least two millenarians in that number suggests the possibility that men of similar views may have been at least as well represented in the rank and file of the radical societies.[42]

The minutes of the S.C.I. show how deeply committed Harwood was to the radical movement. Probably because of the Norwich background, his name frequently appears in connection with the provincial reform societies. He was chairman of the meeting on March 23, 1792, when the society received from Sheffield a ringing endorsement of Paine's *The Rights of Man* as well as an expression of gratitude to John Horne

Tooke "for his meritorious support of our lawful privileges, as a firm advocate of our natural and just rights." In answer, Harwood signed a minute to his "brothers, and fellow-labourers in the same cause," in which he reaffirmed "that the people of this country are not, as Mr. Burke terms them, *Swine*; but rational beings, better qualified to separate truth from error than himself, possessing more honesty, and less craft." He was also in attendance on May 11, 1792, when the society approved an address hailing the Jacobins as "brothers" and expressing the belief that the new friendship between Frenchmen and Englishmen was the "offspring of no earthly court."[43]

Because of his relationship with Horne Tooke, Harwood was questioned closely at his trial in 1795 about the reformer's political views. He testified that his friend had a profound regard for the king, Lords, and Commons but believed that the House of Commons was badly in need of reform. Harwood said that Horne Tooke particularly abhorred the borough mongers. As a remedy, Horne Tooke proposed "to a great number of friends, that they should all stand for the different rotten boroughs, and that each should petition against the members who might be supposed to have brought the original interest of it. I proposed myself to be one, I believe Mr. Maxwell was another, Mr. Walker, of Manchester, another, and I believe there were some others who were very desirous of doing it; he said, by this means only we could ever expect a reform; and it was only by such a reform that we could ever expect any good to this country."[44]

Thus, Harwood is a link in the radical coalition's joining the infidel and the millenarian, each of whom drew on the rich imagery of the Bible to articulate his political objectives in the 1790s, although with widely differing motives. In William Sharp and his friend and fellow engraver William Blake, we will see two more millenarians committed to reform politics. But, also, by inquiring into their political and religious attitudes, we will be able to better understand why the alliance between the infidels and millenarians fell apart, leading Sharp, Harwood, and possibly many others, ultimately, into the Southcottian movement.

WILLIAM SHARP

William Sharp, like his contemporaries William Blake and Thomas Bewick, is yet another in the tradition of radical engravers which includes W. J. Linton and Walter Crane.[45] Sharp was born in London in 1749, the son of a gunmaker. His father recognized his precocious ability and apprenticed him to an engraver of fire arms. After his apprenticeship expired, he was able to establish himself independently, although his training had been inadequate for the career he desired. As his biographer, W. S. Baker, points out, "he may be classed among those who have worked themselves into distinction by their native powers of observation, perseverance and industry." Because he escaped the inhibiting influence of a school of engraving and had to learn for himself the subtleties of his craft, "he was the founder of his own style, the intelligent pupil of his own labor and experience." His first success was an engraving of a painting by Benjamin West, *Alfred the Great, dividing his loaf with the Pilgrim*, which was published in 1782. By 1787, an inheritance from his brother enabled him to begin publishing his own work, a step he was moved to take because of dissatisfaction with his fees from the print dealers. In 1814 his fame as an engraver was recognized by the Imperial Academy of Vienna and the Royal Academy of Bavaria, both of which elected him a member. He refused Sir Joshua Reynolds' invitation to become an associate engraver of the Royal Academy, however, because of the stigma which Sharp and all engravers felt at their ineligibility to become royal academicians.[46] Blake summarized this feeling of bitterness and hostility:

Having spent the Vigour of my Youth & Genius under the Opression of Sr. Joshua & his Gang of Cunning Hired Knaves Without Employment & as much as could possibly be Without Bread, The Reader must Expect to Read in all my Remarks on these Books [Reynolds' Discourses] Nothing but Indignation & Resentment. While Sr. Joshua was rolling in Riches, Barry was Poor & Unemploy'd except by his own Energy; Mortimer was call'd a Madman, & only Portrait Painting applauded & rewarded by the Rich & Great. Reynolds & Gainsborough Blotted & Blurred one against the other & Divided all the English World between them. Fuseli, Indignant, almost hid himself. I am hid.[47]

Sharp and Blake were products of the same restless milieu of London artisans and came in contact with each other many times over the years. David Erdman has suggested a parallel between the evolution of Sharp's career and "Blake's progression from Wilkite patriotism in the 1770s to humanitarian Christianity in the late 1780s to political radicalism in the 1790s."[48] Certainly it is clear that Blake was not a fantastic anomaly but that he sprang instead from a vital subculture, highly sensitive to the shocks of the contemporary world.[49] The one tantalizing hint we have that the poet's genius might have flowed into the same stream as that of Sharp is in the diary of Henry Crabb Robinson. On January 30, 1815, not long after Joanna's death, Robinson records a story he heard from John Flaxman that Sharp "endeavoured to make a convert of Blake the engraver [to Joanna Southcott], but . . . such men as Blake are not fond of playing the second fiddle—Hence Blake himself a seer of visions & a dreamer of dreams would not do homage to a rival claimant of the privilege of prophecy." [50]

A second friend who may have supplied information to Blake about Joanna was William Owen Pugh, the Welsh lexicographer who belonged to Joanna's inner circle of advisers, as did Sharp and Harwood. Robert Southey remembered, in 1830, that "my old acquaintance William Owen, now Owen Pugh, who, for love of his native tongue, composed a most laborious Welsh Dictionary, without the slightest remuneration for his labour, when he was in straitened circumstances, and has, since he became rich translated *Paradise Lost* into Welsh verse, found our Blake after the death of Joanna Southcote, one of whose four-and-twenty elders he was. Poor Owen found everything which he wished to find in the Bardic system, and there he found Blake's notions, and thus Blake and his wife were persuaded that his dreams were old patriarchial truths, long forgotten, and now revealed." [51] There is also a suggestion that Blake knew a third Southcottian, John Pye, another engraver who rose to prominence in the London Southcottian church after Joanna's death. [52]

Blake's short poem "On the Virginity of the Virgin Mary & Johanna Southcott" is the one tangible piece of evidence of his interest and it has been characteristically misinterpreted. He wrote:

> Whate'er is done to her she cannot know,
> And if you'll ask her she will swear it so.
> Whether 'tis good or evil none's to blame:
> No one can take the pride, no one the shame. [53]

John Gordon Davies argues that Blake's poem is proof of his disbelief in the Virgin Birth because the poet linked the virginity of Mary with that of Joanna whose announced pregnancy by the Holy Spirit ended so lamentably. [54] In fact, Blake wrote this quatrain sometime between 1800 and 1803, at least eleven years before Joanna's "pregnancy." It is more plausible that the four lines exemplify Blake's complete tolerance of spiritual communications, no matter how *outré*. Sharp may even have approached the poet about Joanna with a certain confidence, relying on knowledge of his friend gained over thirty-five years. He undoubtedly knew of his fellow Southcottian Owen Pugh's influence on Blake and of Blake's own interest in the prophetess, which extended over a ten-year period (i.e., from the date of the poem).

If Blake listened, he was not gullible. The poet would have required support for the prophetess' claims. He asked in *Milton* if "Whitefield & Westley" were prophets or "were they Idiots or Madmen?" There was one test, "shew us Miracles!" [55] It is true that the miracle Blake required was not something marvelous, the "arbitrary command of the agent upon the patient."[56] The ones which Whitefield and Wesley performed were those of "men who devote Their life's whole comfort to intire scorn & injury & death." And the poet asked, "Can you have greater Miracles than these?"[57] But Blake declared that "Jesus could not do miracles where unbelief hindered, hence we must conclude that the man who holds miracles to be ceased puts it out of his own power to ever witness one."[58] For this reason, Blake may have been at least neutral toward Joanna's claims until they were either proved or disproved. Even if no miracle was forthcoming and Shiloh was not born in 1814 (although Sharp believed that a spiritual birth took place), Blake would not have ridiculed her experience. He wrote in 1788, "No man was ever truly superstitious who was not truly religious as far as he knew," and "True superstition is ignorant honesty & this is beloved of god and man."[59]

Sharp, like Blake, was a visionary. At a dinner given by Thomas Holcroft, Crabb Robinson noted that Sharp asked his host to come out of the room and then proceeded to tell him that Bonaparte's life had been spared in a battle the previous day in Germany. He had received the communication the night before "by authority."[60] Sharp also knew "from authority" that Flaxman was from the "seed of Abraham" and had a great role to play in the accomplishment of Richard Brothers' mission to restore the Jews to the Holy Land.[61] Holcroft told of a third incident, in 1798: "Last summer [Sharp] had retired to a lonely place near or at Kilburn; and there he himself had been absolutely favoured with a revelation, communicating to him personally, beyond all doubt, the revolutions that are immediately to happen."[62]

A number of enterprises bound Blake and Sharp together in the last decade of the century. They both subscribed to Jacob Duché's *Discourses on Various Subjects*, which appeared in 1779. Duché had inquired into the "mysticism of Jacob Behmen and William Law" and became "interested in the visions of Swedenborg" a few years after the publication of the *Discourses*.[63] Sharp engraved the plates for the work and even paid twelve pounds of the printing expenses.[64] Blake and Sharp were associated in several engraving projects—Lavater's *Physiognomy* in 1789, Johnson's Milton in 1791,[65] and, abortively, a new edition of Hume's *History of England*.[66] The two of them worked under Henry Fuseli's supervision on the Milton project. The painter wrote to a friend in Liverpool on May 29, 1792:

Sharp has had his picture (the picture itself, not a Copy) nearly these two months and is busy in the aquafortis part of both plates. We have contrived a roller for him from the design of Mr. [Tom] Paine, who is a Mechanic as well as a Demogorgon, to enable him to place it, for it is 13 feet high by a width of 10; & though his house is larger than those of most Engravers it was too high to enter any of his rooms. . . . Of the Second Number Adam & Eve observed by Satan; and Satan taking his flight upwards from chaos which is of the same dimensions with Sharp's and intended for Blake, are much advanced; and upon the whole Sketches of a number of Subjects are ready and wait for execution on Canvas.[67]

Finally, the names of both Sharp and Blake appeared on a testimonial to celebrate the merits of a new device to prevent forgeries of banknotes.[68]

The relationship between the two men seems to have been more than a casual one. Erdman suggests that Sharp "may have stimulated Blake's interest in the New Church [of Swedenborg]" and "*may* in this period have encouraged his interest in Paine and Barlow."[69] Possibly it was John Flaxman, a close friend of both, instead of Sharp who first interested Blake in the New Church. Both Sharp and Flaxman were members of "the Theosophical Society, instituted for the Purpose of promoting the Heavenly Doctrines of the New Jerusalem by translating, printing, and publishing the Theological Writings of the Honourable Emmanuel Swedenborg."[70] As for Blake's relationship with Paine, it is more indirect than it once seemed. No longer is it possible to believe the attractive story that the poet's warning enabled Paine to leave for France twenty minutes ahead of the authorities, although the tale still has its adherents.[71] On the other hand, association with Sharp could well have put Blake in contact with the reformer, for Paine and Sharp had both professional and political contacts with each other.

Fuseli, Blake's close friend, stands witness of one encounter between the two men: "Paine was an excellent mechanic,"[72] the painter recalled, and "when Sharpe was about to engrave my picture of 'The Contest of Satan, Sin, and Death' [late in 1790], he employed a carpenter to construct a roller to raise or [lower it] at pleasure; in this, after several ineffectual attempts, he did not succeed to the expectations of Sharpe, who mentioned the circumstance in the hearing of Paine; he instantly offered his services, and set to work upon it, and soon accomplished all, and indeed more than the engraver had anticipated."[73] It seems unlikely that Paine would perform an apparently onerous chore for a random acquaintance.

In addition, Sharp and Paine both belonged to the Society for Constitutional Information. On several occasions, the minutebooks of the society reveal that they attended meetings together at the Crown and Anchor.[74] Possibly, the engraver's membership in a committee to investigate

Paine's prosecution even forms the kernel of reality in the famous story about Blake and Paine.[75]

Therefore, Sharp could well have brought Blake into the radical ambience which Paine and Barlow helped to create and which suffuses so much of Blake's poetry. Blake prided himself on being a "Liberty Boy,"[76] certain that "Liberty" was "the charter'd right of Englishmen"[77] and was being jeopardized by a corrupt government. Gilchrist called him "an ardent member of the New School, a vehement republican and sympathizer with the Revolution, hater and contemner of kings and kingcraft."[78] This certainly parallels Crabb Robinson's description of Sharp. The diarist called the engraver "a violent Jacobin and an extreme and passionate partisan of the Republicans."[79]

The development of Sharp's political attitudes is clearly revealed in his work. In 1780, beneath a liberty cap and a "Don't Tread on Me" rattlesnake, he engraved a portrait of George Washington, "Commander in Chief of ye armies of ye United States of America." Two years later, he engraved "Alfred the Great" after Benjamin West's painting which reminds of the obsession of the preindustrial radical movement with the "lost rights" enjoyed by Englishmen under Alfred. In 1782,[80] Thomas Stothard designed and Sharp engraved the "Declaration of Rights" on a plate inscribed to the Society for Constitutional Information.[81] In 1791, Sharp published as well as engraved a portrait of Thomas Erskine, the defender of Hardy and Horne Tooke in 1794, and a fellow member of the Society of Friends of the People.[82] In the thirteen-month period from April 20, 1793, until May 14, 1794 (Sharp was one of the eleven who attended the last meeting of the S.C.I. on May 9, 1794),[83] he engraved two portraits of Paine from George Romney's painting; one of Thomas Walker, the founder of the Manchester Constitutional Society who was tried for treason in April 1794 at the Lancaster assizes; and one of Daniel Eaton, tried for selling Part II of *The Rights of Man* in 1793 and for alleged libel of George III a year later.[84]

Unlike Blake, Sharp did not limit his radicalism to a few personal gestures and his art. Horne Tooke introduced him to the Society for Constitutional Information. Their friendship began when Horne Tooke asked the engraver to teach his craft to his two daughters at Wimbledon. Sharp stayed at Horne Tooke's house "very constantly" in the summer, working on his own projects and instructing his two students.[85] Sharp, along with reformer Major Cartwright, Dr. Towers, and a few others, belonged to the Society of Friends of the People as well as the S.C.I. The former was the most moderate of the various London reform societies in the 1790s, its membership reaching from the Earl of Lauderdale and Charles Grey at its upper end to Sharp, "the celebrated engraver," at its lower,[86] and the only one that links directly with the Reform Bill movement of the 1830s. It was curious company for a "violent Jacobin" to keep.

At the trial of Horne Tooke in 1794, Vicary Gibbs, Erskine's lieutenant, underlined Sharp's role in the Society for Constitutional Information:

Consider who M. Sharpe is; he is a member of the Constitutional Society; in that character he must have known a great deal of the proceedings of that society: he was a member of the committee of conference; in that character he must have known all that passed at the meeting of the delegates from the two societies: he was a member of the committee of co-operation; in that character he must have known all that had passed in that committee, which was to . . . be the immediate agent for perfecting the treasonable purposes which existed in the minds of the rest [i.e., the prosecution's case]—not only of perfecting the treasonable purposes, but he is stated in the indictment to be one of those with whom Mr. Tooke and the others conspired to bring about the deposition of the King.

In fact, it was not at all clear why Sharp was not being tried for treason alongside Horne Tooke, Hardy, Holcroft, and the nine others. The solicitor general asserted that the Committee of Correspondence was responsible for the management of the S.C.I. Of its six members, only Sharp and John Pearson escaped being indicted for high treason. Gibbs said, "Certainly everything that passed, he knew, and certainly none of the others could be traitors if Mr. Sharpe was not."[87]

Sharp was compromised the most by his membership in a delegation to the London Corresponding Society which met on April 11, 1794, at John Thelwall's house to publish its resolutions concerning the prospect of a British Convention. In calmer times such a gathering might possibly have been acceptable as an extraparliamentary pressure group, but in 1794 the word *convention* inevitably conjured up the specter of the National Convention in France. Not long after the meeting, the grand jury returned a true bill against the four members from the Society for Constitutional Information who served with Sharp on the committee, Jeremiah Joyce, Thomas Wardle, Stewart Kyd, and Thomas Holcroft.[88]

An incident occurring a year before throws yet more light on Sharp's place at the center of the radical experience in London and makes it even more surprising that he was not charged later. Three days before John Frost left to take up his commission to represent the S.C.I. at the French National Convention, he fell into an altercation as he was finishing dinner and was heard to say, "I am for equality; I see no reason why one man should be greater than another; I would have no King; and the Constitution of this country is a bad one."[89] After returning from

France, he was tried for sedition and convicted.[90] Upon his release, the *Oracle* reported that "*Citizen* William Sharp, the engraver" was one of those who put up £250 as a guarantee of Frost's good behavior.[91] When one considers that Blake, although "hid," never made much more than £100 a year as an engraver and "sometimes" as little as £50,[92] this seems to have been a remarkable personal commitment on Sharp's part.[93]

The last great moment in the fourteen-year history of the Society for Constitutional Information was its anniversary dinner on May 2, 1794, at the Crown and Anchor. Some three hundred gathered to listen to speeches, sing revolutionary songs, and make perfervid toasts. In the course of the dinner and between toasts a band played "Çà Ira," the "Carmagnol," the "Marsellois March," the "Democrat," "and a new piece of music, called the 'FREE CONSTITUTION.'" Sharp was one of thirteen stewards who composed the toasts, which received "unbounded applause." The first was to "THE RIGHTS OF MAN," then came "A Free Constitution," "The Swine of England, the Rabble of Scotland, and the Wretches of Ireland,"[94] "Equal Laws and Liberty," "May Despotism be trodden under the Hoofs of the Swinish Multitude," "THE ARMIES CONTENDING FOR LIBERTY," "Wisdom, Firmness, and Unanimity to all the Patriotic Societies in Great Britain," and "To the reign of Peace and Liberty." Others were to "That steady Friend to Liberty, John Horne Tooke," and, of course, "Thomas Paine."[95]

The following Friday, May 9, the S.C.I. met unknowingly for the final time. Sharp, Horne Tooke, and nine others attended and read Thomas Muir's letter written on the *Surprise*, the last item recorded in the minutebooks of the society. Muir had been convicted by a Scottish court and was on his way to Australia when he composed his letter. Addressing it "to the Members of the Society for Constitutional Information in London," he said that it "is an object of high consolation to my mind" that "the spirit of Freedom, is not extinguished, but still retains its former Energy in defiance of the Artifices and of the violence of Despotism."[96]

At noon on the next Friday, Horne Tooke found himself in the coils of that same despotism. Sharp fared better in that he was not imprisoned. Horne Tooke wrote in his diary for June 7, 1794, "Sharp is still in custody at his own house."[97] An incident occurred at Sharp's which may have caused Holcroft's arrest. While under surveillance at his home, Holcroft paid the engraver a visit which resulted in an altercation between himself and Sharp's guard, who thought the writer was attempting to help his friend escape. The guard was doubled and shortly afterward Holcroft indicted.[98]

The Privy Council interviewed Sharp several times. The reported results of the interrogations were markedly contradictory. On one occasion, Sharp was supposed to have interrupted to ask Pitt and Dundas and their colleagues if they would like to subscribe to a work which Horne Tooke intended to undertake. Sharp's biographer, W. S. Baker, said, "A hearty laugh at the singularity of the proposal ensued, and he was soon after liberated." Baker also said, however, that Sharp had been caught "dabbling a little (it could be no more) in the politics of Thomas Paine and Horne Tooke."[99] In fact, Baker demonstrates no knowledge of the engraver's political activities. Horne Tooke heard an account of another interrogation of Sharp by the Privy Council which had a considerably different tone. He wrote in his diary: "Sunday, June 22 [1794] Mr. Pitt at Privy Council quarrelled last week with Mr. W. H. Sharp. Sharp words were passed on both sides. Reeves[100] said—'Well we can do without his evidence. Let him be sent to prison, & hanged with the rest of them in the Tower.' Mr. Pitt ordered him to be sent to the Tower. Lord Grenville opposed it."[101]

With the witch hunt for the radicals in full cry, the Privy Council records actually reveal that Sharp chose to play neither the buffoon nor the hero in such perilous circumstances. He constantly skirted the questions asked him by pleading forgetfulness or saying that he had left the meeting early the night on which some controversial piece of business had taken place. When he could be pinned down, the engraver said that he had not supported the convention held in Scotland. As to his membership on the committee which met with the L.C.S. delegates, he argued that he had been selected only because of his friendship with Horne Tooke. Sharp admitted that in correspondence he and Horne Tooke addressed each other as "*Citizen*" but he felt this was innocent enough, adding that he disapproved of "French Equality" as well as "the Idea of a Convention." Sharp informed the council that "many" supported the egalitarian principles of the French Revolution, naming Holcroft as one. As evidence, Sharp said that the dramatist believed that "no Man should have a Coach till he was grown old." The engraver remarked he was "afraid" of those "who wanted to overset everything," and that he and Horne Tooke were "denounced" by "the violent members" for not concurring "in these Bold measures." Sharp stretched the credulity of his examiners too far when he told them that he had approved the playing of "Ça Ira" at the banquet only because it was said that an English regiment had charged the French to that tune. The Privy Council admonished Sharp that when he returned for further questioning he should "speak the whole truth openly[,] fairly[,] and candidly, not disguising and endeavouring to mislead by giving colour to words, as he had just done on expressing his approbation of Ça Ira, as if it was a question of music, and not of political sentiment." They might well have repeated the admonition at another interview when Sharp was asked what he understood by the toast "The Armies of Europe contending for Liberty." The engraver replied that he believed it referred to the Polish Revolution, which he "liked," and certainly did not refer to the French armies, which he admitted lamely, "He sometimes thought ill of . . . , sometimes well." [102]

When called to testify at Horne Tooke's trial, Sharp said that the purpose of the S.C.I. was parliamentary reform, and force had never been discussed as a possible means of achieving it. [103] The engraver's political views coincided with those of the society, according to Thomas Symonds, who knew Sharp "very well." [104] Also, Sharp had signed the Declaration of the Friends of the People of April 11, 1792, which had been read into the testimony at Hardy's trial. It stated that "the persons who have signed their names to this agreement, think, that these two fundamental measures"—free elections and more equal representation and shorter parliaments—"will furnish the power and the means of correcting the abuses, which appear to them to have arisen from a neglect of the acknowledged principles of the constitution, and of accomplishing those subordinate objects of reform, which they deem to be essential to the liberties of the people, and to the good government of the kingdom." Like Horne Tooke, Sharp seemed to believe that "every thing would be right" if parliamentary reform were obtained. [105]

The jury required just eight minutes to acquit Horne Tooke. His acquittal, following that of Hardy, showed the prosecution how untenable were its ambitions. [106] The government, however, had clearly revealed the seriousness of its intentions to crush the reformers. Nevertheless, the radical movement continued to make itself vigorously felt between the State Trials and the Two Acts and, afterward, more fitfully until it went underground to reemerge later at a more congenial time. But for many, probably including Sharp and Harwood, active participation in radical politics had ceased.

The question to be answered is where did the millenarian strand lead once it had disentangled itself from the reform movement. At his trial, Horne Tooke asked the engraver, "I believe you have some peculiar ways of thinking of religion of your own?" To which Sharp replied simply, "I have my own ways." [107] Again, Sharp's work offers us a clue to his thinking. On May 14, 1794, two days before Horne Tooke's arrest, Sharp's engraving of a portrait of Daniel Eaton appeared. A few months after the trials, on April 16, 1795, Sharp unveiled a portrait of "RICHARD BROTHERS, PRINCE OF THE HEBREWS." In the margin of the engraving appeared the words "Fully believing this to be the man whom God has appointed; I engrave his likeness, [signed] William Sharp." [108] The faces of the two men stand juxtaposed, one the radical bookseller and the other a half-pay naval lieutenant turned prophet, who called himself the "Nephew of the Almighty." Between the two lay the trauma of the State Trials and the appearance of Brothers' first book, *Revealed Knowledge*.

VII

Joanna's Herald

A CHOSEN PERSON

The Reverend Joseph Lomas Towers can help us understand why a millenarian could, at least at first, imagine a powerful ally in the reform societies. But Towers' work, although offering a map to the disoriented in a complex and troubled time, made no claim to divine inspiration. Millenarians could see the hieroglyphs of their age—political revolution, high prices, and a variety of natural catastrophes—dissolve into meanings which might be quickly and passionately grasped. This new or more sharply focused understanding, however, only positioned them for the start of their journey to the New Jerusalem. Sooner or later God would have to designate a leader to conduct them on their way. As one distressed soul said: "If religion is essential to the happiness of all mankind it is contrary to every principle of divine justice and goodness, that we should ever be left without some chosen guide in paths of mystery and perplexity, where our eternal salvation depends on the clearest knowledge of divine promise and prophesy." As a result, mankind could expect at a time that "is now pregnant with the greatest events in politics and religion" to look for "some chosen person."[1]

In 1794, Richard Brothers published a book which claimed that he was in possession of "revealed knowledge" given to him by God which would allow him to play the long looked for role. Within the next months he was to storm the popular world with prophecies and explanations of events which would suggest to many the seamless relationship between religion and politics. As a result, Brothers, more than any other single individual, would be responsible for the fusing of radical politics and millenarian beliefs into one articulate whole. The effect was sufficiently powerful that on March 4, 1795, orders were issued for his arrest on charges of "treasonable activities."

Six years before these events, Brothers was a naval lieutenant on half-pay who had come to the decision that a military career and the Christian life were incompatible, refusing even to draw his small entitlement because it required him to swear loyalty to the crown and to acknowledge the king as his sovereign lord. The former stipulation would have compelled him to violate the biblical injunction "Swear not at all" and the latter, to admit his absolute fealty to an earthly monarch. Unable to support himself, he was committed to a workhouse in London until his affairs were untangled. In 1792 he warned the government of the dangers of English involvement in the impending war between France and Austria and Prussia. According to Brothers, the opening stages of the struggle between revolutionary France and her enemies were, in fact, the beginning of the fulfillment of the book of Daniel. Unsettled both by the lack of response to his pronouncements and a stay in debtor's prison, he decided to give up prophecy and leave the country. He departed for Bristol on foot but never arrived. Brothers remembered, "God, by his power, stopped the action of every joint and limb, and turned me feelingly around . . . ; commanding me, at the same instant, to return and wait his proper time." He was soon to announce he was "Nephew of the Almighty," the divinely appointed herald of a great and mighty change which was to convulse the world. This change was to include the restoration of the Hebrews to the Promised Land. At the time of the diaspora, according to Brothers, ten of the twelve tribes had come to England where they had intermarried and surrendered their identities. Brothers would restore these "invisible" Jews to their lost patrimony.[2]

Brothers' book *Revealed Knowledge* and subsequent publications outlined his message. The prophet charged that "all nations" faced God's wrath for two reasons, they were at war and condoned swearing. "There is no war in Heaven, neither is there any Swearing," he wrote, and these are "the two [principal] things which Christ, above all others, prohibits in the most positive terms." Signs of God's displeasure had come as early as January 1791 when thunder of unprecedented kind had been heard. "It roared through the streets, and made a noise over London like the falling of mountains of stone." This was the voice of the angel in the eighteenth chapter of Revelation, announcing the divine judgments which were to fall on the city. The date set was August 15, 1793. Because of God's love for His prophet, however, Brothers managed to save the Londoners, the inhabitants of Babylon, from the fate they so richly deserved. When retribution did come, though, "The dead will increase so fast and be in such prodigious numbers . . . , that the living will not be sufficient to bury them, but will leave the bodies exposed to the fowls of Heaven for meat."[3]

Shadowed by images of blood and destruction, Brothers' political views emerged. The revolutionary government of France had gained God's favor by its actions against the Roman Church.[4] With Louis XVI's death, as foretold in Daniel, the institution of the monarchy in France was ended forever, and this was to be but prologue to a "general fall of *European monarchy*."[5] The prophet addressed himself specifically to England's role in the Last Days. He asked, "Will England continue the war any longer against a people that has the judgment of God in their favour?" If the king and his government chose this path, then the consequences would be disastrous. Speaking as God's "nephew," Brothers said unhesitatingly that the deity "shall throw down [forever] the English Monarchy; and from the confusion it will make throughout the country, involve almost every family of wealth in beggary and death."[6] Brothers did not anticipate the destruction of the rich with pleasure, however. If anything, he was irremediably bourgeois in his views. Their wealth and power were necessary if the poor were to have employment and government was to be properly organized. That he was no leveler came clear when he wrote that those who believe "all property should be common and all men equal, the industrious and idle, the master and servant," are mistaken, adding, "how foolish and unjust, how unreasonable, and how absurd to imagine such a thing for a moment."[7]

Though he could reflect with pleasure on the fact of a republic in France and the prospect of the monarchy's end in England as well as other European states, this did not mean that Brothers endorsed a republican form of government or even that he was antimonarchist. Any polity that "was just in its conduct and promoted the welfare of its people" was acceptable. With this kind of conduct on the part of government, "the people cannot be slaves, and where due equality in law is observed in all cases, there can be no oppression."[8] The ultimate safeguard remained that whether republic or monarchy the real authority lay with God and, by delegation, Brothers. He wrote, "I embrace all governments, whether kingdoms, republics, or principalities." But they all must recognize "my power as the temporal representative of the Almighty."[9] It would be Brothers' special charge to lead the "invisible" Jews back to Palestine. Just as David's "obscurity" had proved no obstacle to his becoming ruler of the Jews, so Brothers believed that his anonymity would not be a barrier to his becoming "the visible Governor of the Jews."[10]

Despite his sympathy for the French republic, and indirect condemnation of the English government, Brothers disclaimed any connection with the radical societies. He said, "I have nothing to do with parties, politics, treasons, meetings, or associations of any kind whatever."[11] According to the prophet, he led a retired life so that he could stay away from "the temptation of political discussion."[12] Years later he bitterly declared, "I have never joined with any political meeting, club, society, or religious sect; I never knew any such [distinctions] against the existing form of government, nor would I be acquainted with any such people."[13]

This, however, was not an opinion shared by others. Eliza Williams, who appeared to have some familiarity with his neighborhood and the people who saw him, called Brothers "a frantic leveller, a miserable instrument of a desperate faction, who suggested his prophecies for him, disseminated them, and supported him."[14] In the view of many, the most that could be said in the prophet's defense was that he did not realize he was being used by the radicals. One of Brothers' interrogators granted that he might be "innocent" of Jacobin associations but "in the hands of crafty, ambitious, and designing men" he could become a dangerous instrument.[15] Contrary to his protestation, evidence existed that a lively traffic of people from all classes of society, including John Binns, a leading figure in the London Corresponding Society, pushed constantly against his doors.[16] One of his callers, George Coggan, echoed the prophet's indifference to governmental forms "so long as justice is distributed to all with an impartial hand" but then expressed doubt that this was being done in England. He realized the immense danger he had placed himself in by what, in the circumstances, amounted to intemperate criticism of the government. "At a time when warrants are issued, and mandates sent abroad, for the purpose of apprehending different persons, and committing them to prison, it may be considered the highest piece of folly, resulting from a checkered brain, or an imagination fired with enthusiastic zeal, to bring in my testimony, and inveigh against the conduct of Ministers. As to the principle from whence I conceive that, originates with GOD, and as to my conduct, I only conceive myself accountable to him alone." Coggan warned that if England did not stop thwarting God's will by opposing the French Republic that "ENGLAND itself may be a REPUBLIC too." He pleaded with the government, "Whoever abides by the Scriptures, and derive their political sentiments from thence, must conclude" that they were on a course charted for disaster.[17]

Coggan was prepared to risk prison for his convictions. So too must have been another supporter of the prophet who denounced the government for its prosecution of the leaders of the radical societies. "These virtuous and immaculate men," he thundered, "after having experienced an unparalleled series of oppression," were proved innocent by those "*unbiassed* by interest and authority." Pitt's government could not deceive itself that these were lonely voices, not when Brothers' books were "read with eagerness by all ranks of people, and all seem anxious to convince themselves of the reality of his mission."[18] What must have been genuinely shivering or, depending on one's viewpoint, exhilarating was the prospect of a popular rising on the order of the Gordon riots of fifteen years before. In this regard a follower warned of a self-indulgent and immoral society which had turned its back on the poor. Without food or clothes, "having scarcely a hogstye to dwell in, [they] cannot with all their industry acquire the common necessaries of life." This state of affairs could not, would not continue. "REMEMBER, *the time is at hand*, when the Lord will execute justice and judgments for all that are oppressed." [19]

NATHANIEL BRASSEY HALHED

To some, including Nathaniel Brassey Halhed, M.P. for Lymington, it seemed that the time may have come at the moment of Brothers' arrest on March 4, 1795. Taken into custody on charges of treason, within a few weeks Brothers found himself incarcerated as a lunatic in a private asylum from which he was not to emerge until 1806. Halhed was deeply concerned by the government's behavior, which he feared would only aid and abet "the purposes of injustice." Trembling at the possible effects, he remembered "the flame kindled by Mr. Wilkes about general warrants" and grew particularly gloomy over thoughts of the Gordon riots of 1780 which, he said, were "indelibly impressed on my memory." Anything which might lead to a "similar catastrophe" must be avoided. Yet the government was acting in a manner which could almost guarantee disorder. Its persecution of Brothers would unquestionably lead to an increase in his popularity. Halhed wrote, "In proportion as his case becomes known, it attracts *interest*." [20] However, no one did more to guarantee that Brothers' case *would* attract interest than Halhed himself who, in dramatic circumstances, ensured that Brothers' career would attain an extraordinary and wholly unexpected new prominence.

Halhed was a political figure of minor significance who had achieved reputation in India as a scholar and judge. While abroad he became a friend and ardent supporter of Warren Hastings. Endowed with a warm heart and capacious intellect, he was principled, learned, steadfast in his friendships, and an altogether attractive man. Halhed had been in the same form as Richard Sheridan at Harrow and the two became intimates, collaborating on a play, translating the love epistles of Aristaenetus, and even falling in love with the same woman. [21]

Halhed had long been interested in the study of prophecy. The son of one of his closest friends remembered that "the amount of European, as well as Asiatic lore, which he brought to bear upon these subjects, was immense, nor in a less degree was the ingenuity with which he applied it all."[22] He first became interested in Brothers' prophecies in January of 1795 and began visiting him on a regular basis throughout the winter and early spring. Nevertheless, few were prepared for the course of action he decided upon.

On Tuesday, March 31, 1795, Halhed rose in the House of Commons and spoke for three hours, denouncing the government's action against the prophet and, to the amazement of his listeners, expressing his own belief in Brothers' divine mission. At the beginning of his speech, he said he asked only for "a fair and patient hearing" and, particularly, to be acquitted of any charges of serving his own interests. His "new line of conduct" would, Halhed rightly claimed, only work against his interests. Firmly separating himself from the radicals, he affirmed he had "no sinister intention . . . [and] no intercourse with any men or set of men public or private, whose principles or whose actions have as far as I can judge tended to the detriment of my countrymen." He then got to the point of his speech, expressing his "very great surprise" that Brothers had been seized. He confessed surprise because he had been seeing the prophet regularly for two months and had never found "the slightest symptom that could indicate any bad designs." Nor was Brothers attempting to stir up the mob. Those who flocked to him were "persons of quality and fortune of both sexes" who would never have considered seeing him a single time, much less repeating a visit, "if they could have conceived that they were fostering, encouraging, aiding, and abetting a traitor." The only explanation for their otherwise indefensible action was that the authorities must have been in possession of some "peculiar information" of which he and the prophet's other visitors were unaware. If that was the case, then he submitted to the better judgment of the state. But he wished to be allowed to make a matter of public record what he knew about Brothers.[23]

Brothers, Halhed said, possessed a blameless and sensible character which he and others who knew him, including his navy colleagues, could vouch for. But if the prophet could be vindicated as a private man, what of his public character? To answer this required an examination of his two books. And, Halhed remarked, here the point of friction appeared. "The man was very well apart from his pen and ink, but when he mounted on the Pegasus of Prophecy, he has galloped over all our heads." But *what* of these writings, he asked? Were they any more than an interpretation of scripture, and, if so, in a free nation why did this present a difficulty if the interpretations were "in perfect submission to the laws and police of the country"? England, more than any other state, abounded in commentaries on the prophetic books of the Bible. Some commentators saw "the mysterious and hidden allusions" applying to Rome, or Turkey, or France, or perhaps Germany or Poland. "But if one solitary individual [happens] to pitch on Great Britain as the destined spot for the elucidation of these enigmatical predictions, surely it is not unreasonable that he should request cool and dispassionate investigation of the grounds of his assertion before you condemn him to fire and faggot." Halhed then requested the House to indulge him further while he looked closely at the passage which (he had heard) had caused Brothers' arrest. He then read to an absolutely hushed assembly Brothers' offending words, "The Lord God commands me to say to you, George the Third, King of England, that immediately on my being revealed in London to the Hebrews, as their Prince, and to all nations as their Governor, your Crown must be delivered up to me, that all your power and authority may cease." But Halhed asked his colleagues to compare this with the savage political attacks of the time. "We see greater and more scandalous liberties taken every day with his Majesty in pamphlets, newspapers, print-shops, etc." He reminded his hearers that the king's resignation was contingent on Brothers being "revealed to the people of London." Casting himself as another Moses, the prophet declared the second "revelation" would be similar to the first. As in the case of Moses, a staff would change into a serpent and then return to its original form. If such a "miracle" was the condition which had to be met before the king delivered up his crown and would never occur, as undoubtedly the administration believed, why was Brothers being persecuted? On the other hand, if the "miracle" did take place, then prison would hardly prove an obstacle to the uses God would make of His prophet. Either way the government acted unwisely by taking Brothers into custody.[24]

Up to this point in his speech, Halhed's appearance was that of a rational, discerning man of, as everyone knew, broad and ecumenical interests and with a keen eye for injustice. But could anyone in the world's greatest senate have been prepared for the last stages of Halhed's remarks? Referring to the prophecies generally, Halhed said, "as far as it has come to my knowledge" all that Brothers had predicted had either actually transpired or were in a state in which their completion was still possible. By acknowledging his belief in the prophet, he admitted that in the view of his friends he had condemned himself to "obloquy and disgrace." Nevertheless, he had done the right thing. His conversion to Brothers' cause came as a result of lengthy comparison of scriptures with the prophet's books. He invited his hearers to make the same comparison at the coming parliamentary recess. "This is all I ask."[25] Three weeks later he spoke again in the House and committed himself irrevocably. "I here, in the face of the House, adopt the whole of [Brothers' writings] as my own; I subscribe to every assertion in them, from the first to the last; I make myself a conscious, a willing accomplice to all the guilt contained in them." He then proceeded to compare the grounds of Brothers' arrest with those of the leaders of the radical societies. The House, he said, had been clearly informed by the administration of the basis on which the charges had been brought against Horne Tooke, Hardy, and the others. "The formation of, or connections with popular societies, formed on principles resembling those of the Jacobin Clubs in France, and deemed to be equally subversive of all regular government, were the ostensible plea of their imprisonment." "Here," he said, "is a ground to stand upon." To belong to such an organization "subjects a man to the suspicion of treasonable practices." But, Halhed asked, "was Mr. Brothers the institutor of any such club? Was he even a member of any club at all? I answer authoritatively— No." It still, however, might be charged that, whether members of a radical club or not, there were those susceptible to infection by the virus of treason. Oliver Cromwell had "subverted the Constitutional Government of the country" by his own preaching and that of his field preachers. "I answer," Halhed said, "Mr. Brothers was no preacher; he never assembled nor thought of assembling any congregation whatever."[26]

Yet, the government was also aware of Cromwell's example and understood better than Halhed that the prophet's influence might have dangerous effects. This was in significant measure due to Halhed himself, who had played an important role in adding mightily to Brothers' fame and, because of his own reputation, to his credibility. One government official expressed a widely held opinion when he said that Brothers "would have sunk into oblivion" if he had not been taken up "by an honourable gentleman, whose authority is of too much consequence to be overlooked, and whose writings might give celebrity to a character much inferior to that of the Lieutenant."[27]

Halhed had established to his satisfaction that Brothers should be taken seriously as a prophet, that he had been unjustly detained, and that he offered no threat to the government. On the last point, he proved manifestly mistaken. Evidence existed that the infidels were taking maximum advantage of Brothers to further their political purposes. The Duke of Portland received a letter from the mayor of Hastings which announced the appearance of a stranger suspected of circulating threatening letters and seditious handbills. He "is employ'd generally in reading Paine's 'Rights of Man,' Brother's 'Prophecies' . . . his conversation is extremely indecent in speaking of the King or Government and . . . he has taken infinite pains to mix with the soldiers . . . giving them money to drink &c."[28] One who offered an "argument in support

of infidelity" acknowledged Brothers' influence on the radical movement and bemoaned the divisiveness which had resulted. He said in a
sarcastic vein, Brothers' "system . . . connects religion and politics,
bloodshed and peace, famine and plenty, together, in a mass, to suit all
dispositions and inclinations. I have only to say to the chosen, PROMUL-
GATE, and to the infidel, BELIEVE; for King Richard Brothers is surely a
Democrat and a Prophet." He urged his fellow radicals to throw off the
"superstitious doctrines" which had beset their efforts to bring about
political reform.

But that our reformers and revolutionists, a great part of whom will not submit
to the supposed imposition of the mystery of a Trinity, or the existence of a
Saviour, should promulgate his doctrines, is not perhaps so surprising when we
perceive their motives. Notwithstanding he so closely blends religion and politics together, which is a thing they pretend so much to detest, and which should
be detested—notwithstanding he fulminates destruction to every vestige of Mo-
narchial Government, yet he would establish one more powerful than all others
collectively: they pretend to believe him, therefore; because the first part is so
consonant to their ideas, they would hazard the second—thinking, perhaps,
they might more easily cope with one. It is the desire of the most violent and ill
principled men to create distrust, disorder, and anarchy; and for that purpose, a
more proper instrument could not be found than Mr. Brothers; and I really
think he is that passive tool of some men of the above description, who would
"ride in the whirlwind / and direct the storm!"

He referred to Brothers' "insidious doctrine" which "under the pretended sanctity of his manners" and aided by "his specious reasoning
on scriptural causes for some late events," as well as "his pretensions to
inspiration, and his solutions of holy writ in predicting those events
which are hidden under the veil of futurity," had resulted in "many converts." Although this might appear a happy development to reformers,
in reality it was only a mare's nest, weakening and deflecting the efforts
of men like himself to bring about necessary political change. If Pitt and
his unreformed Parliament were to be combated in such perilous times,
men of courage and clear judgment were required. He wrote, "The endeavours of those men on whom Mr. Pitt and HIS House of Representa-
tives (I will not say, the People's) so abundantly lavish the appellation of
Jacobins that it is rung as the *tocsin* of terror all over the Kingdom, are
not to be put in the scale of competition with the exertions of Mr. Pitt,
in accelerating the subversions of the constitution of England." He appealed to the "good sense" of the radicals "to renounce those superstitious doctrines, which shew not your wisdom so much as your timid-
ity, and which tend to debase the spirit of men who would be free."

Finally, he encouraged his readers to be courageous and firm, perseverant and resolute "when tribulation arrives." [29]

There were others, though, who believed that the infidels were the ones weakening and misdirecting the radical movement and that only when their influence was removed would the Christian vision of a world transformed regain its integrity and power.

THE AGE OF REASON

Tom Paine's *Age of Reason* appeared for the first time in England in 1795. This event may have been the decisive influence on William Sharp's outlook. At this same time, a candidate was being recommended to the London Corresponding Society as "*A good Democrat and a Deist*," or additionally, "that he is no Christian." [30] Paine's book, the second part written while he was in a Paris prison, was a not particularly novel exercise in biblical criticism. It was written, however, with his peculiar energy and style. In attacking the Bible, and thus labeling the popular radical movement with infidelity, Paine estranged himself and all that he seemed to represent from a large body of radical opinion. Certainly Sharp reacted strongly against Paine's deism. In 1806, the engraver wrote a pamphlet entitled *An Answer to the World*, in which he defended his allegiance to Joanna and revealed irreconcilable differences between his position and that of his one-time colleague. Sharp was only too aware of the "alarming extent" to which infidelity had increased. "Not only the reality of a devil is universally denied; but the divinity of Jesus Christ is openly attacked." And yet, the engraver said, "he is considered as an *object of worship*, because he was a BETTER MAN than *others*." The contradiction seemed so apparent. How could the infidels admire a man for "purity of character" when by refusing to acknowledge his divine birth they stigmatized him as an imposter and Mary "a degraded woman." [31]

Sharp's views and those of Paine played in counterpoint to each other. Measured against Paine's contempt for the Bible was Sharp's belief that "the Bible is a divine collection of records on purpose to shew to man the effects of his fallen state, that in the end, from the fountain of all goodness, he may see also the *origin of evil and its end*." Sharp asked how could "any man, whether philosopher or atheist, If he has heart to reflect at all, suppose that all those events in the Bible can be inventions? or they are not true?" But such men were all around him. He had to gloomily admit "*there is scarcely faith to be found!*" Paine indicted the Bible as a long chronicle of cruelty and brutality. Sharp's reply was that "many infidels have blamed the Bible, in recording so much evil, instead of admiring it for its impartiality, in shewing what man has been, and what he is under the powers of darkness." Paine complained that the Bible authorized the despotism of kingcraft and priestcraft, whereas only a democratic republic in which humans governed themselves could be rationally defended. Sharp argued, indirectly, that the best proof for democracy was the biblical injunction that all must love each other as they love themselves. Those who turned away from God into deism or atheism only sought a pretext to reject this fundamental egalitarian precept and to elevate themselves above their fellow humans. The infidel, then, was at bottom antidemocratic.[32]

Sharp did not mention the name of his former colleague in his pamphlet, but Joanna had no reason to be as reticent. In *An Answer to Thomas Paine's Third Part of the Age of Reason*, Joanna focused Sharp's general charge, comparing Paine with Nebuchadnezzar "who wanted to impress upon the minds of the people an elevated sense of his greatness." This is impossible, she said, because "there is no elevated state, that man can set up in himself, but the Lord by his power can overthrow and prove that there is a God who dwelleth in the heavens above and amongst the inhabitants of the earth below." Speaking for Sharp probably as much as for herself, she said: "In Thomas Paine's 'Age of Reason,' I shall point out his folly, and the darkness of his understanding concerning the scriptures, knowing that his former publications hurt many weak minds, and have made many become atheists; because his reasoning is so artful, and wickedly contrived to make a mock of the scriptures, and which men, by carelessly reading, may not discern his folly; and therefore they are carried away with his pernicious doctrines."[33]

Joanna admitted that she had never read any of Paine's books before, although she had heard "much talk" of his various publications "and the injury they have done to many."[34] In the small Methodist community in Exeter, Joanna must have known and remembered Mr. Cross who had been so pious that he accompanied criminals to their executions in Heavitree, where Joanna once worked, but fell away from religion when he began reading Tom Paine. The historian of Exeter Methodism remembered, "The incendiary publications of Thomas Paine had kindled in his breast a strong desire for political change; and, as his republican zeal increased in warmth and fierceness, his religious ardour abated in the same proportion, until he became an avowed unbeliever." It was even rumored that Cross had burned his Bible.[35] The prophetess hoped to save those like Cross who had succumbed to the radical's artful reasoning. She described how much "comfort and consolation" there is in the scriptures "that Paine hath despised."[36]

Joanna blamed the agonized condition of the country on Paine and his supporters. Their infidelity had brought God's judgments on England. She quoted a newspaper story which reflected on the overwhelming misery "of the great majority of the people." The journalist expressed shock over "the sudden and most exorbitant advance in the price of every necessary of life which may well confound our understanding, and strike us with dismay; because, under this calamitous state of things, we know not which way to turn, or how to act." Joanna's attention moved to another page of the paper which had an account of the pillorying of the intrepid Daniel Eaton for publishing Paine's *Age of Reason*. "Instead of pelting, as is usual in similar cases," the story read, ". . . Every individual appeared more eager than another to cheer and encourage the unfortunate sufferer. At intervals he addressed the multitude, who huzzaed him, as if he had been complimenting a candidate at a popular election." The relationship between the two news stories seemed perfectly clear to Joanna. The land was burdened with sorrow and misery because of "the conduct of the public, in caressing a man for doing all in his power to suppress the word of God."[37]

Joanna warmly approved of William Cobbett's condemnation of Paine in the *Weekly Register*. It was Cobbett's belief "that every churchman has a right to call upon the minister of his own parish for an antidote against this deadly poison." Cobbett estimated that at least fifteen thousand people had milled around Eaton as he stood in the pillory "from whom he received every possible mark of compassion and of applause." If this were so, then Joanna was horrified to think of how many more in the kingdom shared Paine's views on scripture. She was convinced "this pernicious doctrine is increasing, like a mighty torrent amongst mankind." There could only be one haven from such iniquity: "joy in believing, and consolation within, which proceedeth from the Lord, that the world can neither give nor take away."[38]

For his part, Blake joined in condemning deism even as he supported Paine. It is true that the poet defended Paine as a better Christian than Bishop Watson, the author of an attack on *The Age of Reason*, but he also said, "You, O Deists, profess yourselves the Enemies of Christianity, and you are so: you are also the Enemies of the Human Race & of Universal Nature." "Natural Religion" and "Natural Philosophy" were only euphemisms for the worship of Satan, "Natural Morality" nothing more than "Self-Righteousness, the Selfish Virtues of the Natural Heart." Its crimes were comprehensive. Deism "was the Religion of the Pharisees who murder'd Jesus." It was responsible for the gravity of the contemporary situation. "Those who Martyr others or who cause War are Deists, but never can be Forgivers of Sin. The Glory of Christianity is To Conquer by Forgiveness. All the Destruction, therefore, in Christian Europe has arisen from Deism, which is Natural Religion." [39]

Sharp also came to his last conclusion. Men could claim to be enlightened, he said, only if peace and goodwill prevailed. The fact that they patently did not, made a mockery of the Western World's pretence of being superior to such uncivilized societies as "the Indians, Savages" and "Hottentots." Backward civilizations such as these might be guilty of strife on a small scale but nothing like that of "the enlightened world," which continues "to extend their wars, their mischief, and their crimes, to every part of the globe." The reason for this contradiction was that the civilized world "in general deny all revelation," and, therefore, "their crimes" result because they have divorced learning from revealed Christianity, even though the laws derived from the Bible ensure "the safety of their persons and property." [40]

If learning meant the denial of Christianity, then Sharp judged that men must turn to the unlearned for truth. He was merciless on scholars who pursued knowledge "only that their dear selves may be admired," borrowing an expression from Joanna in comparing them with "honey covering over a dish full of dirt." Sharp turned to excoriate "a certain class of men who call themselves philosophers." Some denied the existence of God altogether but most were deists. They formed a "numerous" group, "not only among the philosophers and great writers of the present day" but even among professing Christians. In an attempt to illuminate the error of these learned sceptics, he turned to a rhetorical address made to mankind by Joanna's Spirit, which, he felt, proved the existence of an intelligent Creator:

> But first let thy original be trac'd
> And tell ME then what mighty thing thou wast.
> When to the potent world MY WORD gave birth,
> And fixed my centre on the floating earth,
> Didst thou assist ME with one single thought,
> Of my ideas rectify in ought? [41]

As a believer in "universal Redemption, and the universal Love of Christ" Sharp felt himself opposed by "Philosophers, Deists and Arians, Atheists and puritanical Calvinists." [42] He said, "It is the fashion of the present age to deny every thing but outward nature: all spiritual wisdom and miracles are denied." [43] The polarization between his own position and that of the "Naturalists" and "Religionists," as he categorized his adversaries, was complete. He confessed special knowledge about the "Naturalists." They were "literary characters of this present age, who profess to be Atheists, and who employ their pens either, as they presumptuously say, for the improvement of the public, or the support of their families." Sharp said, "I have personally known such men, although I once doubted the possibility that they could exist." [44] With this remark, Sharp must have only confirmed what in fact had taken place years before, his estrangement from the Godwin–Horne Tooke circle. [45] The "atheists" he was referring to included Godwin and Holcroft, both avowed unbelievers. Out of friendship or, more likely, a sense of shared commitment to nonviolence and the belief that the propagation of truth would in itself bring about the millennium, Sharp attempted to convince Holcroft to alter his ways and to follow him in the direction he had taken. In his diary for February 20, 1799, Holcroft recorded that he called on Sharp to buy a print, "The Sortie Made by the Garrison of Gibralter," [46] "which [Sharp] said, if I kept, would become of great value, for it was the last on such a subject, meaning the destruction of war, that would ever be published." Sharp told the dramatist that human learning lay at the root of the world's tribulations: "The wisdom of man, he said, counteracting the wisdom of the Creator, had occasioned all our miseries: but the tongue of wisdom was now subdued,—meaning Egypt, which was not only a slip of land resembling a tongue, but the place in which the learning of the world originated. Thus, by the help of a pun and a metaphor, he had double proof, which he accepts as indubitable. Syria, Palestine, and all these countries are soon to be revolutionized; and those who do not take up arms against their fellow men, are to meet at the grand millennium." Holcroft was amused at Sharp's earnestness but also interested, in a speculative and self-mocking way. "Notwithstanding my cross-questioning him, he has a strong desire to make a convert of me, and, knowing the principles of peaceful benevolence which I hold, has no small hopes of succeeding." The dramatist said of Sharp, "He is a worthy and excellent man, and, in spite of this insanity, has an acute, strong, and inquiring mind." [47] In a few years' time, Holcroft's son-in-law, Colonel Harwood, would give evidence that he, too, had been inflicted with this insanity.

We have already seen that Sharp attempted to convert Blake to Joanna's following. He also approached another in his own circle, John Flaxman, the sculptor and intimate of Blake, about his beliefs. Flaxman possessed a high regard for Sharp, as did Horne Tooke [48] and Holcroft. Writing to his father from Rome on July 22, 1794, the sculptor sent his love to Sharp and said, "The newspapers have informed us that our friend Mr. Sharp the Engraver has been examined on suspicion [of treason], but from what I know of him I think his character so excellent that I cannot believe anything will be found against him."[49] Although Flaxman was a Swedenborgian and "a profound mystic," like Blake he chose not to follow rival prophets. The sculptor told Crabb Robinson in 1799 that Sharp had once made an appeal to him to join Richard Brothers' crusade to the Holy Land. There, in 1798, Jerusalem was to have been rebuilt in fulfillment of prophecy. Those invited were the "Visible Hebrews," the contemporary Jews, and the "Invisible Hebrews," those who had been separated from the Jewish people long before and were only now rediscovering their true identity.[50]

The consistent theme running throughout the various evolutions in Sharp's career is his belief that the world was in the throes of the Last Days, as manifested by the American and French revolutions, the continuing turbulence in Europe, and the spread of infidelity, and that, as a Christian, he had a responsibility to cooperate in the building up of the New Jerusalem. As an early Swedenborgian with Flaxman, he would have agreed with what the sculptor wrote on January 26, 1790: "I am fully sensible of the present changes in Europe being necessary to the present Season of the Church, at the same time that they testify the truth of E:S's [Emanuel Swedenborg's] mission."[51] It seems reasonable to believe that the millennial rhetoric which suffused reform activity led Sharp from the New Church to the Society for Constitutional Information, which he joined in the early spring of 1792. Three factors *may* then have caused him to break with radical politics in 1794 and 1795. The "success" of the state trials could have been interpreted as a demonstration of divine disapproval of radical activity. The fall of Robespierre in the summer of 1794 meant the end of the "republic of virtue" and, despite the bloodshed and highly ritualized denunciations of Christianity (a millenarian could insert Catholicism for Christianity), that part of the revolution with which it was easiest to feel an ally. Finally, and most importantly, the appearance of *The Age of Reason* could have signaled the discrediting of a false prophet and *Revealed Knowledge* the arrival of a new one, Richard Brothers.

In 1801, Sharp read the first of Joanna's publications, *The Strange Effects of Faith; With Remarkable Prophecies (Made in 1792, &c) of Things Which Are to Come*, and went to Exeter to investigate her claims. Three years later he sent a letter to an unnamed bishop, possibly Bishop Hurd, who was deeply interested in prophecy, in which he said, "I think it proper to inform your Lordship that Mrs. Joanna Southcott most certainly writes from a Spirit invisible." In the engraver's opinion, "the whole tendency of her writings proves that the millenium, or Kingdom of Christ, is at hand." [52] He underlined his commitment to Joanna in 1806:

The present awful state of the world has been increasing in calamities, ever since the year 1792, *the very year* when the SPIRIT OF PROPHECY *was given* to Joanna. Let any person only compare the state of this nation, beginning at that year 1792, with what it is at present; let them well consider the burdens that have increased upon the people: the sufferings many must have gone through, by dearth and scarcity, and an uncommon increase of national taxes and other heavy expenses! Let every person, whether they believe in Prophecies or not, only place the TWO DATES together—that is, 1792 and this year 1806; then let them view the events that have happened on the CONTINENT OF EUROPE, between those periods of time.

When men reflect "upon what has happened within the PERIOD of the last thirteen years," Sharp wrote, "they must conclude, that some GREAT and MIGHTY change is about to take place." [53]

By 1813, Napoleon had long since supplanted the Pope in the lexicon of prophecy as the Beast of Revelation. France was no longer the inspiration but rather the deadly adversary of the people of God. Sharp wrote a letter to the Reverend Joseph Pomeroy, a Church of England clergyman who had supported Joanna in her first years of prophesying but then attempted to disassociate himself from her, which revealed his change in stance. The engraver, once thought to be "a violent Jacobin and an extreme and passionate partisan of the Republicans," told the backsliding parson, "You are departing from your allegiance to your King, by bringing his church, which forms a part of his government, and the bishops, into contempt, at a time when we are threatened with every calamity from a powerful and ambitious enemy." He asked Pomeroy, "Why, Rev. Sir, do you continue silent? Why will you suffer people to have the least cause to suspect you to be a traitor to your King and country!" [54] Perhaps the final irony was the relationship which Joanna drew between the suffering of the kingdom and the huge popular support accorded to Daniel Eaton (the radical whose portrait Sharp had engraved in 1794) by the thousands who attended his pillorying in 1812 for publishing *The Age of Reason*. Joanna asked, "What blessings have we any right to expect from God, to relieve our burdens, when we see the scriptures despised, and men so encouraged to write against the word of God?" [55]

By publishing *The Age of Reason*, Eaton identified himself with Tom Paine as an infidel. It was, at last, probably because of infidelity that Sharp broke his political and personal ties with reform. His estrangement from the infidels had a dramatic effect on his outlook. Radical politics were discredited as a medium in which Christians could play an active role. It was clear now that truth could not be obtained from the learned, "the philosophers," because learning, like radicalism, had been contaminated by infidelity. Therefore, Sharp believed that God was likely to make His will known to those who arrived at the truth intuitively, like himself, Flaxman, and Blake, or someone among the uneducated. Because Sharp was by temperament a subject and not a "mental prince" like Blake,[56] nor possessed of Flaxman's regard for the opinion of others, he energetically sought among the rival prophets to find the one whom God wished him to support: "I have the natural pride of man, and have no desire to be an object of ridicule; but whatever pain or mortification the pride of character, or reputation, may produce in me, it is my superior duty to adhere to truth. The mockery of the world I must endure; the pity of my friends, who would promote every worldly advantage for my interest, I must feel, and many, I know, are sorry for me, believing me to be a deluded man. It is my sincere wish that they may throw aside their prejudices, as I have done, and endeavour at least to prove me in error." No one disparaged Isaac Newton, he said, "for believing the Bible to be the Book of Divine Wisdom," nor did anyone pity the great physicist "for his belief in prophecies and divine revelation." Sharp asked why he should be censured for believing substantially the same thing.[57] He did not strike back at his critics, as Blake did at Flaxman:

> I mock thee not, tho' I by thee am Mocked.
> Thou call'st me Madman, but I call thee Blockhead.[58]

As Sharp turned away from radical politics, his vision of a transformed world retreated inward. At the point when this abstraction no longer obtruded on reality, it became devoid of any revolutionary or reform potential it once possessed. "It is a spiritual operation only," he said, "that can renovate the mind and heart of man by a new birth; for in the end all things must become new; that is, a new heart and an enlightened understanding." His vision was both humane and comprehensive but no longer practically effective. "As the light spreads forth—human learning must disappear, where it does not promote the love of God above all things, and of our neighbours as ourselves— All the human race are now invited to be brethren, and to love one another; for every difficulty will be removed." "The *English nation*," he said, "will be the first redeemed." Then, "The Lord's Kingdom will come on earth as it is in heaven."[59]

VIII

The Last Redoubt

Eighteen hundred years ago,
I suffered death on Calvery,
I suffered death on Calvery
For to redeem the world;
And the world shall very soon be free,
And shall wear the Cap of Liberty;
Then all shall happy be,
When Satan down is hurl'd!

The standard of me—the Lord,
Is hoisted in England!
To show the slumbering world,
The day is near at hand.
—Songs of Zion for the Millennium[1]

VICTORY

In 1798, four years before Joanna left Exeter for London, her Spirit announced that God chose Richard Brothers first as His prophet "and afterwards, upon his falling from the Lord, He gave the Spirit of prophecy" to her.[2] It seems certain that, as the long years of the prophet's imprisonment stretched out, his followers, leaderless and confused, turned in large numbers to Joanna. In this sense, Brothers "broke the ground all through" for the prophetess.[3] Of the seven who interviewed her in Exeter at Christmas in 1801, all except Peter Morrison were his supporters. One Southcottian noted that "many of us had been believers of him."[4]

Although Brothers' career apparently made a powerful impression on Joanna while she was still in Devonshire, she did not actually read any of his writings until after arriving in London.[5] Even then, it is not clear to what extent she seriously informed herself about his views. On July 10, 1802, she could say, "We were all seated in Mr. Beecraft's parlour, busily reading Mr. Brothers's Prophecies."[6] And yet, as late as April 1806, the month he was released, Joanna claimed, "I have read over Mr. Brothers' Books which I never read in my life till now."[7] Whether she read his publications or they were read to her or they simply charged the atmosphere in which she lived, Joanna understood Brothers' message well enough to know it offered a challenge to her position. On the one hand, she expressed perplexity. "I was never told what of his books was right and what was wrong. I cannot decide upon them." On the other hand, however, her ambiguous feelings could quickly melt away under the hot glare of certainty. Brothers' writings were "full of blasphemy that shocked me, and I marvelled how it was said in my writings that the Lord had ever visited him at all."[8] They were "erronious," she said, and the prophet "deranged in his senses."[9]

The principal charge she hurled at Brothers was that he had succumbed to "spiritual pride" and, as a result, forfeited God's favor.[10] Joanna's Spirit asserted, "I [will not] give my power to man to govern and rule my people. For then they would be looking to the creature and not to the Creator." The prophet's ambition to rule over the faithful had come to seem indistinguishable from that of Bonaparte, "who judges all power is given to him as Brothers thought it was given to him." Neither Brothers nor any other mortal was to be the "prince and Saviour."[11] God, not humans, would reign over the millennial kingdom.

Of course, the motivations behind Joanna's attitude toward the imprisoned prophet are only too easy to understand. She felt jealous of the special relationship he claimed with God and, consequently, eager to exact retribution on him for the threat he posed to her status. Reassurance from the Spirit came forth soothingly, as always, and she heard him whisper, "I loved none but thee."[12] Nevertheless, Joanna was forced to maneuver carefully or run the risk of alienating the rival prophet's followers. Her Spirit helped speed the efforts at accommodation by saying, "Let no one blame theirselves for their belief in Brothers; it was I the Lord work'd in their hearts."[13] However, on one issue she could certainly meet his supporters forthrightly and sympathetically. Despite the fact that Brothers deservedly lost God's support, nothing justified the government's persecution of him. Stupidly and cruelly, Pitt and his administration determined to punish Brothers for telling them the truth, that God disapproved of the war with France. Because he had the misfortune to be the messenger bearing bad tidings, they required that he suffer. But there were wider and even unhappier ramifications. The whole country had been forced to suffer because of the government's action. "I was told when he was put into prison that the curse of God would fall on the Land." Its evidence was everywhere: "Thousands have died for want." If the will of God continued to be thwarted and Brothers was not released, the famine would envelop the rich as well as the poor, she warned.[14]

Brothers' release, therefore, came to be a matter of the highest priority. Her Spirit told her simply, "I sent thee to London to free him."[15] According to William Sharp's journal, three days after her arrival from Exeter she was writing to Nathaniel Halhed, asking that he "consider . . . the most proper mode of making an application to the Parliament House [in order to] procure the freedom of Mr. Brothers." Within the week, Sharp had a "most agreeable interview" with Sir Richard Ford, an undersecretary of state and chief police magistrate for London, whom he informed of Joanna's appearance in the city. The engraver told Ford that Joanna had been commanded by her Spirit to secure Brothers' release. Revealing that prophecy could still bear political implications, Sharp warned Sir Richard that he hoped "to prevent any calamity falling upon the Government in particular and the Nation at large," which might well take place if Brothers' confinement continued. Then Sharp presented Ford "with the whole of Joanna's books," parts of which they looked through together.[16]

Joanna's widely circulated demands for the prophet's release helped confirm Brothers' followers in their new loyalty to her. At first, she had to accept her role as his coadjutor. Foley, Sharp, Turner, and Halhed continued to believe that *both* she and Brothers were divinely inspired, that he was the new Adam to her new Eve. On June 12, 1802, three weeks after the prophetess had taken up residence in London, a group of her supporters drank a toast to Brothers in her presence. Only Peter Morrison abstained.[17] Inexorably, however, she moved to force a decision between Brothers and herself.

On November 10, 1802, Nathaniel Halhed received his seal, apparently acknowledging his faith in the prophetess.[18] Joanna told him five weeks later, "I am now ordered to write to you as your Faith for a long time has been to believe in Mr. Brothers and me as being both directed by the Spirit of the Lord." In his "last publication," however, she said it was clear that Brothers had abandoned the pathways of the Spirit. "His Book must shame every one that is endowed with reason and religion," and continued, "one would scarce believe a man in his right senses could write such a book." According to her, it "must mortify his friends and give his enemies room to triumph over him." She compared Brothers' fall from grace with that of Adam. Adam could blame "the woman," but Brothers only had himself to fault.[19] But Halhed proved reluctant to abandon the prophet, even in the face of a visit by Joanna's brother to promote her interests.[20] At this point, the Spirit intervened and assured the prophetess that she should go to him herself, if "not this Week, go the following Week," and he would come round. Two days later, on December 19, she called on him with Foley and Sharp, and he became "at liberty" to leave his house where he had felt himself a prisoner for ten years,[21] apparently freed by the testimony of his faith in Joanna.

However, not until the spring of 1806, a few weeks before Brothers' release, did Joanna discover that Halhed and the prophet had finally parted ways. By this time, Brothers was under the influence of John Finlayson, a Scottish lawyer who abandoned his practice to become the prophet's adviser and whom Joanna despised. Finlayson apparently blocked any attempt of the prophet's old supporters to approach him. Foley and Sharp joined Halhed in bitterly turning away from a man who had once consumed their hopes and dreams and who had now retreated forever into a private world of his own, guarded over by his new aide.[22]

With the last remnants of Brothers' support crumbling, Joanna could afford to be magnanimous to her rival. If he submitted to her leadership, everyone "in a happy union will all be united together." If he persisted in opposition, however, the Spirit said, "His end [will] be without honor and all his followers will perish and come to nothing that join with him against thee."[23] Joanna's Spirit railed particularly at the prophet for his contemptible use of Sharp, "who was his faithful Friend."[24] In the summer of 1806, the engraver told Joanna he was going to destroy all the prints he had made of Brothers. Instead, she suggested that his name simply be defaced and, with it, the legend, "Prince of the Hebrews." This meant victory. The prophetess said, "I sent for one of the Prints & I painted his name over in three Red Streaks & compleatly blotted out his name with the Red paint knowing it was the Blood of Christ that must cleanse us from all Sin & bring in the Redemption to Man."[25] The following month, Foley, too, threw his support unconditionally to Joanna. He wrote to Peter Morrison of "the errors & shocking Crimes" which Brothers had committed against the Lord. But, hope still remained for him. Joanna's Spirit said that he might be saved "if he humbles himself & sincerely repents."[26]

The prospect of a contrite Brothers bending his knee to Joanna in order to join her movement and guarantee his freedom did not please everyone. At the height of the fever to possess her seals in 1804, rumors were circulating that their distribution was a stratagem designed to determine the strength of Joanna's following. As one believer related the story, "When we find ourselvs Sufficiently Strong we shall go and Rescue Richd. Brothers from prison, and then attempt to overturn the Govt."[27] The interview which Sharp had previously had with Sir Richard Ford could hardly have reassured the authorities on this score.

NO BETTER SUBJECTS

The government kept a wary eye on the Southcottian movement, just as it had on Brothers and his following. The Privy Council had ordered Brothers' arrest for "maliciously publishing fantastical prophecies with intent to cause disturbances." On two occasions Elias Carpenter was arrested, but each time he was released.[28] In December 1803, both Elias Carpenter and Joseph Prescott were subjected to "a long and pointed examination for 3 hours & a half in a private Room" by Sir Richard Ford. Apparently, Joseph's paintings were considered particularly dangerous because Ford threatened him with imprisonment if he drew any more of his visions. Joseph replied "with Great Innocence and without Fear" that he would do as God commanded him.[29]

A few agitated souls did believe that Joanna and her lieutenants were gathering their support for an insurrection. One anonymous author raised visions of the peasant revolts of the past when he wrote that Joanna "excites amongst her subjects an expectation that they are, by-and-by, to be *marshaled in battle array, to conquer a kingdom for themselves, with sticks and staves*!" His concern grew increasingly strident: "There are, it seems, tens of thousands ready to march at the command of a woman whom they esteem a Prophetess—the Oracle of God; and let me ask, what may not the zeal of such fanatics lead them to attempt? fanatics who, like the *Fifth Monarchy Men*, not merely expect that Christ must reign personally on the Earth, but believe that they, his favourites, must fight for, and win a kingdom for themselves!"[30] A clergyman charged that Joanna "was evidently an instrument in the hands of the enemy, to collect together a number of people and promote a rebellion against the government."[31] Elias Carpenter could well affirm that, of the "various ideas" held about the large numbers of people constantly coming to his house, "some suppose that it has a political design."[32] Enemies even called the prophetess "Bonaparte's *Brother*."[33]

Because of these imputations, Joanna, Carpenter, Sharp, and other Southcottians were anxious to affirm their political orthodoxy. They complied with the laws of the nation because the laws emanated from the king, to whom God had given His authority. "Rebellion is as Iniquity and Idolatry," Joanna's Spirit said.[34] According to her, "the Sealed People do not trouble themselves about politics or parties and have no connection with desperate Men but it is their duty to avoid contention or strife."[35] She declared in a pamphlet published in 1807, "His majesty has no better subjects in his kingdom, or who wish more for the perfect happiness of the nation, than the true believers in my visitation."[36] The

Spirit argued that his command had been "to be peaceable with all men, as far as in you lie." He asked Joanna, "Is there a word of rebellion in thy writings that I have ordered or commanded?"[37] Elias Carpenter echoed Joanna's loyal sentiments. "With political subjects I never interfere," he said and expressed his hope "that in happiness and peace, our beloved sovereign may sway the sceptre for very many years yet to come" and in time that "he may participate in the glorious change."[38] Sir Richard Ford agreed that there was little to fear from the Southcottians. After his interview with Carpenter, he said to a fellow magistrate, "The principles of these Gentlemen (however erroneous) seem founded with so much Love to their fellow Creatures, and the Good of the World at Large; that was it not for my Official Capacity—I should think it no Disgrace to Belong to Men of such Inofensive principles."[39]

Earlier in 1803, Prime Minister Henry Addington received a letter from another of Joanna's followers, Richard Law, who may well have been correct in describing his epistle as "*the most extraordinary . . . ever* Penned . . . *to a PRIME MINISTER.*" Law warned that Addington must divest himself of his false councillors who "make black appear white, and . . . adorn the most ugly falsehood with the lovely robes of truth." After this was done, he must turn to those "who trust not to their own wisdom, not to the wisdom of any man, but are learned in the writings of Joanna Southcott." He urged the prime minister to "take their advice . . . and only theirs." Far from being treacherous, his new councillors would be "the most loyal men in the united kingdom." Indeed, "so far from their being prone in the least to sedition, they would not hear an expression of that nature fall from the lips of any one, without giving in return a necessary reproof, and suitable admonition." If there were any danger "that might threaten you from any dark scheme, or wicked plot the disaffected and designing might contrive," such men as these "if kind providence led them to discover the same . . . would with the greatest pleasure, and without loss of time, acquaint you with it." Addington was told "the day is near at hand when you will have a sufficient specimen of their loyalty and attachment to you. For it is the sealed number that must gain the victory, and ultimately vanquish the enemy."[40]

The sealed were well suited to protect England because only they knew how to deal with the principle of evil which animated her enemies and which earlier had overtaken the French Revolution. Napoleon was not a mere flesh-and-blood enemy but the Beast of Revelation. The "mutiny in France" had been sanctioned by God, the Spirit said, as the first blow against the Roman Catholic powers in Europe.[41] But the French proved to be as irreligious after the revolution as they had before. Because the country was "divided in heart" and "the stronger party" was for Satan, France surrendered to the Beast, the evil prince promised in the book of Revelation who would seek to overwhelm the people of God. The Beast, of course, was Napoleon, who was "no Monarch of France . . . but set up by a lawless people." The French had become "madmen, who broke all the laws of their country; cut off their king, and cut off all who had a right to the crown." [42] The struggle with France, therefore, had become a holy war, to be waged on two fronts, one spiritual and one temporal. That it would be successful there was no doubt. Speaking for all those who derived their optimism from the prophetic books of the Bible, Lewis Mayer, a writer on prophecy but an ardent opponent of Joanna, said that "as Bonaparte is collecting the antichristian nations into a political body, to subdue and govern the whole earth, it is a matter of no small consolation to Britons to be enabled to trace out in prophecy so many assurances that his schemes will finally prove abortive, and terminate in the destruction of his usurped empire." [43]

The futility of seeking a resolution to the war with France, either by military victory or by peaceful negotiation, was demonstrated by the fate of the old antagonists William Pitt and Charles James Fox. Pitt wished "to Conquer in War, and gain every Victory over his Enemy, and he died disappointed in Every scheme that he had laid." Fox went "the Other Way." He sought peace, "and now all his hopes have failed him the same. [He] will not see the day or the hour that he wished for to complete happiness to this Land & bring in a Settled peace." Victory and peace would come one day, the Spirit said, but "know it is I the Lord who have all power in my hands to Complete your happiness and your Victory." [44]

The spiritual struggle which the Southcottians urged against France is described most dramatically in a pamphlet published in 1803. It was addressed to the bishops and the clergy, with information "WORTHY THE CONSIDERATION OF ALL RANKS AND DENOMINATIONS AT THIS DANGEROUS CRISIS." On the frontispiece are four exclamations: "England is threatened!!! Our Sovereign in danger!!! The Enemy at the door!!! What shall we do to be saved!!!" The author wrote: "A nation like our's, favoured by Providence with the assistance of enlightened men, has much to hope from the explanations of its spiritual guides. It is to them all thinking men will look for that armour which (I firmly believe) can alone protect and defend us." He was convinced "that a prophetess arises in the west, as did our Saviour in the east," and asked, "Shall we reject her?" If rejected, "great and essential reasons should be assigned for it; as she offers us, by command of the Holy Spirit, a *seal of safety* in these times of danger, without exacting anything, but that we *pray for the coming of Christ's kingdom and the destruction of Satan's.*" The mortal combat between England and France was only an outward manifestation of the real struggle between good and evil. "The safety of England," therefore, "will depend, not on the sword, but on the righteousness of its people." The pamphlet ended, "Friendship—affection of every kind—loyalty—love of our sovereign—our country—but above all, love for the cause of God—all cry aloud to us. . . . Let *all* take up arms, and fight not merely with an arm of flesh, but with the sword of the SPIRIT." [45]

Addington's correspondent, Richard Law, informed the prime minister that, if the nation would only announce its belief in Christ's coming, "then Bonaparte will be defeated in his attempts against this country, and you will gain over his arms the most brilliant victories." He told Addington that his support of Joanna "will do infinitely more to save the nation, than all the ships in the navy, or all the armies that can be raised. It will gain you eternal fame, the brightest renown, and render your name at once illustrious and immortal, to the latest posterity." In his concluding remarks, Law said that Addington should not think him "a poor solitary maniac, not worth your notice." "If I am out of my senses," he said, "I am not singular in that respect; for I can assure you, there are great numbers in the nation who believe the same as I do; and there are thousands in the land who have already signed for Christ's kingdom to come; and before another year is past there will be tens of thousands." He hoped the prime minister would become "one of the happy number." [46]

Confusion arose among the believers as to whether they should actually take up arms against Napoleon and his armies or whether they should devote themselves exclusively to spiritual exercises to bring about his downfall. This had come about because Joanna had at first said they "should have nothing to do with the contentions of the nation." [47] Elias Carpenter upheld the pacifist position:

Say not, that we are disaffected to government, because we cannot fight.—We are, of all his majesty's subjects, the ablest supporters of it. We are enlisted under an invincible leader, who is about to strike at the root of the evil: O, that every soldier in this kingdom was but fairly enlisted in our corps, they would then have no need to fire a gun. Gideons' lamps and pitchers then would be sufficient to put our enemies to flight. Standing on our shores, and blowing rams-horns, would make them fall in their passage to us;—innocent, but powerful weapons the Lord furnishes those with, who put their trust in him. [48]

The issue was resolved on the activist side, however. Joanna referred to

Joseph Prescott's painting of the rider with the upraised, two-edged sword to convince her followers that they had a temporal as well as a spiritual battle to wage in the Last Days.[49] Believers, like unbelievers, had to obey "the Command of their King and Country" or they themselves would be the cause of contention in the land. God was "a Man of war" and believers "must be men of war." If they shunned the field of battle, then others would rightly call them cowards and say, "These men were of no use."[50] Joanna wrote to Sharp on July 25, 1803, however, and told him that her followers were allowed to take part only in defensive action; that is, they could fight only if England were invaded.[51] Under these conditions, believers were permitted to join parish associations of volunteers.[52] The Spirit attempted to clarify the situation for the prophetess:

> So now unto my friends I say the same,
> Your King's command must be obeyed by them.
> And so the armour I do bid them wear,
> These are the very words I said before,
> That he who had no sword must go and buy;
> I said the time to use it then was nigh;
>
> . . . .
>
> Then if my sword doth in your land appear,
> How can my followers it refuse to wear?
> To draw the sword, yourselves for to defend;
>
> . . . .
>
> And now let them like valiant soldiers stand.
> And every foe shall now before them fall:
> This is thy Prophecies, I tell you all;
>
> . . . .
>
> And true believers nothing have to fear;

"France's ruin," Joanna was told, "is hastening on."[53]

The foreign enemy had been identified and instructions issued as to how to deal with him. Of at least equal importance, however, was the cause of England's domestic agony. The reason that the harvests failed, the poor were starving and unemployed, and infidelity was spreading throughout the nation lay in England's failure to prepare itself for Christ's coming. By ignoring or rejecting the prophetess' message, the unbelievers had brought terrible suffering on the people. In the past, this reasoning had been sufficient to justify insurrection against the ungodly and the institutions with which they were identified.

As we have noted, this was not to be the direction which the Southcottian movement took, in part because of the French example. In a collection of Southcottian broadsheets in the John Rylands Library, there is a song called "Church and King" which was sung to the tune of "Rule Britannia." The song includes a verse in which Joseph Priestley is pictured looking at the "bleeding corpse of France," where "wild anarchy" reigns, and continues:

> Yet *Priestley*, Faction's darling child,
>   Enjoys this sanguinary scene,
> And celebrates with transports wild,
>   The *wrongs*, miscall'd *the rights* of men.
>
>   . . . .
>
> Go, democratic demons, go!
>   In France your horrid banquet keep!
> Feast on degraded *Prelates* woe,
>   And drink the tears that *Monarchs* weep.
> Our Church is built on Truth's firm ROCK,
>   And mocks each sacrilegious hand;
> In spite of each *electric shock*,
>   The heav'n defended steeples stand.[54]

Joanna meditated on the dreadful consequences of the French Revolution. "We may see by the French Revolution" that it has given no happiness to mankind. It had "only deluged Europe with blood: and were Buonaparte and his followers to be destroyed tomorrow, sin and sorrow would remain the same." Joanna argued, "No revolution against men can bring in this glorious and happy period, which is promised in the Scriptures of Truth." "Let us reflect," she said, "on all the revolutions, and all the destruction, which have happened to tyrants, in ages back, and see if it completed the happiness of man; or if tears were wiped away from off all faces; and all the earth praised the Lord. This was never done by the revolutions of men; neither will it ever be accomplished by any revolution which man can point out."[55] It is Satan who must be destroyed, the prophetess declared, for Satan had been responsible for human woes since the beginning, when he tempted Eve in the Garden of Eden. Now he was struggling to turn mortals away from God at another climactic moment in the history of the race. "He is the cause of your sorrows, the cause of your sins, and the cause of your misery," Joanna warned.[56] "This is the revolution we must have in our hearts, against his power and his devices, and plead the promises of God." Believers will speak "in psalms, hymns, and spiritual songs, making melody in our hearts unto the Lord, that we may be sincere, and without offence, till the day of Christ."[57] Joanna was told by her Spirit during a stay in Old Swinford that her followers would be "workers . . . with

God" in establishing His heavenly kingdom. But they would "work," the Spirit said, only by demonstrating their "love and zeal . . . and their desire for Me, and My Kingdom."[58] Humans will be delivered from their suffering by God, who will "do more and better for man then it is possible for [them] to do for theirselves, or to do one for the other."[59]

That Joanna refused to advocate a violent transfer of power from humans to God did not make her condemnation of the contemporary scene any less severe. A believer understood this when he scored Joanna's critics as "brave defenders of the existing system of all things."[60] According to the Spirit, those who "are against MY PEACEABLE REIGN, and longing to have all things remain as they are," will shortly have "sorrow and misery" descend upon them.[61] Among them were tyrannical governments that restricted human liberties. A hymn which Joanna's followers sang in their meeting places concluded with the verse:

> Behold! earth's monarchs now combine,
> With their proud nobles, to decree;
> Pride, wealth, and pow'r together join,
> To quench the flame of liberty.[62]

The Southcottians wanted to bring about thoroughgoing change but only by adapting their desires to the conventional political tradition of Englishmen. The lists which the sealed were asked to sign were petitions meant to bring about change in the political order by appealing to the ultimate source of power. One who called himself "a Lover of Truth" underlined the meaning of the lists of believers. "Reader," he said, "when you petition your governors upon worldly affairs, do you not first give your name to a rough petition, then sign a petition properly drawn up, and then wait the result? Then why should you marvel that the Lord should deal with men after the manner of men?"[63] The lists also served as poll records by which men and women voted for God or Satan to rule over them. "Satan said he would stand or fall by Election, as a member of Parliament," the Spirit said, so "I then held him to his word, and ORDERED THE SEALING to appear, to try the votes." The returns had come in, "and not one List hath man brought for [Satan]: so he is cast without a man to vote for his reign."[64]

But on the inaugural day of the new regime, "the day of Christ," the existing government would be overthrown and society completely reorganized. Elias Carpenter declared that "our leveling system" would be much more comprehensive than that of the French: "The high must be brought down, and the humble exalted, until we meet in a pleasant plane of equality. What a neighbouring nation hath been grasping at in shadow, we shall have in substance, when our Lord establishes his kingdom: it will be complete happiness, neither too much or too little with any; but like the manna gathered by the children of Israel, he that gathers much will have nothing over, and he that gathers little have no lack." [65] George III would be compelled to surrender his kingdom to God. [66] He and the other monarchs of the world would be allowed to retain their crowns, but no longer would they exercise absolute authority over their subjects. Christ would guide them in making "just decrees." [67] Joanna said: "In reading over the reigns of the Kings, and meditating upon the reign of Kings in all nations, . . . [I concluded] there is no government that has been so well established for the happiness of mankind, as the government that is brought in by the Gospel." [68]

Some of the believers thought that Christ would raise them to positions of absolute authority in the new polity. But their hopes were to be dashed. God judged subjects as well as sovereigns unfit to govern without restrictions in the New World. The Spirit said: "Only land back thy thoughts when kings ruled by an arbitrary power, how fatal were the effects to the subjects; but how much more fatal would this be if man was taught to believe I had given all power into the hands of a man that I had set over them." Napoleon was the outstanding example of a man raised from the people to a position of absolute power. His corrupt and tyrannical rule served as a warning for all. According to the Spirit,

> Earthly princes, all must leave,
> And to the heavenly all must cleave,
> And with my kingdom to appear
> Ere man is crowned with glory here.
> It is the victory of your God
> Must gain the kingdom as I've said,
> Then to my saints I'll give it free
> When their desires are all for me,
> And see the folly they have done.
> To fix their happiness in man
> Who had no power to fix his own
> When I begin to unthrone
> The thoughts of men that swell on high,
> To think in them all power does lie. [69]

In a letter of April 2, 1806, however, Joanna consoled the believers with her conviction that, although none of them would enjoy supreme power, those who were alive at the Second Coming "will be made rulers over many places as priests unto the Lord." [70]

SHILOH

Everything became prologue to the moment in 1814 when Joanna stunned her following by announcing that she was pregnant by her divine spouse. The Spirit told her, "This year, in the sixty-fifth year of thy age, thou shalt have a SON, by the power of the MOST HIGH." The child's name was to be Shiloh. Like Solomon's son he would "judge thy people with righteousness, and thy poor with judgment. . . . He shall spare the poor and needy, and shall save the souls of the needy. He shall redeem their souls from deceit and violence; and precious shall their blood be in his sight."[71] A prophecy remembered from the sixteenth century could have helped convince the followers that the birth of Shiloh was necessary to fulfill Joanna's mission. It read, "An old Woman Shall conceive and Bare a Conqueror, But He Shall not Stay with you Nor Eat of your victuals nor Lie [in] the Little Bed you have prepared for Him."[72]

But, to Joanna, the announcement of her pregnancy represented a last desperate effort to galvanize her following and to vindicate the truth of her claims. Although believers continued to declare their faith in Joanna's divine mission, recruitment slowed considerably after the spectacular growth of the early years. In order to flourish, the Southcottian movement required a backdrop of disaster, of "judgments," and, by the fall of 1813, news was disquietingly good. Believers were growing restive, and their questions increasingly strident. How long, how long must the people of God wait for His kingdom to be established?

Joanna's Spirit pushed and provoked her to the final catastrophe. "Now discern from the papers," the Spirit said, "how great is their boasting as though all their dangers were over, as though peace and plenty were already established, and the bright sunshine was over your land, that ye have nothing now to fear." Then, he said, "I now tell thee many of the believers, will begin to grow jealous that thou art deceived, and they are deceiving theirselves to believe in my visitation to thee." But, he promised, there will be "a sudden surprise cometh upon them to shew them plain."[73]

The "sudden surprise" came on October 11, 1813, when she experienced a "powerful visitation . . . working upon my body." She grew "alarmed and filled with different fears" that it was the "power of evil" which had made love to her. The Spirit offered the reassurance that Satan could not invade the human body without causing pain, which she had not felt.[74] Less kindly, he added that the prophetess was no longer attractive enough to draw an evil spirit as her lover.

> If doubts in thee do so arise,
> I tell thee 'tis to make thee wise

How youthful days thou must call back,
For wisdom here I say thoust lack,
To think a Spirit would appear,
In love to thee thou now dost fear;
When every bloom of youth is gone,
Thy folley thou dost now discern,
If Spirits could such power gain,
They'd come before old age was seen.
Because I say it would be so,
[Too] much like men would spirits go.

The reason for the pregnancy was easy to discover, she said. The coming of the Kingdom of Heaven meant "the coming of the Bridegroom, and a marriage union." Christ "will Pour out His Spirit upon all Flesh so some likeness of His Spirit after the manner of men in the flesh must be felt by the woman." [75] At Christmas, while meditating on the Virgin Mary, she felt her body shake and "a sensation that is impossible for me to describe upon my womb." [76] The infant Shiloh's existence was now beyond challenge.

Confusion between the roles of Shiloh and Christ was inevitable. The Spirit did not go very far in resolving it when he said that because Christ was a "*guilty malefactor*" Shiloh "will be preferred as a PRINCE and a SAVIOUR: and then the FATHER will be honoured for the SON's sake." [77] It seems that Shiloh was to be assigned duty as Christ's proconsul, to further prepare the way for the Second Advent. He would reign on earth as a king. Under his leadership the defeat of the powers of darkness would be completed. A secondary consideration was that he would satisfy the Jews' yearning for their own Messiah.

But, despite the eagerness to believe, proof for Joanna's incredible claim was necessary. To all appearances, the prophetess was indeed pregnant. In the spring of 1814, George Turner wrote back to Yorkshire, "I can only say she increases much in size and I think will be a beautiful sight by the time she is Eight months." [78] Toward the end of the summer, Ann Underwood could tell the Leeds merchant that Joanna's "women friends are well satisfied as they can feel the Child as strong to move as they ever felt one of their own outwardly." She conceded, however, that it was "necessary to have the Judgment of medical men in this case." [79] Subsequently, the verisimilitude of the course of Joanna's false pregnancy was sufficient to convince seventeen of the twenty-one physicians who examined her, including a leading London surgeon, Richard Reece, that the aged prophetess was indeed pregnant. This, even in the face of her refusal to allow any who attended her to conduct an internal examination.[80] The outcome of the examinations did much to encourage new believers but little to discourage the lively and scabrous speculation concerning the possibility of Joanna's pregnancy "without the interposition of a supernatural power."[81] This Joanna attempted to forestall by surrounding herself with a phalanx of women believers who were in constant attendance upon her.

News of the startling developments had, of course, reached Old Swinford. In August, Foley decided to travel to London and find out for himself Joanna's condition. He kept a diary from July 16 to August 26, and the entries reveal the same irrepressible good humor which made him such a valued companion during his undergraduate days. There are references to "a very agreeable journey" and "a fine and pleasant morning" which do less justice to the circumstances of his travel and the weather than to his general outlook on life. Upon his arrival in London, on Thursday, August 18, he found accommodations in the New Road and then went to see Joanna around noon. His diary entry reveals some lurking apprehensions. But, he could write happily, "Joanna (thank God) was large and far gone in pregnancy." She told him of the opinion offered by her attending physicians and advised him to interview them himself, which he did. The prophetess seemed in "high spirits" and continued so in the next few days. Foley found that others had purposes similar to his own. George Turner and Thomas Senior had come from Leeds, and the Reverend Samuel Eyre from Bristol. Other worthies whom Foley saw were Edmund Baker, William Owen Pugh, William Roundell Wetherell, Samuel Hirst, Daniel Roberts, and Colonel Harwood.[82]

Events, at last, seemed to be moving quickly. Joanna had instructed the believers to find her suitable lodgings for her accouchement. The Spirit said that a public advertisement must be placed for "thou dost not wish to deceive or impose upon the Publick." The house had to be "large enough to entertain many for 2 or 3 months." For when Shiloh was born, the Spirit said, "many respectable Gentlemen and Ladies will be truly convinced by the Birth of the Child, and will become faithful Friends and true Believers, and wish to See thee after the Child is born." When that happened, at long last her journey would be at an end. "And then thou will have nothing to fear of being established in a comfortable Situation."[83]

THE LAST DAYS

The effect of Joanna's announcement on her following was electric, causing some to leave the movement in horror but convincing the remainder that the decisive moment, after years of waiting, had at last come. In addition, many new followers were now coming in. Joanna reported, "Thousands are now desirous of having" the seals.[84] Years later, Samuel Jowett remembered the intoxication of those months:

Our eyes were so dazzled with the glorious prospect set before us, of those things taking place immediately, that were then made known; we became like the man taken out of a dark room, and placed in the radiant beams of the sparkling sun, the light so overpowering him that he could not see:—so it was with us—the idea of having one of the GODHEAD to reign over us was overwhelming, after being so long tyrannized over by man, under evil influence; that we could not calmly and deliberately consider what was delivered unto us, because of the bright shining picture of the illustrious era which was presented to our view.[85]

In response to the popular demand, a brief *Life* of the prophetess quickly ran through eleven editions.[86] The *Leeds Mercury* announced solemnly on October 15 that local publishers would bring out a "Memoir" on the prophetess "in a few days" costing one shilling. It would have "*a correct Portrait*" of Joanna and a rendering "of the *superb Crib.*" The *Mercury* said, "We understand the compiler has totally rejected the calumny and abuse which disgrace many other publications on the subject."[87]

Who were these new converts rushing to acquire the seals and to profess their belief in the coming of King Shiloh? On October 8, 1814, the *Manchester Gazette* published an article about a local workman who had joined the Southcottians, subtitling it "Deplorable effects of Religious Delusion." The article was intended as a cautionary tale against the folly of those flocking to the movement. According to the *Gazette*: "A man for many years the faithful and industrious servant of most respectable manufacturers in the North of England, where he lived in comfort and contentment, in an evil hour went to hear the preachers delegated by this woman; and becoming infatuated with doctrines that held forth the time to be near," when the laborer would no longer live by the sweat of his brow, gave up his employment, "much against the wishes of his masters." His brother-in-law who worked in the same factory attempted to dissuade him from his disastrous course. But, the *Gazette* continued, "at this period the coming of Shiloh, and actual commencement of the Millennium, was announced among the Johannian Votaries." This news "ravished" the workman "with visions of eternal ease, health and happiness, visions that displayed before him rivers of wine, milk, and honey, of themselves perpetually flowing to fill the cans and pitchers of the faithful." The result was that, "about five weeks ago, he set out on foot for London" with a bundle containing all his worldly possessions slung over his shoulder, in order to be present at Shiloh's birth. A series of misadventures in the capital led to the man's disillusionment and ultimately his destitution, his life being saved only through charity. The shocking thing, said the *Gazette*, was that his was not an isolated case: "Thousands are daily verging to the same point of fanatical idiocy." Carefully, the article concluded, "The subject is becoming too serious to be jested with."

In a letter to the *Times* on September 2, 1814, an outraged "J.W." commented on the enormous influx of provincial believers into the metropolis: "It is a fact, that, in consequence of what the newspapers have for some time been relating about this woman, shoals of enthusiasts, with more money in their pockets than brains in their skulls, are now pouring into London and its vicinity, to behold this chosen vessel!"

So many imposters appeared in London claiming to be Joanna, in order to exploit the credulity of the growing number of followers, that the prophetess had her portrait distributed so that all would know what she looked like.[88] The problem of mistaken identity had first presented itself several years before. In a letter of August 29, 1811, Joanna said that she wanted to have her "Likeness" made "as there are women of Bad Character going about London, calling themselves Joanna Southcott, by which means I have been represented as being a Strange looking woman." She asked Sharp to undertake the task and was well pleased with the result. "Mr. Sharp have succeeded very well in taking it as they all say it is a Striking Likeness, and he is going to Engrave it." Some of the followers raised objections to the whole enterprise on the grounds that it would lead to image worship. But the matter was settled when the Spirit gave his approval. "If men Judged aright it would draw their hearts to long for My Kingdom to Rejoice in My People that Sorrow and Sighing must be done away." He reminded Joanna, however, that "if men look at thy Likeness only as an Idol to worship" they would commit sin.[89]

In eager anticipation of Shiloh's birth, her followers began sending Joanna a number of elaborate gifts for the expected child. Among them were "laced caps, embroidered bibs, and worked robes, a mohair mantle, which cost £150;—an elegant silver cup and salver, with a lid, on which is placed a ball representing the globe, upon which is perched a dove, with an olive branch." A Birmingham engraver had written on the tray, "Hail, Messiah, Prince of Salem!" Inscribed around the rim of the cup were the words, "Of the increase of his government, and peace there shall be no end." A shield on the body of the cup bore the inscription, "This present was sent as a token of love to the Prince of Peace, from a part of the believers in the divine mission of Joanna Southcott, at Birmingham." One of the goblets which came with the cup had the words:

> Then Palaces shall rise;
>   The joyful Son
> Shall finish what his short-lived
>   Sire began.

In addition to the above, "presents to a very large amount have been sent from various parts of the kingdom."[90] The *Birmingham Commercial Herald* reported that their cost was in "the amount of several thousands of pounds."[91]

The *European Magazine* agreed on the large number of gifts, reporting that the prophetess "has been literally overwhelmed with presents."[92] A "lady of rank" gave Joanna a "solid gold" font along with other objects of similar costliness.[93] The catalogue of gifts was indeed long and fabulous but sometimes exacted at enormous sacrifice. A complaint was heard that "mechanics with large families, and servants who had no other means than what were derived from their wages," made contributions which resulted in "their own evident injury, and that of their distressed relatives." It was "a fact" that a "tradesman" had bankrupted himself by sending the prophetess twenty pounds. Many gifts, however, were of a touchingly humble character. A blind woman gave sixpence, a little girl two roses; from other believers there were individual presents of a comb, a piece of flannel, a night cap, a pair of socks, a dozen napkins, a pin cushion, a shilling, a robe, a shirt, a pair of shoes, "a small foreign gold coin," and scores of other items of similar kind.[94] Finally, because so many of the gifts *were* costly, Joanna refrained from accepting any more.[95]

Unquestionably, the most gorgeous of all the gifts was a crib costing £200. Its frame was "made with satin-wood, richly ornamented with gold; the sides and ends filled with lattice work gilt." Blue satin lined the body of the crib. At its head was a cloth "with a celestial crown of gold embroidered upon it." Beneath the crown "appears the word SHILOH, in *Hebrew characters*, richly drawn, and exhibited in gold spangles." A blue satin canopy hanging over the crib provided the finishing touch. All the gifts were meticulously recorded in a special book, in order, Joanna said, that "if there was a possibility of my being deceived, all persons should have their presents returned to them again."[96]

In August, Joanna instructed Tozer to announce at his Sunday service the closing of the Southcottian chapels in London and throughout the country until the birth of Shiloh. On the last Sunday of the month only a small number of the vast crowd which assembled at Tozer's Duke Street Chapel were able to push their way in.[97] Instead of dispersing, those who were refused admission waited restlessly outside until Tozer had concluded his sermon. The preacher appeared at a side window of the chapel in hopes of satisfying the crowd, but they insisted that he stand where he could be seen by everyone. He moved to a middle window and then proceeded to address them with fiery intensity in his heavy Devonshire accent. A reporter from a London newspaper listened with the throng. According to his notes, the preacher said that

he had been of the Church of England till he felt a strong conviction that great events would take place on the face of the earth. These events which were for its happiness were now about to come to pass. He believed that HE was coming, who would prepare the way for the *millennium*, or the time when all mankind should live in unity and brotherly love with one another—when the sword should be turned into a ploughshare, and the spear into a pruning hook—when the industrious man should live by his industry, and the poor man get his bread without the sweat of his brow. . . . He took occasion to inform them that all mankind would ultimately be saved—that the greatest sinner, after a [suffering] proportioned to his offences, should participate in the general happiness.

To those who interrupted to ask about Joanna's pregnancy, Tozer replied that he understood that Shiloh was to be delivered sometime in the middle of October. The preacher finished, according to the reporter, amid "several rounds of applause" by bowing continuously to the "mob," giving them his thanks, calling down God's blessing on everyone, "and wishing them *their liberty*."[98]

The *Bristol Mirror* reported that the believers had purchased land near Regent's Park in order to erect a palace for King Shiloh.[99] A hymn had even been composed which was to be sung on the day of his birth.

> Shiloh to our faith is given,
>   On this bright auspicious morn;
> Shiloh, choicest gift of heaven,
>   For a faithless world is born.
>
> Ne'er shall war and desolation,
>   Spread o'er earth their purple dye;
> Peace shall shelter ev'ry nation,
>   Faith shall beam in ev'ry eye.
>
> Hail Joanna! favour'd mortal,
>   Chosen maid of heav'n's love;
> Thou canst ope the blessed portal,
>   Of the joyful seats above.

Thou, the voice of heav'n revering,
Canst our future fate descry;
Sounds unknown to mortal hearing,
Sights unseen by mortal eye.

Wicked world for ever doubting,
Soon you'll suffer endless pain;
While the elect, gladly shouting,
Celebrate Messiah's reign.

Arouse! awake! and never slumber,
Of the SACRED SEAL possest,
Haste to be amongst the number
Of the saints, supremely blest.[100]

A London newspaper, the *Sunday Monitor*, suddenly realized that a special readership had materialized overnight. It was to say later, "We had no idea that either Mrs. Southcott, or her doctrines, were of such universal consequence, as they then appeared to be."[101] Even with the American war being waged and "the fate of Europe about to be decided," Joanna was the sole interest "in the minds of many" in the kingdom.[102] The paper said that, if the dome of St. Paul's had collapsed or a fourth of the city been destroyed by an earthquake, the excitement could not have been more intense. "In every street, alley, court, and house, nothing was heard but the name of Southcott."[103] Ballads composed about Shiloh were sung in the streets and at places of public entertainment.[104] Joanna's publications sold as fast as they became available.[105] Toy shops were filled with "Joanna Southcott's Cradles," draped in pink calico with a trim of silver lace and a tiny doll inside representing Shiloh.[106]

The *Times* accused the *Sunday Monitor* of pandering to this highly susceptible audience. For its part, the *Monitor* responded with a burst of self-congratulation for its tolerance and enterprise: "The meed of public applause, and the unparalleled increase of circulation which has attended our impartiality, are the most encouraging tributes which can be paid to our rectitude and independence." Never had the paper's circulation been higher.[107] Its editor welcomed letters from the believers. The paper thus became the clearing house for all news about Joanna's condition, including the voluminous correspondence contributed by several of the physicians who examined her.

Joanna's certainty about her condition remained unassailable. Much reassured, George Turner wrote on March 16, "Now let the Mockers be silent for if she is [a] deceiver herself or is deceived she has now com-

pletely committed herself. So let them wait the issue of the event." [108]
Joanna's adversaries were not prepared to "wait" in Birmingham or
Greenwich, however, where sizable disturbances took place. Her followers were possibly "in danger" in Birmingham, a city which Joanna
called "a bad place." In Greenwich, her preacher, Theodore Turpin, appealed in vain to the magistrates for protection and found the risks of
violence so high that he switched his meeting from the evening to the
afternoon. London, however, was "very quiet." [109] This was to change in
late summer, for, by then, roaming mobs were making life unbearable
for Joanna and her entourage. Ann Underwood said, "We are beset with
men, women, and children, and everyone looking up to the house calling out where is Joanna, and abusing her with shocking expressions." [110]
Foley wrote in his diary on August 22: "There was a great riot in the
evening before Joanna's house, and they threw violently many stones
and brickbats against the house and doors, and *they*, the inhabitants,
were much alarmed. Joanna was told by the Spirit that it would not be
safe for her to continue there long, as her life would be in danger." [111] By
September she felt compelled to move, saying, "I could no longer stay
there in Safety," and went into hiding. [112] The Spirit assured her that she
would deliver before the end of the month. By the close of October, the
believers were growing "very anxious." [113] It had now been a year since
her "visitation" and Shiloh had not yet appeared.

One last, extraordinary development was to transpire, however. Joanna announced that she intended to marry, so that when the child was
born it would not be stigmatized by illegitimacy. She had expressed her
intention to take this step in October, a year before, and had instructed
her preachers to inform the believers of her decision at their meeting
places. [114] The very idea of marriage, regardless of who the partner was,
horrified her, she told Foley, particularly when "never one word of Love
ever passed between him and me in our lives." Perhaps even more staggering was the thought that she would have to surrender "the Power
and Authority," given her by God, "to one that I have no regard for." If
it were her choice, she would not take such a step for "a Million of
Money but as it was the command of the Lord I would not disobey for
the world." [115] Joanna, too, had wearied of waiting for her heavenly
bridegroom to become flesh.

Now that Joanna was unattractive and infirm, and not far from
death, her sexual longings turned back to her youth when her beauty
had made her the heart's desire of the most striking young men of the
neighborhood. The Spirit, whose very existence was due to these un-
acknowledged and unexpressed desires, at last extended his benedic-
tion to a union which, except for circumstances and the torments of

Joanna's personality, should have taken place fifty years before. Her spouse was to be "Noah" but not, he hastened to add, "Noah Bishop." [116] The Noah of Joanna's youth had married, was the father of a grown son, and lived in his native village of Harpford, enjoying a rich, full, and anonymous life which he had once wished above all else to share with Joanna. [117] What his name meant to her in these last months is impossible to say. But, whatever it was, the pressure of the past, of Gittisham, of the abortive meeting at the Sidmouth fair, of the memories of parents and siblings, of her endless duties in household after household, of all that might have been, the memories must have flickered disturbingly. At last, however, everything faded before the brilliant presence of the companion who had given her life its strength and its purpose. She had long ago surrendered herself to her Spirit, and now, as always, she would obey his commands.

But the suitor who finally presented himself was not a "Noah" but one John Smith, steward to the Earl of Darnley, who owned Rock Cottage where Joanna, Jane Townley, and Ann Underwood had lived since 1804. Smith's "great friend" was a man named George Troup, a staunch Southcottian, native of Blockley, and for forty years a page to the Prince of Wales. There is even a story that Troup so interested the prince regent in Joanna that he paid a visit to her in Blockley "to assure himself of the truth of her claims, and made some generous gifts to help the Cause." [118]

Smith declared his honorable intentions, and, for the first and last time, her Spirit encouraged a match, telling her not to refuse his offer as he was "a Very Respectable [man]." On Saturday morning, November 12, 1814, Smith came to see the prophetess "and they had a great deal of conversation together." Because he wanted to settle everything at once a marriage contract was drawn up. Then, Ann Underwood reported later, Smith read through his part of the service "and She Repeated her part of the ceremony in the presence of Me and another." [119] The marriage agreement was to be abrogated, however, if Joanna did not give birth to a child.

The *Monitor* began issuing an "Official Bulletin," which was dispatched regularly to the provincial press. As a response to the "many most pressing enquiries relative to Mrs. SOUTHCOTT," thousands of believers in London and the rest of the kingdom consumed such morsels of information as contained in the bulletin sent out for December 4, 1814:

On Thursday night Mrs. Southcott rested better than she had done for some weeks past, being entirely free from pain and restlessness, and she continued so on Friday, having neither sickness nor pain. Last night, however, she became very restless and uneasy; she took one of the opium pills, which composed her till near two o'clock in the morning, when she awaked in very great pain, and continued so for an hour; it then went off, and she slept for a short time, then waking in great pain. In this manner she has continued the whole day. The pain is not of a long duration as she very soon goes to sleep again.

Though her sickness has not returned, her appetite does not improve. She is free from fever but is faint and low.

Saturday Night, 8 o'clock.

Joanna, in fact, was dying. As the middle of October came and went, and her health deteriorated, the prophetess began to be fitfully pessimistic about the pregnancy. But her faith always managed to reassert itself. Colonel Harwood assured her that everything was in order, she was not dying, and soon she would give birth to Shiloh. On December 12, he wrote to Edmund Baker that the growing scepticism of the physicians should be ignored: "All that happens is far out of the common practice of medical men, and they know nothing about it." He advised believers not to be asking "Abstract Questions, . . . for we know nothing but what we are taught of the Lord." For his part, he refused to despair. He told Baker that he "with all true believers will see her as promised, with the child in her arms & milk in her breasts." [120] Dr. Reece continued his visits, but his confidence in his original diagnosis began to waver. Sharp, who Reece had discovered was "a plain honest man, of deep thought and great research," remained steadfast. "He was fully prepossessed that the child would establish the Millennium, and would not hear a word against her pregnancy, though apparently a real practical Christian." In response to the doctor's dejection, Sharp merely said that Reece's judgment was "*professional*" while his was "*spiritual*." [121]

Sometime on the evening of Christmas day, a Sunday, Joanna turned to Ann Underwood and asked how she was, then squeezed her hand, and whispered, "I am not afraid to appear before my God, as I have done nothing but what I believed to be in true obedience to my Lord." [122] Her words then became indistinguishable.

Two nights later Colonel Harwood gave up his vigil by her bedside at one o'clock and asked the nurse to notify him if she became worse. It was impossible to be hopeful, however, because her breath was coming with increasing difficulty. He was hurriedly called at three o'clock and sat quietly by Joanna's bed watching her for the next hour. He told his wife, "I saw her last breath go from her mouth, exactly as the Clock struck four." [123]

However, the colonel was not yet ready for despair about the fulfillment of her mission or, indeed, about Joanna. He wrote the next day, "I shall always think of what I have done, & what I am doing, as a duty

. . . to the Almighty." And, still, God possessed the power, as He had shown with Lazarus, to carry out "the great work" and "raise his Instrument" from the dead.[124] Following Joanna's directions, Colonel Harwood, Sharp, and the others refused to allow a medical examination to settle the matter of her pregnancy and determine the cause of her death, if indeed she was dead, until a period of four days elapsed. "No force" during this time "should be used to Extricate the child," she had warned. At the end of that time it would be clear "to the full Satisfaction of her friends" if "actual Death" had taken place.[125]

In the course of the autopsy which followed, one physician attributed her symptoms of vomiting and loss of appetite to "biliary obstructions," and the enlargement of her body to the simple accumulation of fat. The appearance of fetal movement "must have arisen from flatus escaping from one intestine to another." The increased size of her breasts was due to "glandular enlargement."[126] There was no evidence of a child. The attending physicians signed a statement that, after their examination, they could report "no part [of her body] exhibiting any Visible appearance of disease sufficient to have occasioned death."[127] Sharp said a year later, "No one could tell the cause of her Death, and to this day it remains unknown."[128]

The body was placed in a plain coffin, the lid screwed down, and pitch used to seal it tight. Because of the press of the increasingly disorderly crowds outside, the coffin did not leave the house until midnight, when it was carried to an undertaker on Oxford Street, remaining there until the second day of the new year, when a hearse, drawn by two horses, came to take it to a cemetery in St. John's Wood. Every effort was made to prevent any information about the details of the actual burial becoming public. None of her followers were informed, and only a few of the inner circle. As the church service was read, three figures stood apart from the grave, in mute witness to the proceedings. They were disguised by heavy coats buttoned to the chin, raised collars, and handkerchiefs pulled over the lower parts of their faces. One of them was Colonel Harwood. The few curiosity seekers who stood close to the grave had no idea that the coffin being lowered into the ground contained the body of Joanna Southcott.[129]

CONCLUSION

With her death, Joanna was finally beyond the reach of her Spirit. However, Phillip Pullen, the compiler of the Southcottian hymnal, heard Dr. Reece exclaim upon examining Joanna a few days before she died that the child was "gone." With this unwitting encouragement, the believers suddenly took heart. On the day of Joanna's death had not news come that peace with America had been declared? Did this not possess some great and awful meaning? It was clear that God was "about to do a great work." Joanna had been mistaken but not deceived. King Shiloh was to have a spiritual birth rather than a temporal one.[130] William Sharp said confidently, "On Christmas Day the Child was born or about that time." He wrote to Foley, "I have not a Particle of doubt on my mind that the Power who created all things caused this wonderful Event to take place for our final restoration to happiness."[131] Soon, King Shiloh would return to earth as a conquering prince, just as Joanna had prophesied. Many believers, therefore, recovered from the excitement and disappointment surrounding Joanna's pregnancy. They reassumed their characteristic posture of quiet expectation, content to wait until their day of deliverance finally came.

Nothing could better illustrate that Joanna had touched a need both real and enduring in the consciousness of thousands of English men and women. Upon this fragile base—the belief that Shiloh's birth had been spiritual instead of temporal—the Southcottian movement continued to exist, if not flourish, following new prophets into the wilderness of the nineteenth and twentieth centuries. It is not my intention to trace the esoteric, though fascinating, attenuations of the sect after Joanna's death,[132] but rather to consider several of its larger implications: first, the movement's antirationalism and, second, the way in which it reflected ongoing attitudes toward social and political change.

During the long agony of Joanna's dying, Ann Underwood described in a letter the presence of two visitors of unusual distinction at the prophetess' bedside. One was Count Lieven, the Russian ambassador to London, and the other Count Orloff, aide-de-camp to the Emperor Alexander: "They behaved in the most feeling, and polite manner, bowing to her. . . . There was something of the appearance of a serious Awe as they went up to the Bed. The ambassador, when he took his leave, stood at the foot of the bed and wished her a happy Deliverance [of the promised child]." In any event, their visit was to be kept secret "for if it was Known, the Newspapers would have it Directly, and the abominable Caricaturers, and very likely our house beset with enquirers, more then it is at present."[133] Since Lieven was the husband of the famous diarist and salon figure Dolly Lieven, it would seem reasonable to discount the visit as that of two curiosity seekers, regardless of their distinction. But it is impossible to do so, considering the monarch whom they served, the Emperor Alexander, who himself had mystical visions and was at that moment struggling to effect a Holy Alliance with the avowed purpose of establishing the Kingdom of God on Earth. The czar received the publications of mystics and enthusiasts from all over Europe. When Alexander was in London in June 1814, Count Lieven accompanied him to a "good and solemn" meeting of the Quakers where the seriousness of the emperor's attitude was greatly heartening to the Friends who conducted the service.[134] A year after Joanna's death, Alexander himself was under the guidance of a prophetess, the Baroness Von Krudener. In the fall of 1815 in Paris, the czar "spent his free evenings in Krudener's salon where they read the Bible, prayed, recounted their dreams and visions, and on occasions listened to the hostess's prophecies."[135]

Joanna's audience was plebian and Madame Von Krudener's aristocratic,[136] but their needs were those of the age—intellectual and emotional security in a convulsed and incomprehensible world. Reason was no longer the unerring guide it had been in the eighteenth century. One of Joanna's followers momentarily set aside his concerns with scriptural exegesis and the imminence of the Second Coming to reflect this sense of betrayal by the world view of the eighteenth century, with its complacent reliance on rational certitudes: "In the search of truth we should shake off all prejudices of the nursery and the schools, nay, even of customs and climates: let us think for ourselves, and divest ourselves of the world as though alone; and in the remotest desert. Let the religion of nature, and the light of reason, be attended to; but not wholly *trusted*."[137]

As long as truth could be searched for with the light of reason in one hand and the light of the spirit in the other, men like Holcroft and Paine, and Sharp, Harwood, and Blake, could travel the same route together. The moment they diverged may have come in 1795 when, in addition to the trauma of the state trials, the words "Deist" and "Democrat" became synonymous. Infidelity, it seemed, had overtaken the radical cause by a *coup de main*, deflecting it from its purpose, which was to assist in building the New Jerusalem on earth. The New Jerusalem was not a metaphor, as Holcroft understood it, but as tangible as Brothers' request for "300 shiploads of timber" along with 20,000 tents and "a rug and blanket or two blankets to each tent" which the prophet had made of the kings of Denmark, Sweden, and Prussia.[138] When the millenarians split off from the radical forces, they turned inward on their journey to the Heavenly City, with only the light of the spirit to illuminate the enveloping darkness. They came to rely on their "feelings" and "spiritual guides" for direction. In this development we can see the springs of the romantic movement welling up from below. "To be properly understood," Dr. Kitson Clark has said, "romanticism must be considered not only as something which affected some of the leading minds of the day, it must be considered as a popular movement, even a vulgar movement."[139] Sharp and Harwood no less than Wordsworth sought out the uneducated for enlightenment in the belief that knowledge and worldly experience hopelessly clouded the perception of truth.

This quietist posture, one of *waiting* for deliverance from the suffering and injustice of the world, continued to play a significant role in shaping the character of radicalism in the first half of the nineteenth century. Edward Gibbon Wakefield, a diplomat and political writer, described the attitudes of those most excited by the stormy progress of the Reform Bill of 1832. He did this in order to explain why there was little reason to fear a civil insurrection in the capital: "The rabble have had, and still have, but confused notions of the object and means of a rebellion. Their extreme ignorance and rudeness disqualify them from thinking on any subject; and such ideas as they form, it is very difficult to extract from them. What I know of them is, that they have a vague expectation of some great change which is to banish misery from the land."[140] Ten years later, Southcottian W. B. Harrison saw humans still yearning to be freed from the prison of their circumstances, differing only in the direction in which they looked for a deliverer: "Is not one part trusting in the wisdom of the Duke of Wellington, and Sir Robert Peel; another in that of Lord Melbourne, and Lord John Russell? Is not a very numerous portion of the people looking for deliverance through a repeal of the corn and provision laws, and probably a still more numerous portion to the charter, as a panacea for all the ills under which they are now suffering?" If his readers took Harrison's advice, they would put their confidence in "the Lord of Hosts."[141]

Wakefield identified those projecting all their hopes toward some vague, salvific power as "the rabble," completely unknown to the upper classes and the government. "Specimens," he said, were costermongers, slaughterers of cattle, drovers, dealers in dogs' meat and dead bodies, cads, bricklayers, chimney sweepers, nightmen, and scavengers. These "helots of society,"[142] however, were not unknown to Joanna, herself once described as one of those whom "society" had "so neglected and despised as scarcely to be considered human beings."[143] Nor were they strangers to Robert Owen, "the prophet of the poor," of whose followers Wakefield said, "Truly they are fanatics,—in a religion, of which the essence is the salvation of mankind in this world."[144]

Joanna helped to prepare a receptive audience for Owen, the New Lanark factory owner and social reformer who founded the Grand National Consolidated Trade Union.[145] *Sherwin's Register* suggested that Owen and Joanna took advantage of the same impressionable audience when it compared the philanthropist with the prophetess who "deluded thousands for the moment, by telling them that a Shiloh was about to come into the world; a Prince of Peace, under whose standard all the nations of the earth were to unite; by telling them that . . . swords were to be converted into ploughshares." [146] So close was the general identification in the popular mind that E. P. Thompson believes Owen could be charged with throwing "the mantle of Joanna Southcott across his shoulders." [147]

Although Owen was a thoroughgoing utopian, he was not a Christian. Using the language of the Bible as a medium to communicate with his following, he allegorized its imagery to illustrate his concept of social change. Like Joanna, he appropriated for himself the role of the prophet or illuminist, the one who had a spiritual superiority to his following. In a passage from his autobiography he traced

the history . . . of the progress of the mission to prepare the population of the world for this great and glorious change, which, when accomplished, will yet more demonstrate the knowledge, wisdom, and goodness of the Eternal Creating Power of the Universe. . . . In other words, and to simplify the subject, the mission of my life appears to be, to prepare the population of the world to understand the vast importance of the second creation of humanity. . . . In taking a calm retrospect of my life from the earliest remembered period of it to the present hour, there appears to me to have been a succession of extraordinary or out-of-the-usual-way events, forming connected links of a chain, to compel me to proceed onward to complete a mission, of which I have been an impelled agent, without merit or demerit of any kind on my part . . . man may now be made a terrestrial angel of goodness and wisdom, and to inhabit a terrestrial paradise . . . the earth will gradually be made a fit abode for superior men and women, under a New Dispensation, which will make the earth a paradise and its inhabitants angels. [148]

A direct link between the Southcottian and Owenite movements exists in the remarkable person of James Elishama Smith. Smith edited *Crisis*, the principal Owenite publication, from the fall of 1833 until it expired in the summer of 1834. His two predecessors had been Robert Dale Owen, the philanthropist's son, and Owen himself. Four years before Smith took up the editorship of the journal, he had joined the Southcottian movement and "totally involved himself in the sect." [149] In the year following his conversion, Smith wrote: "Little did I think, New Year before last, there was a people in the country who were taught by revelation a doctrine so closely allied to my own. I never had heard of them. Yet I discovered, by the grace of God, such doctrines as they hold, and, of course, must have been led and taught by the same Spirit which teaches them, for it was such doctrine as never man taught or heard of before, being hid in the mysterious language of Scripture, and reserved for the latter days to be brought forth to the light." [150] Smith retained some detachment, however, and within two years he left the movement, although it appeared at one time that he was aspiring to its overall leadership. He went to London where he attracted a large following at the Rotunda by preaching a radical Christianity which included the dispossession of the wealthy and a redistribution of goods. From there, he found his way into the Owenite movement. On September 14, 1833, Smith wrote in *Crisis* defending his alliance with Owen, an infidel: "Mr. Owen is a disciple of Nature, and only opposes Revelation so far as he thinks it disagrees with Nature; but he is perfectly willing . . . to see the two reconciled, for the leading feature of his system is 'unity.' Did Mr. Owen not desire such a result, he would never have given encouragement to me. . . . If Nature and Revelation can be married together, it must be a most social union. Now they can and desire to be so united, and I now publish the banns. . . . Revelation is the bridegroom, and a stern, mystical old gentleman he is. Nature is the bride, the free woman." [151]

Ultimately, tensions arose which were similar to those experienced by Sharp and Harwood in the S.C.I. in the 1790s. On August 1, 1834, Smith wrote to his brother telling him that he had left "Owen's party." He said, "It is probable I am now nearly done with the Infidels. . . . I shall most probably be back to the Believing again." [152] Within a week after the publication of the last issue of the *Crisis*, Smith had become the editor of a family religious magazine, *The Shepherd*. "No one," John Saville has said, "could possibly guess that the editors of the two papers were the same man." [153] Forty years before, William Sharp's portraits of Daniel Eaton and Richard Brothers had stood just as incongruously side by side. In the case of both Sharp and Smith, the reasons for their extraordinary *volte face* were the same. Millenarians could still be active in radical politics but their relationship with the infidels would remain tentative and exploratory until they either shed their religious beliefs or retreated from the arena altogether. Sharp and Smith took the latter way.

The Southcottian movement was many sided, and it is impossible to assign any single explanation for its extraordinary success. Certainly, there is evidence of disturbed psychology at work, in both Joanna's case and those of her followers whose fantasies encroached all too successfully on their perception of reality. There is ample evidence that the "poor and oppressed" *were* prominent in her following. These were men and women victimized by the massive social and economic dislocation taking place in the country, particularly in the hardship years of 1800–1801. Although there is no specific evidence of a correlation between the distress of 1810–1813, which saw food riots shift dramatically to the manufacturing cities of the Midlands and North, and

Southcottian recruitment, surely these hard times served as a potent backdrop to the last spectacular year of the movement.[154] It is also true, as Clarke Garrett and others have emphasized, that there were those for whom the apocalyptic tradition offered a thoroughly rational and convincing interpretation of events. Even though it was a tradition in the process of being discredited, its adherents should be judged no more harshly than those who have embraced any number of other imperfect cosmologies in their efforts to better understand and come to terms with the worlds in which we live.

The extraordinary feminist appeal of the movement entitles Joanna to some mention with her great contemporary, Mary Wollstonecraft, William Godwin's wife and the author of the pioneering text of the women's movement, *A Vindication of the Rights of Woman*. Joanna as well as Mary devoted her life to pushing against the restricted opportunities available to women. In a different but no less valid sense, Joanna, as Mary, became one of the most remarkable women of her age, relying on what she saw as the truth of her own experience to establish a vivid, original, and fully realized identity for herself, and her sex, within the traditional perspectives of popular piety.

Joanna Southcott did not intend the institutions of English society to crumble when she announced the millennium. The prophetess and her following posed no active threat to the established order. Her insistence on maintaining her affiliation with the Church of England reflects the deep conservatism of village life which she never really escaped. Joanna offered what she herself needed, a haven at a time of crisis and vast cultural dislocation, where those who saw angels coming out of the sun with drawn swords and fiery dragons in the air could find solace. But if Joanna did not actively seek to change the order of the world she knew, by implication her anticipation of the millennium condemned it as a derelict existence from which mortals must be freed. "Is it a new thing for a Woman to deliver her people?" she asked. "Did not Esther do it? Did not Judith do it?"[155] Although Joanna failed in her attempt, behind her lingered the promise that someday Shiloh, the conquering prince, would return to earth and lead his people to the Heavenly City, which will never cease to beckon as long as men and women find themselves exiles in the City of Man.

At this last redoubt, Joanna's followers raised their voices to the promise of the future, not the memories of the past:

> The glorious Flag of Liberty,
> Which heads all Zion's host;
> Jesus suffered death on Calvery,

To redeem the world that's lost;
And Shiloh, he shall reign the King,
Of everlasting peace;
When Christ shall reign a thousand years
All sorrow it shall cease.

God's spirit now does strive again,
His standard is unfurl'd,
Joanna's children again shall bid
Defiance to the world![156]

Appendices

AN ANALYSIS OF THE SOUTHCOTTIAN SCROLLS

The following figures are derived from scrolls in the Joanna Southcott Collection in the Humanities Research Center at the University of Texas at Austin with the exception of those for Dowlish in Somerset and Teddington in Middlesex, which are taken from lists in the Southcott Collection in the Greater London Record Office. The figures for "single" and "family" categories are necessarily tentative. Followers whose surnames fall in sequence or, in the case of the London lists, ones who though out of sequence have the same addresses were assigned to "family" groups. All others were considered "single." These "single" and "family" classifications must, therefore, be used with care.

Many of the towns on the Southcottian scrolls are unidentified by county. Unless otherwise noted, they have been assigned to a county on the basis of obvious association (such as Exeter in Devonshire), deduction from other evidence, or, if a choice had to be made, where there are known to be significant concentrations of Southcottians.

*One asterisk denotes those towns which are identified by county on the scrolls and which appear in the *Gazetteer of the British Isles* 9th ed. (Edinburgh, 1966).

**Two asterisks denote those towns which are identified by county on the scrolls but apparently in error (i.e., they do not appear in the gazetteer).

Unidentifiable: All towns which are unidentified on the scrolls, which do not appear in the gazetteer, or whose location is otherwise uncertain.

APPENDIX A
Totals by Town

	Single Men	Single Women	Questions	Families Men	Families Women	Families Units	Total Believers
Bedfordshire							
Shefford		1					1
**Stefford		1					1
*Woburn	1						1
Berkshire							
—	1						1
Buckinghamshire							
**Dagenham	1						1
Cambridgeshire							
Cambridge		1					1
**Compton		1					1
Cheshire							
Macclesfield	6	23		3	3	3	35
Cumberland							
—	2	1		7	5	5	15
**Inton					2	1	2
**Netherwasdale		10			2	1	12
Derbyshire							
Ashover	1	3		3	4	2	11
Blackwell	3	3		4	5	3	15
Chesterfield	18	42	1	6	4	5	71
Pinxton	2	1		2	3	2	8
Devon							
Ashburton	10	23		3	14	3	50
Barnstaple		11			6	2	17
Bigbury	13	45		6	26	13	90
Brixham	16	55		9	20	13	100
Brixton	1						1
Christow	1			3	2	2	6
Crediton	3	15			15	5	33
*Dawlish	1						1
East Ogwell		1					1
Exeter	19	82		19	25	21	145
Exmouth	2	2		7	10	8	21
Ilfracombe	5	7		3	5	4	20
*Kenn	6	13		3	5	4	27
Kingsbridge	1			1	1	1	3
Newton Abbot		7		2	2	2	11

APPENDIX A (*Continued*)

	Single Men	Single Women	Questions	Families Men	Families Women	Units	Total Believers
*Northam	1						1
Plymouth	25	121	1	3	19	11	169
Rattery		1		1	2	1	4
South Brent	1			1	1	1	3
*South Molton	1						1
Staverton	1	9		1	1	1	12
Stokenham	1	1		1	1	1	4
*Tiverton	11	31		4	16	9	62
Topsham	4	4		1	1	1	10
*Totnes	10	25		9	13	9	57
Essex							
—	2	1		1	1	1	5
**Barton	1						1
*Dagenham		1					1
*Rainham				3	2	2	5
Gloucestershire							
Bristol	24	25		7	11	9	67
**Higham				1	1	1	2
*Tewkesbury		2					2
Hampshire							
Gosport		1					1
Portsmouth	1						1
Wight, Isle of	1	2		2		1	5
*East Meon		1					1
Herefordshire							
*Linton	1	1					2
Hertfordshire							
*Ashridge				1	1	1	2
Gaddesden	1	12		5	5	2	23
Little Gaddesden	2	2		6	6	6	16
*West Mill		1					1
Kent							
—				1	1	1	2
**Chainey		1					1
Chatham		25			2	1	27
*Cranbrook	1						1
*Dymchurch		1					1
**Farmingham		1					1

APPENDIX A (*Continued*)

	Single Men	Single Women	Questions	Families Men	Families Women	Families Units	Total Believers
Gravesend	66	90		18	37	25	211
*Ospringe	2			1	1	1	4
**Teversham	1						1
Lancashire							
Ashton-Under-Lyne	70	72	3	24	31	24	200
Bury	19	23					42
Clayton	3	13		5	12	6	33
Coln[e]	13	7	1	7	8	6	36
Manchester	5	18		3	17	8	43
**Noyna		9			3	1	12
Stockport	26	71		12	12	12	121
Sunny Bank	4	1		2	2	2	9
*Warrington	17	34		17	19	17	87
Leicestershire							
*Husbands Bosworth		2					2
Leicester	16	19		1	8	4	44
Loughborough					3	1	3
London	520	821	26	308	408	317	2,083
Middlesex							
**Grousley Elinton		1					1
*Teddington	19	25	2	35	44	35	125
Twickenham	1						1
Uxbridge		1					1
Norfolk							
Norwich	1				2	1	3
Northamptonshire							
Welford	5	7		1	1	1	14
Northumberland							
Alnwick	7	3		4	6	5	20
Nottinghamshire							
Mansfield	21	25		15	23	18	84
*Newark	12	55	2	4	8	5	81
Nottingham	9	22		11	14	11	56
Worksop	2	7		3	2	2	14
Shropshire							
**Mailey	1						1
Somerset							
—		1					1
Bath	18	39		6	12	8	75

APPENDIX A (*Continued*)

	Single Men	Single Women	Questions	Families Men	Families Women	Families Units	Total Believers
Crewkerne	47	121		46	51	39	265
*Dowlish	147	163	2	26	36	23	374
**Maplestone		1					1
West Chinnock		1					1
*Winscombe					2	1	2
Suffolk							
**Brindestone				1	1	1	2
Sussex							
Brighton		1					1
Warwickshire							
Birmingham		8					8
**Strewley	1						1
Worcestershire							
**Blockley				2	2	2	4
Yorkshire							
Barnsley	21	22		7	8	5	58
Beverley				3	2	1	5
Bradford	37	52		12	24	15	125
Brodsworth	9	11		9	10	9	39
Cowms	11	17		5	19	11	52
Doncaster	12	18		12	12	11	54
Gilling		3			2	1	5
Halifax	1	5					6
Hatfield							
Woodhouse	11	30		7	8	7	56
Helmsley	2	2		6	3	4	13
*Horton	28	25	1	10	14	11	78
Huddersfield	23	47		11	26	17	107
Hull	5	5		7	9	8	26
Idle & Idle Thorpe	9	27	1	7	19	11	63
**Kenningham				1	2	1	3
Leeds	56	65	1	30	34	31	186
Little Houghton	9	7					16
Marr	7	5		3	5	3	20
Mexbrough	2	1					3
Pontefract	16	23	1	8	14	8	62
Potovens	25	24		10	17	12	76
Pudsey	16	10		6	7	6	39
Sheffield	116	184	1	23	26	18	350
Stainforth	2	19		6	6	6	33

APPENDIX A (*Continued*)

	Single Men	Single Women	Questions	Families Men	Families Women	Families Units	Total Believers
Stockton	9	10		4	2	3	25
*Thorne	12	61		20	27	23	120
Thornhill Lees	24	22		1	9	4	56
Wakefield		15			6	3	21
Whitby	8	8		6	9	7	31
York	11	8		4	4	4	27
Unidentifiable							
Akering		1			3	1	4
Ashford	1						1
Bridgewater		23			11	5	34
Charlestown		79			28	10	107
Gamsey	4	3		3	1	2	11
Horsebrook					3	1	3
Korbrey	3						3
Lidbury		3	1	2	4	2	10
Little Howton	7	9		5	5	5	26
Newcastle	3	4		2	5	2	14
Pittersfield	1	4					5
Santon		2					2
Stockenham		5					5
Sutton	1	5					6
Thonhill	1	2					3
Ireland							
*Granard	4	2		1	1	1	8
Belgium							
Bruges	1						1
Swedish Pomerania	1						1

Totals by County

	Single Men	Single Women	Questions	Families Men	Families Women	Families Units	Total Believers
London	520	821	26	308	408	318	2,083
Yorkshire	482	726	5	218	324	240	1,755
Devon	133	453	1	77	185	112	849
Somerset	212	326	2	78	101	71	719
Lancashire	157	248	4	70	104	76	583
Kent	70	118		20	41	28	249
Nottinghamshire	44	109	2	33	47	36	235
Middlesex	20	27	2	35	44	35	128
Derbyshire	24	49	1	15	16	12	105
Gloucestershire	24	27		8	12	10	71
Leicestershire	16	21		1	11	5	49
Hertfordshire	3	15		12	12	9	42
Cheshire	6	23		3	3	3	35
Cumberland	2	11		7	9	7	29
Northumberland	7	3		4	6	5	20
Northamptonshire	5	7		1	1	1	14
Essex	3	2		4	3	3	12
Hampshire	2	4		2		1	8
Warwickshire	1	8					9
Worcestershire				2	2	2	4
Bedfordshire	1	2					3
Norfolk	1				2	1	3
Cambridgeshire		2					2
Herefordshire	1	1					2
Suffolk				1	1	1	2
Berkshire	1						1
Buckinghamshire	1						1
Shropshire	1						1
Sussex		1					1
Unidentifiable	21	140	1	12	60	28	234
Outside England	6	2		1	1	1	10
Total	1,764	3,146	44	912	1,393	1,005	7,259

Notes

INTRODUCTION

1. The University of Texas at Austin, Joanna Southcott Collection, 340, June 3, 1802, f. 61.

2. Joanna Southcott, *The Strange Effects of Faith. Second Part*, p. 69.

3. E. J. Hobsbawm, *Primitive Rebels*, p. 60.

4. Helen Kazantzakis, *Nikos Kazantzakis*, p. 131.

5. Albert Soboul has written of the *sans culottes* attitude, "The Revolution had been a *gospel*, a holy scripture which would assure the salvation of humanity" ("Religious Sentiment and Popular Cults during the Revolution," in *New Perspectives on the French Revolution*, ed. Jeffry Kaplow, p. 343).

6. S. Whitchurch, *Another Witness! Or Further Testimony in Favor of Richard Brothers*, pp. 4–5.

7. Clarke Garrett, *Respectable Folly*, and W. H. Oliver, *Prophets and Millennialists*.

8. Anthony Lincoln, *Some Political and Social Ideas of English Dissent*, p. 4.

9. Ibid., p. 2.

10. Joseph Priestley, *Essay on the First Principles of Government* (1771), p. 9, quoted in ibid., p. 172.

11. Quoted in ibid., p. 3.

12. *Anti-Jacobin*, I, 629, quoted in ibid., p. 26.

13. Quoted in Isaac Kramnick, "Religion and Radicalism: English Political Theory in the Age of Revolution," *Political Theory* 5 (November 1977): 509.

14. Ibid., p. 523.

15. Thomas Paine, *The Writings of Thomas Paine*, ed. Moncure Conway, I, 118–119.

16. Quoted in E. P. Thompson, *The Making of the English Working Class*, pp. 110–111.

17. William Blake to John Flaxman, September 12, 1800, in *Blake: Complete Writings*, ed. Geoffry Keynes, p. 799.

18. "Annotations to Watson," in ibid., p. 386.

19. Joshua Brooks, comp., *A Dictionary of Writers on the Prophecies*.

20. Joseph Galloway, *Brief Commentaries upon Such Parts of the Revelation and Other Prophecies as Immediately Refer to the Present Times*, p. vi.

21. William Jones, *Popular Commotions Considered as Signs of the Approaching End of the World*, pp. vii, 8.

22. Joseph Priestley, *The Present State of Europe Compared with Ancient Prophecies*, p. 2.

23. George Stead Veitch, *The Genesis of Parliamentary Reform*, p. 219. Priestley referred to his French citizenship and his election as a deputy to the Convention as "these marks of confidence." He called them "the two greatest honours France could bestow on a foreigner."

24. Priestley, *Present State of Europe*, pp. 31, 25–26. Cobbett remembered that when he was a boy he "firmly believed . . . that the Pope was a prodigious woman, dressed in a dreadful robe, which had been made red by being dipped in the blood of Protestants" (*Political Register*, January 13, 1821, quoted in Thompson, *Making of the English Working Class*, p. 36, n. 1).

25. LeRoy Edwin Froom, *The Prophetic Faith of Our Fathers*, II, 649. But see Hillel Schwartz, "The End of the Beginning: Millenarian Studies, 1969–1975," *Religious Studies Review* 2 (July 1976): 1–15.

26. Alexander Pirie, *The French Revolution Exhibited in the Light of the Sacred Oracles*, pp. 149, 254.

27. John Strype, *Memorials of Cranmer* (1812 ed.), I, 91–92, quoted in David Daiches, *The King James Version of the Bible*, p. 38.

28. G. M. Trevelyan, *England under the Stuarts*, p. 57.

29. Blake, "Milton," xxvi. 44, in *Blake*, p. 513. For the continuity of millenarian beliefs, see Hillel Schwartz, *The French Prophets*.

30. T. D. Kendrick, *The Lisbon Earthquake*, pp. 1–23, 142–164. In his "Annotations to Watson," Blake said, "The Earthquakes at Lisbon etc. were the Natural result of Sin" (*Blake*, p. 388).

31. Robert Southey, *Letters from England; By Don Manuel Alvarez Espriella*, III, 263.

32. Blake to Thomas Butts, January 10, 1802, in *Blake*, pp. 812–813.

33. Elie Halévy, *England in 1815*, p. 256.

34. Arthur Young, *The Farmer's Letters to the People of England*, 2d ed. (1771), pp. 353–354, quoted in M. Dorothy George, *London Life in the Eighteenth Century*, p. 153.

35. See Norman Cohn, *The Pursuit of the Millennium*, p. 13, as well as Bryan R. Wilson, *Magic and the Millennium*, pp. 18–69, and J. F. C. Harrison, *The Second Coming*, pp. 8–10.

36. Peter Pindar, *Physic and Delusion!*

37. Balleine regards Joanna as "an unrecorded chapter of Church history," and asks that his book be read "as a footnote to Father Knox's *Enthusiasm*." Only fifty-six of the 151 pages of Balleine's work are directly concerned with Joanna's career.

38. Thompson, *Making of the English Working Class*, pp. 382–389; J. F. C. Harrison, *Robert Owen and the Owenites in Britain and America*, pp. 109–111. I was also very much stimulated by Deborah Valenze's thesis, "Millenarianism in Britain, 1794–1814: The Movements of Richard Brothers and Joanna Southcott."

39. Oliver, *Prophets*, p. 239.

40. Harrison, *Second Coming*, pp. 5, 99, 265.

41. Garrett, *Respectable Folly*, pp. 11–12, 15, 218.

42. Oliver, *Prophets*, p. 14.

43. Harrison, *Second Coming*, p. 221.

44. George Shepperson, "The Comparative Study of Millenarian Movements," in *Millennial Dreams in Action*, ed. Sylvia L. Thrupp, pp. 48–49.

I. THE WOMAN OF REVELATION

1. Joanna Southcott, *The Strange Effects of Faith; With Remarkable Prophecies, Made in 1792, &c. of Things Which Are To Come. Fifth Part*, p. 193.

2. Joanna Southcott, *The Third Book of Wonders, Announcing the Coming of Shiloh; With a Call to the Hebrews*, pp. 62–63. The date of Joanna's baptism, June 6, appears in the Devon and Cornwall Record Society, *The Register of Baptisms, Marriages & Burials of the Parish of Ottery St. Mary, Devon 1601–1837*, Part 1, p. 483. She herself did not know her exact birth date but it was determined by her followers to be April 25. See Mary S. Robertson, "Joanna—The Woman," in *Southcott Express*, March 1927, p. 119.

3. Joanna Southcott, *The Second Book of Wonders, More Marvellous Than the First*, p. 98.

4. Richard Polwhele, *The History of Devonshire*, I, 322. Vancouver reported in 1808 that the total population of the parish was 459. Of this number, 75 were engaged in agriculture and 39 "in Manufactures" (probably lace-making, for which nearby Honiton was famous). Since there were 64 families, the average family size was about 7, corroborating the parish's local reputation for health and longevity (Charles Vancouver, *General View of the Agriculture of the County of Devon*, p. 421).

5. Ibid., p. 325.

6. See Christopher Hussey, "Combe, Devon," *Country Life*, June 9, 1955, pp. 1486–1489; June 16, 1955, pp. 1556–1559.

7. Polwhele, *Devonshire*, p. 325.

8. Ibid., pp. 325–326.

9. Ibid., p. 325.

10. Jim Edwards, private interview held during a visit to Gittisham, Devon. Mr. Edwards was in his seventies at the time of the interview and had worked as a woodman on the Combe estate most of his adult life.

11. Arthur Warne, *Church and Society in Eighteenth Century Devon*, pp. 60–61. The original seating chart can be seen on the wall at the entrance to the church. Of great interest is the fact that the current seating arrangements generally correspond with those of the eighteenth century so that the visitor can get a fine period "feel."

12. Hussey, "Combe," p. 1558. Reymundo Putt's unusual name owed to the fact that his father had been a merchant in Spain.

13. Polwhele, *Devonshire*, pp. 324–325. Polwhele said, "The estates in Gittesham not belonging to the Putts, cannot amount to more than one hundred a-year: and these lands lie at the extremity of the parish."

14. Southcott, *Second Book of Wonders*, pp. 90–93.

15. Ibid., pp. 95–96, 99.

16. Ibid., p. 95.

17. Joanna Southcott, *Copies and Parts of Copies of Letters and Communications, Written from Joanna Southcott, and Transmitted by Miss Townley to Mr. W. Sharp, in London,* p. 10.

18. Southcott, *Second Book of Wonders,* pp. 96–98. "Lady-Day" can refer to a number of different events in the life of the Virgin Mary. It is unclear from Joanna's reference which of the possible dates she is referring to. For example, the Feast of the Annunciation is celebrated on March 25, while the Assumption falls on August 15.

19. Ibid.

20. Southcott, *Copies and Parts of Copies,* p. 13. The term "poorwarden" is unusual. It probably refers to the administration of a local charity. In 1590 the Beaumont family left a legacy of £800 for the relief of the parish poor who were not on the rates. Those responsible for the administration of the trust made weekly payments to their clients. See William White, *History, Gazetteer, and Directory of Devonshire,* p. 228.

21. Southcott, *Copies and Parts of Copies,* p. 11.

22. For a discussion of the uses and technology of the pound house, see Walter Minchinton's article "Poundhouses: A Survey," *Devon Historian* no. 12 (April 1976): 30. William Marshall's classic, *The Rural Economy of the West of England,* I, 224–226, is also useful.

23. Southcott, *Copies and Parts of Copies,* pp. 11–14.

24. U.T., Southcott Collection, 339, [?], 1799, f. 85.

25. Ibid., 438, f. 208.

26. Ibid., 329, November 21, 1804, f. 70. There is also a suggestion that he took a "mistress," which would have been the supreme insult to the memory of Joanna's mother and further reason for her enmity. See Southcott to the Reverend Thomas P. Foley, October 8, 1801, 437, f. 451.

27. Ibid., 339, [?], 1800, f. 109.

28. Elias Carpenter, *Nocturnal Alarm; Being an Essay on Prophecy & Vision,* pp. 66–67.

29. Southcott, *Strange Effects of Faith. Second Part,* p. 69. As advancing age made her father increasingly enfeebled, Joanna became the provider for the two of them. The resulting self-confidence probably explains why her sister could remember that Joanna engaged her father in a lively dialogue concerning matters of "Divinity" and "Philosophy." See U.T., Southcott Collection, 420, June 10, 1808, f. 1. The result was that her father gave initial support to her prophecies. Subsequently, however, he withdrew it (439, July 12, 1799, ff. 47–48).

30. "An Appeal to all Liberal Minded Christians," ibid., 333. This is a brief sketch of Joanna's life written and published by her brother. It is pasted inside item No. 333.

31. Joanna Southcott, *The Full Assurance That the Kingdom of Christ Is at Hand, from the Signs of the Times,* p. 4.

32. Joanna Southcott, *The Answer of the Lord to the Powers of Darkness,* p. 74.

33. Southcott, *Strange Effects of Faith, Fifth Part*, pp. 203–204.

34. U.T., Southcott Collection, 336, May [?], 1796, f. 220.

35. Southcott, *Full Assurance*, pp. 2–3.

36. Southcott, *Second Book of Wonders*, pp. 89–90.

37. Joanna Southcott, *An Answer to a Sermon Published and Preached by Mr. Smith, on Tuesday Evening, March 15, 1808, at Beersheba-Chapel, Prospect-Place, St. George's Field*, p. 64.

38. Southcott, *Second Book of Wonders*, pp. 89–90, 101, 107.

39. M. G. Jones, *The Charity School Movement*, p. 365. *The Account of Charity Schools* noted that there were twenty students attending the parish school in 1724. Sir Thomas Putt, who died in 1686, left provisions in his estate to maintain a teacher for twenty "poor children" (White, *Directory of Devonshire*, p. 228). However, relying on her own experience as principal of a girls' school and a lifetime of scrutiny of Joanna's writings, Alice Seymour, her biographer, speculated that Joanna had been educated by one of the German schoolmasters who settled in England after the Hanoverian Succession. See *Southcott Express*, June 1928, pp. 28–29.

40. U.T., Southcott Collection, 449, f. 22.

41. Southey called Joanna "old, vulgar, and illiterate" (*Letters from England*, III, 237). In William White's *History, Gazetteer, and Directory of the County of Devon, including the City of Exeter*, Joanna is described in a similar vein. "She was an illiterate woman, could neither read nor write, but drank beer and took snuff very freely" (p. 365). Also, see A. J. Howcroft, *Tales of a Pennine People*, p. 65, and Jane Townley, *A Letter from Mrs. Jane Townley to the Editor of the Council of Ten, in Answer to His Remarks and Misrepresentations, Respecting the Mission of Joanna Southcott*, pp. 34–35.

42. It was not solely from maliciousness that Joanna's critics accused her of being illiterate. The likelihood that a woman of her background could read and write was most improbable. The anonymous author [J. G. H.] of a *History of Methodism in North Devon* (London, 1871) said that, in the early nineteenth century, "Many of the farmers and their children, and three-fourths of the labouring classes, were unable to read" (p. 65).

43. Joanna Southcott, *The Controversy of the Spirit with the Worldly Wise, As Given through Joanna Southcott*, p. 3.

44. Joanna Southcott, *The Trial of Joanna Southcott, during Seven Days, Which Commenced on the Fifth, and Ended on the Eleventh, of December, 1804. At the Neckinger House, Bermondsey, Near London*, p. 67.

45. Joanna Southcott, *The Long-Wished-For Revolution Announced to Be at Hand in a Book Lately Published, by L. Mayer, When, as He Says, "God Will Cleanse the Earth by His Judgments, and When All Dominions Shall Serve the Most High,"* p. 93.

46. Joanna refers to Knolles' work as "Knowles's History of the Turks." See *The Continuation of the Prophecies of Joanna Southcott. A Word in Season to a Sinking Kingdom*, p. 7. She describes her reaction to Paine's book in *An Answer to Thomas Paine's Third Part of the Age of Reason, Published by D. I. Eaton*, p. 2. The Spirit also instructed Joanna to read *The History of Josephus*. See U.T.,

Southcott Collection, 117, *Communication by the Small Still Voice on the History of Josephus* (Ms. dtd. 1806, publ. 1856), p. 1.

47. Southcott to Foley, July 19, 1801, in *Letters, &c.* [Divine and Spiritual Letters of Prophecies], p. 11.

48. Elias Carpenter, *An Apology for Faith, and Detection of Existing Errors Subversive of the Truth*, p. 35.

49. R. E. A. Pool to the Editors, History of Religions, Swift Hall, University of Chicago, April 23, 1974 (copy in possession of author). Dr. Pool is a member of faculty at Keynes College, University of Kent, at Canterbury, and a specialist in reading historical documents.

50. U.T., Southcott Collection, 437, f. 12.

51. Foley to Reverend Mr. Pomer[o]y, October [?], 1804, British Library, Add Mss. 47795, f. 15b.

52. Quoted in Emma Grayson, *The King's Son Shiloh, Prince of Peace*, p. 148.

53. Southcott, *Second Book of Wonders*, pp. 108–109, 100–101.

54. Joanna Southcott, *Letters and Communications of Joanna Southcott. The Prophetess of Exeter: Lately Written to Jane Townley*, pp. 27, 34–35, 32.

55. Southcott, *Copies and Parts of Copies*, pp. 14–15.

56. Ibid., p. 15.

57. Ibid., pp. 15–16.

58. Ibid., pp. 17–18.

59. Southcott, *Letters and Communications*, pp. 89–92. The story of Lord Burnet is a traditional folk ballad. One version, "Matty Groves," became popular in the 1960's with the revival of interest in the genre.

60. Ibid., pp. 92–93, 101.

61. Ibid., pp. 108, 101–102.

62. Southcott, *Copies and Parts of Copies*, pp. 84, 90.

63. Ibid., pp. 26–29.

64. U.T., Southcott Collection, 128, *Communication by the "Small Still Voice" in Explanation of Many Scriptures, Especially on the Subject of the Mighty Counsellor, &c.* (Ms. dtd. 1804, publ. 1859), pp. 28–29.

65. J. Jean Hecht, *The Domestic Servant Class in Eighteenth-Century England*, p. 19.

66. *An Address to the P——t in Behalf of the Starving Multitude* (1766), p. 39, quoted in ibid., pp. 9–10.

67. White, *Directory of the County of Devon*, p. 365.

68. Southcott, *Strange Effects of Faith, Second Part*, p. 86.

69. A follower said that Joanna had been under the influence of spiritual advice since 1772. See *A Call from the Most High God, the God of Abraham, the God of Isaac, the God of Jacob, to His Ancient People the Jews*, pp. 5–6. This vague association did not become explicit, however, until twenty years later when she began receiving communications from her Spirit, whom she identified as the second rather than the third member of the Trinity.

70. See, for example, Morton Prince, *The Dissociation of a Personality*, particularly his reference to St. Catherine of Sienna (p. 395). Julian Jaynes offers a

stimulating discussion on this subject in *The Origin of Consciousness in the Breakdown of the Bicameral Mind*, pp. 84–99, 347–364, 375–376, 410. Also of interest is the case of Robert Baxter, in Andrew L. Drummond's *Edward Irving and His Circle*, pp. 255–259.

71. Quoted in Mona Wilson, *The Life of William Blake*, p. 273.

72. Southcott to a friend, October 8, 1803, U.T., Southcott Collection, 339, ff. 118–119.

73. *Mr. Joseph Southcott, the Brother of Joanna Southcott, Will Now Come Forward as Dinah's Brethern Did*, p. 99.

74. U.T., Southcott Collection, 334, December 18, 1796, f. 76.

75. Southcott, *Letters and Communications*, p. 40.

76. *Joseph Southcott*, p. 50.

77. Southcott, *Copies and Parts of Copies*, pp. 80–81.

78. Southcott, *Letters and Communications*, p. 113.

79. Ibid.

80. U.T., Southcott Collection, 334, June 12, 1796, f. 152.

81. Ibid., 339, October 10, 1802, f. 149.

82. Ibid., 332, June 18, 1809, ff. 17–18.

83. Southcott, *Strange Effects of Faith, Second Part*, p. 42.

84. Southcott, *Trial of Joanna Southcott*, p. 60.

85. Anna Eliza Bray, *A Description of the Part of Devonshire Bordering on the Tamar and the Tavy*, I, 330–332, 334; II, 291–292. Anna Eliza Bray (1790–1883) was a popular novelist who gathered significant material about the habits and beliefs of rural Devonians while living in Tavistock with her second husband, the Reverend E. A. Bray. She composed her findings in the form of a series of letters to Robert Southey.

86. See A. G. Endacott, "Devon Folklore," in *The Devonian Year Book for the Year 1937*, pp. 60–61; and H. Syer Cuming, "On Charms Employed in Cattle Disease," *British Archeological Association Journal* 21 (1855): 323–329.

87. See F. C. Tyler, "The Rolling Stone on Gittisham Hill," *Proceedings of the Devon Archaeological Exploration Society* 1 (1929–1932): 70–73, and Arthur W. Fox, "By Hill, Down and Dale," *Papers of the Manchester Literary Club* 57 (1932): 252–253.

88. Bray, *A Description*, II, 46–47.

89. Southcott, *Strange Effects of Faith, Fifth Part*, pp. 194–195.

90. Ibid., pp. 194–195, 197–198.

91. Southcott, *Copies and Part of Copies*, pp. 63–65.

92. Joanna Southcott, *A Word to the Wise; Or a Call to the Nation*, p. 25.

93. Quoted in Ralph Whitlock, *The Folklore of Devon*, p. 42.

94. U.T., Southcott Collection, 334, January 12, 1803, f. 130.

95. Montague Summers, *The Geography of Witchcraft*, p. 153, and Whitlock, *Folklore*, p. 41; R. Trevor Davies, *Four Centuries of Witch Beliefs*, p. 183, n. 1.

96. Keith Thomas, *Religion and the Decline of Magic*, p. 438.

97. Ibid., p. 539. Thomas' generalization rests on Alan Macfarlane's doctoral thesis, which became *Witchcraft in Tudor and Stuart England*.

98. Ibid., pp. 502–534, 557–559.

99. Roger North, *The Autobiography of Roger North*, ed. Augustus Jessopp, III, 130–131. John Wesley came to Devon no fewer than thirty times, including eighteen visits to Exeter. His view on witches is worth recalling because he mirrored popular prejudice on this subject, as in so many others:

It is true, likewise, that the English in general, and indeed most of the men of learning in Europe, have given up all accounts of witches and apparitions, as merely old wives' fables. I am sorry for it; and I willingly take this opportunity of entering my solemn protest against this violent compliment which so many that believe the Bible pay to those who do not believe it. I owe them no such service. I take knowledge these are at the bottom of the outcry which has been raised, and with such insolence spread throughout the nation, in direct opposition not only to the Bible, but to the suffrage of the wisest and best men in all ages and nations. They well know (whether Christians know it or not), that the giving up witchcraft is, in effect, giving up the Bible; and they know, on the other hand, that if but one account of the intercourse of men with separate spirits be admitted, their whole castle in the air (Deism, Atheism, Materialism) falls to the ground. I know no reason, therefore, why we should suffer even this weapon to be wrested out of our hands. Indeed there are numerous arguments besides, which abundantly confute their vain imaginations. But we need not be hooted out of one; neither reason nor religion require this.

One of the Capital objections to all these accounts, which I have known urged over and over, is this, "Did you ever see an apparition yourself?" No; nor did I ever see a murder; yet I believe there is such a thing; yea, and that in one place or another murder is committed every day. Therefore I cannot, as a reasonable man, deny the fact, although I never saw it, and perhaps never may. The testimony of unexceptional witnesses fully convinces me both of the one and the other.

The Journal of the Rev. John Wesley, A.M., ed. Nehemiah Curnock, V, 265–266, quoted in Stuart Andrews, *Methodism and Society*, pp. 119–120.

100. Bray, *A Description*, II, 170; I, 37; II, 276.

101. Joseph Glanville, *Sadducismus*, Preface, quoted in Basil Willey, *The Seventeenth Century Background*, p. 196.

102. Bray, *A Description*, II, 277–278. James Obelkevich also came across this story in his research on popular religion in South Lindsey. See his *Religion and Rural Society*, p. 284.

103. Bray, *A Description*, I, 261; II, 170–171. As late as 1898 an incident occurred in Heavitree where Joanna had worked a century before which demonstrated the enduring vitality of witchcraft beliefs in the West Country: "Two women of the lower classes were quarrelling violently the other evening in Heavitree, a suburb of Exeter. One yelled to the other, 'You wretch, you always keep a black and a white pig, so that you can witch us; you ought to be scragged!' The one so addressed, it seems, has lived in her cottage some twenty years. She has during this period always kept a couple of pigs, one of each colour; and her neighbours consider she does this so that she may enjoy the very

questionable powers of witchcraft. No butcher in the neighbourhood will buy her pigs, as, if he were known to do so, he would certainly lose the local custom on which he relies" (*Notes and Queries*, December 10, 1898, pp. 466–467, quoted in Davies, *Four Centuries*, p. 197).

104. U.T., Southcott Collection, 86, Joanna Southcott, *Astrology and Witchcraft* (Ms. dtd. 1808, published 1853), p. 4. In his study of witchcraft accusations in Essex, Dr. Macfarlane writes "that people surrounded themselves with a wall of magical objects and gestures, intended to ward off evil generally and a witch specifically. Hanging holy writing around the neck, especially the first chapter of St. John's Gospel, was much favoured" (*Witchcraft*, p. 103).

105. Southcott, *Astrology and Witchcraft*, p. 5.

106. Ibid.

107. She observed, "Exeter seems in confusion, in war one against another, about me." See Southcott to the Reverend Stanhope Bruce, January 18, 1802, in *Divine and Spiritual Letters of Prophecies Sent to Reverend Divines, and Other Spiritual Good Men and Women*, p. 74.

108. Joanna Southcott, *A Warning to the World. Joanna Southcott's Prophecies*, p. 33.

109. Ibid., pp. 33–34.

110. *Devon and Exeter Gazette*, January 3, 1920, in the West Country Studies Library (WCSL), Southcott Cuttings, Exeter.

111. George Oliver, *Lives of the Bishops of Exeter*, pp. 164–165.

112. Southcott, *Letters and Communications*, pp. 26–27.

113. Southcott, *Strange Effects of Faith, Second Part*, p. 77.

114. Joanna Southcott, *True Explanations of the Bible. Part the Second*, p. 104.

115. Southcott to George Turner, November 1, 1807, U.T., Southcott Collection, 326, f. 132.

116. Southcott to Jane Townley, June 11, 1804, Greater London Record Office and Library (GLRO), Acc 1040/189, ff. 160–161.

117. *Trewman's Exeter Flying Post*, January 19, 1815.

118. Thomas, *Magic*, pp. 352, 349–350.

119. Ibid., pp. 292–295, 302.

120. *Fairburn's Edition of the Prophetess; Or Southcott and Shiloh*, p. 30.

121. Southcott, *Astrology and Witchcraft*, pp. 1–2.

122. Southcott to William Sharp, February 1, 1802, U.T., Southcott Collection, 328, f. 138.

123. Ibid., f. 137; *Communication on the Comet* (Ms. dtd. 1811, publ. 1859), pp. 4, 3, 1.

124. Southcott, *Astrology and Witchcraft*, p. 3.

125. *The Works of the Rev. William Bridge*, I, 437, quoted in Thomas, *Magic*, p. 363.

126. Southcott, *True Explanations, Part the Second*, p. 191.

127. George Turner, *A Book of Wonders*, p. 75.

128. Richard Polwhele, preface to George Lavington's *The Enthusiasm of Methodists and Papists Considered*, p. cxiv.

129. See Harrison, *Robert Owen*, pp. 98–99; Southcott, *Strange Effects of Faith, Second Part*, p. 42.

130. Southcott, *Answer of the Lord*, p. 75.

131. The question arises as to how Joanna was able to subsidize her publishing activities. Hecht has calculated that a "maid of all work" made approximately eight pounds a year (*Domestic Servant*, p. 149). More important, however, was the income from fees, allowances, and perquisites, which could double a servant's wages (pp. 153, 160). Frequently, a career in service made it possible for a servant to retire and set up a tavern (pp. 188–190). Joanna at one time had the expectation of opening an upholstery shop with her savings. From her own testimony, however, it appears that she was forced to go deeply in debt during 1801, the year in which she published a thousand copies of each of her first five books at the command of the Spirit (*A Continuation of Prophecies*, p. 25). "The thought of gain was never in my view, and what I thought I was commanded of the Lord, I obeyed; but so far from any gains at present, I now stand *one hundred pounds* worse than I should, had I never took pen in hand, and I can prove it to the world." Continuing, she said, "And, that the public may be further satisfied I do not write for gain, I shall make this remark, that it is well known to all my acquaintance, that I can maintain myself by my trade, as decent as any woman of my line of life would wish to live; and should have placed myself in business years since, had I not been ordered to leave all, to follow on to know the Lord, and then I assuredly should know him. So I have done as the merchants do, run all at a venture; and I have done as Peter did, launched into the great deep" (*The Strange Effects of Faith; With Remarkable Prophecies, Made in 1792 &c. of Things Which Are to Come. Fourth Part*). Joanna's financial difficulties were so acute that her sister feared she would be imprisoned for debt (*Warning to the World*, p. 20). Joanna blamed the gravity of her situation on the "usurious extortion" of the man who had advanced her money (*Letters*, p. 11).

132. Southcott, *Warning to the World*, p. 58.

133. Ibid., pp. 1, 3.

134. Joanna said the Spirit told her that if he spoke his own language it would be Latin (*The Second Book of the Sealed Prophecies*, p. 50). "'Tis your own words I do pursue; / For should I always speak in mine / It would be Latin to mankind; / Such Latin they could never read, / Nor understand a word that was said." Suzanne Labrousse also was taken to task for her poor grammar and she, too, knew the experience of automatic handwriting.

135. U.T., Southcott Collection, 336, April 25, 1805, ff. 205, 210.

136. Joanna Southcott, *The Strange Effects of Faith, Third Part*, p. 134.

137. Joanna Southcott, *A Dispute between the Woman and the Powers of Darkness*, p. 9. Actually, the offer was made by "Satan's Friend."

138. Quoted in Wilson, *Life of Blake*, p. 78.

139. U.T., Southcott Collection, 437, f. 160.

140. Dan Wakefield, "Novel Bites Man," *Atlantic Monthly*, August 1970. Wakefield described an experience that occurred while working on a short story: "[I] found myself writing a lyric kind of story I had not planned or

known about. It was the first time I had ever experienced that kind of 'natural' outpouring, as if some secret source in my brain had been unlocked and the words rushed forth as fast as I could put them down. When it was over, I read it through and saw that I didn't have to change anything. It was like a trance or being possessed—or being *in possession*, not of something weird or foreign, but of myself, at last" (pp. 76–77). He is even more explicit when he talks of his novel. "Incredibly, the novel poured out. Fifteen, sometimes twenty pages a day. It was like automatic writing; like I was the secretary simply taking down dictation. It seemed the story was all there written in my head all the time, and I was finally able to see it, hear it, get the words on paper. It was lovely and scary at the same time" (p. 78).

II. THE REACTION OF THE CHURCHES

1. Polwhele, preface to Lavington, *Enthusiasm*, p. cxiv.

2. Joanna Southcott, *Prophecies. A Warning to the Whole World, from the Sealed Prophecies of Joanna Southcott*, p. 35.

3. Southey, *Letters*, III, 238.

4. Thompson, *Making of the English Working Class*, p. 383.

5. Frederick Artz, *Reaction and Revolution*, p. 54.

6. Southcott, *Trial of Joanna Southcott*, p. 140.

7. U.T., Southcott Collection, 333, July 22, 1806, f. 317.

8. Southcott, *Full Assurance*, pp. 11–12.

9. U.T., Southcott Collection, 286, July 7, 1802, f. 1.

10. Joanna Southcott, *Divine and Spiritual Communications, Written by Joanna Southcott*, p. 32.

11. U.T., Southcott Collection, 339, May 21, 1813, f. 224.

12. Southcott, *Divine and Spiritual Communications*, p. 32.

13. Wesley, *Journal*, VI, entry for August 15, 1782, p. 365.

14. Ibid. See V, 503, n. 2, for an epitome of the debate on Saunderson's character. The Rev. F. F. Bretherton, who discovered the preacher's diary, judged that Saunderson had been unjustly criticized for his behavior. L. Tyerman (*The Life and Times of the Rev. John Wesley, M.A.*, III, 42–43) and Crookshank, the historian of the Methodist movement in Ireland, were of a different opinion. For his part, Telford, the editor of Wesley's letters, described Saunderson as "a zealous young man" (*The Letters of the Rev. John Wesley, A.M.*, VI, 30).

15. Wesley (*Letters*) to Miss Cummins, June 8, 1773, VI, 31; to Hannah Ball, September 1, 1773, VI, 38; to Joseph Benson, June 28, 1774, VI, 95; to Charles Wesley, October 28, 1775, VI, 184.

16. Ibid., Mrs. Bennis to Hugh Saunderson, December 4, 1771, V, 190; Wesley to Mrs. Bennis, June 13, 1770, V, 191.

17. Tyerman, *Life and Times*, III, 43–44. This assertion has been challenged, however; see Wesley, *Journal*, V, 503, n. 2. Telford acknowledges that Saunderson is usually thought to have been the recipient but maintains that "more probably" it was meant for Richard Steel (*Letters*, V, 132). In view of Saunderson's later dissipation in Exeter, it can at least be maintained that

Wesley's admonitions would not have been inappropriate if addressed to Saunderson.

18. In the remainder of the famous letter, Wesley exhorts the Irish Methodists to be "active" and "cleanly"; to keep their clothes mended ("Let none ever see a ragged Methodist"); to keep free of lice ("Do not cut off your hair, but clean it, and keep it clean"); to cure themselves of the "itch"; and to stay away from tobacco, snuff, and alcohol (*Letters*, V, 132–134).

19. Wesley, *Journal*, V, 503, n. 2.

20. Ibid., entry for May 13, 1773, and p. 505, n. 2; entry for May 20, 1773, p. 507, n. 1; p. 509, n. 1; p. 516, n. 2.

21. Ibid., VI, entry for June 4, 1774, pp. 23–24. Reflecting on the absurdity of the charges brought against him, Wesley asked rhetorically, "Was not the sheriff strangely overseen?" (p. 24). The thousand-pound fine suffered by Mr. Sutherland represented much less in Scots currency than in English.

22. Wesley (*Letters*) to Mary Bosanquet, May 29, 1775, VI, 151; to Mary Lewis, July 28, 1775, VI, 168.

23. Wesley, *Journal*, VI, entry for May 21, 1780, p. 279.

24. Ibid., entry for August 15, 1782, p. 365.

25. Southcott, *Copies and Parts of Copies*, p. 18.

26. *Joseph Southcott*, p. 71.

27. Southcott, *Copies and Parts of Copies*, p. 18.

28. Ibid., p. 19. Joanna spelled Saunderson's name in several different ways.

29. *Joseph Southcott*, p. 79.

30. Southcott, *Copies and Parts of Copies*, pp. 19–20.

31. *Joseph Southcott*, p. 73. Joanna reported that Marshall "lost his senses years before he died; and I have been told it was shocking to hear the noise he made."

32. Southcott, *Copies and Parts of Copies*, p. 20.

33. *Joseph Southcott*, pp. 80–82.

34. Ibid., p. 81.

35. Ibid., p. 83.

36. U.T., Southcott Collection, 339, May 1, 1801, f. 247.

37. Southcott, *Second Book of Wonders*, p. 84.

38. Quoted in Ronald Knox, *Enthusiasm*, p. 450, and cited in Warne, *Church and Society*, p. 114.

39. Quoted in A. M. Lyles, *Methodism Mocked*, p. 40, and cited in Warne, *Church and Society*, p. 115.

40. Quoted in Andrews, *Methodism and Society*, p. 44.

41. James Lackington, *Memoirs of the First Forty-Five Years of the Life of James Lackington*, pp. 71–72. Until 1744, the rules of the society included a list of questions which had to be addressed to each class member at the weekly meetings. They were (1) What known sin have you committed since our last meeting? (2) What temptations have you met with? (3) How were you delivered? (4) What have you thought, said, or done, of which you doubt whether it be sin or not? (5) Have you nothing you desire to keep secret? (Andrews, *Methodism and Society*, pp. 44–45).

42. Joanna Southcott, *The Strange Effects of Faith: Being a Continuation of Joanna Southcott's Prophecies of Things Which Are to Come*, p. 85.

43. Southcott, *Trial of Joanna Southcott*, pp. 45–46.

44. John Wesley Thomas, *Reminiscences of Methodism in Exeter*, pp. 2, 4, 12. Warne mentions Samuel Wesley's association with Blundell's School (*Church and Society*, p. 106).

45. Quoted in Elijah Chick, *A History of Methodism in Exeter and the Neighborhood*, pp. 24–25.

46. Wesley to Mr. Gidley, January 18, 1776, and July 4, 1778, quoted in Thomas, *Reminiscences*, pp. 14–15.

47. Wesley to Mr. Gidley, April 11, 1779, quoted in Chick, *History*, p. 34.

48. Ibid., p. 36.

49. Quoted in ibid., p. 39.

50. Ibid., p. 44.

51. Southcott, *Continuation of Joanna Southcott's Prophecies*, p. 85. But the *Dictionary of National Biography* maintains that Joanna joined the Methodists the previous Christmas. This is also the date given in a pamphlet published in 1847 (*The Trial, Casting, and Condemnation of the Prince of this World, the Old Serpent, Devil, and Satan*, p. 44). The significance of the earlier date is that, if Joanna's commitment to the Methodists antedated the appearance of her Spirit, her experiences in the society may have played a catalytic role in her personality breakup. It is more likely, however, that she did not join until afterward.

52. Thomas, *Reminiscences*, p. 28.

53. Southcott, *Continuation of Joanna Southcott's Prophecies*, pp. 85–87, 90, 92.

54. Reverend Robert Hawker, *The Life and Writings of the Late Rev. Henry Tanner of Exeter*, pp. 7, 9–13.

55. Ibid., pp. 16–17, 21–22.

56. Ibid., pp. 25–27.

57. Ibid., pp. 53, 186, 53, 61.

58. Ibid., p. 140.

59. Ibid., pp. 167, 170, 183, 215, 125, 128–129.

60. Ibid., p. 36.

61. Thomas, *Reminiscences*, p. 13.

62. Southcott, *Answer to a Sermon Published*, p. 6.

63. Ibid., pp. 7–8.

64. Southcott, *Trial of Joanna Southcott*.

65. Joanna Southcott, *The Book of Wonders, Marvellous and True*, pp. 74–75.

66. Southcott, *Warning to the Whole World*, p. 35.

67. Southcott, *Continuation of Joanna Southcott's Prophecies*, pp. 84–85.

68. This is a constant refrain throughout Joanna's writings. An explicit reference would not properly convey the significance it possessed for her.

69. Southcott to Elias Carpenter, December 5, 1803, U.T., Southcott Collection, 333, f. 37.

70. Ibid., 324, September 13, 1804, f. 95.
71. Southcott, *Second Book of the Sealed Prophecies*, p. 36.
72. U.T., Southcott Collection, 334, December 16, 1803, f. 64.
73. Southcott, *Divine and Spiritual Communications*, p. 38.
74. Southcott, *Warning to the World*, pp. 24—26.
75. U.T., Southcott Collection, 324, September 13, 1804, f. 97.
76. Ibid., 324, f. 103.
77. Southcott, *Trial of Joanna Southcott*, p. 138.
78. Ibid., pp. 138—139.
79. Thomas Babington Macaulay, *Critical and Historical Essays*, II, 143. Macaulay said, "We have seen an old woman, with no talents beyond the cunning of a fortune teller, and with the education of a scullion, exalted into a prophetess, and surrounded by tens of thousands of devoted followers, many of whom were, in station and knowledge, immeasurably her superiors; and all this in the nineteenth century; and all this in London" (p. 131).
80. Southcott, *Strange Effects of Faith. Third Part*, p. 98.
81. Joanna Southcott, *The Strange Effects of Faith; With Remarkable Prophecies (Made in 1792, &c.) of Things Which Are to Come: Also Some Account of My Life* [First Part], p. iv.
82. *Joseph Southcott*, p. 39.
83. Ibid., p. 40. Billingsgate was the London fish market where the language was noted for its abusiveness and coarseness.
84. Southcott, *Trial of Joanna Southcott*, p. xii.
85. Ibid., p. 41.
86. *Joseph Southcott*, pp. 39—40.
87. Joanna Southcott, *The Fifth Book of Wonders, Announcing the Event Having Taken Place, Which Was Promised in the Fourth Book Should Be in May*, pp. 28—29.
88. Joanna Southcott, *Sound an Alarm in My Holy Mountain*, p. 71.
89. Southcott, *Divine and Spiritual Communications*, p. 28.
90. Carpenter, *Nocturnal Alarm*, pp. 69—70.
91. U.T., Southcott Collection, 84, *Communication on Prayer; In Which Is Introduced a Reference to the Conduct of Daniel towards the Priests, in the History of "Bel and the Dragon"* (Ms. dtd. 1804, publ. 1853), p. 6.
92. Southcott to the Reverend Mr. Pomeroy, September 17, 1804, in Southcott, *Second Book of Wonders*, p. 41.
93. Southcott, *Warning to the World*, pp. 64—65.
94. *Joseph Southcott*, p. 37.
95. Southcott to Jane Townley, June 4, 1804, U.T., Southcott Collection, 328, f. 13.
96. *Joseph Southcott*, pp. 39—40.
97. Southcott to Townley, June 2, 1804, in *On the Prayers for the Fast Day, May, 1804*, p. 33.
98. Southcott, *Trial of Joanna Southcott*, p. xii.
99. Southcott to J. Crossley and J. Grimshaw, n.d., U.T., Southcott Collection, 339, f. 296.

100. Joanna Southcott, *Joanna Southcott's Answer to Five Charges in the "Leeds Mercury," Four of Which Are Absolutely False*, p. 20.

101. Southcott to Mr. Warren, October 22, 1807, in U.T., Southcott Collection, 133, *Communication, on the Persecution Caused by the Devil and the Possibility of His Visible Appearance* (Ms. dtd. 1807, publ. 1859), p. 1.

102. William Roundell Wetherell, *A Testimony of Joanna Southcott, the Prophetess*, p. 12.

103. Southcott, *Answer of the Lord*, p. 92.

III. EXETER AND ELSEWHERE: THE BACKGROUND

1. Southcott, *Strange Effects of Faith* [First Part], p. 29. See Michael Barkun's *Disaster and the Millennium*, pp. 34–61.

2. Southcott to a friend, July 19, 1803, U.T., Southcott Collection, 332, f. 28.

3. Ibid., f. 30.

4. Cohn, *Pursuit of the Millennium*, p. 282.

5. Vittorio Lanternari, *The Religions of the Oppressed*, trans. Lisa Sergio, p. 309.

6. Vancouver, *The County of Devon*, p. 359.

7. William Chapple, *A Review of Part of Risdon's Survey of Devon*, pp. 36–51.

8. Ibid., pp. 51–53.

9. Ibid., pp. 44, 54.

10. Vancouver, *County of Devon*, pp. 361–363.

11. W. G. Hoskins and H. P. R. Finberg, *Devonshire Studies*, pp. 425, 427.

12. Ibid., pp. 427–428.

13. W. G. Hoskins, *Industry, Trade and People in Exeter, 1688–1800*, pp. 18–19, 63, 150.

14. Ibid., pp. 53, 40, 36, 42.

15. Ibid., pp. 124, 13–14.

16. Ibid., pp. 12–13, 21.

17. Ibid., pp. 75–77.

18. Ibid., pp. 125–127, 56, 135–136, 141. In his study of millenarian movements in the Middle Ages, Norman Cohn noted "the spectacular rise in prices that preluded the [millenarian] revolution at Münster" (*Pursuit of the Millennium*, p. 282).

19. Hoskins, *Exeter*, p. 147.

20. Alexander Jenkins, *The History and Description of the City of Exeter and Its Environs*, p. 224.

21. Ibid., pp. 224–225.

22. Hoskins, *Exeter*, p. 147.

23. Southcott, *Warning to the World*, p. 35.

24. Ibid., p. 55.

25. Jenkins, *History*, pp. 227–228.

26. Hoskins, *Exeter*, p. 148.

27. Jenkins, *History*, pp. 227–228.

28. Ibid., p. 228.

29. Southcott, *Warning to the Whole World*, p. 56.

30. Jenkins, *History*, pp. 228–229.

31. Southcott, *Answer to Five Charges*, p. 11.

32. Southcott to a friend, July 19, 1803, U.T., Southcott Collection, 332, f. 29.

33. Ibid., 371, 372.

34. Ibid., Southcott to a friend, July 19, 1803, 332, f. 30.

35. Ibid., Southcott to Mr. Taylor, October ?, 1813, f. 38.

36. Charles Lane, *Life of Joanna Southcott*, p. 7.

37. U.T., Southcott Collection, 444, f. 16.

38. R. D. Murphy, "Off the Beaten Track," Typescript, Leeds Reference Library.

39. John Rylands Library, Manchester, Broadsheet No. 340. Also see Alan Booth, "Food Riots in the North-West of England, 1790–1801," *Past and Present* 77 (November 1977): 84–107.

40. British Library, Add Mss. 32633, February 4, 1804, f. 192b.

41. Ibid., Southcott to Mrs. Wilmot, February 7, 1804, f. 195b.

42. Southcott to Mr. and Mrs. Field, August 4, 1803, Gloucestershire Record Office, D3471 1/2, f. 15.

43. Add Mss. 32633, January 22, 1804, f. 203b.

44. Add Mss. 47799, August 11, 1803, f. 89b.

45. *London Courier*, September 19, 1804, quoted in Harry Price, "Joanna Southcott's Box," *Journal of the American Society for Psychical Research*, October 1927, p. 552.

46. "On the Destruction of the Enemy," British Library, Egerton Mss. 2399, n.d., f. 166b.

47. Add Mss. 32633, January 22, 1804, f. 203b.

48. Ibid., August 11, 1803, f. 173a.

49. Ibid., January 22, 1804, f. 185b.

50. Ibid., Southcott to Mrs. Wilmot, February 7, 1804, f. 196a.

51. Southcott to Mrs. Taylor, January 2, 1804, Add Mss. 47794, ff. 17ab.

52. U.T., Southcott Collection, 436, September 2, 1807, ff. 17–18. Also see *Trewman's Exeter Flying Post*, December 25, 1806, p. 4, for the announcement that the first sealing was to be stopped.

53. U.T., Southcott Collection, 439, September 3, 1808, f. 89.

54. Southcott to a friend, September 11, 1808, in Emma Grayson, *Had They Had Knowledge*, p. 169.

55. U.T., Southcott Collection, 444, ff. 9–10.

56. Southcott to George Turner, April 11, 1814, in Grayson, *Had They Had Knowledge*, p. 107.

57. U.T., Southcott Collection, 370, 371, and 372. Most of the names on each scroll are written in the same hand, indicating that they were consolidated from other sources by a secretary. For the purposes of this study, no one has been counted who can be shown to have joined after 1816. One scroll is entitled "Roll of the Believers in London," with dates ranging from March 5, 1809, to

October 23, 1908. There are 1,511 names listed. A second scroll is called "Roll of the Believers" and contains 1,291 names from a large number of towns. There is no date on the scroll, but a watermark reads 1816. A third scroll has the heading "The Roll of Names by the Command of the Lord to George Turner Who Unite to Obey the Lord and Are Waiting His Appearing and His Son Shiloh to Reign Over Us on Earth." It lists 4,062 names. Turner was one of Joanna's principal supporters and was accepted as her successor after her death by some parts of the movement. Unfortunately, there is no date on the scroll. It is of the same character as the previous two, however, and probably was compiled sometime between Joanna's death in December 1814 and January 1817. Turner prophesied that on January 28, 1817, the earthquake predicted in Revelation (6:12) would occur. This raised the Southcottian movement to a final collective pitch of excitement. Turner's rhetoric became decidedly revolutionary as the great day approached. He said, "Those who are not worth a penny now must be lords of the land. No rents must be paid. No postage for letters. No turnpikes. No taxes. Porter a gallon for one half-penny. Ale the same." The earthquake did not occur and Turner was arrested by the government for high treason. A jury found him to be insane, however, and he was confined to a Quaker asylum (G. R. Balleine, *Past Finding Out*, pp. 76–78).

I have integrated three additional lists of believers with the Texas scrolls. One consists of the names of 125 believers from Edmund Baker's congregation at Teddington in Middlesex. The other two are from his Dowlish chapel in Somerset. One, the "Dowlish List of Names," has 304 names. The other, the "Dowlish List of Believers," has 71 names. See the Greater London Record Office and Library, Acc 1040/1-2, 4. (I wish to thank Dr. Maurice Pearton for sending me the information about the Dowlish followers.)

58. February 27, 1806, in *The Scriptures of the Holy Trinity*, p. 35.

59. See Appendices A and B for the membership by town and county. I wish to thank Jane McKean Holahan for her invaluable aid in the preparation of these figures.

60. I am grateful to the staff of the history library and the map room of the County Hall in London for their assistance in helping me locate these followers. Street names have sometimes gone through several changes since the early nineteenth century. Urban development over a 160-year period and the destruction caused by the war posed other difficulties. The following is a list of those parts of the London area and the numbers in which the Southcottians could be found: Barking (19), Barnes (5), Bermondsey (67), Bethnal Green (29), Brompton (1), Camberwell (20), Chelsea (36), the City (104), Clapham (3), Finsbury (54), Hampstead (2), Holborn (87), Hoxton (6), Islington (5), Kennington (9), Kensington (4), Lambeth (96), Marylebone (26), Newington (10), Paddington (6), Peckham (22), Poplar (5), Putney (3), St. Pancras (27), Shoreditch (11), Somers Town (17), Southwark (192), Stepney (67), Walworth (49), Wandsworth (2), and Westminster (143). There were also 9 believers in Greenwich (which have been included in Appendices A and B in the figures for the London believers).

61. George Rudé, *Hanoverian London, 1714–1808*, p. 10.

62. Quoted in George, *London Life*, p. 85.

63. Jane E. Norton's *Guide to the National and Provincial Directories of England and Wales* proved helpful. Among the directories consulted were *Holden's Triennial Directory for 1809, 1810, 1811* (London), the *Manchester and Salford Directory for 1813*, the *Sheffield General Directory* (1817), the *Directory, General and Commercial, of the Town & Borough of Leeds for 1817*, *The Nottingham Directory* (1815), and *Matthews's Annual Bristol Directory for the Year 1815*, all of which are in the British Library.

64. U.T., Southcott Collection, 445, February 19, 1802, f. 562.

65. Reverend Thomas P. Foley to Mr. Taylor, October 15, 1808. Add Mss. 47795, f. 53b.

66. Southcott to Foley, December 10, 1810, Add Mss. 57860.

67. GLRO, Acc 1040/188, f. 415.

68. *Edinburgh Review* 24 (1815): 470.

69. R. Hann, *Charges against Joanna Southcott, and Her Twelve Judges, the Jury, and Four and Twenty Elders*, p. 36.

70. *Chambers Encyclopedia* (London, 1867), IX, 6.

71. Samuel Jowett to Mr. Wyatt [?], [?], 1871, Blockley Antiquarian Society, Blockley, Gloucestershire, 780 (5).

72. Add Mss. 32636, October 13, 1803, f. 33b.

73. Blockley, 515, November 11 and 12, 1802, f. 9.

74. George Turner, *The Armour of God*, p. 20.

75. Foley to R. Bramhall, May 19, 1829, Blockley, 594, f. 1.

76. Harrison, *Second Coming*, p. 221.

77. See Chapter 4 for a discussion of the "sealing" of Joanna's supporters.

78. See Southcott, *Sound an Alarm*, p. 26; Philip Pullen, *Index to the Divine and Spiritual Writings of Joanna Southcott*, p. 170.

79. See Southcott, *Warning to the Whole World*, p. 45.

80. *The Times* (London), August 22, 1814.

81. *Phrenological Journal* 7 (March 1831–September 1832): 360–361. I was directed to this reference by Professor Harrison in his *Robert Owen*, p. 110. Also see "Joanna Southcott," *Penny Cyclopedia* (London, 1842), XXII, 274, and R. Pearse Chope, ed., *The Devonian Year Book for the Year 1916* (London and Bristol). Chope observes that Joanna had 100,000 followers, "more than John Wesley ever had during his lifetime" (p. 50).

82. Edward Walford, *Old and New London*, p. 252.

83. Joanna Southcott, Part V [of the *Controversy between Joanna Southcott and Elias Carpenter*], p. 215.

84. L. Mayer, *The Woman in the Wilderness*, p. 31.

85. Carpenter, *Apology for Faith*, p. 164.

86. John Rylands Library, Broadsheet No. 351. This came from Walworth, Surrey.

87. C. Maurice Davies, *Unorthodox London*, pp. 274–275.

88. It can be established that each of Joanna's first five pamphlets was published in editions of 1,000. Also, the first printing of *A Word to the Wise* has on the colophon page the note, "This thousand to be given away." The second

printing of the edition has a note similarly placed which reads, "This thousand to be sold."

89. This is a total of sixty-six rather than sixty-five pamphlets. In the South-cottian canon, *Letters on Various Subjects from Mrs. Joanna Southcott to Miss Townley* is included with *Prayers for the Fast Day*, although the works are quite different and were sold separately.

90. West Country Studies Library, Exeter, Southcott Collection, bookseller's notation.

91. Richard D. Altick, *The English Common Reader*, pp. 70, 75, 69. The Cheap Repository Tracts, many of which were the work of Hannah Moore, sold for 1/2 d., 1 d., and 1 1/2 d., a fraction of the cost of Joanna's pamphlets. For the place that Joanna's work has in the popular literature of the eighteenth century, see Deborah M. Valenze, "Prophecy and Popular Literature in Eighteenth-Century England," *Journal of Ecclesiastical History* 29, no. 1 (January 1978): 89–90.

92. See Bryan R. Wilson, *Sects and Society*, p. 298. However, of the 123 identifiable names of the Teddington Church, 69 are women (56 percent) and 54 are men (44 percent), indicating a considerably narrower distribution. See GLRO, Acc 1040/2.

93. Southcott, *Controversy of the Spirit*, p. 35.

94. Southcott, *Trial of Joanna Southcott*, p. 143.

95. Southcott, *Strange Effects of Faith*, p. iv.

96. Add Mss. 32637, June 23, 1805, f. 42b.

97. Halévy, *England in 1815*, p. 279.

98. Wilson, *Sects and Society*, p. 301.

99. These figures are highly tentative. Followers whose surnames fall in sequence on the Southcottian scrolls or, in the case of the London lists, ones who though out of sequence have the same addresses were assigned to "family groups." All others were considered "single." The resulting figures for "single" men and "single" women are more valid for the latter. A man might with little reflection join the movement as the family representative. This would be less true for women.

100. Hecht, *Domestic Servant Class*, pp. 19–20.

101. Southcott, *Warning to the World*, p. 76.

102. George Turner, *The Assurance of the Kingdom*, p. 139.

103. Southcott, *Trial of Joanna Southcott*, pp. 139–140.

104. [24 signers] to Reverend Mr. Pomeroy, October 17, 1804, in Joanna Southcott, *The True Explanation of the Bible Revealed by Divine Communications to Joanna Southcott*, pp. 75, 78–79.

105. U.T., Southcott Collection, 340, October 18, 1807, f. 29.

106. June 28, 1804 in *Scriptures of the Holy Trinity*, p. 180.

107. U.T., Southcott Collection, 70, *Communication by the Small Still Voice*, p. 8.

108. Elias Carpenter, *Who Are the Deluded? Or Mystery Unmasked*, pp. 36–37.

IV. OLD WINE IN NEW BOTTLES

1. See R. A. Baldwin, *The Jezreelites*, p. 15.

2. W. B. Harrison, *A Letter Addressed to an Eminent Clergyman of the Established Church of England*, p. 73.

3. U.T., Southcott Collection, 331, September 2, 1808, f. 51.

4. Add Mss. 47800, February 23, 1815, f. 211a.

5. Henry Gunning, *Reminiscences of the University, Town, and County of Cambridge from the Year 1780*, I, 69.

6. Worcestershire Record Office, entry for February 24, 1803, BA 3762, 899.31 (parcel 137.v).

7. H. J. Haden, "Thomas Philip Foley," *Notes and Queries*, July 5, 1952, p. 297.

8. Priestley, *Present State of Europe*, pp. xiii–xiv.

9. Quoted in Alice Seymour and Mary S. Robertson, eds., *Watch* no. 4 (1937): 11–12.

10. Reverend Thomas P. Foley to William Phillips, April 3, 1802, Add Mss. 47795, f. 1a.

11. See Gunning, *Reminiscences*, pp. 69–71, and *Notes and Queries*, August 20, 1887, p. 154.

12. Add Mss. 32634, January 24, 1804, f. 98b.

13. Foley to Mr. Taylor, n.d., Add Mss. 47795, f. 75a.

14. Ibid., Foley to Charles Taylor, September 11 [?], 1807, f. 47a.

15. Add Mss. 32634, June 16, 1803, f. 98a.

16. Foley to William Phillips, April 3, 1802, Add Mss. 47795, ff. 2ab.

17. See his letters to Mrs. Foley, January 31, 1812, Add Mss. 57860, and to William Phillips, April 3, 1802, Add Mss. 47795, f. 1a.

18. U.T., Southcott Collection, 444, ff. 19–20.

19. Foley to Mrs. Foley, September 11, 1806, Add Mss. 47795, f. 35a.

20. Ibid., Foley to Mrs. Taylor, October 31, 1803, f. 7a.

21. Ibid., Elizabeth Foley to Miss Taylor, December 8, 1803, f. 8a.

22. Ibid., Foley to Mr. Taylor, January 26, 1805, f. 17b.

23. Ibid., Foley to Mr. Taylor, February 5, 1806, f. 25a.

24. Ibid., Foley to Mr. Taylor, July 6, 1805, f. 20a.

25. Ibid., Foley to Peter Morrison, August 15, 1806, f. 30a.

26. Ibid., Foley to Major Pidcock, February 23, 1807, f. 43b, and January 26, 1807, f. 43a.

27. E. J. Field to Foley, April 14, 1808, and Foley to Field, April 18, 1808. Add Mss. 57860.

28. U.T., Southcott Collection, 444, ff. 14–21.

29. Jane Townley to the Bishop of London, May 22, 1804, Add Mss. 32636, f. 67a.

30. For an account of Jane Townley's relationship with Joanna see *Council of Ten*, pp. 4–10. There is a short sketch of her life in the December 1927 issue of the *Southcott Express*, pp. 192–196.

31. Southcott to Foley, May 10, 1804, Add Mss. 32636, ff. 49 ab. She tells

Foley, "I have . . . a perfect happy companion in Miss Townley, and also in her servant." In a letter from Foley in the same year, it is made clear that Joanna lived by Townley's "Bounty and Kindness" (see Add Mss. 47797, f. 84b). Richard Law estimated that her income was over £700 a year (see his letter to her, July 17 [?], 1816, Add Mss. 47796, f. 16a).

32. Townley to Mr. Bradley, May 28, 1812, U.T., Southcott Collection, 435, f. 23. Miss Townley comments that Christ will not reign in person but "in Spirit" upon His return to earth. This is an unusual example of her speaking in her own voice about a controversial matter.

33. Townley, *Council of Ten*, p. 29.

34. Townley to Mrs. Taylor, June 22, 1804, Add Mss. 47794, f. 21b.

35. Townley, *Council of Ten*, p. 29.

36. Charles Barnard to Edmund Baker, October 26, 1814, GLRO, Acc 1040/25, f. 3.

37. Mary S. Robertson, "Ann Underwood," *Southcott Express*, March 1928, p. 17.

38. Ann Underwood to Joshua Lowe, February 3, 1814. Acc 1040/184, ff. 112–116.

39. Richard Law to Townley, May 10, 1816, Add Mss. 47796, ff. 1b, 3ab.

40. Ibid., Law to Townley, June 23, 1816, f. 8b; to Townley, December 1817, f. 53a; to Townley, November 22, 1818, ff. 63ab.

41. Ibid., Law to Townley, November 22, 1818, ff. 63ab; to Ann Underwood, November 27, 1818, ff. 64ab; to Townley, November 28, 1818, f. 66a; to Underwood, May 21, 1817, f. 27b; to Underwood, November 13, 1817, f. 48b. Law was certainly an unstable character, but this last mutation may have been a clumsy joke on his part.

42. Southcott to Mrs. Taylor, October 29, 1802, Add Mss. 47794, f. 5a.

43. Foley to Mr. Robert Taylor, May 25, 1802, Add Mss. 47795, f. 4a.

44. U.T., Southcott Collection, 335, November 18, 1804, f. 35.

45. Quoted in Lavinia E. C. Jones, ed. *Commentary upon the Prayers and Ordinances of the English Protestant Church*, p. 10.

46. Southcott to a friend, December 2, 1811, U.T., Southcott Collection, 334, ff. 59–60. For the point of view of a magistrate faced with application for a license from a Southcottian preacher, see *Gentleman's Magazine* 85 (January 1815): 38.

47. Add Mss. 47794, February 8, 1809, ff. 116ab.

48. Southcott to Foley, March 24, 1812, Add Mss. 57860, f. 3.

49. U.T., Southcott Collection, 331, September 2, 1808, ff. 51–52, 55; Townley to Mr. Turner, June 28, 1809 [?], 332, f. 15.

50. Blockley Antiquarian Society, Blockley, Gloucestershire, BA515, entry for January 18, 1803, f. 64.

51. U.T., Southcott Collection, 113, *Extract from a Letter Addressed to Mr. G. Woolcott, of Exeter* (Ms. dtd. 1806, publ. 1854), pp. 1–2.

52. Townley to a friend, June 22, 1809, U.T., Southcott Collection, 332, ff. 10–11.

53. Southcott to S. Entwissle, October 30, 1805, Add Mss. 47797, f. 103b.

54. Southcott, *Warning to the World*, p. 18.

55. Southcott, *Copies and Parts of Copies*, p. 32.

56. Townley, *Council of Ten*, p. 8.

57. Foley to Elias Carpenter, October 28, 1805, Add Mss. 47795, f. 22b.

58. Southcott to E. J. Field, August 4, 1803, Gloucestershire Record Office, D3471 I/2, f. 12.

59. Southcott to Peter Morrison, May 20, 1805, Add Mss. 47794, ff. 57ab.

60. Foley to a friend, January 22, 1810, U.T., Southcott Collection, 445, f. 547.

61. Southcott to Peter Morrison, September 8, 1806, Add Mss. 47794, ff. 83ab.

62. Southcott to George Brough, November 21, 1806, Add Mss. 47797, f. 129a.

63. Southcott to a friend, May 24, 1809, University of Manchester, John Rylands Library, R20862, f. 250.

64. Southcott to [?], September 27, 1806, Add Mss. 47794, f. 85a.

65. Southcott to a friend, May 24, 1809, John Rylands Library, R20862, f. 251.

66. Southcott to Peter Morrison, September 8, 1806, Add Mss. 47794, f. 84a. She said, "My heart is wounded with the complaints I hear, which is more concerning you then I hear from all the others."

67. "The Oath," June 14, 1804, John Rylands Library, R20862, f. 103.

68. U.T., Southcott Collection, 333, December 5, 1803, ff. 34–37.

69. Southcott, *True Explanations. Second*, p. 186.

70. *Leeds Mercury*, October 22, 1803, p. 3.

71. The Southcott Collection at the University of Texas at Austin includes fifty-two seals. Only eight, however, have been opened.

72. Southcott, *Divine and Spiritual Communications*, p. 20.

73. Joanna Southcott, *A Caution and Instruction to the Sealed, That They May Know for What They Are Sealed*, pp. 2, 10. The passages in Revelation are from Chapter 7, verses 3–9. Verse 4 reads, "And I heard the number of them which were sealed: *and there were* sealed an hundred *and* forty *and* four thousand of all the tribes of the children of Israel."

74. *Leeds Mercury*, October 29, 1803, p. 2.

75. Ibid., October 22, 1803, p. 3.

76. John Crossley and William Jowett, *A Vindication of Joanna Southcott's Writings*, p. 18.

77. U.T., Southcott Collection, 324, June 4, 1808, ff. 20, 24.

78. Southcott, *Warning to the World*, p. 12.

79. *The Life and Prophecies of Joanna Southcott, from her Infancy to the Present Time*, p. 18; U.T., Southcott Collection, 114, *Extract from a Letter Respecting the Seals Being Put into the Coffin with the Individual Who Leaves the Earth* (Ms. dtd. 1808, publ. 1854).

80. Grayson, *Had They Had Knowledge*, p. 177.

81. Southcott, *Sound an Alarm*, p. 26.

82. *Making of the English Working Class*, p. 385.

83. According to *Devon Notes and Queries* 11 (January 1902–October 1903): 241, "She is said to have sold between six and seven thousand of them, some at 12s., but most of them at a guinea." Also see *Notes and Queries*, May 1, 1909, p. 353, and, more recently, P. Thompson, "'Your Own Messiahs' in the West," *Devon Life*, April 1976, p. 40. There are numerous other examples of this widespread belief. In one account, William Sharp was supposed to have been a prominent vendor of the seals (see Southcott Cuttings, September 16, 1814, in the West Country Studies Library [WCSL], Exeter).

84. Add Mss. 32636, April 3, 1805, f. 156a.

85. Lord Byron to John Murray, September 7, 1814, in Thomas Moore, *The Letters and Journals of Lord Byron*, p. 432.

86. Southcott, *Copies and Parts of Copies*, p. 44. Joanna ordered E. J. Field to inform the Yorkshire believers to "strictly scrutinize" all who applied for seals and to ensure that each applicant had access to a copy of her book *Sound an Alarm* (see his letter to Mr. Hirst, August 2, 1806, in Grayson, *Had They Had Knowledge*, p. 149).

87. George Turner, *A Vindication for the Honour of God, in Answer to J. Aked, Halifax*, p. 40.

88. T. C. Turberville, *Worcestershire in the Nineteenth Century*, p. 233.

89. Harrison, *Letter to an Eminent Clergyman*, p. 16.

90. *Leeds Mercury*, September 3, 1814.

91. *Sunday Monitor*, December 11, 1814.

92. Southcott to George Turner, n.d., quoted in the *Southcott Express*, December 1927, pp. 183, 186.

93. Foley to the public, n.d., U.T., Southcott Collection, 324, f. 59. A reporter stated that he had purchased a seal from one of Joanna's supporters. According to him, she had "become almost as general a topic of conversation, in the metropolis, as the late Jubilee" (see the *Wakefield and Halifax Journal*, August 26, 1814).

94. Southcott, *Answer to Five Charges*, p. 18.

95. Southcott to a friend, n.d., U.T., Southcott Collection, 298, f. 6.

96. Southcott, *Sound an Alarm*, p. 52.

97. Field to Mr. Hirst, August 2, 1806, quoted in Grayson, *Had They Had Knowledge*, p. 149.

98. See John Crossley, *The Master and Scholar Refuted*, p. 1, and Southcott to Mr. John Bedford, May 7, 1810, Add Mss. 47794, f. 120b. If the believer could not read, then the two books were required to be read to him or her (see Southcott to Mr. Jowett, July 14, 1808, GLRO, Acc 1040/184, f. 265, and a communication from her Spirit, British Library, Egerton Mss. 2399, August 2, 1806, f. 103a).

99. Add Mss. 32634, June 9, 1806, ff. 301ab.

100. Eusebius, *A Letter to His Grace the Lord Archbishop of Canterbury, Relative to the Impious Blasphemies of the Late Imposter Joanna Southcott, and Her Followers*, p. 10.

101. WCSL, Southcott Cuttings, *Kirby's Wonderful Museum*, p. 341.

102. Southcott to Foley, December 21, 1812, Add Mss. 57860.

103. "On the Conduct of the Methodists," January 30, 1805, quoted in the *'Express' Leaflet*, no. 42, p. 283.

104. Southcott to Mr. Jowett, July 14, 1808, GLRO, Acc 1040/184, f. 274.

105. See Southcott to Peter Morrison, May 20, 1805, Add Mss. 47794, ff. 57ab. One of the principal difficulties was their desire to come to London. The Spirit had to forbid "some of the Friends [who] made application to come" to the city.

106. *Southcott Despatch* no. 37 (1922): 2.

107. John Rylands Library, R20862, July 12, 1805, f. 415.

108. "The Love Feast," December 11, 1804, in *Southcott Despatch* no. 38 (1922): 8.

109. U.T., Southcott Collection, 331, September 2, 1808, ff. 50–51.

110. Southcott, *Warning to the Whole World*, p. 99.

111. Southcott to Townley, May 29, 1804, in *Prayers for the Fast Day*, p. 43.

112. Southcott, *Trial of Joanna Southcott*, pp. 132–133.

113. Philip Pullen, *Hymns, or Spiritual Songs, Composed from the Prophetic Writings of Joanna Southcott*.

114. Field to Mrs. Taylor, January 23, 1804, Add Mss. 47797, f. 59b. Also see "Religious Imposter Detected," n.d., John Rylands Library, Broadsheet No. 354, n.d., p. 3.

115. Field to Mrs. Taylor, January 23, 1804, Add Mss. 47797, f. 59b. Although disappointingly devoid of any genuinely interesting information or reflection on Joanna's movement, the following works suggest something of the German interest in the prophetess: *Johanne Soutgate. Die neue Prophetin in England*; D. August Hermann Niemeyer, *Beobachtungen auf Reisen in und ausser Deutschland*; and C. F. Zimpel, *Das Sonnenweib einem Schlüssel zum richtigen Verstandniss der Bibel*.

116. Add Mss. 47797, f. 60a. Also see Brent Forth, *And the Lord Spake unto Joanna Southcott*, pp. 22–23, and, particularly, *Order of Service for January 12th. The Uplifting of Hands. According to the Command Given to Joanna Southcott*.

117. Foley to a friend, January 22, 1810, U.T., Southcott Collection, 445, f. 548. Foley wrote to Charles Taylor on November 22, 1808, that the leader of the Bristol Southcottians, Samuel Eyre, who was an Oxford M.A., had a meeting room which would hold three hundred and had "sometimes above 100 attend him" (see Add Mss. 47795, f. 56a, and, for biographical information on Eyre, Foster's *Aluminae Oxoniensis*, p. 442, in Blockley, 793).

118. U.T., Southcott Collection, Southcott to Stone, Sibley & others, April 15, 1812, 438, f. 435, and "Instructions for the Sealed people, as to their meetings . . . ," n.d., 441.

119. Joanna Southcott to Mr. Lucas, December 2, 1811, in L. E. C. Jones, *Commentary*, p. 12.

120. Southcott to a friend, February 8, 1811, U.T., Southcott Collection, 447, ff. 351–352.

121. Southcott to a friend, February 8, 1811, GLRO, Acc 1040/190, ff. 8, 5–6.

122. John Rylands Library, Broadsheet No. 347, December 13, 1814 (extract from a letter to Jane Townley), and Alice Seymour, comp., *The Voice in the Wilderness*, p. 43. According to Miss Seymour, the simplicity of dress was meant to encourage humility among the believers. This is particularly ironic in view of the fact that members of later offshoot movements were to be spectacularly visible because of their unusual costume and hair styles. In the Ashton-Under-Lyne reference library is an interesting manuscript notebook kept "by a follower of Joanna Southcott." Its dates, December 15, 1829, to May 20, 1830, suggest that the author was undoubtedly a supporter of John Wroe, who, like Joanna, found Ashton unusually sympathetic to millenarian claims. The notebook is replete with amazingly detailed descriptions of jewelry and ornaments to be worn by the devout. Also see *The Life and Journal of John Wroe*; Howcroft, *Tales of a Pennine People*, pp. 65–91; Winifred M. Bowman, *England in Ashton-Under-Lyne*, pp. 235–240; and William Chadwick, *Reminiscences of Mottram*, pp. 47, 77.

123. Southcott to Mr. and Mrs. Taylor, December 22, 1802, Add Mss. 47794, f. 7b.

124. Southcott to Foley, March 16, 1812, Add Mss. 57860, f. 2a.

125. Southcott to Reverend Bull, November 16, 1802, GLRO, Acc 1040/185, f. 523.

126. Joanna's literal interpretation of "bride," "bridegroom," and "Marriage" in Revelation and other books of the New Testament was, of course, at variance with the conventional explanation that they were "general symbols of the close bond and mystical unity between Christ and His Church" (see Baldwin, *The Jezreelites*, p. 12).

127. "The faith of the Believers in the Divine Mission of Joanna Southcott," Add Mss. 47803E, f. 3a.

128. R. Southam to Miss Gibson, July 18, 1811, GLRO, Acc 1040/23a, f. 3.

129. *Transactions of the Panacea Society with the Archbishops and Bishops of the Church of England*, p. 79. This is a publication by Joanna's twentieth-century followers.

130. Baldwin, *The Jezreelites*, p. 12.

131. John Evans, M.A., to the Right Honourable Lord Erskine, late Lord High Chancellor of Great Britain, 1814, in *Two Witnesses* no. 34 (1917): 3–5. Evans claimed his summary of Southcottian beliefs was "the most intelligible account of her opinions as well as of her religious views hitherto submitted to the public attention." The fact that the letter is reprinted without challenge in a twentieth-century Southcottian periodical suggests that he was correct.

132. Ibid.

133. Sidney Lee, ed., *Dictionary of National Biography* (London, 1898), LIII, 278.

134. Add Mss. 47800, September 2, 1808, f. 127a.

135. Southcott Collection, WCSL, bookseller's notation.

136. Field to Mrs. Taylor, March 10, 1803, Add Mss. 47797, f. 34a.

137. Ibid., 47795, September 21, 1807, f. 47a.

138. Ibid., 32635, 1796, f. 175b.

139. Ibid., 47800, July 6, 1807, f. 102a.

140. See Acc 1040/2 in the GLRO. See also n. 99, chap. 3.

141. For example, see *Flindell's Western Luminary*, September 13, 1814, p. 8.

142. For Joanna's attitude toward financial gain, see *Strange Effects of Faith; Fourth Part*, p. 186. William Sharp sent money collected from sympathizers to help defray the costs of publication expenses and served as a go-between for loans (Joanna wrote, "I shall take it as a favor if the gentleman you mentioned will lend me £10, or, £15"). See her letters to Sharp of September 12, 1801 (U.T., Southcott Collection, 449, f. 15), November 16, 1801 (ibid., 437, f. 454); for a version of the imbroglio which Sharp found himself in as a result of his efforts to raise money, see *An Account of the Trials on Bills of Exchange, Wherein the Deceit of Mr. John King and His Confederates, under the Pretence of Lending Money Is Exposed, and Their Arts Brought to Light*.

143. See "Joanna Southcott's Will" in WCSL, Southcott Cuttings, and *Kirby's Wonderful Museum*, in which there is a copy of the will and the later codicil, pp. 356–363. Also, see a letter in Blockley, 780 (15), dated November 21, 1812 which gives the details of the annuity which she received.

144. See Grayson, *King's Son Shiloh*, pp. 267–269, for the conclusions of a twentieth-century Southcottian on Joanna's finances. A letter from Joanna to William Sharp is of interest on this point. On January 22, 1804, she wrote to him, "I shall be glad to know, if there is any money in Stock, towards paying the printing, as I desired it to be laid up for that purpose" (see Add Mss. 47799, f. 116a).

145. Southcott to Miss Eveleigh, September 20, 1810, Add Mss. 47794, f. 122a.

146. Worcestershire Record Office, entry for November 17, 1810, BA 3762.899.31 (parcel 137.v).

147. Field to Peter Morrison, May 5, 1807, Add Mss. 47797, f. 143a.

148. Southcott to Miss Eveleigh, August 17, 1808, Add Mss. 47794, f. 114a.

149. Southcott to Foley, February 16, 1807, Add Mss. 57860, f. 3.

150. Worcestershire Record Office, BA 3762.899.31 (parcel 137.v).

151. Southcott to Mrs. Symons, October 8, 1803, Add Mss. 47794, f. 9a.

152. Ibid., Southcott to Mrs. Taylor, September 4, 1804, f. 35a.

153. Ibid., Southcott to Miss Eveleigh, September 20, 1810, f. 122a.

154. Southcott to George Turner, March 10, 1806, Blockley, 516(27), f. 125.

155. Foley to Mr. Taylor, December 9, 1803, Add Mss. 47795, f. 9b.

V. TRUE BELIEVERS

1. Theodore Turpin, *Extracts from Sermons Preached at Different Chapels in the Years 1812, 1813, and 1814*, p. 4.

2. *Sunday Monitor*, November 13, 1814.

3. U.T., Southcott Collection, 128, *Communication by the "Small Still Voice*," p. 27.

4. Daniel Roberts, *Observations Relative to the Divine Mission of Joanna*

Southcott with a Detail of the Proceedings of the People Called Quakers, against a Member, for his Belief, pp. 1, 4, 23. The Quakers ejected Roberts from their society because of his belief in Joanna.

5. Harrison, *Letter to an Eminent Clergyman,* p. 42.

6. Amraphel, *Truth's Humble Appeal unto All Men,* pp. 10, 6.

7. Southcott, *Book of Wonders,* p. 64.

8. Add Mss. 47794, ff. 65b–66a.

9. Mr. Baylee to Reverend T. P. Foley, June 4, 1806, U.T., Southcott Collection, 336, f. 129.

10. Carpenter, *Nocturnal Alarm,* pp. 74–75, 68–69.

11. *A Letter Addressed to the Rev. T. P. Foley,* p. 36.

12. Turpin, *Extracts from Sermons,* p. 40.

13. Crossley and Jowett, *Vindication of Joanna Southcott's Writings,* p. 17.

14. W. B. H[arrison], *A Letter Addressed to a Friend, Proving from Reason and Scripture, That a Further Divine Revelation Will Be Given for the Instruction and Direction of Mankind Previous to the Establishment of Christ's Kingdom on Earth,* pp. 45–47.

15. British Library, 1801, Egerton Mss., 2399, f. 22a.

16. J. Aiken, *Joanna Southcott,* p. 3.

17. Add Mss. 47800, 1805, f. 41a.

18. *Pulman's Weekly News,* November, [?], in Southcott Cuttings, WCSL.

19. Thompson, "'Your Own Messiahs,'" p. 41. Also see Paul McGuire's *The Tower Mystery,* p. 16. This otherwise unimportant novel is interesting because of its familiarity with the local history of Somerset. A "scholar" is introduced who has all the right qualifications for a guide. "He knows the name of every hill and field in his neighborhood and why it was named; he knows the date of every cottage in the village and the troubles of every cottager. He can distinguish the cider of Chard from the cider of Devon." While walking in Crewkerne, the narrator and the "scholar" pass a carter who prompts the "scholar" to remember the area's intimate association with the Southcottian movement. According to him, the carter's great-grandfather had been the first convert to Joanna's cause in the neighborhood, and then he told his companion, "Joanna was great guns in South Somerset, you know," proceeding to point out the descendants of the original followers "all the afternoon."

20. Reverend Hoadley Ash to Southcott, September 28, 1807, in Seymour, *Voice in the Wilderness,* pp. 78–80.

21. Harrison, *Letter to an Eminent Clergyman,* pp. 5–6.

22. Wetherell, *Testimony of Joanna Southcott,* p. 10.

23. Carpenter, *Who Are the Deluded?,* p. 17.

24. Lamplugh Hird to Earl Fitzwilliam, March 19, 1801, Fitzwilliam Papers, Sheffield Reference Library, f. 45/8.

25. Foley to a friend, May 6, 1808, Add Mss. 47795, ff. 51ab. Mr. R. D. Murphy, a student of Leeds Southcottianism, has also found that many converts to Joanna's movement were Methodists (see his typescript, "Off the Beaten Track," in the Leeds Reference Library).

26. Add Mss. 47795, ff. 51ab.

27. Southcott, *Strange Effects of Faith* [First Part], p. 25.

28. Carpenter, *Nocturnal Alarm*, p. 63.

29. Fellow travelers of these distraught souls were the inevitable charlatans who succeeded in stigmatizing the Southcottian movement with their crimes. One was Mary Bateman, a wise woman with a particularly odious reputation, who lived in a Leeds suburb. According to one source (Johnson Grant, *Grant's History of the English Church*, p. 451), she had been a follower of Swedenborg and Richard Brothers. Her command over her audience had little to do with intellectual persuasion, however. She played unscrupulously on the credulity of those who were "from the most ignorant and poverty-stricken class" (in the view of Mr. R. D. Murphy). On Saturday, January 26, 1806, her hen was supposed to have laid an egg with the words "CHRIST IS COMING" inscribed on it lengthways. The hen was not reluctant to provide additional eggs with the same astonishing rubric. Murphy has explained that the trick was accomplished "by inserting into the hen's ovary eggs on which messages had been written in dilute acid which, after a few minutes, turned brown and became visible. The writing was done and the eggs put in place just as the audience was reaching the peak of its expectation; naturally the hen expelled the egg as quickly as possible" ("Off the Beaten Track").

Joanna hesitated to lend her prestige to this nonsense but she finally capitulated. "If the thing were real, I thought the warning was striking to all, as the crowing of the cock reproved the denial of Peter. And so I thought from the hen—it reproved an unbelieving world that denied the coming of their Lord." One of the reasons she pronounced the story credible was that her father had once assured her of the truth of an equally incredible tale. According to him, an employer had gotten his servant girl pregnant. When he tried to pressure her into naming a fellow servant as the father of her unborn child, she refused. But the child was born with "the name of the master written on the child's thigh, which every one must know was the wondrous working of the Lord to confound the unjust master, who denied the child being his own" (U.T., Southcott Collection, 143, *Communication in Answer to a Circumstance Which Caused Some Dispute* [Ms. dtd. 1806, publ. 1860], p. 2).

In 1808 a jury convicted Mary Bateman of murder. That a strain of self-delusion was mixed into the wise woman's career became evident at her execution. "She dressed in white," an account said, "fully expecting deliverance from the fatal tree. She suffered in the presence of 20,000 spectators, most of whom were watching for the coming of an Angel to rescue her" (quoted in Balleine, *Past Finding Out*, p. 55). She had earlier obtained one of Joanna's seals which, in the light of her subsequent notoriety, caused serious damage to the reputation of the Southcottian sect and was probably an important factor in Joanna's decision to stop the practice for a time. For Joanna's attitude toward her see her letter of April 1, 1809 (U.T., Southcott Collection, 420, ff. 1, 7, 16). Also see Harrison, *Second Coming*, pp. 122–124.

30. Southcott, *Sound An Alarm*, p. 36.

31. *A Circumstance Which Caused Dispute*, pp. 1, 6–7.

32. U.T., Southcott Collection, 133, *Communication, on the Persecution*

Caused by the Devil and the Possibility of His Visible Appearance (Ms. dtd. 1807, publ. 1859), pp. 2–3.

33. Ibid., p. 3.

34. Ibid., 134, *Communication, How to Contend with Evil Spirits, An Extract* (Ms. dtd. 1807, publ. 1859), pp. 1–2.

35. Ibid., 336, April 18, 1801, ff. 180–181, 184.

36. The U.T. Southcott Collection contains fourteen paintings which may quite possibly be the originals painted by Joseph Prescott. If not, they are duplicates of his work.

37. Carpenter, *Apology for Faith*, p. 35.

38. Ibid., pp. 11–14.

39. Ibid., p. 13.

40. Carpenter, *Nocturnal Alarm*, pp. 91, 97–98. A third visionary Carpenter brought into his circle was known as the Spiritual Searcher.

41. Amraphel, *Truth's Humble Appeal*, pp. 4, 3.

42. Southcott to a friend, July 19, 1803, U.T., Southcott Collection, 332, f. 28.

43. Joanna Southcott, *The Second Book of Visions*, p. 37.

44. *Memoirs of the Life and Mission of Joanna Southcott . . . To Which Is Added a Sketch of the Rev. W. Tozer*, p. 15.

45. Southcott, *Warning to the Whole World*, p. 114.

46. S. Catherine Carpenter, *Are These Things So? Being Remarks on "Demonocracy Detected,"* p. 11.

47. Southcott, *The Continuation of the Prophecies*, p. 19; U.T., Southcott Collection, 382.

48. Southcott, *The Continuation of the Prophecies*, pp. 35–36; U.T., Southcott Collection, 384.

49. Southcott, *Second Book of Visions*, pp. 35–36; U.T., Southcott Collection, 393.

50. Southcott, *Warning to the World*, pp. 85–86; U.T., Southcott Collection, 391.

51. Carpenter, *Who Are the Deluded?*, pp. 21, 24–27, 29–30, 32. Also see Thomas Dowland, *Divine and Spiritual Communications through T. Dowland to E. Carpenter for the British Nation*.

52. Carpenter, *Who Are the Deluded?*, pp. 35, 51.

53. Ibid., p. 47.

54. Carpenter, *Nocturnal Alarm*, pp. 63–64.

55. Carpenter, *Apology for Faith*, p. 28; Part II, *Missionary Magazine*, p. 113. (Carpenter's pamphlet *An Apology for Faith* was published in two parts, the second of which is *Missionary Magazine*.)

56. Carpenter, *Apology for Faith*, pp. 25–26, 42.

57. Southcott to a friend, n.d., U.T., Southcott Collection, 298, f. 70.

58. Carpenter, Part II, *Missionary Magazine*, p. 145; *Apology for Faith*, p. 62.

59. U.T., Southcott Collection, 120, *Communication on the Old and Young Prophet* (Ms. dtd. 1802, publ. 1859), p. 4.

60. "Milton," xxii, 50–53, in Blake, *Complete Writings*, p. 506.

61. Southcott, *Divine and Spiritual Communications*, pp. 27–29.

62. U.T., Southcott Collection, 122, *Communication upon the Teachings of Baron Swedenborg* (Ms. dtd. 1802, publ. 1859), p. 1.

63. Ibid., Southcott to a friend, July 19, 1803, 332, ff. 31–32.

64. *Teachings of Baron Swedenborg*, pp. 1–2.

65. U.T., Southcott Collection, 329, July 10, 1802, f. 121.

66. Southcott, *Warning to the Whole World*, p. 99.

67. *Teachings of Baron Swedenborg*, p. 2.

68. Ibid., pp. 2–3.

69. U.T., Southcott Collection, 121, *Communication in Answer to Baron Swedenborg's Description of Heaven* (Ms. dtd. 1802, publ. 1859), pp. 6–7.

70. Southcott, *A Word to the Wise*, p. 2.

71. U.T., Southcott Collection, 334 [last page]. The inscription was copied from a tombstone in Milton Church Yard, Kent.

72. Southcott, *Second Book of the Sealed Prophecies*, p. 11.

73. Southcott, *Trial of Joanna Southcott*, p. 109.

74. Southcott, *Second Book of the Sealed Prophecies*, p. 131.

75. Southcott, *Trial of Joanna Southcott*, p. 107.

76. U.T., Southcott Collection, 299, [?], 1797, f. 2.

77. Ibid., 283.

78. Joanna Southcott, *Copies of Letters Sent to the Clergy of Exeter, from 1796 to 1800, with Communications and Prophecies Put in the Newspapers in 1813*, p. 54.

79. U.T., Southcott Collection, 333, September 17, 1805, f. 86.

80. *Scriptures of the Holy Trinity*, p. 181.

81. U.T., Southcott Collection, 299, [?], 1797, f. 2.

82. Southcott, *Strange Effects of Faith. Third Part*, p. 134.

83. Southcott, *Trial of Joanna Southcott*, p. xxxiv.

84. Southcott, *Warning to the World*, p. 65.

85. Southcott, *Trial of Joanna Southcott*, p. xxx.

86. *A Letter Addressed to the Rev. T. P. Foley*, p. 54.

87. Southcott, *A Word to the Wise*, p. 1.

88. U.T., Southcott Collection, 126, *Communication on the Folly of Deception* (Ms. dtd. 1803, publ. 1859), p. 1.

89. Southcott, *Second Book of the Sealed Prophecies*, p. 102.

90. Southcott, *Copies and Parts of Copies*, p. 60.

91. Southcott to a friend, December 2, 1811, U.T., Southcott Collection, 334, f. 61.

92. Southcott to Reverend Mr. Pomeroy, March 23, 1800, in Southcott, *Letters to the Clergy of Exeter*, p. 27.

93. U.T., Southcott Collection, 336, September 5, 1804, ff. 98–99.

94. Southcott, *Second Book of the Sealed Prophecies*, p. 130.

95. William Frend, *Peace and Union Recommended to the Associated Bodies of Republicans and Anti-Republicans*, pp. 47–48.

96. Thomas Taylor, *An Additional Testimony Given to Vindicate the Truth of the Prophecies of Richard Brothers*, pp. 10–17.

97. "Remarks on Mr. Thomas Senior's Dream," n.d., GLRO, Acc 1040/194, f. 299.

98. Southcott to Mr. Long, [?], 1805, U.T., Southcott Collection, 336, ff. 201–202.

99. Jane Townley to Mrs. Taylor, September 4, 1804, Add Mss. 47794, f. 35a.

100. Richard Law to Townley, July 14, 1816, Add Mss. 47796, ff. 14b–15a.

101. Christiana Blunt, *A Midnight Dialogue between Joanna Southcott and Satan, Translated from a Luciferian Manuscript*, p. 4.

102. Southcott to a friend, December 2, 1811, U.T., Southcott Collection, 334, f. 62.

103. Ibid., 328, [?], 1804, f. 59.

104. Ibid., Southcott to Long, [?], 1805, 336, f. 202.

105. Southcott, *Strange Effects of Faith. Third Part*, p. 120.

106. Southcott, *Strange Effects of Faith* [First Part], p. 37.

107. G. Bennett, *A Warning to the Nation, from the Prophecies of Joanna Southcott*, p. 10.

108. Southcott, *How to Contend with Evil Spirits*, p. 2.

109. Southcott to a friend, March 25, 1806, U.T., Southcott Collection, 336, ff. 134–135.

110. Joanna Southcott, *True Explanations of the Bible. Part the Sixth*, p. 529.

111. Southcott, *A Continuation of Prophecies*, p. 15.

112. Southcott, *Warning to the World*, p. 68.

113. September 27, 1806, Add Mss. 47794, f. 85a. Through internal evidence it seems clear that the letter is meant for Peter Morrison.

114. U.T., Southcott Collection, 131, *Copy of a Letter; England May Be a Happy Land; Also the Warning Given by Mr. Brothers* (Ms. dtd. 1806, publ. 1859), pp. 4, 9–10.

115. Roberts, *Observations*, p. 62.

116. Pullen, *Hymns, or Spiritual Songs*, p. 194.

117. U.T., Southcott Collection, February 21, 1804, 436, f. 132.

VI. THE POLITICS OF THE MILLENNIUM

1. A Convert, *The Age of Prophecy! Or, Further Testimony of the Mission of Richard Brothers*, p. 7.

2. Duke of Portland to Earl Fitzwilliam, March 9, 1801, Sheffield Reference Library, Fitzwilliam Papers, f. 45(a).

3. Ibid., March 18, 1801, f. 45/7.

4. See E. P. Thompson's "An Army of Redressers" in *Making of the English Working Class*. But also see F. K. Donnelly and J. L. Baxter, "Sheffield and the English Revolutionary Tradition, 1791–1820," *International Review of Social History* no. 20 (part 3, 1975): 398–423, and Marianne Elliott, "The 'Despard Conspiracy' Reconsidered," *Past and Present* no. 75 (May 1977): 46–61.

5. Fitzwilliam Papers, March 18, 1801, f. 45/7.

6. Ibid., Lamplugh Hird to Earl Fitzwilliam, March 19, 1801, f. 45/8. Nathaniel Brassey Halhed, however, said six years before that Brothers "never assembled nor thought of assembling any congregation whatever," suggesting that whatever organization and leadership was provided took place without the prophet's guidance. Also, after March 1795, he was confined to an asylum. See *The Second Speech of Nathaniel Brassey Halhed Esq.*, p. 14.

7. A. D. Harvey, *Britain in the Early Nineteenth Century*, p. 104.

8. Carl B. Cone, *English Jacobins*, pp. 106–107, 123–124.

9. P. A. Brown, *The French Revolution in English History*, p. 151.

10. Edward Royle, *Radical Politics, 1790–1900*, p. 4. Also see Albert Goodwin, *The Friends of Liberty*, pp. 483–485.

11. W. S. Baker calls Sharp "the greatest historical engraver that England has yet produced" in *William Sharp*, p. 10; this is a slight study with only rudimentary biographical information but a helpful list of Sharp's works. Baker completely misunderstands the nature of his subject's radicalism. Crabb Robinson possessed one of the most famous of Sharp's engravings, "The Doctors of the Church" [after Guido], which he called a "masterpiece." He said, "I am no connoisseur certainly, and perhaps have no delicate sense of the beauty of engraving; but I never look on this specimen without a lively pleasure" (*Diary, Reminiscences, and Correspondence of Henry Crabb Robinson*, ed. T. Sadler, I, 53).

12. Public Record Office (PRO), Treasury Solicitor's Papers (TS), 11/961 (minutebook of the Society for Constitutional Information).

13. Ibid., 11/962.

14. T. B. Howell, comp., cont. by Thomas James Howell after 1793, *A Complete Collection of State Trials*, XXV, 253.

15. Royle, *Radical Politics*, p. 18.

16. Reverend Joseph Lomas Towers, *Illustrations of Prophecy*, II, 664–665.

17. Ibid., I, iii.

18. Cone, *English Jacobins*, p. 141.

19. Dr. Joseph Towers, *Thoughts on the Commencement of a New Parliament*.

20. Richard Price, *Observations on the Importance of the American Revolution*, 2d ed. (Philadelphia, 1785), p. 61, and *The Evidence for a Future Period of Improvement in the State of Mankind* (London, 1787), pp. 25, 53, quoted in Rodney M. Baine, *Thomas Holcroft and the Revolutionary Novel*, p. 47.

21. Brooks, *Dictionary of Writers*, p. lxxi.

22. Towers, *Illustrations of Prophecy*, I, 47.

23. Howell, *State Trials*, XXIV, 1214–1215.

24. Ibid., XXIV, 783.

25. William Hamilton Reid, *The Rise and Dissolution of the Infidel Societies in This Metropolis*, pp. 5, 8, 14, 2.

26. Towers mentions only "a contemporary work on prophecy by a Mr. Fleming" (See Froom, *Faith of Our Fathers*, II, 642–643, 645–647, 649, 820). Froom also mentions Towers' work (pp. 723–724).

27. Towers, *Illustrations of Prophecy*, I, vi, v, vii–viii, 11.

28. William Hazlitt, *The Spirit of the Age*, pp. 79, 82, 83.

29. Alexander Stephens, *Memoir of John Horne Tooke*, II, 264–266.

30. Ibid., pp. 267–270.

31. Howell, *State Trials*, XXV, 438.

32. Ibid., col. 434.

33. Thomas Holcroft, *Memoirs of the Late Thomas Holcroft*, ed. by William Hazlitt, p. 184. William Godwin recorded the event in his diary; the entry for April 3, 1796, reads, "Harwood marries" (consulted the microfilm copy in the possession of the Bodleian Library, Oxford University).

34. In his *Thomas Holcroft and the Revolutionary Novel*, Rodney Baine discusses in a note the discrepancies which have arisen in dating the beginning of their friendship (p. 115). He criticizes C. Kegan Paul, *William Godwin: His Friends and Contemporaries*, for citing a letter dated February 1785 from Holcroft to Godwin, which indicates that their intimacy had already begun, and then subsequently assigning later dates to it. Baine refers to Godwin's own statement that he did not meet Holcroft until his "thirty-first year," which would have been 1787 (p. 11).

35. Holcroft, *Memoirs*, p. 184.

36. David Fleisher, *William Godwin: A Study in Liberalism*, p. 17.

37. Paul, *William Godwin*, I, 357, 64–65, quoted in Baine, *Holcroft*, pp. 11, 44.

38. Leslie Stephen, *History of English Thought in the Eighteenth Century*, II, 224–229.

39. Quoted in Thompson, *Making of the English Working Class*, pp. 110–111.

40. Holcroft, *Memoirs*, pp. 152–153.

41. It is frequently impossible to distinguish William Sharp from Richard Sharp, either in Godwin's diary or in the minutes of the Society for Constitutional Information. Richard Sharp, known as "Conversation Sharp," was active in radical and literary circles and became M.P. for Castle Rising, 1806–1812. The following selections from Godwin's diary are often cryptic, for the most part mundane, but in their evocation of the ebb and flow of life during these years they reveal much, particularly the danger of sharply contrasting "the intellectual deep freeze around Godwin" with "the bubbling world of experimental artisans in which the revolutionary mystic William Blake had his being," as Gwyn Williams has done (*Artisans and Sans-Culottes*, p. 67). Godwin was interested in Sharp's work. He recorded on October 20, 1792, that he went to "see Romney's Paine, Fuseli's Devil, & Trumbull's Gibralter, at Sharpe's [Sharp was engraving each of these]." On May 3, 1802, he went to an exhibition which included Sharp's work, and on February 18, 1808, he noted that he had seen the engraver's new prospectus. There were many meals and much conversation: January 20, 1793, "Dine at H Tooke's, with Holcroft, Sharpe, Banks & Jardine"; July 16, 1796, "Ride to Reepham [in Norfolk] to . . . sup at Tooke Harwood's; sleep"; November 4, 1796, "dine at HTs [Horne Tooke's] with Harwood"—visits: May 24, 1794 [in the midst of the arrests], "call on Sharp with Holcroft"; October 2, 1794, "call on Sharp, adv. Holcroft"; late June 1794,

"Call on T. Harwood"; August 18, 1802, "Call on Sharp engraver"—exchange of letters: February 28, 1803, "Write to Harwood"; April 14, 15, 17, 1806, "Write to Sharp"—meetings which may have been either random or planned: April 8, 1802, "Meet Tho Campbel & Sharp eng[raver]"; January 19, 1805, "meet Sharp"; March 12, 1805, "meet Sharpe, Barrel & Wordsworth: tea at Turners"—and, finally, advice given: December 1793, "adv. Sharpe"; August 28, 1798, "adv. Harwoods"; March 27, 1809, "adv. Harwood."

42. Howell, *State Trials*, XXIV and XXV, trials of Hardy and Tooke.

43. Ibid., for Harwood's involvement in the S.C.I., see XXV, 135–136; XXIV, 540–541, 547; XXV, 150–151, 437–438; XXIV, 551–552; XXV, 438–439, 511. Also see n. 94.

44. Ibid., XXV, 435.

45. E. P. Thompson highlights this radical tradition among engravers in "History from Below," *Times Literary Supplement*, April 7, 1966, pp. 279–280.

46. Baker, *William Sharp*, pp. 10–11, 13, 16–17, 32–33.

47. William Blake, "Annotations to Sir Joshua Reynolds's Discourses," in *Complete Writings*, p. 445.

48. David V. Erdman, *Blake: Prophet against Empire*, p. 175.

49. For a pioneering study in this regard, see Jacob Bronowski, *William Blake: A Man without a Mask*.

50. Robinson, *Diary*, entry for January 30, 1815, in G. E. Bentley, Jr., *Blake Records*, p. 235.

51. E. Dowden, ed., *The Correspondence of Robert Southey with Caroline Bowles* (London and Dublin, 1881), pp. 193–194, quoted in Bentley, *Blake Records*, p. 399. Bentley points out an egregious error in Southey's chronology. Southey's single visit to Blake was in 1811. At that time the Blakes told him of Owen Pugh's influence but this was three years *before* Joanna's death.

52. E. J. Chance to "Dr. Uncle," undated, in Bentley, *Blake Records*, p. 365. It reads in part, "Mr. Pye & Mr. Field called but left no message—." Pye's companion may well have been E. J. Field, Joanna's one-time London agent.

53. Blake, "Poems from the Note-Book 1800–3," in *Complete Writings*, p. 418. For another explanation of Blake's rejection of the prophetess, see Morton D. Paley, "The Prince of the Hebrews and the Woman Clothed with the Sun," in *William Blake: Essays in Honour of Sir Geoffrey Keynes*, ed. Morton D. Paley and Michael Phillips, pp. 280–293. The basis of the poet's resistance, Paley believes, was his "life long opposition to the doctrine of the Virgin Birth, with its concomitant elevation of celibacy and denial of the erotic." He gets around the problem of the early date by asserting that Joanna's first works were filled "with veiled predictions" about the prospective birth of Shiloh (p. 285).

54. John Gordon Davies, *The Theology of William Blake*, p. 111.

55. Blake, "Milton," xxii. 61–62, in *Complete Writings*, p. 506.

56. Blake, "Annotations to Watson," in ibid., p. 391.

57. Blake, "Milton," xxiii. 1, 2, in ibid., p. 506.

58. Blake, "Annotations to Watson," in ibid., p. 391.

59. Blake, "Annotations to Lavater," in ibid., p. 75.

60. Robinson, *Diary*, I, p. 54.

61. Ibid., pp. 53–54.
62. Holcroft, *Memoirs*, p. 254.
63. Erdman, *Prophet*, p. 12, n. 19.
64. G. E. Bentley, Jr., and Martin K. Nurmi, *A Blake Bibliography*, p. 205.
65. Erdman, *Prophet*, p. 159, n. 33.
66. Bentley, *Blake Records*, p. 46.
67. Ibid., pp. 46–47.
68. Ibid., p. 58.
69. Erdman, *Prophet*, pp. 159–160.
70. G. E. Bentley, Jr., "Blake's Engravings and His Friendship with Flaxman," *Studies in Bibliography* 12 (1959): 166.
71. Royle, *Radical Politics*, p. 20.
72. Paine went to France in 1787 to promote his invention of an iron bridge. Godwin recorded in his diary for November 27, 1791: "sup at Nicholson's, talk of self-interest, Paine's bridge."
73. John Knowles, *Life and Writings of Henry Fuseli* (London, 1831), I, 375–376, quoted in Erdman, *Prophet*, p. 161.
74. For example, Sharp and Paine were definitely together at the meetings on May 4, May 18, and May 25, 1792, and probably March 16, April 20, and July 13, of that year. Harwood was present on March 16, May 4, May 18, and July 13. In addition, he attended with Paine on March 30, 1792, when Sharp was absent (Howell, *State Trials*, XXIV, XXV, Hardy and Tooke). Paine and "Sharpe" are identified as friends in an undated letter from Thomas Cooper to Horne Tooke. Cooper had been asked by the Manchester Constitutional Society to "abridge Paine" and was writing to Tooke for advice. "Sharpe, I hear, is not in town; Paine is in France; and I do not know of any friend of his but yourself, to whom I can send my proposed abridgement for his opinion." Although William Sharp engraved a portrait of the Manchester reformer, Thomas Walker, a friend and colleague of Cooper, it is highly unlikely that he is the Sharpe being referred to in the letter. Though undated, it was written before August 29, 1791. Sharp did not join the S.C.I. until the spring of the following year, although he engraved an emblem for the society as early as 1782. Therefore, it is undoubtedly Richard Sharp to whom the reference is made (Howell, *State Trials*, XXV, 120–122).
75. Erdman was one of the first to notice the improbabilities in the story about Paine and Blake (*Prophet*, pp. 154–155). He suggests that "behind the business of Blake's warning Paine in 1792 may lie the fact that Sharp was on a committee of the S.C.I. which was directed on May 18 to 'inquire into the rumour of [government] prosecution of Paine' and which reported on June 22 that an information had been filed against him" (p. 159). It was a committee of seven which included, besides "Mr. Sharpe," Horne Tooke, John Frost, Lord Daer, and three others (Howell, *State Trials*, XXV, 104).
76. Alexander Gilchrist, *Life of William Blake*, pp. 92–94, quoted in Bentley, *Blake Records*, p. 40.
77. Blake, "King Edward the Third," 1.9 in *Complete Writings*, p. 18.
78. See Gilchrist, *Blake*, pp. 92–94, in Bentley, *Blake Records*, p. 40.

79. Robinson, *Diary*, I, 54.

80. Erdman, *Prophet*, p. 36. He dates the engraving of the plate in 1782.

81. Sharp engraved the inscription at the express invitation of his "friend" Major Cartwright, the author of the Declaration of Rights. Cartwright's niece described Sharp as her uncle's "political associate." She wrote, "Though his frequent endeavours to convert Major Cartwright to a belief in his favourite prophets and prophetesses were fruitless, yet their friendly intercourse continued through life; and Sharp often expressed a great desire to engrave the portrait of the reformer" (see F. D. Cartwright, *The Life and Correspondence of Major Cartwright*, I, 135–136).

82. Howell, *State Trials*, XXIV, 1024–1025. Among the signers of a Declaration of the Friends of the People on behalf of parliamentary reform made on April 11, 1792, were Charles Grey, at the time M.P. for Northumberland, Major Cartwright, Richard Sharp, and Dr. Towers, as well as Erskine and William Sharp. The William Harwood who signed is not William Tooke Harwood. The latter told the attorney general that he was not a member of the society (ibid., XXV, 435).

83. Ibid., 565–566.

84. Baker, *William Sharp*, pp. 68–69, 71, 78.

85. Howell, *State Trials*, XXV, 248.

86. See note 82.

87. Howell, *State Trials*, XXV, 467, 305, 66, 481.

88. Ibid., see XXIV, 951, 564–565; XXV, 67; XXIV, 951; XXV, 586–587.

89. See Lucyle Werkmeister, *A Newspaper History of England, 1792–1793*, p. 135.

90. G. S. Veitch clears up serious discrepancies in the D.N.B. entry on Frost in his *The Genesis of Parliamentary Reform*, pp. 270–271.

91. Werkmeister, *Newspaper History*, pp. 463–464.

92. Bentley, *Blake Records*, p. 608.

93. Perhaps Sharp was assisted by the famous moneylender John King, known as "Jew" King. He was married to Lady Lanesborough and had at one time been a protégé of Tom Paine. In 1783 he wrote *Thoughts on the Difficulties and Distresses in Which the Peace of 1783 Has Involved the People of England*. When King apostasized, Paine wrote to him, "I don't know anything these many years, that surprised, and hurt me more, than the sentiments you published in the Courtly HERALD. . . . You have gone back from all you ever said" (Werkmeister, *Newspaper History*, pp. 33, 196). Sharp and two friends were swindled when they went to King for financial assistance fourteen years later. Joanna wrote a pamphlet describing the affair (*Trials on Bills of Exchange*).

94. This had to do with Burke's reference to the "swinish multitude." A pamphlet confiscated at Hardy's was entitled the RIGHTS OF SWINE and signed "A FRIEND TO THE POOR." See Howell, *State Trials*, XXIV, 745–748.

95. Ibid., XXIV, 571–572; XXV, 253.

96. PRO, TS, 11/962 (minutebook of the S.C.I.).

97. "Horne Tooke's Diary," *Notes and Queries*, January 9, 1897, p. 21; January 23, 1897, p. 61.

98. Holcroft, *Memoirs*, pp. 172–173.

99. Baker, *William Sharp*, pp. 20–21. The story is related somewhat differently in the obituary of Sharp which appeared in the *Annual Register* 66 (1824): 228–230. In this version, the engraver is supposed to have asked the Privy Council if they wished to subscribe to his portrait of General Kosciusko.

100. John Reeves had founded and ably organized the Crown and Anchor Association. The "Association" was intended to protect "Liberty and Property against republicans and levellers." The room in which it met was directly over that of the Society for Constitutional Information.

101. *Notes and Queries*, February 6, 1897, p. 103.

102. Privy Council, 1/22/A36(b)/2257 and TS11/960/2062. Sharp was questioned by the Privy Council on four separate occasions, May 24, June 6, June 9, and June 11.

103. Howell, *State Trials*, XXV, 253, 248, 255.

104. Ibid., cols. 425, 721.

105. Ibid., XXIV, 1023–1025.

106. Ibid., XXV, 743, 745–746.

107. Ibid., col. 254.

108. Baker, *William Sharp*, pp. 78–79.

VII. JOANNA'S HERALD

1. Richard Brothers, *Wonderful Prophecies*, pp. 15–16.

2. See Richard Brothers, *An Exposition of the Trinity*, p. 18, and *A Revealed Knowledge of the Prophecies and Times, Book the Second*, p. 74. For a sketch of the prophet's career, Cecil Roth's *The Nephew of the Almighty* is of slight interest, but see Garrett's *Respectable Folly*, pp. 179–207, and Alexander Gordon's biography of the prophet in *The Dictionary of National Biography*. Mel Scult's *Millennial Expectations and Jewish Liberties*, pp. 71–89, throws some additional light on the period.

3. Brothers, *Revealed Knowledge*, pp. 22, 64, 39–40, 49–50, 52, 48.

4. G. Coggan, *A Testimony of Richard Brothers*, pp. 4–6. Coggan, a devoted follower of Brothers, provides a clear statement of the prophet's views on the Bourbon regime's shortcomings and, particularly, France's rescue from "Popish darkness, delusion, superstition, ignorance, and folly" by the revolutionaries. A Roman Catholic could, however, also support reform in England and revolution in France as evidenced by Dr. Francis Plowden who was active in the S.C.I. See *Church and State*, pp. 579–580, and for more information on Plowden, C. F. Triebner's *Five Letters to the Critical Reviewers*. Triebner was the minister of a German Lutheran congregation who violently opposed the revolution in France, believing that it was inspired by the papacy. He was convinced that Brothers was an instrument of sedition (see *Cursory and Introductory Thoughts on Richard Brothers' Prophecies*).

5. Richard Brothers, *A Revealed Knowledge of the Prophecies and Times, Book the Second*, p. 19.

6. Ibid., p. 21.

7. Richard Brothers, *Wisdom and Duty*, p. 27. This was actually written in 1801.

8. Ibid., p. 16. As Clarke Garrett points out, however, Brothers took an increasingly sanguine view of the institution of monarchy in his later writings (*Respectable Folly*, p. 213).

9. Richard Brothers, *A Letter from Mr. Brothers to Miss Cott*, p. 63.

10. Brothers, *Revealed Knowledge, First*, p. 51.

11. Brothers, *Miss Cott*, p. 64.

12. Brothers, *Revealed Knowledge, Second*, p. 25.

13. Richard Brothers, *A Poem on the Creation*, p. vii.

14. Eliza Williams, *The Prophecies of Brothers Confuted*, pp. 16–17. For other opinions concerning the danger of Brothers' influence, see William Sales, *Truth or Not Truth; Or a Discourse on Prophets*, pp. 7–8 and Henry Spencer, *A Vindication of the Prophecies of Mr. Brothers and the Scripture Exposition of Mr. Halhed*, pp. 19, 32. Some idea of the popular response to Brothers' prophecies can be found in the memoirs of John Binns, a leading member of the London Corresponding Society. Binns took refuge in a bar on the stormy night of June 4, 1795. He discovered fifty or sixty men, women, and children huddled together who believed Brothers' prophecy that London would be destroyed that day was coming true. "It seemed to me," Binns said, "that every one in the room knew something of Brothers' prophecy, and of the time at which it was to be fulfilled. . . . There was a general feeling and expression of alarm" (*Recollections* [Philadelphia, 1854], pp. 48–50, quoted in Garrett, *Respectable Folly*, p. 206).

15. Joseph Moser, *Anecdotes of Richard Brothers*, p. 34.

16. Halhed, *Second Speech*, p. 15. This apparently provided the basis for the comments in *Chambers's Edinburgh Journal*, "Richard Brothers, the Mad Prophet," December 18, 1849, p. 380. According to this sketch, Brothers' followers were "neither few in numbers, nor confined to the ranks of the unwise and uneducated" (a copy may be found in the Harry Price Library, University of London). See n. 14 for Binns' awareness of Brothers' influence. He visited the prophet periodically.

17. Coggan, *A Testimony*, pp. 37–39, 44, 46.

18. Henry Francis Offley, *Richard Brothers, Neither a Madman nor an Impostor*, pp. 3, xv.

19. Taylor, *Additional Testimony*, pp. 13–14.

20. Nathaniel Brassey Halhed, *Two Letters to the Right Honourable Lord Loughborough*, pp. 4–5.

21. John Henry Blunt, D.D., ed., *Dictionary of Sects, Heresies, Ecclesiastical Parties, and Schools of Religious Thought* (1891), p. 569; Elijah Barwell Impey, *Memoirs of Sir Elijah Impey*, pp. 355–359; Thomas Moore, *Memoirs of the Life of the Right Honourable Richard Brinsley Sheridan*, I, 16–44; Walter K. Kelly, ed., *Erotica*, p. vi.

22. Impey, *Memoirs*, p. 357.

23. *Mr. Halhed's Speech in the House of Commons*, pp. 3–4.

24. Ibid., pp. 4–7.

25. Ibid., pp. 7–8.

26. Halhed, *Second Speech*, pp. 11–14.

27. Moser, *Anecdotes*, p. 32. For other evidence, see *A Crumb of Comfort for the People*, pp. 5–6, 27; J. Crease, *Prophecies Fulfilling*, p. 6; and David Levi, *Letters to Nathaniel Brassey Halhed, M.P.*, pp. 1–2, 39, 48.

28. Quoted in E. P. Thompson, "The Crime of Anonymity," in *Albion's Fatal Tree*, p. 291.

29. Convert, *Age of Prophecy!*, pp. 40, 46, 39–41. For an extreme criticism of Halhed's support of Brothers, published by Daniel Eaton, see *Doubts of Infidels*.

30. Reid, *Rise and Dissolution*, p. 9.

31. [William Sharp], *An Answer to the World, for Putting in Print a Book in 1804, Called "Copies and Parts of Copies of Letters and Communications, Written from Joanna Southcott,"* and *Transmitted by Miss Townley to Mr. W. Sharp in London*, p. 53.

32. Ibid., pp. 30, 50–51, 30, 21.

33. Southcott, *Answer to Age of Reason*, pp. 23–24, 2.

34. Ibid., p. 2.

35. Thomas, *Reminiscences*, p. 22.

36. Southcott, *Answer to Age of Reason*, p. 13.

37. Ibid., pp. 24–25.

38. Ibid., pp. 38–39, 41–42, 44.

39. Blake, "Jerusalem" [To the Deists], in *Complete Writings*, pp. 682–683.

40. [Sharp], *Answer to the World*, p. 12.

41. Ibid., pp. 13, 19–20.

42. Ibid., p. 22.

43. [William Sharp, introd.], *Divine and Spiritual Communications*, p. v.

44. [Sharp], *Answer to the World*, p. 34.

45. It is true, however, that Sharp's name (as well as Harwood's) continued to appear at intervals in Godwin's diary until the engraver's death in 1824.

46. The print is identified in the edition of the *Life of Holcroft*, edited by Elbridge Colby (London, 1925), II, 246, quoted in Erdman, *Prophet*, p. 342.

47. Holcroft, *Memoirs*, pp. 253–254.

48. At his trial, Tooke said to the engraver, "Mr. Sharpe the gentlemen who have called you as a witness appear to have as good an opinion of you as I have. It is said that I nominated you to some delegation: do you think that I did it because I had a good opinion of you?" Sharp answered, "Yes" (Howell, *State Trials*, XXV, 247).

49. Bentley, "Blake's Engravings," p. 166.

50. Roth, *Nephew of the Almighty*, pp. 49–50.

51. Bentley, "Blake's Engravings," p. 166.

52. William Sharp to Bishop [?], June 28, 1804 in Southcott, *Copies and Parts of Copies*, p. 29.

53. [Sharp], *Answer to the World*, pp. 6–7.

54. Sharp to Reverend Joseph Pomeroy, September 28, 1804, in Southcott, *Second Book of Wonders*, pp. 53–54.

55. Southcott, *Answer to Age of Reason*, p. 25.

56. Blake wrote, "I must Create a System or be enslav'd by another Man's. / I will not Reason & Compare: my business is to Create" (see "Jerusalem," plate 10.20−21, in *Complete Writings*, p. 629.

57. [Sharp], *Divine and Spiritual Communications*, pp. vii−viii.

58. Blake, "To F[laxman]," in *Complete Writings*, p. 539. Another whose experience closely corresponds with that of Sharp is Coleridge. The poet had pronounced radical sympathies, and for much the same reasons as the millenarians. In his lectures on theology, he challenged "the prejudices of the 'infidels' among his supporters, by grounding his own idiosyncratic reformism upon Christian precept and revelation." He may have been involved with the Bristol Constitutional Society. In the Prospectus of *The Watchman*, which ceased to exist after its tenth number in May 1796, he announced that his "chief objects" were "to cooperate (1) with the WHIG CLUB in procuring a repeal [of the Two Acts] and (2) with the PATRIOTIC SOCIETIES, for obtaining a Right of Suffrage general and frequent." Coleridge also lectured energetically against the acts in Bristol and became a close friend of John Thelwall. It would seem that, "taken together, these facts suggest that the curve of Coleridge's commitment, in 1795−96, took him very close indeed to the popular societies—or towards their more intellectual component." But Coleridge's "trajectory," like that of Sharp's, was deflected away into mystical utopianism. The evidence tantalizingly suggests that their reasons may have been similar. In 1817 Coleridge gave this explanation for the demise of *The Watchman*: "I made enemies of all my Jacobin and democratic patrons . . . disgusted by their infidelity and their adoption of French morals with French psilosophy." He wrote to his brother, the Reverend Charles Coleridge, in March 1798, "I wish to be a good man & a Christian—but I am no Whig, no Reformist, no Republican." Ten years later he said, "I may safely defy my worst enemy to shew, in any of my few writings, the least bias to Irreligion, Immorality, or Jacobinism." Like Sharp, he recoiled from Godwin's deism. *Political Justice* drove him to the frenzied declaration: "Your principles are villainous ones! I would not entrust my wife or sister to you—Think you, I would entrust my country?" ("Bliss Was It in That Dawn: The Matter of Coleridge's Revolutionary Youth and How It Became Obscured," *Times Literary Supplement*, August 6, 1971, pp. 929−932).

59. [Sharp], *Divine and Spiritual Communications*, pp. vi, ix, x, viii.

VIII. THE LAST REDOUBT

1. John Rylands Library, Broadsheet No. 362.

2. Add Mss. 47799, May 18, 1798, f. 34b. An Exeter friend of Joanna, Mrs. Minifie, said that she "had spoken in his favour some years before." See U.T., Southcott Collection, 439, May 19, 1798, f. 64.

3. Joanna Southcott, *A Communication Given to Joanna, in Answer to Mr. Brothers' Last Book, Published the End of This Year, 1802*, p. 8.

4. Reverend T. P. Foley to the Reverend Stanhope Bruce, September 4, 1803 [?], GLRO, Acc 1040/187, f. 127b.

5. Jane Townley to Mr. Hows, February 2, 1818, Add Mss. 26038, f. 67b.

6. Ibid., 47801B, July 10, 1802, f. 13a.

7. U.T., Southcott Collection, 439, April 29, 1806, f. 197.

8. Ibid., Southcott to a friend, April 2, 1806, 447, f. 217. Brothers was not passive in the face of Joanna's challenge. He asserted that the sealing "is only a metaphorical term," which did not refer to "an artificial seal or the signing of names on paper," and, moreover, that she was of the wrong sex to play such an important role. "It's a HE, *not a She*," he said. See *A Letter to His Majesty and One to Her Majesty* (London, 1802), pp. 16, 13, quoted by Morton D. Paley, "The Prince of the Hebrews and the Woman Clothed with the Sun," in *William Blake*, ed. Paley and Phillips, p. 281.

9. U.T., Southcott·Collection, 439, April 29, 1806, f. 197.

10. Ibid., 437, May 5, 1803, f. 120.

11. John Rylands Library, R20862, ff. 370, 373.

12. U.T., Southcott Collection, 445, July 12, 1802, f. 710.

13. Southcott to Foley, May 26, 1806, Add Mss. 57860, f. 1a.

14. Letter to Both Houses of Parliament, 1802, Add Mss. 47802, ff. 8b–9a.

15. U.T., Southcott Collection, 455, July 30, 1803, f. 14.

16. See entries for May 23, 26, 28, in Add Mss. 57860. On June 7, he called on Lord Stanhope with whom he "had a long and agreeable interview."

17. Ibid.

18. U.T., Southcott Collection, 447, May 17, 1803, f. 206.

19. Southcott to Nathaniel Halhed, December 18, 1802, GLRO, Acc 1040/185, ff. 697–699.

20. U.T., Southcott Collection, 455, December 17, 1804, ff. 1, 4.

21. Add Mss. 32636, December 19, 1804, ff. 125b–126a.

22. Southcott to a friend, March 25, 1806, U.T., Southcott Collection, 446, f. 243; and Southcott to a friend, May 14, 1806, ibid., 446, f. 229. For further evidence of her attitude toward Finlayson, see Joanna's letter to a friend, June 5, 1806, Add Mss. 47794, f. 80a. For mention of one of his sexual misadventures, see E. J. Field's letter to Peter Morrison, May 5, 1807, Add Mss. 47797, f. 144a.

23. U.T., Southcott Collection, 446, April 19, 1806, ff. 226–227.

24. Add Mss. 57860, June [?], 1806, f. 8a.

25. Southcott to Foley, August 19, 1806, Add Mss. 57860, f. 1a. According to the letter, Sharp came to see her with news of his decision on July 8.

26. Foley to Peter Morrison, August 15, 1806, Add Mss. 47795, f. 30a.

27. Field to Mrs. Taylor, January 23, 1804, Add Mss. 47797, f. 59a. Field called this charge "ridiculous and absurd."

28. Balleine, *Past Finding Out*, pp. 34–35, 47.

29. Field to Mrs. Taylor, January 23, 1804, Add Mss. 47797, f. 59a.

30. *A Letter Addressed to the Reverend T. P. Foley*, pp. 36, 56.

31. Southcott, *Trial of Joanna Southcott*, p. xii.

32. Carpenter, *Nocturnal Alarm*, p. 9.

33. Southcott, *Warning to the World*, p. 74.

34. [Thomas Foley], *The Answer of the Rev. Thomas P. Foley, to the World*, p. 27.

35. U.T., Southcott Collection, 415, n.d., f. 44. In 1819 the Reverend T. P. Foley wrote that "we the true followers of Joanna Southcott have *nothing* to do with Politics in any shape, or way, whatever. We only wish to see satan's Kingdom destroyed, & our Blessed Lord's Kingdom of love & peace & righteousness established over the whole world" (see his letter to the Reverend F. Jennings, August 30, 1819, Add Mss. 47795, f. 87b). Three years later, Jane Townley learned that the ever difficult Peter Morrison was taking a radical political position. She lashed out at him "for your Rebellion against the King and rulers" and said it "is acting in compleat opposion to Joanna's visitation." Townley said she was "ordered to reprove all who are not Loyal." See her letter to Peter Morison (an alternative spelling of his name), August 6, 1822, Add Mss. 47802, f. 16b.

Twentieth-century Southcottians reiterate these views of Joanna's political attitudes. She is called an "anti-Revolutionist" by Rachel Fox in her *Joanna Southcott's Place in History: A Forecast*, p. 1. In 1921 Alice Seymour admonished the striking coal miners by referring to Joanna's declaration that "the only revolution that can be attended with happiness to mankind, is to wish for the destruction of our *Spiritual Enemy*." Joanna's biographer said of the miners, "They have yet to learn there must be government—there must be order—or there is no peace or happiness for any community" (see *Southcott Despatch* no. 27, p. 2).

36. Southcott, *Trials on Bills of Exchange*, p. 54.

37. Southcott, *Trial of Joanna Southcott*, p. xiv.

38. Carpenter, *Nocturnal Alarm*, p. 9.

39. Field to Mrs. Taylor, January 23, 1804, Add Mss. 47797, f. 59b.

40. Richard Law, *Copy of an Epistle of the Most Extraordinary Nature*, pp. 17, 11–12.

41. Southcott, *Strange Effects of Faith; Fourth Part*, p. 180.

42. U.T., Southcott Collection, 70, *Communication by the Small Still Voice*, pp. 14, 5.

43. L. Mayer, *A Hint to England; Or, a Prophetic Mirror*, p. 32.

44. Add Mss. 32637, September 11, 1806, f. 128b.

45. F. Lewis, *An Address to the Clergy, Particularly the Bench of Bishops*, pp. 3, 15, 18, 22.

46. Law, *Copy of an Epistle*, pp. 12–13, 18, 17.

47. U.T., Southcott Collection, 74, *Communication on the Temporal and Spiritual Sword* (Ms. dtd. 1803, publ. 1853), p. 2.

48. Carpenter, *Nocturnal Alarm*, p. 103.

49. Southcott to Mr. Sharpe, July 27, 1803, in *Temporal and Spiritual Sword*, p. 5.

50. U.T., Southcott Collection, 333, July 26, 1803, ff. 59–61.

51. *Temporal and Spiritual Sword*, p. 1.

52. U.T., Southcott Collection, 124, *Answer to Mr. Carpenter's Letters, and the Chapters in the Bible, Which He Sent to Joanna* (Ms. dtd. 1803, publ. 1859), p. 15.

53. *Temporal and Spiritual Sword*, p. 3.

54. John Rylands Library, Broadsheet No. 323.

55. Southcott, *Long-Wished-For Revolution*, p. 9.

56. Joanna Southcott, *True Explanations of the Bible. Part the Seventh*, p. 587.

57. Southcott, *Long-Wished-For Revolution*, pp. 10, 12.

58. U.T., Southcott Collection, 437, August 6, 1803, f. 417.

59. Ibid., 327, February 12, 1806, f. 121.

60. Amraphel, *Truth's Humble Appeal*, p. 4.

61. *Joseph Southcott*, p. 101.

62. Pullen, *Hymns, or Spiritual Songs*, p. 201.

63. *Scriptures Which Shew for What Christ Died*, p. 34.

64. Southcott, *Sound an Alarm*, p. 24.

65. Carpenter, *Nocturnal Alarm*, p. 109.

66. U.T., Southcott Collection, 106, *Communication Sent to Mr. Pomeroy* (Ms. dtd. 1794[?], publ. 1853), p. 3.

67. Southcott, *Third Book of Wonders*, p. 57.

68. Joanna Southcott, *True Explanation. First*, p. 27.

69. U.T., Southcott Collection, 132, *Communication in Answer to Mr. Brothers's Book and a Vision He Had of Two Suns* (Ms. dtd. 1806, publ. 1859), pp. 7, 9.

70. Ibid., 131, *Copy of a Letter: England May Be a Happy Land; Also the Warning Given by Mr. Brothers* (Ms. dtd. 1806, publ. 1859), p. 2.

71. Southcott, *Third Book of Wonders*, pp. 4, 52. The meaning of "Shiloh" is most obscure. The Authorized Version of the Bible has Jacob say, in Genesis, "The sceptre shall not depart from Judah, until Shiloh come." Otherwise, Shiloh is mentioned only as a town. Balleine demonstrates how the translations of the verse have varied from Bible to Bible. He concludes that the Authorized Version has a mistranslation of the passage and thus "led the Southcottians very wildly astray" (see *Past Finding Out*, pp. 142–143). Professor J. D. M. Derrett links the Shiloh belief of the Southcottians to a reference in *The Testament of the Twelve Patriarchs*, an example of Jewish Hellenistic Apocalyptic, which appeared in 1706 and may have been in Joanna's possession at Blockley (see A. W. Exell, *Joanna Southcott at Blockley and The Rock Cottage Relics*, pp. 37, 63–68). More to the point, as Clarke Garrett suggests, is that Brothers had called himself "the Shiloh," which is "probably" why Joanna was moved to appropriate the name for the child if, as she believed, God had chosen her to succeed Brothers (see *Respectable Folly*, pp. 214–215). Garrett's analysis of Brothers' career is the best informed and most penetrating that has yet appeared, but also see J. F. C. Harrison's *Second Coming*, pp. 57–85.

Another episode which may have provided a precedent for Joanna is a story that she heard in March 1807 concerning a woman who claimed she had conceived by the Holy Ghost and was going to give birth to the man child. Ironically, the Spirit's observation was that "these are Lying wonders from the Devil who now works in various ways to bring Prophecies into scorn and Contempt." It was a device by the devil to deceive "the simple and unwary." Joanna commented, "The meaning of the man Child Being Born hath a spiritual alusion of

Being Born by faith." Therefore, no actual child was meant to appear (see Southcott to a friend, March 12, 1807, U.T., Southcott Collection, 435, f. 24).

72. "A Prophecy Given in the 16th Century," U.T., Southcott Collection, 323.

73. Ibid., Southcott to a friend, December 16, 1813, 436, f. 50.

74. Add Mss. 26038, February 11, 1814, f. 63a.

75. U.T., Southcott Collection, 436, February 28, 1814, ff. 149–150, 146.

76. Add Mss. 26038, February 11, 1814, f. 63a.

77. Joanna Southcott, *The Fourth Book of Wonders, Being the Answer of the Lord to the Hebrews*, p. 42.

78. George Turner to Thomas Senior, March 16, 1814, GLRO, Acc 1040/193, f. 64.

79. Ann Underwood to Turner, August 6, 1814, ibid., Acc 1040/193, ff. 72–73.

80. Foley's diary entry for August 21, 1814 in Grayson, *King's Son Shiloh*, p. 221.

81. *The Plymouth Literary Magazine; Or, Devon and Cornwall Scientific Repository* (Plymouth, 1814), p. 158.

82. In Grayson, *King's Son Shiloh*, pp. 216–223.

83. U.T., Southcott Collection, 335, September 15, 1814, ff. 15–16.

84. Joanna Southcott, *Prophecies Announcing the Birth of the Prince of Peace, Extracted from the Works of Joanna Southcott*, p. 39.

85. Samuel Jowett, *To the Believers in Joanna Southcott's Visitation*, p. 7.

86. John Fairburn, *The Life of Joanna Southcott, the Prophetess.*

87. *Leeds Mercury*, October 15, 1814. This is undoubtedly a version of John Fairburn's *Life.*

88. Southcott, *Third Book of Wonders*, p. 63.

89. U.T., Southcott Collection, 326, ff. 98–99, 101, 104–106.

90. Fairburn, *Life*, pp. 15–16.

91. Quoted in the Bristol *Mirror*, August 27, 1814, p. 4.

92. *European Magazine and London Review* 66 (July–December 1814): 177.

93. WCSL, Southcott Cuttings.

94. R. S. Kirby, *Kirby's Wonderful and Eccentric Museum*, pp. 355–356, 359–363.

95. Fairburn, *Life*, p. 16.

96. Ibid., pp. 16–17, 37. The gifts were returned by Joanna's secretary, Ann Underwood. See Townley, *Council of Ten*, p. 35.

97. Tozer was by trade a lath render. He had built the chapel himself, opening it in the spring of 1805. According to a critic, Tozer said that he had "no presentiment of the numbers who congregate to hear him, or he would have erected a larger place of worship" (*Life and Prophecies of Joanna Southcott*, p. 15).

98. *Sunday Monitor* [London], September 4, 1814.

99. Bristol *Mirror*, January 7, 1815, p. 2.

100. *Fairburn's Edition of the Prophetess*, pp. 51–52.

101. *Sunday Monitor*, November 6, 1814.

102. Ibid., September 11, 1814.

103. Ibid., November 6, 1814.

104. Eusebius, *Letter to His Grace*, p. 12.

105. Turner to Thomas Senior, March 16, 1814, GLRO, Acc 1040/193, f. 62.

106. H. Syer Cuming to Reverend Walter Begley, March 5, 1888, Harry Price Library. Cuming knew several Southcottians. His father claimed to have once seen Joanna, and said, "The most ill-looking Portrait of Joanna must be regarded as a flattering likeness, and villainy and craft was expressed in her visage." His parish, Cuming said, "was considered one of the great centres of the Southcottian Heresy."

107. *Sunday Monitor*, January 1, 1815.

108. Turner to Mr. Senior, March 16, 1814, GLRO, Acc 1040/193, f. 63.

109. Ibid., Underwood to friends, March 11, 1814, f. 54.

110. Ibid., Underwood to George Turner, August 6, 1814, GLRO, Acc 1040/193, ff. 70–71.

111. August 22, 1814 in Grayson, *King's Son Shiloh*, pp. 221–222.

112. Southcott to friends, September 3, 1814, Add Mss. 32636, f. 208a.

113. Charles Barnard to Edmund Baker, October 26, 1814, GLRO, Acc 1040/25, f. 2.

114. Southcott to a friend, October 18, 1813, GLRO, Acc 1040/186, ff. 1167–1168, 1180.

115. Ibid., October 18, 1813, ff. 818–819.

116. Southcott to friends, October 19, 1813, Add Mss. 32636, f. 206b.

117. *Devon and Exeter Gazette*, September 20, 1926, WCSL, Southcott Cuttings.

118. Seymour, *Voice in the Wilderness*, p. viii.

119. Underwood to Foley, November 14, 1814, Add Mss. 47800, f. 206a. Foley received all the news of the fall and winter by mail. He and his wife, Elizabeth, wanted to be present at Shiloh's birth but the Spirit advised against it. Joanna promised that he could baptize the child. See her letter to him of October 5, Add Mss. 32635, ff. 189b, 190b. For further information on Smith, see Exell, *Joanna Southcott*, pp. 45–46.

120. Col. W. Tooke Harwood to Edmund Baker, December 12, 1814, GLRO, Acc 1040/29, ff. 1–2.

121. Quoted in Seymour, *Express*, II, 387, 389.

122. *Southcott Express*, September 1927, p. 157. This information is contained in a letter from Alice Seymour.

123. Harwood to Ann Harwood, December 28, 1814, U.T., Southcott Collection, 255.

124. Ibid.

125. Add Mss. 47800, November 19, 1814, f. 177b.

126. P. Mathias, *The Case of Johanna Southcott*, pp. 6, 15–17.

127. Add Mss. 47800, f. 178b. However, Dr. Reece came under particularly biting attack. The *Edinburgh Review* asked how he could have lent his prestige to such idiocy without an internal examination of the prophetess. Reece, the *Review* charged, "contributed more than any one man to encourage the proph-

etess and her disciples, and to make converts to her delusion" (see *Edinburgh Review* 24 (1815): 466). He defended himself in his *A Correct Statement of . . . the Last Illness and Death of Mrs. Southcott*, which has some interesting comments about Sharp and Joanna.

128. William Sharp to Foley, December 25, 1815, GLRO, Acc 1040/190, f. 118.

129. See *Notes and Queries*, April 16, 1904, p. 302; Add Mss. 26039, ff. 55a–55b; Forth, *The Lord Spake*, p. 111; and Kirby, *Wonderful Museum*, pp. 353–354.

130. *A Full Account of the Death of Joanna Southcott on Tuesday, December 27, 1814*, p. 3; Reece, *A Correct Statement*, pp. 87, 91, 106, and *A Complete Refutation of the Statements and Remarks Published by Dr. Reece, Relative to Mrs. Southcott*, pp. 30–31. Reece meant by his statement that all visible signs of Joanna's pregnancy had disappeared. Two alternate explanations for Shiloh's failure to appear were suggested: (1) the child's birth had been postponed because of the unbelief of the bishops and (2) a temporal birth had never been intended. According to this second theory, Shiloh was already alive and had only to be recognized. Townley and Underwood soon believed that the Reverend Joseph Pomeroy would manifest himself as the promised hero. Pomeroy was nominated because Joanna had long prophesied a great role for him in the movement which he had never fulfilled (see Balleine, *Past Finding Out*, pp. 68–69).

131. Sharp to Foley, December 25, 1815, GLRO, Acc 1040/190, f. 118.

132. For the course of the Southcottian movement after Joanna's death see Balleine, *Past Finding Out*, pp. 67–147. His book contains a particularly interesting "Table of Southcottian Sects" (p. 147). Also see P. G. Rogers, *The Sixth Trumpeter*, and, especially, Harrison's *Second Coming*.

The Panacea Society in Bedford, England, still actively distributes Joanna's works and periodically places advertisements calling on the bishops to gather and open Joanna's famous "box." The box allegedly contains a large number of Joanna's prophecies which are to be opened only in the presence of twenty-four bishops. Failure to do so will cause the country's ruin. A number of such "boxes," either spurious or containing only a few of Joanna's writings, have surfaced over the years. One of them fell into the possession of Harry Price, founder and honorary director of the National Laboratory of Psychical Research, who opened it on a carefully stage-managed occasion at Westminster Hall in June 1927. The box contained a number of random items, such as coins, a horse pistol, pamphlets on prophecy, including one of Brothers', and, most interestingly, a copy of a 1765 novel called *The Surprises of Love* by John Cleland, which Price says was annotated in Joanna's hand.

Although Price gave the box and his whole remarkable library on psychic phenomena to the University of London, the novel apparently disappeared. Therefore, it is impossible to determine whether the prophetess owned it. The principal story is one that would particularly appeal to Joanna. It concerns two young people, Letitia and Frederic, who meet in disguise at Greenwich Park. Although well born and rich, she is dressed as a servant, as is her new friend, who is equally well to do. It was Frederic's intention to debauch as many of the most attractive young women of the servant class as he could manage. Instead, he falls in love with Letitia, their identities are revealed, and, of course, they live happily ever after. Of even more interest is another story in the collection. In it, a baronet's son falls in love with a farmer's adopted daughter who is employed as a servant. Subsequently, it is revealed that she is the granddaughter of a nobleman. Similarly, other stories in the volume deal with mistaken identity, as in the previous examples, principally concerning a young and beautiful woman who is either dissimulating that she is a poor servant or, in fact, genuinely thinks she is. In each case, she attracts a wealthy, upper-class suitor who marries her.

For the story of the box, see Price's *Leaves from a Psychist's Case-Book*, pp. 287–304. For the history of the real box, see Mary S. Robertson, *Authentic History of the "Great Box" of Sealed Writings Left by Joanna Southcott*. It was safeguarded at one time or another by Sharp, Pugh, Foley, and Foley's son.

133. U.T., Southcott Collection, 330, ff. 52–53.

134. Quoted in Leonid I. Strakhovsky, *Alexander I of Russia*, p. 183. The comment was made by Stephen Grellet who saw Lieven and others with Alexander at the meeting.

135. E. M. Almedingen, *The Emperor Alexander I*, p. 167.

136. Jane Townley emphasized this distinction in 1823 when she said, "The believers in Joanna have never expressed themselves, as I know of, against Madame Krudener; for in fact they know nothing about her" (*Council of Ten*, p. 30).

137. Lewis, *Address to the Clergy*, p. 12.

138. Brothers, *Miss Cott*, p. 89.

139. G. Kitson Clark, "The Romantic Element: 1830–1850," in *Studies in Social History: A Tribute to G. M. Trevelyan*, ed. J. H. Plumb, pp. 236–237.

140. Edward Gibbon Wakefield, *Householders in Danger from the Populace*, p. 7.

141. Harrison, *Letter to an Eminent Clergyman*, p. 93.

142. Wakefield, *Householders in Danger*, p. 7.

143. Southcott, *True Explanation of the Bible, First*, p. 64.

144. Wakefield, *Householders in Danger*, p. 10.

145. Professor Harrison has thrown much light on the "millennial matrix" from which Owen's appeal evolved. He argues that the Owenites were, in fact, a millennial sect with Owen as "a leader whose teaching was accepted by followers, and which did not institutionally survive his death" (see Harrison, *Robert Owen*, pp. 102, 136).

146. Quoted in Thompson, *Making of the English Working Class*, p. 787.

147. Ibid.

148. *Life*, 1a xlii–xliii, quoted by W. H. Oliver, "Owen in 1817: The Millennialist Moment," in *Robert Owen: Prophet of the Poor*, ed. Sidney Pollard and John Salt, p. 181.

149. John Saville, "J. E. Smith and the Owenite Movement, 1833–1834," in ibid., p. 117. Also see Oliver, *Prophets*, pp. 197–203.

150. W. Anderson Smith, *'Shepherd' Smith, the Universalist: The Story of a*

Mind (1892), p. 52, quoted in Saville, "J. E. Smith," p. 118.

151. *Crisis*, September 14, 1833, quoted in Harrison, *Robert Owen*, pp. 118–119.

152. *'Shepherd' Smith,* p. 112, quoted in Saville, "J. E. Smith," p. 138.

153. Ibid., p. 138. See also Oliver, *Prophets*, pp. 197–217.

154. See J. Stevenson, "Food Riots in England, 1792–1818," in *Popular Protest and Public Order*, ed. R. Quinault and J. Stevenson, pp. 45–46.

155. Southcott, *Warning to the World*, p. 52.

156. John Rylands Library, Broadsheet No. 361.

Bibliography

A NOTE ON SOURCES

J. F. C. Harrison once complained that "a chronic shortage of primary materials hampers all studies of the common people. They simply did not leave the quantities of literary evidence that the letter-writing classes bequeathed to posterity." [1] A social scientist, Michael Barkun, sounds much the same lament. "We rarely have the feeling of seeing millenarian movements through the eyes of their own members. Rather, the data almost always comes filtered through the consciousness of outsiders, be they administrators, clerics, travelers, or scholars." [2] Certainly the problems which Professors Harrison and Barkun perceive are real, but they do not apply in the case of Joanna Southcott and her followers. Unlike any other contemporary movement of its kind, the Southcottians left behind a plenitude of published and manuscript sources.

However, even the few who have managed to make their way through the dense thicket of Joanna's published writings have failed to make satisfactory use of her unpublished materials, which were circulated in the form of "correspondence books" among believers both during and long after her lifetime. The principal Southcottian collections can be found in the Humanities Research Center, University of Texas at Austin; the British Library; and the Greater London Record Office. Smaller but important holdings are in the possession of the Blockley Antiquarian Society, Blockley, Gloucestershire; the Burnet Morris Collection, West Country Studies Library, Exeter; the Gloucestershire and Worcestershire Record Offices; the Harry Price Library, University of London; and the John Rylands University Library of Manchester.

1. J. F. C. Harrison, "A Knife and Fork Question? Some Recent Writing on the History of Social Movements," *Victorian Studies* 18 (December 1974): 220.
2. Barkun, *Disaster and the Millennium*, p. 131.

WORKS EITHER BY JOANNA SOUTHCOTT OR CONSIDERED PART
OF HER CANON IN THE ORDER RECOGNIZED BY HER FOLLOWING

The Strange Effects of Faith; With Remarkable Prophecies (Made in 1792, &c.) of Things Which Are to Come: Also Some Account of My Life [First Part]. Exeter, [1801].

The Strange Effects of Faith. Second Part. Exeter, [1801].

The Strange Effects of Faith. Third Part. Exeter, [1801].

The Strange Effects of Faith; With Remarkable Prophecies, Made in 1792 &c. of Things Which Are to Come. Fourth Part. Exeter, [1801].

The Strange Effects of Faith; With Remarkable Prophecies, Made in 1792, &c. of Things Which Are to Come. Fifth Part. Exeter, [1801].

The Strange Effects of Faith; With Remarkable Prophecies, Made in 1792, &c. of Things Which Are to Come. Sixth Part. Exeter, 1802.

A Continuation of Prophecies, by Joanna Southcott, from the Year 1792, to the Present Time. Exeter, [1802].

The Strange Effects of Faith; Being a Continuation of Joanna Southcott's Prophecies of Things Which Are to Come. London, [1802].

Letters, &c. [Divine and Spiritual Letters of Prophecies]. London, 1801.

Divine and Spiritual Letters of Prophecies Sent to Reverend Divines, and Other Spiritual Good Men and Women, That Are Now Ordered to Be Put in Print by Divine Command for the Good of the Public, and to Try the Wisdom of Mankind to What Spirit They Will Allude This Strange Revelation. London, n.d.

A Dispute between the Woman and the Powers of Darkness. London, [1802].

The Answer of the Lord to the Powers of Darkness. London, 1802.

A Communication Given to Joanna, in Answer to Mr. Brothers' Last Book, Published the End of This Year, 1802. London, [1802].

Prophecies. A Warning to the Whole World, from the Sealed Prophecies of Joanna Southcott, and Other Communications Given since the Writings Were Opened on the 12th of January, 1803. London, [1803].

The First Book of the Sealed Prophecies. London, n.d.

The Continuation of the Prophecies of Joanna Southcott. A Word in Season to a Sinking Kingdom. London, [1803].

The Second Book of Visions. London, [1803].

A Word to the Wise; Or a Call to the Nation, That They May Know the Days of Their Visitation from the Prophecies That Are Given to Joanna Southcott, with the Reasons Assigned Why the Spirit of Prophecy Is Given to a Woman; And Which Is Explained from the Scriptures in the Following Pages. Stourbridge, 1803.

Divine and Spiritual Communications, Written by Joanna Southcott: On the Prayers of the Church of England; The Conduct of the Clergy, and Calvinistic Methodists, with Other Particulars. London, 1803.

Sound an Alarm in My Holy Mountain. Leeds, [1804].

A Warning to the World. Joanna Southcott's Prophecies. London, 1804.

On the Prayers for the Fast Day, May, 1804. London, 1804.

Letters on Various Subjects from Mrs. Joanna Southcott to Miss Townley. London, 1804.

Copies and Parts of Copies of Letters and Communications, Written from Joanna Southcott, and Transmitted by Miss Townley to Mr. W. Sharp, in London. London, 1804.

Mr. Joseph Southcott, the Brother of Joanna Southcott, Will Now Come For-

ward as Dinah's Brethren Did; That They Shall Not Deal with His Sister, as They Would With a Harlot; For So They Are Now Dealing with Her. And He Will Prove to the World Where the Adultery Is Committed, by Men Who Are "Uncircumcised in Heart and Life"; and Now He Will Expend All That He Has In the World, If Required, in the Honest Defense of Her Character—Till He Has Slain the Uncircumcised Philistines, and Entirely Freed His Sister from the "Reproaches of Their Adultery." London, 1804.

Letters and Communications of Joanna Southcott. The Prophetess of Exeter: Lately Written to Jane Townley. Stourbridge, 1804.

The Trial of Joanna Southcott, during Seven Days, Which Commenced on the Fifth, and Ended on the Eleventh, of December, 1804. At the Neckinger House, Bermondsey, Near London. London, 1804.

Joanna Southcott's Answer to Garrett's Book, Entitled "Demonocracy Detected —Visionary Enthusiasm Corrected; or, Sixpennyworth of Good Advice Selected from the Scriptures of Truth: By the Rev. Jeremiah Learnoult Garrett, Author of 'Rays of Everlasting Light.'" Also, Remarks on An Engraved Print, Published by the Said Garrett of His Own Head: With Marvelous and Wonderful Accompaniments, Wherein the Demon is Detected, Dissected—Who Soon Will Be Corrected, and All His Adherents Rejected. London, [1805].

Joanna Southcott's Answer to Five Charges in the "Leeds Mercury," Four of Which Are Absolutely False; But as in the First Charge, Her Accuser Might Have Some Room for Cavilling, She Wishes to Make Every Allowance; And Give a Clear Answer, How That Was Misunderstood: And Not Only to Answer the Four False Charges That Are Brought against Her; But She Has Brought Four Charges against Her Adversaries, Which Will Be Seen in the Following Pages. London, [1805].

The True Explanation of the Bible Revealed by Divine Communications to Joanna Southcott. Part the First. To Which Are Added Letters to and from the Rev. Mr. Pomeroy. London, 1804.

True Explanations of the Bible. Part the Second. London, [1804].

True Explanations of the Bible. Part the Third. London, [1804].

True Explanations of the Bible. Part the Fourth. Disputes and Controversies With Mankind. London, n.d.

True Explanations of the Bible. Part the Fifth. London, n.d.

True Explanations of the Bible. Part the Sixth. London, [1805].

An Explanation of the Parables Published in 1804. London, [1806].

The Kingdom of Christ is at Hand. Being an Answer to a Book, Dated April 8, 1805, Printed at Halifax in Yorkshire, and Signed a Lover of the Truth of God; By Joanna Southcott: With an Explanation How the Lord Pleaded with Men in Past Ages, and How He Will Plead with All Flesh at His Second Coming; Also an Examination of Baptism, and the Use and Meaning of Church Ordinances, and of the Sealing of the People, in These Latter Days. London, n.d.

The Second Book of the Sealed Prophecies. London, [1805].

The Answer of the Rev. Thomas P. Foley, to the World, Who Hath Blamed His Faith in Believing It Was a Command from the Lord to Put in Print Such Para-

bles, As He Printed Last Year at Stourbridge, under the Title "What Manner of Communications are These?" Oldswinford, 1805. [By Thomas Foley.]

The Controversy between Joanna Southcott and Elias Carpenter, One of Her Judges, Made Public. Part I. London, [1805].

Part II [of the *Controversy between Joanna Southcott and Elias Carpenter*]. London, [1805].

Part III [of the *Controversy between Joanna Southcott and Elias Carpenter*]. London, [1805].

Part IV [of the *Controversy between Joanna Southcott and Elias Carpenter*]. London, [1805].

Part V [of the *Controversy between Joanna Southcott and Elias Carpenter*]. London, [1805].

An Answer to the World, for Putting in Print a Book in 1804, Called "Copies and Parts of Copies of Letters and Communications, Written from Joanna Southcott," and Transmitted by Miss Townley to Mr. W. Sharp in London. Beginning with the Parable of the Little Flock of Sheep: In Which Reasons Are Given, in Answer to the Mockery and Ridicule of Men, for Printing the Parables and Fables, Which Were Published from Divine Command in That Book. London, 1806. [By William Sharp.]

The Full Assurance That the Kingdom of Christ Is at Hand, from the Signs of the Times. London, [1806].

The Long-Wished-For Revolution Announced to Be at Hand in a Book Lately Published, by L. Mayer, When, as He Says, "God Will Cleanse the Earth by His Judgments, and When All Dominions Shall Serve the Most High." Explained by Joanna Southcott; With Letters to Her, from the Author of That Book, and Her Answers; to Which Are Added Observations upon His Wrong Application of the Scripture Prophecies in General, and His Ignorance, Particularly in Wishing for a Period of Judgments, Without Explaining What Will Bring This Happy Deliverance in the End, Which Shall Be to the Glory of God, and to the Good of the Whole Human Race, by Being United to His Spirit, and Bearing His Image, and Satan Cast Out, So That the Earth May Be at Rest for One Thousand Years. London, 1806.

Answer to Mr. Brothers' Book, Published in September 1806, and Observations on His Former Writings; also, a Letter Sent to Mr. Huntington with Remarks on the Calvinist and Roman Catholic Doctrines, &c. and the Unbelief of the Jews at the Destruction of Jerusalem. London, [1806].

A Caution and Instruction to the Sealed, That They May Know for What They Are Sealed. London, [1807].

An Account of the Trials on Bills of Exchange, Wherein the Deceit of Mr. John King and His Confederates, under the Pretence of Lending Money Is Exposed, and Their Arts Brought to Light. London, [1807].

An Answer to a Sermon Published and Preached by Mr. Smith, on Tuesday Evening, March 15, 1808, at Beersheba-Chapel, Prospect-Place, St. George's Field. London, [1808].

No Title [*Answer to False Doctrines, and the Crying Sins of the Nation*]. London, 1808.

A True Picture of the World and A Looking-Glass For All Men. London, [1809].

True Explanations of the Bible. Part the Seventh. London, 1810.

The Controversy of the Spirit with the Worldly Wise, As Given through Joanna Southcott. London, 1811.

A Continuation of the Controversy with the Worldly Wise. London, 1811.

An Answer to Thomas Paine's Third Part of the Age of Reason, Published by D. I. Eaton; Likewise to S. Lane, a Calvinistic Preacher, at Yeovil, in Somersetshire; And to Hewson Clarke, Editor of "The Scourge," and Late of Emanuael [sic] *College, Cambridge.* London, [1812].

The Book of Wonders, Marvellous and True. London, 1813.

The Second Book of Wonders, More Marvellous Than the First. London, 1813.

Copies of Letters Sent to the Clergy of Exeter, from 1796 to 1800, with Communications and Prophecies Put in the Newspapers in 1813. London, 1813.

Wisdom Excelleth the Weapons of War, and Herein Is Shewn That Judgments Are the Strange Works of the Lord, But Mercy His Darling Attribute. London, 1814.

The Third Book of Wonders, Announcing the Coming of Shiloh; With a Call to the Hebrews. London, 1814.

The Fourth Book of Wonders, Being the Answer of the Lord to the Hebrews. London, 1814.

The Fifth Book of Wonders, Announcing the Event Having Taken Place, Which Was Promised in the Fourth Book Should Be in May. With a Further Explanation of the Four Former Books; Also an Answer to the Address of the Rev. James Hearn, Curate of Brixham, Devon; and to the Mockery of Others. London, 1814.

A Communication Sent in a Letter to the Reverend Mr. P. in 1797, with an Explanation Thereon Now. London, 1814.

Prophecies Announcing the Birth of the Prince of Peace, Extracted from the Works of Joanna Southcott; To Which Are Added a Few Remarks Thereon, Made by Herself. London, [1814].

PRIMARY WORKS

Aiken, J. *Joanna Southcott.* N.p., n.d.

Amraphel. *Truth's Humble Appeal unto All Men.* London, [1804].

Annual Register, 1806, 1809, 1814, 1815, 1824.

Bennett, G. *A Warning to the Nation, from the Prophecies of Joanna Southcott.* London, n.d.

Bicheno, James. *The Probable Progress and Issue of the Commotions Which Have Agitated Europe since the French Revolution, Argued from the Aspect of Things, and the Writings of the Prophets.* London, 1797.

———. *The Signs of the Times: Or the Overthrow of the Papal Tyranny in France, the Prelude of Destruction to Popery and Despotism; But of Peace to Mankind.* London, 1793.

Blake, William. *Blake: Complete Writings*. Edited by Geoffrey Keynes. Oxford: Oxford University Press, 1969.

Blunt, Christiana. *A Midnight Dialogue between Joanna Southcott and Satan, Translated from a Luciferian Manuscript*. 2d ed. London, 1814.

Bray, Anna Eliza. *A Description of the Part of Devonshire Bordering on the Tamar and the Tavy*. 3 vols. London, 1836.

Brooks, Joshua, comp. *A Dictionary of Writers on the Prophecies*. London, 1835.

Brothers, Richard. *An Exposition of the Trinity*. London, 1795.

————. *A Letter from Mr. Brothers to Miss Cott*. London, 1798.

————. *A Poem on the Creation*. London, 1806.

————. *A Revealed Knowledge of the Prophecies and Times, Book the First*. London, 1794.

————. *A Revealed Knowledge of the Prophecies and Times, Book the Second*. London, 1794.

————. *Wisdom and Duty*. London, 1805.

————. *Wonderful Prophecies*. London, 1795.

A Call from the Most High God, the God of Abraham, the God of Isaac, the God of Jacob, to His Ancient People the Jews, Scattered throughout the Earth, by His Holy Spirit to the Bride, As Promised through the Prophets, the Gospel and the Apostles, to the Gentile Church. London, 1845.

Carpenter, Elias. *An Apology for Faith, and Detection of Existing Errors Subversive of the Truth. With a Selection of Communications from the Invisible World; Announcing the Redeemer's Triumphant Appearance*. 2 pts. London, 1814.

————. *The Extraordinary Case of a Piccadilly Patient; or, Dr. Reece Physick'd, by Six Female Physicians*. London, 1815.

————. *Nocturnal Alarm; Being an Essay on Prophecy & Vision: Or a Brief Examination of Some Remarkable Things under Those Heads Which Have Recently Appeared in the World: And Which, from Their Extraordinary Import, Seem Worthy of the Enquiry and Consideration of All Serious and Well-Disposed Christians*. London, 1803.

————. *Who Are the Deluded? Or Mystery Unmasked: Being a Few Extracts From a Faithful Record of Spiritual Teachings: Viz. Revelations and Visions, Communicated to a Deceased Character: Submitted, with Humility, to Those Who Wish to Explore the Truth and Detect Error*. London, 1805.

Carpenter, S. Catherine. *Are These Things So? Being Remarks on "Demonocracy Detected": Shewing the Erroneous Statements of that Author, and Proving the Scriptural Opinions of Joanna Southcott, and Those in Faith United with Her*. London, 1805.

Cartwright, F. D. *The Life and Correspondence of Major Cartwright*. 2 vols. London, 1826.

Chapple, William. *A Review of Part of Risdon's Survey of Devon*. Exeter, 1785.

Coggan, G. *A Testimony of Richard Brothers*. London, 1795.

A Convert. The Age of Prophecy! Or, Further Testimony of the Mission of Richard Brothers. London, 1795.

Crease, J. *Prophecies Fulfilling: Or, the Dawn of the Perfect Day.* London, 1795.

Crossley, John. *Letters and Observations, to Ministers.* Bradford, 1814.

———. *The Master and Scholar Refuted.* London, 1810.

———. and William Jowett. *A Vindication of Joanna Southcott's Writings; Being a Reply to an Anonymous Pamphlet Published against Her at Halifax.* Leeds, 1805.

A Crumb of Comfort for the People. London, 1795.

Day to Day Service of Worship: According to the Command Given to Joanna Southcott, the Spirit of Truth. [New Plymouth: New Zealand Branch of the Southcottian Movement], 1969.

Doubts of Infidels. London, 1795.

Dowland, Thomas. *Divine and Spiritual Communications through T. Dowland to E. Carpenter for the British Nation.* London, 1848.

Eusebius. *A Letter to His Grace the Lord Archbishop of Canterbury, Relative to the Impious Blasphemies of the Late Imposter Joanna Southcott, and Her Followers.* London, 1815.

Fairburn, John. *The Life of Joanna Southcott, the Prophetess.* 11th ed. London, 1814.

Fairburn's Edition of the Prophetess; Or Southcott and Shiloh. London, 1814.

Fairburn's Edition of the Prophetess; Or Southcott and Shiloh; No. 2. London, 1814.

Fielden, Thomas. *An Exposition of the Fallacies and Absurdities of that Deluded Church Generally Known as Christian Israelites, or "Johannas."* Rawtenstall, 1850[?].

Frend, William. *Peace and Union Recommended to the Associated Bodies of Republicans and Anti-Republicans.* 2d ed. Cambridge, 1793.

A Full Account of the Death of Joanna Southcott on Tuesday, December 27, 1814. N.p., 1814.

Galloway, Joseph. *Brief Commentaries upon Such Parts of the Revelation and Other Prophecies as Immediately Refer to the Present Times.* London, 1802.

Gilchrist, Alexander. *Life of William Blake.* London and Cambridge, 1863.

Grant, Johnson. *Grant's History of the English Church.* London, 1814.

Grayson, Emma. *Had They Had Knowledge.* New Plymouth: New Zealand Branch of the Southcottian Movement, 1974.

———. *The King's Son Shiloh, Prince of Peace.* New Plymouth: New Zealand Branch of the Southcottian Movement, 1972.

Gunning, Henry. *Reminiscences of the University, Town, and County of Cambridge from the Year 1780.* Vol. 1. London, 1854.

Halhed, Nathaniel Brassey. *The Second Speech of Nathaniel Brassey Halhed Esq.* London, 1795.

———. *Two Letters to the Right Honourable Lord Loughborough, Lord High Chancellor of England, on the Present Confinement of Richard Brothers, in a Private Mad-House.* London, 1795.

———. *The Whole of the Testimonies to the Authenticity of the Prophecies and*

Mission of Richard Brothers, as Prince and Prophet of the Hebrews. London, 1795.

Hann, R. *Charges against Joanna Southcott, and Her Twelve Judges, the Jury, and Four and Twenty Elders,* N.p., 1804.

H[arrison], W. B. *A Letter Addressed to a Friend, Proving from Reason and Scripture, That a Further Divine Revelation Will Be Given for the Instruction and Direction of Mankind, Previous to the Establishment of Christ's Kingdom on Earth.* Manchester, 1832.

————. *A Letter Addressed to an Eminent Clergyman of the Established Church of England, Explaining the Nature and Object of the Divine Mission of the Late Joanna Southcott.* Leeds, 1842.

Hawker, Reverend Robert. *The Life and Writings of the Late Rev. Henry Tanner of Exeter.* London, 1807.

Hazlitt, William. *The Plain Speaker.* London, 1826.

————. *The Spirit of the Age.* 4th ed. London, 1886.

Hodgkins, B. *A Few Plain Remarks on the Pretended Prophecies and Delusions of a Modern Prophetess.* 2d ed. Birmingham, 1813.

Holcroft, Thomas. *Memoirs of the Late Thomas Holcroft.* Edited by William Hazlitt. London, 1852.

"Horne Tooke's Diary." *Notes and Queries,* January 9, 1897, pp. 21–22; January 23, 1897, pp. 61–62; February 6, 1897, pp. 103–104.

Howell, T. B., comp.; cont. by Thomas James Howell after 1793, *A Complete Collection of State Trials.* London, 1818.

Impey, Elijah Barwell. *Memoirs of Sir Elijah Impey.* London, 1846.

Jenkins, Alexander. *The History and Description of the City of Exeter and Its Environs.* Exeter, 1806.

Johanne Soutgate. Die neue Prophetin in England. 2 pts. Edinburgh, 1805.

Jones, Lavinia E. C., ed. *Commentary upon the Prayers and Ordinances of the English Protestant Church, Extracted from Revelations Given by the Small Still Voice in London, during the Years 1801 to 1814.* Bradford, [1863?].

Jones, William. *Popular Commotions Considered as Signs of the Approaching End of the World.* London, 1790.

Jowett, Samuel. *To the Believers in Joanna Southcott's Visitation.* Leeds, 1844.

Kelly, Walter K., ed. *Erotica. The Elegies of Propertius, the Satyricon of Petronius Arbiter, . . . To which Are Added, the Love Epistles of Aristaenetus.* London, 1854.

Kirby, R. S. *Kirby's Wonderful and Eccentric Museum; Or Magazine of Remarkable Characters, Including All the Curiosities of Nature and Art, from the Remotest Period to the Present Time, Drawn from Every Authentic Source.* London, 1820.

Lackington, James. *Memoirs of the First Forty-Five Years of the Life of James Lackington.* 13th ed. London, [1810].

Lavington, George. *The Enthusiasm of Methodists and Papists Considered. With Notes, Introduction, and Appendix by . . . R. Polwhele.* London, 1820.

Law, Richard. *Copy of an Epistle of the Most Extraordinary Nature; Sent to the*

Right Honourable Henry Addington, Prime Minister of the United Kingdom, on Affairs of the Utmost Importance. July 19, 1803. London, n.d.

A Letter Addressed to the Rev. T. P. Foley. London, 1813.

Levi, David. *Letters to Nathaniel Brassey Halhed, M.P.* London, 1795.

Lewis, F. *An Address to the Clergy, Particularly the Bench of Bishops; Containing Some Important Facts Worthy the Consideration of All Ranks and Denominations at This Dangerous Crisis.* London, 1803.

The Life and Death of Joanna Southcott; With the Particulars of Her Will, and an Account of Her Dissection. London, 1815.

The Life and Journal of John Wroe. Ashton-Under-Lyne, 1829.

The Life and Prophecies of Joanna Southcott. London, 1814.

The Life and Prophecies of Joanna Southcott, from her Infancy to the Present Time. London, 1815.

Marshall, William. *The Rural Economy of the West of England.* 2 vols. London, 1796.

Mathias, P. *The Case of Joanna Southcott.* London, 1815.

Mayer, L. *A Hint to England; Or, a Prophetic Mirror; Containing an Explanation of Prophecy That Relates to the French Nation, and the Threatened Invasion.* London, 1803.

———. *The Woman in the Wilderness, or, the Wonderful Woman, with her Wonderful Seal, Wonderful Spirit, and Wonderful Child, Who "Is to Rule the Nations with a Rod of Iron."* London, 1806.

Memoirs of the Life and Mission of Joanna Southcott . . . To Which Is Added a Sketch of the Rev. W. Tozer. London, 1814.

Moore, Thomas. *The Letters and Journals of Lord Byron.* London, 1875.

———. *Memoirs of the Life of the Right Honourable Richard Brinsley Sheridan.* Vol. 1. London, 1825.

More, Hannah. *The Works of Hannah More.* New York, 1830.

Moser, Joseph. *Anecdotes of Richard Brothers.* London, 1795.

Mr. Halhed's Speech in the House of Commons. London, 1795.

Narrative of a Trial between Sir J. H. Astley, Bart., and Colonel W. T. Harwood. Norwich, 1803.

Niemeyer, D. August Hermann. *Beobachtungen auf Reisen in und ausser Deutschland.* 2d ed. Vol. 2. Halle, 1822.

North, Roger. *The Autobiography of Roger North.* Edited by Augustus Jessopp. London, 1890.

Offley, Henry Francis. *Richard Brothers, Neither a Madman nor an Impostor.* London, 1795.

Order of Service for January 12th. The Uplifting of Hands. According to the Command Given to Joanna Southcott. Plymouth, 1913.

Paine, Thomas. *The Writings of Thomas Paine.* Edited by Moncure Conway. New York and London, 1894.

The Picture of London For 1815. London, 1815.

Pindar, Peter. *Physic and Delusion! Or, Jezebel and the Doctors! A Farce in Two Acts.* London, 1814.

Pirie, Alexander. *The French Revolution Exhibited in the Light of the Sacred Oracles; Or, a Series of Lectures on the Prophecies Now Fulfilling.* Perth, 1795.

Plowden, Francis. *Church and State: Being an Inquiry into the Origin, Nature, and Extent of Ecclesiastical and Civil Authority.* London, 1795.

Polwhele, Richard. *The History of Devonshire.* Vol. 1. London, 1797.

Priestley, Joseph. *The Present State of Europe Compared with Ancient Prophecies.* London, 1794.

Pullen, Philip. *Hymns, or Spiritual Songs, Composed from the Prophetic Writings of Joanna Southcott.* 4th ed. London, 1814.

————. *Index to the Divine and Spiritual Writings of Joanna Southcott.* London, 1815.

Readings from Joanna Southcott's Publications: Prayers and Communications [New Plymouth: New Zealand Branch of the Southcottian Movement], 1970.

Reece, Richard. *A Complete Refutation of the Statements and Remarks Published by Dr. Reece, Relative to Mrs. Southcott.* London, [1815].

————. *A Correct Statement of . . . the Last Illness and Death of Mrs. Southcott.* London, 1815.

Reid, William Hamilton. *The Rise and Dissolution of the Infidel Societies in This Metropolis.* 2d ed. London, 1800.

Roberts, Daniel. *Observations Relative to the Divine Mission of Joanna Southcott with a Detail of the Proceedings of the People Called Quakers, against a Member, for his Belief.* London, 1807.

Robinson, Henry Crabb. *Diary, Reminiscences, and Correspondence of Henry Crabb Robinson.* 3 vols. Edited by T. Sadler. London, 1869.

Sales, William. *Truth or Not Truth; Or a Discourse on Prophets: With a Testimony of One.* London, 1795.

The Scriptures of the Holy Trinity. The New Testament Explained in England by the Voice of the Spirit of Christ. Part IV. Hebrews to Timothy. London, n.d.

Scriptures Which Shew for What Christ Died; Also Which Shew His Second Coming, to Bruise Satan's Head, and to Establish His Peaceable Kingdom on Earth. The Difference Shewn of Christ's Second Coming and Last Coming; And the Difference of the First Resurrection and the General Resurrection. Likewise the Remarkable Events of 1811, Selected from the Newspapers. London, 1812.

Seymour, Alice, comp. *The Voice in the Wilderness: The Gospel of The Holy Spirit As Given to Joanna Southcott by the Spirit of Truth.* Ashford, Middlesex: J. Stitt, 1933.

Sibley, Samuel. *A Copy of the Articles of Faith, as Acknowledged and Believed by the Children of the Faithful, Belonging to the House of Faith, Or, Philadelphian Church; Well Known by the Name of the Followers of the Divine Mission of Joanna Southcott.* London, 1819.

Southey, Robert. *Letters from England; By Don Manuel Alvarez Espriella.* 3 vols. London, 1807.

Spencer, Henry. *A Vindication of the Prophecies of Mr. Brothers and the Scripture Exposition of Mr. Halhed.* London, 1795.

Stephens, Alexander. *Memoir of John Horne Tooke.* 2 vols. London, 1813.

Taylor, Thomas. *An Additional Testimony Given to Vindicate the Truth of the Prophecies of Richard Brothers.* London, 1795.

Towers, Dr. Joseph. *Thoughts on the Commencement of a New Parliament. With . . . Remarks on the Letter of the Right Hon. Edmund Burke, on the Revolution in France.* London, 1790.

Towers, Reverend Joseph Lomas. *Illustrations of Prophecy.* 2 vols. London, 1796.

Townley, Jane. *A Letter from Mrs. Jane Townley to the Editor of the Council of Ten, in Answer to His Remarks and Misrepresentations Respecting the Mission of Joanna Southcott.* 2d ed. London, 1823.

The Trial, Casting, and Condemnation of the Prince of This World, the Old Serpent, Devil, and Satan. London, 1847.

Triebner, C. F. *Cursory and Introductory Thoughts on Richard Brothers' Prophecies.* London, 1795.

———. *Five Letters to the Critical Reviewers.* London, 1796.

Turberville, T. C. *Worcestershire in the Nineteenth Century.* London, 1852.

Turnbull, Joseph. *Unbelief and Credulity. A Sermon Occasioned by the Death of Mrs. Joanna Southcott, Preached at Her Native Place, Ottery Saint Mary, Devon on Lord's-Day Evening, the 8th of January, 1815.* Chard, 1815.

Turner, George. *The Armour of God.* London, 1821.

———. *The Assurance of the Kingdom.* London, 1819.

———. *A Book of Wonders.* London, 1817.

———. *A Vindication for the Honour of God, in Answer to J. Aked, Halifax.* Leeds, 1807.

Turpin, Theodore. *Extracts from Sermons Preached at Different Chapels in the Years 1812, 1813, and 1814.* London, 1825.

Vancouver, Charles. *General View of the Agriculture of the County of Devon.* London, 1808.

Wakefield, Edward Gibbon. *Householders in Danger from the Populace.* London, 1832 [?].

Webster, Thomas. *Reasons for the Fall of Man.* London, 1804.

Wesley, John. *The Journal of the Rev. John Wesley, A.M.* Edited by Nehemiah Curnock. 8 vols. London: Epworth Press, 1914; reprinted 1938.

———. *The Letters of the Rev. John Wesley, A.M.* Edited by John Telford. 8 vols. London: Epworth Press, 1931.

Wetherell, William Roundell. *A Testimony of Joanna Southcott, the Prophetess; Sent by the Lord, To Warn the People of His Coming.* London, n.d.

Whitchurch, S. *Another Witness! Or Further Testimony in Favor of Richard Brothers.* London, 1795.

White, William. *History, Gazetteer, and Directory of Devonshire.* Sheffield, 1850.

———. *History, Gazetteer, and Directory of the County of Devon, including the City of Exeter.* Sheffield, 1878.

Williams, Eliza. *The Prophecies of Brothers Confuted*. London, 1795.

Wilson, Henry, and James Caulfield. *The Book of Wonderful Characters: Memoirs and Anecdotes of Remarkable and Eccentric Persons in All Ages and Countries*. London, [1870?].

Wollstonecraft, Mary. *A Vindication of the Rights of Woman*. New York: W. W. Norton, 1967.

Zimpfel, C. F. *Das Sonnenweib einem Schlüssel zum richtigen Verstandniss der Bibel*. N.p., 1861.

SECONDARY WORKS

Abrams, M. H. "English Romanticism: The Spirit of the Age." In *Romanticism Reconsidered*, edited by Northrop Frye, pp. 26–72. New York: Columbia University Press, 1963.

Almedingen, E. M. *The Emperor Alexander I*. New York: Vanguard Press, 1964.

Altick, Richard D. *The English Common Reader*. Chicago: University of Chicago Press, 1957.

Andrews, Edward Deming. *The People Called Shakers*. New York: Oxford University Press, 1953.

Andrews, Stuart. *Methodism and Society*. London: Longman, 1970.

Armytage, W. H. G. *Heavens Below: Utopian Experiments in England, 1560– 1960*. Toronto: University of Toronto Press, 1961.

Artz, Frederick. *Reaction and Revolution*. New York: Harper Torchbooks, 1966.

Baine, Rodney M. *Thomas Holcroft and the Revolutionary Novel*. Athens: University of Georgia Press, 1965.

Baker, W. S. *William Sharp*. Philadelphia, 1875.

Baldwin, R. A. *The Jezreelites*. Orpington, Kent: Lambarde Press, 1962.

Balleine, G. R. *Past Finding Out: The Tragic Story of Joanna Southcott and Her Successors*. London: S.P.C.K., 1956.

Barkun, Michael. *Disaster and the Millennium*. New Haven and London: Yale University Press, 1974.

————. "Movements of Total Transformation: An Introduction." *American Behavioral Scientist* 16, no. 2 (November–December 1972): 145–151.

Bentley, G. E., Jr. *Blake Records*. Oxford: Clarendon Press, 1969.

————. "Blake's Engravings and His Friendship with Flaxman." *Studies in Bibliography* 12 (1959): 161–188.

Bentley, G. E., Jr., and Martin K. Nurmi. *A Blake Bibliography*. Minneapolis: University of Minnesota Press, 1964.

Best, G. F. A. "Popular Protestantism in Victorian Britain." In *Ideas and Institutions of Victorian Britain*, edited by Robert Robson, pp. 115–142. London: G. Bell & Sons, 1967.

"Bliss Was It in That Dawn: The Matter of Coleridge's Revolutionary Youth and How It Became Obscured." *Times Literary Supplement*, August 6, 1971, pp. 929–932.

Bowman, Winifred M. *England in Ashton-Under-Lyne*. Altrincham: John Sherratt, 1960.

Blunt, John Henry, D.D., ed. *Dictionary of Sects, Heresies, Ecclesiastical Parties, and Schools of Religious Thought*. N.p., 1891.

Booth, Alan. "Food Riots in the North-West of England, 1790–1801." *Past and Present* 77 (November 1977): 84–107.

Bridenthal, Renate, and Claudia Koonz, eds. *Becoming Visible: Women in European History*. Boston: Houghton Mifflin, 1977.

Brockett, Allan. *Nonconformity in Exeter, 1650–1875*. Manchester: Manchester University Press, 1962.

Bronowski, Jacob. *William Blake: A Man without a Mask*. London: Secker & Warburg, 1944.

Brown, P. A. *The French Revolution in English History*. London: C. Lockwood & Son, 1918.

Burridge, Kenelm. *New Heaven, New Earth*. New York: Schocken Books, 1969.

Capp, Bernard. *The Fifth Monarchy Men: A Study in Seventeenth-Century English Millenarianism*. London: Faber and Faber, 1972.

———. "*Godly Rule* and English Millenarianism." *Past and Present* 52 (August 1971): 106–117.

———. "The Millennium and Eschatology in England." *Past and Present* 57 (November 1972): 156–162.

Carpenter, S. C. *Eighteenth Century Church and People*. London: John Murray, 1959.

Cecil, Lord David. *The Stricken Deer*. London: Constable & Co., 1929.

Chadwick, William. *Reminiscences of Mottram*. Stalybridge, 1860's [?].

Chick, Elijah. *A History of Methodism in Exeter and the Neighborhood. From the Year 1739 until 1907*. Exeter: S. Drayton & Sons, 1907.

Cohn, Norman. *The Pursuit of the Millennium*. 3d ed. London: Paladin, 1970.

Cole, G. D. H., and Raymond Postgate. *The Common People*. London: Methuen & Co., 1956.

Cone, Carl B. *English Jacobins*. New York: Scribner, 1968.

Cross, Whitney R. *The Burned-over District. The Social and Intellectual History of Enthusiastic Religion in Western New York, 1801–1850*. Ithaca: Cornell University Press, 1950.

Cuming, H. Syer. "On Charms Employed in Cattle Disease." *British Archeological Association Journal* 21 (1855): 323–329.

Daiches, David. *The King James Version of the English Bible*. Chicago: University of Chicago Press, 1941.

Davies, C. Maurice. *Unorthodox London or Phases of Religious Life in the Metropolis*. 2d ed. London, 1874.

Davies, John Gordon. *The Theology of William Blake*. Oxford: Clarendon Press, 1948.

Davies, R. Trevor. *Four Centuries of Witch Beliefs*. London: Methuen & Co., 1947.

Drummond, Andrew L. *Edward Irving and His Circle*. London: J. Clarke & Co., [1937].

Emsley, Clive. *British Society and the French Wars, 1793–1815*. London and Basingstoke: Macmillan Press, 1979.

Endacott, A. G. "Devon Folklore." In *The Devonian Year Book for the Year 1937*, edited by Francis A. Perry, pp. 57–66. London: London Devonian Association, 1938.

Erdman, David V. *Blake: Prophet against Empire*. Rev. ed. Garden City, N.Y.: Anchor Books, 1969.

Exell, A. W. *Joanna Southcott at Blockley and The Rock Cottage Relics*. Shipston-on-Stour: Blockley Antiquarian Society, 1977.

Festinger, Leon, Henry W. Riecken, and Stanley Schacter. *When Prophecy Fails*. Minneapolis: University of Minnesota Press, 1956.

Fleisher, David. *William Godwin: A Study in Liberalism*. London: George Allen & Unwin, 1951.

Forth, Brent. *And the Lord Spake unto Joanna Southcott*. London, [1937].

Fox, Arthur W. "By Hill, Down and Dale." *Papers of the Manchester Literary Club* 57 (1932): 252–254.

Fox, Rachel. *Joanna Southcott's Place in History: A Forecast*. Plymouth, 1925.

Froom, LeRoy Edwin. *The Prophetic Faith of Our Fathers*. 4 vols. Washington, D.C.: Review and Herald, 1946–1954.

Garrett, Clarke. *Respectable Folly: Millenarians and the French Revolution in France and England*. Baltimore & London: Johns Hopkins University Press, 1975.

Geertz, Hildred, and Keith Thomas. "An Anthropology of Religion and Magic: Two Views." *Journal of Interdisciplinary History* 6, no. 1 (Summer 1975): 71–109.

George, M. Dorothy. *London Life in the Eighteenth Century*. New York and Evanston: Harper Torchbooks, 1964.

Gilbert, Alan D. *Religion and Society in Industrial England: Church, Chapel and Social Change, 1740–1914*. New York: Longman, 1976.

Gill, F. C. *The Romantic Movement and Methodism*. London: Epworth Press, 1937.

Glock, Charles Y. "The Role of Deprivation in the Origin and Evolution of Religious Groups." In *Religion and Social Conflict*, edited by Robert Lee and Martin E. Marty, pp. 24–36. New York: Oxford University Press, 1964.

Goodwin, Albert. *The Friends of Liberty*. Cambridge, Mass.: Harvard University Press, 1979.

Baring-Gould, S. *Devonshire Characters and Strange Events*. London: John Lane, 1908.

H., J. G. *History of Methodism in North Devon*. London, 1871.

Haden, H. J. "Thomas Philip Foley." *Notes and Queries*, July 5, 1952, pp. 294–298.

Halévy, Elie. *England in 1815*. 2d ed. London: Ernest Benn, and New York: Barnes & Noble, 1949; reprinted 1970.

Harrison, J. F. C. *The Early Victorians, 1832–1851*. London: Weidenfield & Nicolson, 1971.

———. "A Knife and Fork Question? Some Recent Writing on the History of Social Movements." *Victorian Studies* 18 (December 1974): 219–224.

———. *Robert Owen and the Owenites in Britain and America*. London: Routledge & Kegan Paul, 1969.

———. *The Second Coming*. London & Henley: Routledge & Kegan Paul, 1979.

Harvey, A. D. *Britain in the Early Nineteenth Century*. London: B. T. Batsford, 1978.

Hecht, J. Jean. *The Domestic Servant Class in Eighteenth-Century England*. London: Routledge & Kegan Paul, 1956.

Hill, Christopher. *Antichrist in Seventeenth-Century England*. London: Oxford University Press, 1971.

———. *The World Turned Upside Down: Radical Ideas during the English Revolution*. London: Temple Smith, 1972.

Hill, Michael. *A Sociology of Religion*. London: Heinemann, Educational, 1973.

Hirst, Désirée. *Hidden Riches: Traditional Symbolism from the Renaissance to Blake*. New York: Barnes & Noble, 1964.

Hobsbawm, E. J. *Labouring Men*. Garden City, N.Y.: Anchor Books, 1967.

———. *Primitive Rebels*, 3d ed. Manchester: Manchester University Press, 1971.

Hoskins, W. G. *Industry, Trade and People in Exeter, 1688–1800*. 2d ed. Exeter: University of Exeter Press, 1968.

———, and H. P. R. Finberg. *Devonshire Studies*. London: Jonathan Cape, 1952.

Howcroft, A. J. *Tales of a Pennine People*. Oldham: Whitehead & Co., 1923.

Hussey, Christopher. "Combe, Devon." *Country Life*, June 9, 1955, pp. 1486–1489; June 16, 1955, pp. 1556–1559.

James, William. *The Varieties of Religious Experience*. New York: Longmans, Green, & Co., 1902.

Jaynes, Julian. *The Origin of Consciousness in the Breakdown of the Bicameral Mind*. Boston: Houghton Mifflin, 1976.

Jones, M. G. *The Charity School Movement*. Hamden, Conn.: Archon Books, 1964.

Juretic, George. "Digger No Millenarian: The Revolutionizing of Gerard Winstanley." *Journal of the History of Ideas* 36, no. 2 (April–June 1975): 263–280.

Kazantzakis, Helen. *Nikos Kazantzakis*. New York: Simon and Schuster, 1968.

Kendrick, T. D. *The Lisbon Earthquake*. London: Methuen & Co., 1956.

Kiernan, V. "Evangelicalism and the French Revolution." *Past and Present* 1 (February 1952): 44–56.

Kitson Clark, G. *The Making of Victorian England*. London: Methuen & Co., 1962.

———. "The Romantic Element: 1830–1850." In *Studies in Social History: A Tribute to G. M. Trevelyan*, edited by J. H. Plumb, pp. 209–239. London: Longmans, Green, & Co., 1955.

Knight, Frida. *University Rebel: The Life of William Frend, 1757–1841*. London: Gollancz, 1971.

Knox, Ronald. *Enthusiasm*. New York: Oxford University Press, 1961.

Kramnick, Isaac. "Religion and Radicalism: English Political Theory in the Age of Revolution." *Political Theory* 5, no. 4 (November 1977): 505–534.

Lamont, William M. *Godly Rule: Politics and Religion, 1603–1660*. London: Macmillan, 1969.

———. *Richard Baxter & the Millennium: Protestant Imperialism & the English Revolution*. London: Croom Helm, 1979.

Lane, Charles. *Life of Joanna Southcott* and *Bibliography of Joanna Southcott*. Reprint. Exeter: Transactions of the Devonshire Association for the Advancement of Science, Literature and Art, 1912.

Lanternari, Vittorio. *The Religions of the Oppressed: A Study of Modern Messianic Cults*. Translated by Lisa Sergio. London: MacGibbon & Kee, 1963.

Lawrence, D. H. *Apocalypse*. New York: Viking Press, 1932.

Lincoln, Anthony. *Some Political and Social Ideas of English Dissent 1763–1800*. Cambridge: At the University Press, 1938.

Macaulay, Thomas Babington. *Critical and Historical Essays*. 2 vols. London, 1854.

Maccoby, Simon. *English Radicalism, 1786–1832*. London: George Allen & Unwin, 1955.

Macfarlane, Alan. *Witchcraft in Tudor and Stuart England*. London: Routledge & Kegan Paul, 1970.

McGuire, Paul. *The Tower Mystery*. London: Skeffington & Son, 1932.

Malinowski, Bronislaw. *Magic, Science and Religion and Other Essays*. Garden City, N.Y.: Anchor Books, 1954.

Mannheim, Karl. *Ideology and Utopia*. London: Kegan Paul & Co., 1936.

Matthews, Ronald. *English Messiahs: Studies of Six English Religious Pretenders, 1656–1927*. London: Methuen & Co., 1936.

"Millennialists and the New Society." *Times Literary Supplement*, April 2, 1970, pp. 361–362.

Morton, Arthur L. *The World of the Ranters: Religious Radicalism in the English Revolution*. London: Lawrence & Wishart, 1970.

Murphy, R. D. "Off the Beaten Track." Typescript. Leeds Reference Library.

Norton, Jane E. *Guide to the National and Provincial Directories of England and Wales*. London: Royal Historical Society, 1950.

Obelkevich, James. *Religion and Rural Society: South Lindsey, 1825–75*. Oxford: Clarendon Press, 1976.

Oliver, George. *Lives of the Bishops of Exeter*. Exeter, 1861.

Oliver, W. H. "Owen in 1817: The Millennialist Moment." In *Robert Owen: Prophet of the Poor*, edited by Sidney Pollard and John Salt, pp. 166–187. London and Basingstoke: Macmillan, 1971.

———. *Prophets and Millennialists*. Auckland & Oxford: Auckland University Press and Oxford University Press, 1978.

Paley, Morton D., and Michael Phillips. *William Blake: Essays in Honour of Sir Geoffrey Keynes*. Oxford: Clarendon Press, 1973.

Paul, C. Kegan. *William Godwin: His Friends and Contemporaries.* 2 vols. London, 1876.

Perkin, Harold. *The Origins of Modern English Society, 1780–1880.* London: Routledge & Kegan Paul, 1969.

Price, Harry. *Leaves from a Psychist's Case-Book.* London: Victor Gollancz, 1933.

Prince, Morton. *The Dissociation of a Personality.* New York: Longmans & Co., 1906.

Robertson, Mary S. "Ann Underwood." *Southcott Express,* March 1928, pp. 17–23.

———. *Authentic History of the "Great Box" of Sealed Writings Left by Joanna Southcott.* Plymouth, 1925.

———. "Jane Townley." *Southcott Express,* December 1927, pp. 192–196.

———. "Joanna—The Woman." *Southcott Express,* Pt. 1, March 1927, pp. 118–121; Pt. 2, June 1927, pp. 141–147; Pt. 3, September 1927, pp. 166–172.

Rogers, P. G. *Battle in Bossenden Wood: The Strange Story of Sir William Courtenay.* London: Oxford University Press, 1961.

———. *The Sixth Trumpeter: The Story of Jezreel and His Tower.* London: Oxford University Press, 1963.

Rosen, George. "Social Change and Psychopathology in the Emotional Climate of Millennial Movements." *American Behavioral Scientist* 16 (November–December 1972): 153–167.

Roth, Cecil. *The Nephew of the Almighty.* London: Edward Goldston, 1933.

Rowbotham, Sheila. *Hidden From History: Rediscovering Women in History from the 17th Century to the Present.* New York: Vintage, 1976.

Royle, Edward. *Radical Politics, 1790–1900: Religion and Unbelief.* London: Longman, 1971.

Rudé, George. *Hanoverian London, 1714–1808.* London: Secker & Warburg, 1971.

Sandeen, Ernest R. *The Roots of Fundamentalism: British and American Millenarianism, 1800–1930.* Chicago: University of Chicago Press, 1970.

Saville, John. "J. E. Smith and the Owenite Movement, 1833–1834." In *Robert Owen: Prophet of the Poor,* edited by Sidney Pollard and John Salt, pp. 115–144. London, 1971.

Schwartz, Hillel. "The End of the Beginning: Millenarian Studies, 1969–1975." *Religious Studies Review* 2, no. 3 (July 1976): 1–15.

———. *The French Prophets.* Berkeley, Los Angeles, London: University of California Press, 1980.

Scult, Mel. *Millennial Expectations and Jewish Liberties.* Leiden: Brill, 1978.

Seymour, Alice. *The Express.* 2 vols. London: Simpkin, Marshall, Hamilton, Kent and Company, 1909.

Shepherd, T. B. *Methodism and the Literature of the Eighteenth Century.* London: Epworth Press, 1940.

Smith, Alan. "Popular Religion." *Past and Present* 40 (July 1968): 181–186.

———. *The Established Church and Popular Religion, 1750–1850.* London: Longman, 1970.

Soboul, Albert. "Religious Sentiments and Popular Cults during the Revolution." In *New Perspectives on the French Revolution*, edited by Jeffry Kaplow, pp. 338–350. New York: Wiley, 1965.

Stephen, Leslie. *History of English Thought in the Eighteenth Century*. 2 vols. Reprint. London: Harbinger, 1962.

Stevenson, J. "Food Riots in England, 1792–1818." In *Popular Protest and Public Order: Six Studies in British History, 1790–1920*, edited by R. Quinault and J. Stevenson, pp. 33–74. London: George Allen & Unwin, 1974.

Stone, Lawrence. *The Family, Sex and Marriage in England, 1500–1800*. New York: Harper & Row, 1977.

Strakhovsky, Leonid I. *Alexander I of Russia*. New York: W. W. Norton & Co., 1947.

Summers, Montague. *The Geography of Witchcraft*. London: Kegan Paul & Co., 1927.

Sykes, Norman. *Church and State in England in the Eighteenth Century*. London: University Press, 1934.

Thomas, John Wesley. *Reminiscences of Methodism in Exeter*. N.p., [1870].

Thomas, Keith. *Religion and the Decline of Magic*. London: Weidenfield & Nicolson, 1971.

Thomis, Malcolm I., and Peter Holt. *Threats of Revolution in Britain, 1789–1848*. London and Basingstoke: Macmillan Press, 1977.

Thompson, E. P. "History from Below." *Times Literary Supplement*, April 7, 1966, pp. 279–280.

———. *The Making of the English Working Class*. New York: Vintage Books, 1963.

———. "The Moral Economy of the English Crowd in the Eighteenth Century." *Past and Present* 50 (February 1971): 76–136.

———. "Patrician Society, Plebeian Culture." *Journal of Social History* 7 (Summer, 1974): 382–405.

———, et al. *Albion's Fatal Tree: Crime & Society in Eighteenth Century England*. New York: Pantheon, 1976.

Thompson, P. "'Your Own Messiahs' in the West." *Devon Life*, April 1976, pp. 40–41.

Thrupp, Sylvia L., ed. *Millennial Dreams in Action*. New York: Schocken Books, 1970.

Timbs, John. *English Eccentrics and Eccentricities*. 2 vols. London, 1875.

Transactions of the Panacea Society with the Archbishops and Bishops of the Church of England. London: Panacea Society, 1935[?].

Trevelyan, G. M. *England under the Stuarts*. 21st ed. London: Methuen, 1965.

Tuveson, Ernest Lee. *Millennium and Utopia*. Berkeley: University of California Press, 1949.

———. *Redeemer Nation*. Chicago: University of Chicago Press, 1968.

Tyerman, L. *The Life and Times of the Rev. John Wesley, M.A.* 3 vols. New York, 1872–1875.

Tyler, F. C. "The Rolling Stone on Gittisham Hill." *Proceedings of the Devon*

Archaeological Exploration Society 1 (1929–1932): 70–73.

Valenze, Deborah. "Millenarianism in Britain, 1794–1814: The Movements of Richard Brothers and Joanna Southcott." Senior Honors Thesis, Harvard College, 1975.

————. "Prophecy and Popular Literature in Eighteenth-Century England." *Journal of Ecclesiastical History* 29, no. 1 (January 1978): 75–92.

Veitch, George Stead. *The Genesis of Parliamentary Reform.* Reprinted. London: Constable & Co., 1965.

Walford, Edward. *Old and New London: A Narrative of Its History, Its People, and Its Places.* London, n.d.

Walsh, John. "Methodism at the End of the Eighteenth Century." In *A History of the Methodist Church in Great Britain,* edited by Rupert Davies and Gordon Rupp, pp. 277–315. London: Epworth Press, 1965.

Warne, Arthur. *Church and Society in Eighteenth Century Devon.* Newton Abbot: David & Charles, 1969.

Wearmouth, Robert F. *Methodism and the Common People of the Eighteenth Century.* London: Epworth Press, 1945.

————. *Methodism and the Working-Class Movements of England, 1800–1850.* London: Epworth Press, 1937.

Webb, R. K. *The British Working Class Reader, 1790–1848.* London: George Allen & Unwin, 1955.

————. *Modern England.* New York and Toronto: Dodd, Mead, 1969.

Werkmeister, Lucyle. *A Newspaper History of England, 1792–1793.* Lincoln: University of Nebraska Press, 1967.

Whitlock, Ralph. *The Folklore of Devon.* London: Batsford, 1977.

Whitworth, John McKelvie. *God's Blueprints.* London and Boston: Routledge & Kegan Paul, 1975.

Wickham, E. R. *Church and People in an Industrial City.* London: Lutterworth Press, 1957.

Willey, Basil. *The Eighteenth Century Background.* Boston: Beacon Press, 1966.

————. *The Seventeenth Century Background.* Garden City, N.Y.: Anchor Books, 1953.

Williams, Gwyn A. *Artisans and Sans-Culottes.* New York: W. W. Norton & Co., 1968.

Wilson, Bryan R. *Magic and the Millennium.* New York, Evanston, San Francisco, London: Harper & Row, 1973.

————. *Sects and Society.* London: William Heinemann, 1961.

Wilson, Mona. *The Life of William Blake.* 3d ed. London: Oxford University Press, 1971.

Wisbey, Herbert A., Jr. *Pioneer Prophetess: Jemima Wilkinson, the Publick Universal Friend.* Ithaca: Cornell University Press, 1964.

Wright, Eugene Patrick, comp. *A Catalogue of the Joanna Southcott Collection at The University of Texas.* Austin: Humanities Research Center, University of Texas, 1968.

Yeo, Eileen. "Robert Owen and Radical Culture." In *Robert Owen: Prophet of the Poor*. Edited by Sidney Pollard and John Salt. London: Macmillan, 1971.

Zygmunt, Joseph F. "When Prophecies Fail: A Theoretical Perspective on the Comparative Evidence." *American Behavioral Scientist* 16 (November–December 1972): 245–268.

Index